Between Human and Divine

Between Human and Divine

The Catholic Vision in Contemporary Literature

■ ■ ■

edited by

Mary R. Reichardt

THE CATHOLIC UNIVERSITY OF AMERICA PRESS

Washington, D.C.

Designed and typeset by Kachergis Book Design
Printed and bound by Thomson-Shore

Library of Congress Cataloging-in-Publication Data
Between human and divine : the Catholic vision in
contemporary literature / edited by Mary R. Reichardt.
p. cm.
Includes bibliographical references and index.
ISBN 978-0-8132-1739-0 (cloth : alk. paper)
1. American literature—Catholic authors—History and
criticism.   2. English literature—Catholic authors—
History and criticism.   3. Catholic literature—History
and criticism.   4. Catholic Church—In literature.
5. Catholics in literature.   6. Christianity in
literature.   I. Reichardt, Mary R.   II. Title.
PS153.C3B47 2010
809´.8921282—dc22   2009040261

Contents

Contents

Between Human and Divine

Introduction

Mary R. Reichardt

Flannery O'Connor once remarked that all fiction that portrays reality as it is truly seen and experienced in the world may be considered Catholic fiction.[1] I have long been pondering this statement because there is, in its essence, something quite accurate about it. If a close and contemplative gaze on human beings interacting with their world is the authors' domain, then a writer, no matter what his or her religious beliefs, shares that which is deeply integral to the Catholic vision. For over two thousand years, this vision has fostered a rich variety of artistic expressions. Throughout the ages and across many cultures, it has compelled artists to commit to palette or paper the human experience in the world and to render palpable the mystery of the meeting point of the human and the divine. Accordingly, the Catholic Church upholds artistic creation as a worthwhile—even necessary—enterprise, as a vehicle by which truth is communicated and grace may be given. An enduring connection between religion and art thus exists, and this connection may pertain even if a work of art does not consist of overtly religious subject matter. In his 1999 *Letter to Artists,* Pope John Paul II affirms that art is "a wholly valid approach to the realm of faith," and that "even when they explore the darkest depths of the soul or the most unsettling aspects of evil, artists give voice in a way to the universal desire for redemption."[2]

Having survived the upheaval of Vatican II, the long and diverse tradition of Catholic literary art is not only alive and well today but, indeed, thriving. Yet as a teacher and scholar of Catholic literature, I find few readers, Catholic or not, who can name contemporary authors or texts in this tradition. This book, therefore, grew out of a felt need. The first collection of scholarly essays to be published on a wide variety of contemporary Catholic

---

1. Flannery O'Connor, *Mystery and Manners,* ed. Sally and Robert Fitzgerald (New York: Farrar, Straus, and Giroux, 1962), 172.
2. Pope John Paul II, *Letter to Artists* (1999), www.vatican.va.

literary works, its aim is to introduce readers who may already be familiar with some aspects of earlier Catholic literature to recent and emerging writers and texts in the tradition. Although a few essays examine some works from the 1970s in the context of an author's development, this volume focuses primarily on literature produced between the years 1980 and 2007, a period well after the initial chaos of Vatican II and one marked by the increasing complexities of the postmodern world. Each of the fifteen essays presented here was written by a literary scholar expressly for this collection. Each presents an informative critical perspective on a given work or works and each, in some manner, addresses the questions, "what, specifically, makes *this* a work of Catholic literature?" and "how does it both fit into and help shape the Catholic literary tradition?" The answers to these questions and the critical methodology used necessarily vary according to the individual critic's intent and perspective.

This volume does not claim to exhaust the field; there are other worthwhile recent authors and texts in the Catholic tradition that might have been included but for the necessary limitations inherent in producing such a collection. In the broad and diverse range of works represented here, however, readers will find a veritable treasure trove of contemporary Catholic writing, one that will provide a substantial basis for continuing exploration. Genres covered include fiction, poetry, and literary nonfiction, and authors include those from the United States, Spain, Canada, Australia, England, Ireland, and Japan. Because many of these writers and works may be new to the reader, the essays are purposely partly introductory in nature providing, where appropriate, brief author biographies and plot overviews. Thus, this collection will appeal not only to literary scholars but to all readers interested in the intersection of religion and literature in general and in Catholic literature in particular. It furthers the study of the fascinating ways in which religion, culture, social change, and tradition are shaped by the imaginative process. It also contributes to scholarship in the area by extending the parameters of the Catholic literary tradition into the present, demonstrating that such literature is flourishing today even if its subject matter, thematic concerns, and writing techniques show new and intriguing shifts in direction.

Like the Catholic faith itself, Catholic literature has long demonstrated its adaptability to many time periods and cultures, genres and styles. While for good reason readers may be wary of so-called religious literature, expecting either bleary sentiment or heavy-handed didacticism, the best of Catholic literature is, first of all, excellent literary art that may be enjoyed by all readers, Catholic or not. Like all good art, Catholic writing is both experimental and expansive, "extend[ing] the Catholic vision into uncharted areas and contested dimensions of experience . . . [and] driven at times to explore volatile and shadowy areas that orthodoxy has shied away from."[3] Indeed, a profound understanding of the sacramental and incarnational basis of Catholicism invites such expansiveness ever deeper into the heart of mystery, with all the paradox, ambiguity, and morally gray areas such exploration involves. It is impossible, therefore, to offer a single definition of "Catholic literature," and the phrase is variously defined by scholars in the field. Some maintain that Catholic literature is that which necessarily portrays Catholic characters or events, or that its author must be a baptized, believing Catholic. Others, such as in the O'Connor remark beginning this introduction, take a far more liberal view. My own definition avoids, I think, the pitfalls of these two extremes, the first that cancels out much worthwhile writing, especially contemporary writing, and the second that is ultimately too broad to be workable. As I have defined it for the purpose of assembling this collection, a work of Catholic literature is that which employs the history, traditions, culture, theology, and/or spirituality of Catholicism in a substantial and informed manner. Whether it involves Catholic subject matter or not, and whether its author is a Catholic or not, such literature is substantially grounded in a deep and realistic understanding of at least some aspects of the Catholic faith, Catholic life, or the Catholic tradition.

In fact, if any generalization may be made, late twentieth- and early twenty-first-century Catholic literature is defined less by its treatment of overtly Catholic subject matter than by a particular Catholic vision applied to its subject matter. This is an important distinction. More than half a century ago, disconcerted by their naïve reaction to her fiction, O'Connor noted with a certain degree of bitterness her Catholic readers' inability to really *read*, to look beyond their expectation that the obvious paraphernalia of Catholic life—priests, nuns, the sacraments, and the like—will appear in a literary work and grasp the depth and subtlety of the Catholic perspective conveyed. While some of the literary works here depict Catholic figures and themes, others do not, and thus for these latter works in particular one must look more closely to discover this underlying Catholic perspective. While it

3. Albert Gelpi, "The Catholic Presence in American Culture," *American Literary History* 11, no. 1 (1999): 202–3.

varies according to an author's particular beliefs and sensibilities, this vision primarily involves a certain way of seeing the world, one based on the
Church's strongly incarnational and sacramental emphasis. Because the Son
of God, Jesus Christ, was incarnated as a human being and went through
all human experiences from birth to death to effect our salvation, Catholic
thought regards all created matter and all aspects of human life on Earth as
imbued with meaning and, indeed, as the very arena in which we find redemption. To Catholics, in a famous formula, grace builds upon nature: it
does not scorn nature or destroy it but transforms it. An incarnational approach to the world—the sense that all created things and human history
have been sanctified by Christ's entrance into them—is essential to Catholic
thought and, as Catholic writers have noted, compels the artist to pay close
attention to even the minutia of life and to portray it realistically. And en-
gaging reality as it is usually means an intense encounter with suffering and
evil. Indeed, the mystery of the Cross remains at the heart of Catholic thinking and Catholic writing.

Closely related to this incarnational perspective is the Catholic emphasis
on sacramentality. Since God is the creator of all things, all things are good
to at least some degree in and of themselves and are loved and sustained by
God. Thus all things, events, and experiences can "tell" of God and have the
power to communicate something of God. Catholicism's central sacrament,
the Eucharist, strongly conveys the faith's emphasis on God's immanence
in the world rather than absence from it: the Real Presence of God is palpable in the world, here and now. A sacramental sensibility finds significance
in all of creation at the same time that it constantly draws a line from that
creation back to the Creator. Such an anagogical, integrative habit of mind
characterizes the Catholic perspective. Thus, at the very least, one can say
that a defining feature of a Catholic vision and one that sets it apart from
strictly deterministic theories is that it is open to supernatural mystery, the
existence of another world beyond that of the senses to which human beings
are ultimately oriented. No matter how they penetrate the heart of darkness
or how cynical their view of human nature is, for writers imbued with this
type of Catholic vision, the watchword remains one of hope, for the vision is
ultimately an affirmative one.

What I have laid out here are some general but essential elements of a
Catholic perspective, one that informs much Catholic literature throughout
the ages. Although the origins of Catholic literature broadly defined may be

said to date back, for example, to the third-century martyrdom narrative *The Passion of Sts. Perpetua and Felicity,* or to Saint Augustine's fourth-century autobiography *Confessions,* and although such genres as Catholic poetry and drama have existed for centuries, Catholic fiction is a fairly recent phenomenon. Like the evolution of the novel in general, early Catholic fiction went through a highly self-conscious phase. Mid-nineteenth-century novels such as English author John Henry's Newman's *Loss and Gain, The Story of a Convert* (1848) and his American counterpart Orestes Brownson's *The Spirit-Rapper, An Autobiography* (1854) tended toward a didacticism that reflected the authors' uneasy status in non-Catholic societies. But imaginative literature in the Catholic tradition came into its own during the first half of the twentieth century with a remarkable outpouring of mature works. Authors such as Paul Claudel, Sigrid Undset, François Mauriac, Georges Bernanos, Graham Greene, Dorothy Sayers, Evelyn Waugh, Muriel Spark, J. R. R. Tolkien, and others created literary art of the highest caliber. As some scholars have suggested, the stable, unchanging rituals and doctrines of Catholicism of the pre–Vatican II period provided writers with the security to leave off the defensiveness that characterized earlier fiction and express a far more complex, sophisticated understanding of Catholicism as it really is lived, with all its failings and flaws, its joys and hopes. Whether born Catholic or, in many cases, converts to the faith, these authors took the truth claims of the Catholic Church seriously and captured the reality of Catholic experience while simultaneously conveying a strong sense of the transcendent dimensions of the faith. But the kind of confident, triumphalist endings of, for example, the multiple conversions and re-conversions that conclude Waugh's *Brideshead Revisited* or the new priest that suddenly appears on the final page of Greene's *The Power and Glory* hardly seem possible today.

For many, the watershed event of Vatican II (1962–65) inaugurated a welcome embrace of modernity, a new emphasis on ecumenical efforts and social justice initiatives, and a greater stress on the responsibility of the laity. But it also ushered in a period of unsettling change and a reexamination of what had appeared to be unalterable truths. While the Council did not alter Church doctrine in significant ways, the effect on the life of the average Catholic was considerable. In the United States, the Council corresponded with the antiauthoritarianism and individualism of the 1960s and produced a generation of Catholics who relied increasingly on the dictates of their consciences to adjudicate moral matters rather than on the teaching authority of the Church. For writers who bridged the period, such as Mary Gordon, there seemed to be a clear demarcation between the "old" Church and the "new" Church, and an identity crisis of sorts ensued.

The works of Flannery O'Connor present, I think, an interesting transition point from the old to the new. O'Connor died in 1964, in the midst of the Council, and her stories record the period of enormous social and economic change in the American South during the 1950s and early 1960s. O'Connor helped reshape the pattern and possibilities of Catholic literature, and it is fair to say that the majority of post–Vatican II writers in the Catholic tradition have been influenced by her in some way. Eschewing with few exceptions the obvious trappings of Catholic characters or events, and breaking with the earlier period's tendency toward triumphalist endings, O'Connor exhibits a postmodern consciousness in her close studies of self-reliant individuals interacting in fragmented families and in social situations fraught with race and class tensions. Yet at the same time her stories reject postmodern relativism and insist on the existence of a supernatural reality—the ragged Jesus hovering just behind the dark tree line of the woods. Although they try hard to resist, O'Connor's characters are brought face to face with a truth much larger than themselves, shattering their myopic visions and revealing to themselves who they really are from God's point of view. Acting as judge, O'Connor's narrators still show full confidence that such absolute truth exists.

Over the last thirty years, Catholic literature has taken a wide variety of forms. In a postmodern world where monolithic conceptions of the truth appear increasingly fragmented, and in a secular society characterized by materialism, moral relativity, and rapid technological change, there is a pronounced theme in much of this work of loss and of the need to regain and renew a sense of the sacred and an authentic spiritual integrity of the human person. Whether it uses postmodern techniques or not, today's Catholic literature shows itself still in search of meaning, discontent with reductionist theories of human nature, and in quest of that which can transform and restore what has been broken. In a desacralized world, there is often a strong desire to recover a sacramental sense of creation. Thus, although reframed, the age-old questions remain. Where will healing be found for our deepest ills? How can one maintain faith in a secular world? Why do we suffer so much and how can we deal with it? The answers to these questions are largely sought through individual experience and not by immediately appealing, as in the past, to Church doctrine or authority. If priests or nuns appear in contemporary fiction, they are typically depicted as more-or-less ordinary folk, merely other fellow strugglers in life. If the triumphant confidence that the Church has all the answers is largely eroded, contemporary Catholic fiction still expresses restless discontent with the kind of overriding moral relativism and crass materialism that characterizes contemporary life.

We turn now to a brief tour of the critical essays in this collection in the order in which they appear.

In such novels as *Charming Billy* (1998) and *After This* (2006), American author Alice McDermott focuses on, as Patricia L. Schnapp puts it in "Shades of Redemption in Alice McDermott's Novels," "our determination to be redeemed." In the ordinary, flawed, Irish-American lives and generational stories that McDermott portrays, the impact of everyday mistakes and disappointments as well as the larger issues of the loss of love and of death are determining factors in her characters' lives. Yet, as McDermott suggests, such things can be redeemed—they *are* significant, and they point to a larger meaning, a part of a plan. All is not lost, no matter how bleak the circumstances, and even the most humble and seemingly frustrated life has dignity. Taken from the Marian prayer *Salve Regina,* the title of *After This* echoes the plea "After this our exile, show unto us the blessed fruit of thy womb Jesus," suggesting the essential hope conveyed through the author's close gaze on her human characters. "She yearns over them with such attentiveness that every detail about them becomes fascinating for her and a way to help readers see, understand, and consequently sympathize with each one," writes Schnapp.

The postmodern novels of British writer David Lodge move thematically in concert with Vatican II, as Daniel S. Lenoski maintains in "*How Far Can You Go?* to *Therapy:* Catholicism and Postmodernism in the Novels of David Lodge." Bridging the gap between the "high tradition" of pre–Vatican II Catholicism characterized by dark dramas of sin and salvation and the postconciliar "popular tradition" that focuses on ordinary, prosaic Catholic lives, *How Far Can You Go?* (1981) and *Therapy* (1995) record the shift in the Church from the vertical and absolute to the horizontal and far more ambiguous domestic world. In this world, daily matters of sex and the body, especially in the lives of Catholic couples who have weathered the sexual revolution, take center stage. While often comedic, Lodge's novels deal with serious issues of the possibilities of faith and the Church's continued viability in contemporary society. As Lenoski puts it,. "How far can you go in *aggiornamento* before your religion loses definition and significance? How far can you go in your commitment to the secular world before the sacred is destroyed rather than fostered?" While Lodge's narration is often undercut by postmodern destabilizing elements, resulting in layers of ambiguity, Lenoski argues that the resultant openness, paradox, and ontological questioning is not antithetical but rather integral to Catholic thought.

The work of poet Mary Karr, who hails from Texas, records her gradual conversion to the Catholic faith, according to Robert P. Lewis in "'Descending Theology': The Poetry of Mary Karr." Karr's most recent collection, *Sinners Welcome* (2006), states Lewis, "translates much of the familiar material of Karr's earlier poems into an altogether new key," a more inward gaze and a more conscious search for a religious answer to the emptiness and cynicism expressed in her earlier poetry. From volume to volume, beginning with the 1987 *Abacus,* Karr's poems mark a spiritual journey and the increasing descent into self and memory that, in the incarnational pattern, is the necessary prelude to the ascent of faith. Lewis notes the transformation in tone especially in *Viper Rum* (1998): it is, he states, "the surprise of grace—the grace of her growing awareness of the incarnate presence of Christ at one with her joys, but especially with her sufferings." For Karr, the possibility of grace comes especially through the body, and her poems record the profound connection between *eros* and *caritas*. As her essay on religion and art in *Sinners Welcome* puts it, for Karr prayer and poetry are "facing altars."

The question of why an orthodox tradition of the Catholic novel as seen, for example, in England and France failed to emerge in Ireland is addressed by Eamon Maher in "An Irish Catholic Novel? The Example of Brian Moore and John McGahern." Focusing on the contemporary writing of Moore, a Belfast native, and McGahern, who was raised in Leitrim, Maher examines how, after Irish independence, the close ties between Church and State in Ireland produced a "stifling blend of nationalism and conservative Catholicism" and a corresponding stranglehold on artistic freedom. Maher notes how Moore and McGahern naturally moved toward dissent from such heavy-handed nationalist and cultural Catholicism, and their novels, Moore's *Catholics* (1972) and *Cold Heaven* (1985), and McGahern's *That They May Face the Rising Sun* (2002), capture the moment of change between an oppressive, anti-intellectual religious atmosphere and Ireland's rapid secularization. Although religious skeptics, both Moore and McGahern write fiction preoccupied with religious questions and with a Catholicism that must regain meaning and spiritual vitality if it is to survive. Their fiction offers insight into the troubled and complex history of the Catholic Church in Ireland. "If we are in fact living in a 'post-Catholic' Ireland," writes Maher, "it makes the fictions of Moore and McGahern all the more valuable as chronicles of a society that no longer exists."

Like many historical novels, Spanish writer Miguel Delibes's *The Heretic* (1998) examines a critical moment in the past in order to provide insight into the present. Set in the early sixteenth century during the Spanish Inquisition, the novel depicts the tensions between the Catholic Church and the growing Protestant movement, and it argues for the positive reciprocal influence of both reformations, the Protestant and Catholic Counter-Reformations, on each other. As Salvador A. Oropesa explains in "The Never-Ending Reformation: Miguel Delibes's *The Heretic*," Delibes was deeply troubled by the Church's complicity and compromise with the Franco regime of the 1930s and 40s, and he spent much of his writing career, culminating in *The Heretic,* examining the repercussions of this period on Spain's religious and political situation, especially as a country with a strong traditionalist—and often intolerant—national Catholic identity. *The Heretic* examines the Catholic value of freedom of conscience and how the violation in the past of such a basic right resulted not only in the schism between Protestants and Catholics but also in Spain's lingering cultural definition of the "other."

Nan Metzger and Wendy A. Weaver's essay, "Some Contexts for Current Catholic Women's Memoir: Patricia Hampl and Her Contemporaries," explores a number of memoirs that have, in a real sense, followed the lead of Minnesota author Patricia Hampl. Catholic autobiography is an ancient and enduring genre, and Metzger and Weaver note how contemporary memoirs are influenced by the legacy of such writers as Augustine, Teresa of Avila, and Edith Stein. Yet while the broad outlines of the age-old spiritual journey remain similar, current Catholic women's memoirs express struggles with faith in ways that alter the traditional conversion plot to reflect postmodern ambiguity and resistance to formal strictures of definition. A number of current memoirists, including Hampl, came of age during the 1960s and were influenced by the period's radical individualism, feminist resistance, and rebellion against traditional religious practice. Over the course of her intertwined memoirs, however, Hampl expresses a spiritual longing that eventually results in a re-embracing of Catholic practice and a corresponding reshaping and reinterpreting of past events. Besides Hampl's memoirs such as *A Romantic Education* (1981), *Virgin Time: In Search of the Contemplative Life* (1992), and *The Florist's Daughter* (2007), this essay also discusses several other recent memoirs, most notably Beverly Donofrio's *Riding in Cars with Boys* (1990) and *Looking for Mary: Or, the Blessed Mother and Me* (2000).

Also a midwestern native, Jon Hassler exhibits a profoundly Catholic perspective in his fiction, from his early success, *Staggerford* (1977), through his novel more directly informed by Catholic subject matter, *North of Hope* (1996), and up to the recent *The Life and Death of Nancy Clancy's Nephew* (2004). Whether Hassler's subject matter is overtly Catholic or not, critic Ed Block, in "'A Ransom of Cholers': Catastrophe, Consolation, and Catholicism in Jon Hassler's *Staggerford, North of Hope,* and *The Life and Death of Nancy Clancy's Nephew*," examines the various elements that contribute to Hassler's pervasive Catholic worldview. A capacity for wonder in the face of mystery, an attunement to the rhythms of the seasons and of nature based on a liturgical sense of time, and hope in the yet unrevealed meaning of the pathos of small-town lives—these elements form part of the Catholic perspective and are expressed in the gentle satire yet close attentiveness that Hassler bestows on his subjects. As a result, Hassler's stories convey the sense that, despite the sadness and frustration of his characters' lives, things are not merely random or chaotic but are overseen by a loving God, and a promise of unity and meaning lies just behind the veil. Using a line borrowed from a Theodore Roethke poem, "things throw light on things," Block explains how this view contributes to Hassler's sacramental understanding of the world.

In "Our Litany: The Varied Voices and Common Vision of Three Contemporary Catholic Poets," Gary M. Bouchard argues that in approaching Catholic poetry today, we first need to learn how to read. The poems of American Dana Gioia, Native American Sherman Alexie, and Ireland native Desmond Egan display little if any Catholic imagery, but they suggest Catholic themes clothed in the ironic, objectified mode of today's poetry. To Bouchard, such poets are no less profound in the depth of their religious sensibility than those who deal in more overtly religious subject matter. If it is true that the impetus for poetry often stems from the experience of loss or incompleteness, then the works in Gioia's *Interrogations at Noon* (2001), Egan's *Selected Poems* (1992), and Alexie's *The Summer of Black Widows* (1996), point to the Catholic theme of longing for the grace of healing and redemption in the face of human failing and imperfections. A sacramental worldview that regards ordinary things as sacred, as the locus of meaning, underscores their poetry. Although very different writers, all three exhibit a contemplative stance in regard to their subject matter, one that does not preach or moralize but rather exhibits wonder or poses questions in the face of an often harsh reality.

This introduction mentioned British writer Graham Greene's 1940 novel *The Power and the Glory* as an example of the type of pre–Vatican II fiction that gave way to a far more ambiguous perception of Catholicism after the Council. But Greene's long and multifaceted writing career witnesses to the fact that the author went through many moods and changes in his approach to the Catholic faith. His last major work, *Monsignor Quixote* (1982), is significant in his Catholic canon, argues Michael G. Brennan in "Graham Greene's *Monsignor Quixote:* A Pilgrimage of Doubt and Reason toward Faith and Belief," because it marks Greene's shift from the skepticism about Catholicism in his middle years to a new acceptance of the possibility of grace and redemption, even if a muted one. A gently comic picaresque parody of Cervantes's famous character, *Monsignor Quixote* takes as its protagonist a priest whose travels, relationships, and spirituality may be seen as indicative of the author's resignation to the mysteries of divine authority, states Brennan, and the book's frequent self-referential aspects show an aging author coming full circle as he ponders the intersection of self, spirituality, and writing. *Monsignor Quixote* may be viewed, therefore, as an allegory of Greene's personal pilgrimage toward death and his increased hope for a new life.

British Catholic writing is alive and well today, according to J. C. Whitehouse in "Contemporary British Catholic Writers: Alice Thomas Ellis, Piers Paul Read, William Brodrick, and Jonathan Tulloch." After a discussion of some of the aspects that distinguish pre–Vatican II from post–Vatican II literature, Whitehouse examines the novels of four writers who, despite exemplifying contemporary shifts in theme and style, focus on what still remains at the heart of Catholicism, a deep probing of the interior life and the spiritual longings that illuminate humanity's essential mystery. Alice Thomas Ellis's *The Sin Eater* (1977) and *The Inn at the Edge of the World* (1990) use satire as a "useful correction for illusion, self-deception, sentimentality, and bland self-satisfaction," states Whitehouse, but her novels also convey a palpable sense of a divine presence behind the everyday reality upon which she casts her sharp eye. Piers Paul Read's novels, such as *A Season in the West* (1988), depict the disordered sexuality and existential mess characters make of their lives in the chaos of the modern world, but through a type of Augustinian lens Read envisions their movement toward God as initiated by their shame and disgust. A search for truth—faith seeking understanding—marks William Brodrick's recent novels, *The Sixth Lamentation* (2003) and *The Gardens of the Dead* (2006), both of which focus on the presence of mystery and the intimations of the God and meaning behind it. And Jonathan Tulloch's *The Season Ticket* (2000) and *Give Us This Day* (2005) examine Irish immigrant Catholics in East England who struggle with poverty and degradation but who find faith in the midst of the brutal reality of their everyday existence.

Nancy Ann Watanabe's "The Contemporary Catholic Bildungsroman: Passionate Conviction in Shūsaku Endō's *The Samurai* and Mary Gordon's *Men and Angels*" discusses contemporary permutations of the Bildungsroman genre in two very different artists. Japanese writer Endō's historical novel *The Samurai* (1992) and American writer Gordon's feminist-inflected *Men and Angels* (1995) both study the plight of the Christian individual in a non-Christian society and express, according to Watanabe, a "revolutionary sort of universalism that parallels the [post–Vatican II] ecumenical movement in the Roman Catholic Church." The Christian individual's faith is sharply tested in light of society's values and even leads to martyrdom of one sort or another but serves to challenge material and secular norms and reorient the lives of those who have little or no religious outlook. Endō and Gordon's novels extend the traditional genre of the Bildungsroman into new territory, exploring the development and education of the spiritual self as it is both nurtured and challenged by its encounters with society.

British poet Elizabeth Jennings (*New Collected Poems*, 2002) and Australian poet Les Murray (*Collected Poems*, 2002) may be seen as participating in the tradition of a sacramental and incarnational poetry stemming from Gerard Manley Hopkins, writes Stephen McInerney in "'Art with Its Largesse and Its Own Restraint': The Sacramental Poetics of Elizabeth Jennings and Les Murray." The sacramental poet is concerned with the interaction between the everyday and the absolute. God's imminence in the world through the Incarnation and in the Real Presence of the Eucharist, and the corresponding mystery of embodiment, is evident in Jennings's poetry, which often portrays the essential belief in a God who is with us here and now and yet also the Christian paradox that the kingdom of God is not yet fully realized. As a poet, Jennings is both a frank realist and a writer full of sacramental joy. Les Murray's poetry, like that of Jennings, is rooted in the sacred and reifies into sacramental shape the ordinary, mundane details of life. A convert to Catholicism especially because of his belief in the Eucharist—the transformation of ordinary elements into the divine—Murray views the poet, too, as a type of priest and the poem as a sacrifice that points to the mystery of "presence" in the world.

Davin Heckman's "The Estrangement of Emilio Sandoz, SJ: Othering in Mary Doria Russell's *The Sparrow*" considers why Jesuit priests so often appear in works of science fiction such as Russell's *The Sparrow* (1996). Although a convert from Catholicism to Judaism, Russell used Jesuits in this novel to explore profound questions of faith in the postmodern world. Because they are perpetual outsiders, the Jesuits fit naturally, states Heckman, into the uneasy place of "cognitive estrangement" that underscores the genre of science fiction. The entire progression of Jesuit training, focusing on Ignatius's *Spiritual Exercises*, is designed to estrange the person increasingly from his surroundings, expand his perspective, and compel him to interrogate himself in relation to the cosmos. Russell's protagonist, Emilio Sandoz, SJ, is a typical postmodern subject teetering uneasily on the border between the apparent opposites of faith and reason while plunged into a personal and ethical tragedy from which there seems no redemption. But, Heckman argues, as the Jesuit order was founded to usher in a new Christian humanism, a worldview that integrated faith with reason, so in the sensibility of Emilio Sandoz one can discover a powerful corrective to today's dialectical thinking that pits faith against reason. In a postmodern world torn by such binary thinking, the "estranged" role of the Catholic may offer an alternative vision.

Canadian author Michael D. O'Brien has devoted his writing career to depicting "compelling epiphanies of man's true face restored to the *imago Dei*—the image and likeness of God in us," states Dominic Manganiello in "Restoring the *Imago Dei:* Transcendental Realism in the Fiction of Michael D. O'Brien." The reality that humankind is made in its Creator's image, lost when Adam fell and restored through Christ, underlines the Catholic themes in *Father Elijah: An Apocalypse* (1996) and *Strangers and Sojourners: A Novel* (1997), both works in O'Brien's *The Children of the Last Days* series. A futuristic thriller that pits a Catholic priest against an atheistic president, *Father Elijah* explores the culture wars that result when a pervasively secular, materialistic society bent on human power-seeking tries to eradicate all notions of a Creator God and of the transcendent origins of human beings. *Strangers and Sojourners* depicts the spiritual pilgrimage of a troubled protagonist who struggles with darkness, despair, and demonic visions before coming to faith and hope. In both works, O'Brien explores the depth of the human soul engaged in the age-old warfare between good and evil and the search to regain an identity grounded in God.

In the collection's final essay, "Maiden Mothers and Little Sisters: The Convent Novel Grows Up," Meoghan B. Cronin considers several recent novels in the context of the long tradition of fiction focused on nuns and convent life. American authors Ron Hansen's *Mariette in Ecstasy* (1991) and Mark Salzman's *Lying Awake* (2000), and British author Michèle Roberts's *Daughters of the House* (1992), present postmodern stories that explore complex issues of female identity, generational relationships, and sexual and spiritual identity in the uniquely all-female environment of the convent. In each of these novels, the protagonist experiences extraordinary spiritual and mystical phenomena that upset relationships and disrupt the carefully controlled rhythms of the nuns' lives. While none of the works shut down the possibility of a real encounter with the divine, all are concerned with the layers of subjectivity through which such phenomena are experienced and interpreted. This layered subjectivity lends itself to multiple postmodern forms of telling, including personal journals, letters, reports, extracts, poems, and the like, all indicating different viewpoints and highlighting the deep ambiguity of such interactions. The experience of the divine comes through the physical, and the intermingling of the sensual and the spiritual leads each author to question the extent to which a woman must sacrifice the self in order to give herself to God.

In extending Catholic thought, culture, and tradition into the present day, contemporary Catholic literature throws new light on a world that often seems close to abandoning God all together. As many have noted, in a postmodern world where the primacy of reason has disintegrated, the arts may actually grow in significance as a means of reimaging the current cultural shift. Despite a variety of contemporary forms and themes, Catholic literature continues to draw on tradition in emphasizing the human encounter with transcendence and mystery, and in exploring ultimate questions in light of the incarnational and sacramental basis of the faith. As does all art, its prophetic voice can help point the way toward a new synthesis of culture and faith, making all things new in Christ.

CHAPTER 1

Shades of Redemption in Alice McDermott's Novels

Patricia L. Schnapp, RSM

It would be hard to imagine a course offered in American Catholic literature today that did not include one of Alice McDermott's novels. Because she draws on her Irish-Catholic background for many of her novels' settings, they are replete with references to the Mass, rosaries, novenas, and the rituals and sacramentals that give the Catholicism she has been immersed in most of her life its distinctive character. But do such references alone make a work of fiction "Catholic"? In his collection of essays *A Stay against Confusion,* Catholic author and critic Ron Hansen writes of his belief that all great novels possess a certain sacramentality. Both fiction and religion, he maintains, share "the unquenchable yearning to achieve the impossible, fathom the unfathomable, hold on to what is fleeting and evanescent." Above all, fiction should, in Hansen's words, convey a sense that "life has great significance, that something is going on here that matters."[1] It is especially this latter point that links Hansen to Alice McDermott. For those reflecting on what defines a "Catholic novel," McDermott's works make a particularly interesting case study.

Not surprisingly, critics have not always been in agreement about McDermott's theological convictions. In his critical study *The Catholic Imagination in American Literature,* Ross Labrie has, in fact, suggested that, despite her Irish-American Catholic background, McDermott's novels reflect a clinical detachment in her treatment of Catholicism rather than a committed embrace of it.[2] In a more recent critique, Joseph O'Neill considers one of McDermott's difficulties as a writer to be her inability to "credit the significance

---

1. Ron Hansen, *A Stay against Confusion* (New York: HarperCollins, 2002), 2, 12, 13.
2. Ross Labrie, *The Catholic Imagination in American Literature* (Columbia: University of Missouri Press, 1997), 277.

of the human travails she describes with such care."[3] Similarly, Paul Gray, in his *New York Times* review of McDermott's novel *After This*, can find no other message in the novel than "Life goes on," and he questions why, if that's all the author has to say, readers should bother with such stories at all.[4] These critiques infer that McDermott is a so-called cultural Catholic, one who grew up immersed in a Catholic world and aware of its preoccupations and language, and who therefore mines this intimate knowledge while not subscribing to the faith with serious commitment. Contradicting this assessment of McDermott as essentially a secular writer, however, Peter Quinn praises her "exquisite examinations of life, death, love, disappointment, and Christian hope." He believes that she has brilliantly made her own Catholicity "indistinguishable from the catholicity of her literary imagination, a clement, loving, and sweet (but never saccharine) embrace of all that is human."[5]

While McDermott has confessed to being "not a very good Catholic," she has also spoken of reassessing her faith in recent years.[6] One of the catalysts for this was the birth of her children. When she was a fledgling author, however, it was literature itself that became for McDermott—as for the young James Joyce—the "altar at which she was willing to worship," chiefly because it seemed to her that "through literature all the questions my Catholic upbringing had taught me to ask were raised and explored and illustrated in a far more compelling and intelligent way than ever I had heard in the old familiar gospel or from a Sunday morning pulpit."[7] These were, of course, the Big Questions: Why are we here? How should we act toward each other? How do we deal with death and other losses? As she explains, McDermott concluded that literature speaks most effectively of the longings of the human heart. Further, it gives shape to the chaotic elements in our lives, putting "context and purpose and significance" into each gesture, action, and detail. It gives, in her words, "form to our existence" and makes out of our human tales something that will "stand against time." In doing so, fiction reveals "our determination not to be trumped by death," which McDermott significantly calls "our determination to be redeemed."[8] It was only later in her life that McDermott discovered that the questions she most wanted to ask as a novelist were the very questions for which her Catholic

3. Joseph O'Neill, "New Fiction," *Atlantic Monthly* 298, no. 3 (2006): 110.

4. Paul Gray, "Family Album," *New York Times Book Review*, Sept. 10, 2006, 15.

5. Peter Quinn, "Clement and Loving," *Commonweal* 133, no. 18 (2006): 25.

6. Alice McDermott, "The Lunatic in the Pew," *Boston College Magazine* 64, no. 3 (2003): 35.

7. Alice McDermott, "Confessions of a Reluctant Catholic," *Commonweal* 127, no. 3 (2000): 14.

8. Ibid.

faith provided answers. Eventually, she also realized that Catholicism was her "first language,"[9] the "native language of her spirit,"[10] and the one that gives her a way of thinking about matters of the spirit.[11] It is not just through her language, however, that McDermott's immersion in her faith is reflected. Rather, McDermott herself has frequently claimed that her works are indeed about faith, hope, and love. Through writing, she states, she realized that, in dealing with such themes as family connections, loneliness, and death, she must also deal with religion, even if her religious sensibility is not always made explicit in each novel.[12] Even her craft in capturing the Irish-American community so punctiliously is less important to her than what is going on in her characters' hearts. "I don't want to be a social scientist," she says. "The spirituality that is tied to Catholicism is much more important to me."[13]

The grandchild of Irish immigrants on both sides of the family, McDermott grew up in the 1960s with her two brothers in an Irish-Catholic enclave on Long Island, New York. With both parents being first generation Irish-Americans, she knew firsthand "how Irish-Americans in the New York area talk, what kind of couches they buy, and what kind of plastic slipcovers they put on the couches."[14] This intimate knowledge of the community she writes about frees her, she says, from having to do research, so she can spend her time on other aspects of writing.[15] McDermott also acknowledges the influence of her home life on her formation as a writer. Because her two older brothers had dominant personalities, she often found it hard to get into family conversations. This led her to become a careful listener. In addition, her father was a great observer of people, often taking the children to the mall where they would all sit and just watch shoppers go by. Her father's comments as they returned home persuaded McDermott that if she paid careful enough attention to others, she'd see amusing things. This led her to become a careful observer.[16] Both of these propensities have had bountiful literary consequences.

9. McDermott, "Lunatic," 36.
10. McDermott, "Confessions," 15.
11. Tom Deignan, "The CRAIC: Alice McDermott; Reluctantly Irish?" *Irish Voice* 13, no. 50 (1999): 17. ProQuest. Wayne State University Library.
12. "Alice McDermott Interview," failbetter.com 22 (Fall 2006): 1.
13. Teresa K. Weaver, "Books: Multilayered Stories Are Writer's Forte," *Atlantic Journal-Constitution,* April 21, 2002: sec. F4, p. 4.
14. Ibid.
15. Jill Rendelstein, "Picture Perfect," *The World and I* 15, no. 3 (2000): 284. ProQuest. Wayne State University Library.
16. Ibid., 285.

After graduating from Catholic grade and high schools, McDermott attended the State University of New York at Oswego. It was there that a writing professor announced to her: "I've got bad news . . . you're a writer."[17] In 1975, McDermott received her bachelor's degree from Oswego and entered the graduate writing program at the University of New Hampshire, where she met her future husband. After receiving her master's degree in 1978, she taught at the University of California at San Diego and at American University in Washington, D.C. She has also been a writer-in-residence at Lynchburg and Hollins Colleges in Virginia, a lecturer in English at the University of New Hampshire, and a professor of writing at Johns Hopkins University. She now lives with her husband and three children in Bethesda, Maryland.

McDermott speaks easily about the craft of writing. She is interested in how her characters live, think, and speak, and especially in how they create meaning out of their own experience. Perhaps her literary manifesto was expressed most succinctly in a 2003 interview: "Incident (in novels and in life) is momentary, and temporary, but the memory of an incident, the story told about it, the meaning it takes on or loses over time, is life-long and fluid, and that's what interests me and what I hope will prove interesting to readers."[18] One of McDermott's strongest convictions, and what she feels gives a certain superiority to fiction over nonfiction, is that the novel can give shape and meaning to what in real life may often seem simply random and senseless. Fiction can also allow the reader to "enter into another universe, a way to see the world anew, to hear an internal voice that is not our own." This, she believes, is "the stuff that endures."[19] Few writers, in fact, make it easier than McDermott to enter another world. Her deftly drawn characters and settings, realistic and lavish with detail, place readers in McDermott's universe so successfully that they feel the chill in the air or see the dandruff on the shoulder of a turquoise cashmere sweater.

McDermott's novels, densely textured and lyrically written with a poet's gift for language, certainly capitalize on her Irish-Catholic background. But Catholicism is found in far more than just the fictional culture in which her works are largely set. Her novels spring, as authentic Catholic fiction does, "from a mind familiar with the creed, with the paradox of the Trinity, with belief in the Eucharistic presence, and . . . with the crucial tenets of 'forgive-

---

17. Eileen McNamara, "Alice McDermott: Novelist; Eileen McNamara: Columnist," *Irish America* 15, no. 5 (1999): 122. ProQuest. Wayne State University Library.

18. Carole Burns, "Off the Page: Alice McDermott," *Washington Post Live Online*, Oct. 2, 2003, 6.

19. Ibid.

ness of sins' and 'life everlasting.'"[20] While McDermott's novels, then, are concerned with the great themes of suffering, forgiveness, hope, belief, charity, sin, and redemption, thus underscoring her essentially Catholic vision, it is the latter theme, redemption, that is for McDermott most significant. The concept of redemption can be a helpful lens in analyzing the specifically Catholic texture of her work, for this theme resonates with the claims of traditional Church theology. God's mercy is always available. Regardless of our actions or circumstances, we—in the words of Karl Rahner—"swim in grace." Certainly, in all McDermott's work a "rhythm of fall and redemption," though sometimes faltering, pulsates persistently.[21] It is, in fact, the constant insistence on redemption, or at least the possibility of redemption, that radiates from McDermott's embrace of her characters, ordinary and flawed as they are, and becomes a leitmotif recurring in all her works. To a rare degree, McDermott conveys a sense that all lives have significance; indeed, that every detail of every life has significance. McDermott redeems her struggling characters—both adults and children—from the dustbin of lackluster and paltry roles upon the stage of their lives and magically lures readers into caring for them because *she* cares for them. She yearns over them with such attentiveness that every detail about them becomes fascinating for her and a way to help readers see, understand, and consequently sympathize with each one.

Redemption is, of course, a semantically multifaceted term, its meanings ranging across a continuum between the secular and the sacred. Standard dictionaries list its first meaning as simply "to buy back," but other definitions include to "help overcome something detrimental," "release from blame or debt," "compensate for," and the theological "free from the consequences of sin." The *New Catholic Encyclopedia* gives as its primary definition "the mystery of God's deliverance of mankind from the evil of sin" and, consequently, God's restoration of us to the state of grace by an act of divine power and merciful love. Yet the *New Catholic Encyclopedia* also acknowledges that "no single theory of the Redemption has ever been total or complete."[22] Obviously, this evocative and open-ended term has purely secular meanings, but its theological ones are also protean enough to vindicate the latitude with which McDermott uses the word. The very term "redemption," then, is broad

20. Daniel McVeigh and Patricia Schnapp, eds., *The Best American Catholic Short Stories* (New York: Rowman and Littlefield, 2007), xvi.

21. Ibid., xvii.

22. E. L. Peterman, "Redemption (Theology of)," in *New Catholic Encyclopedia*, ed. Bernard L. Marthaler, Richard E. McCarron, and Gregory F. LaNave, 2nd ed. (Detroit: Gale Thompson for the Catholic University of America Press, 2003), 973.

and multifaceted. Even the notion of spiritual redemption implies at least two quite different ideas: that original sin, through divine initiative, has been removed so that humankind can enter heaven, or, most simply, that any mistake or sin, no matter how heinous, can be transcended by grace and thus forgiven. The analogous secular meaning of redemption suggests, among other things, that mistakes can be compensated for and, to some extent, expunged—though sometimes only by an act requiring great effort or sacrifice.

The most frequent sense of "redeem" in McDermott's work is some blend of "release from blame" and "compensate for." Both of these meanings, however, suggest a related implication with more than a coloring of religious significance. This is a belief in the inherent dignity of all persons rooted in our origins and destiny as children of God. It is on the affirmation of this dignity that much of McDermott's authorial intent regarding the concept of redemption is focused. Indeed, McDermott has said that after observing so many characters in fiction and TV shows treated simply as clichés caught in clichéd situations, she is determined to "retrieve" such characters and such situations, to "redeem" simple emotions and illustrate that they *are* important and serious matters.[23] In so using her authorial power to redeem, she is, of course, simultaneously affirming these characters' dignity and the goodness of human life lived on Earth. This affirmation, this gracious gazing upon her characters, permeates McDermott's novels. And her technique is simple: she neither condemns her varied protagonists for their human frailty nor scorns their trite dramas. Rather, through her elaboration of each detail of their appearance and actions, she invests them with significance and worth. In *At Weddings and Wakes* (1992), for instance, the minor character Aunt Agnes is scrutinized as minutely and described as lavishly as a celebrity might be in a tabloid:

A door off the living room opened and Aunt Agnes emerged, broad and tall and severe, in a slim black skirt and pale silk blouse, stockings, and flat black slippers embroidered with red and gold. She accepted a kiss from each of the children (her perfume thick and mellow, the perfume that filled theater lobbies and office buildings) and then moved to the silver cart, where she slid open a small door and one by one took out three stubby glasses etched with white lilies.[24]

The imagery here reflects McDermott's characteristic technique of layering detail upon detail, but it also shows her admiration for playwriting in which

23. Kim Heron, "Redeeming Simple Emotions," *New York Times Book Review*, April 19, 1987, 29.
24. Alice McDermott, *At Weddings and Wakes* (New York: Random House, 1992), 27.

the visual aspect of the narrative is crucial and, typically, given meticulous attention in stage directions by the author.

Indeed, sympathy and respect color McDermott's efforts to redeem her characters and are reflected in distinctive ways in each of her novels. Her first novel, *A Bigamist's Daughter* (1982), focuses on a young editor at a vanity press. The title character Elizabeth has a significant revelation through the manuscript of a client (and, eventually, her lover) who has written a novel about a bigamist. While McDermott does not show her mastery of tone uniformly here and occasionally the novel seems mired in repetition, it demonstrates that she had already acquired her stylistic assurance and meticulous craft. In this work, to some extent at least, the antiheroine Elizabeth is "redeemed" through flashbacks to her childhood. The habitual absence of her father leads to her subsequent inability to make commitments, and the novel's conclusion illustrates the degree to which Elizabeth is an emotional victim, disabled in a crucially important way. Still, Elizabeth is the least satisfying and lovable of McDermott's central characters, and the novel is too self-conscious about its excessive bedroom undressing—a beginner's concession, perhaps, to popular tastes and not one repeated in any other of her subsequent works. Despite its shortcomings, *A Bigamist's Daughter* explores with care and insight the long shadow of crippled affection that typically begins in childhood and creates not only truncated emotions but cynicism about the possibilities of love. If readers are impatient with Elizabeth, they are likely also to forgive her—to "redeem" her—through their understanding of her constantly frustrated love for her father, which, the author insists, has resulted in her incapacity to trust any other love.

That Night (1987), McDermott's second novel and the only one so far to be filmed, begins dramatically. From the first sentence, the reader is introduced to the distinctive signature style of McDermott's narrative voice. Here, her intensification, phrase by vivid phrase, of the import of the event around which the novel pivots is reminiscent of the descriptions of William Faulkner:

That night when he came to claim her, he stood on the short lawn before her house, his knees bent, his fists driven into his thighs, and bellowed her name with such passion that even the friends who surrounded him, who had come to support him, to drag her from the house, to murder her family if they had to, let the chains they carried go limp in their hands.[25]

25. Alice McDermott, *That Night* (New York: Random House, 1987), 3.

Set in the 1960s, *That Night* is the not-uncommon story of two teens from dys-functional families involved in a high school romance that leaves the girl, Sheryl, pregnant. According to the convention of the time, she is sent away to have the baby, while the narrator, a ten-year-old neighbor at the time of the title incident who watched it from next door, records their story in care-ful detail. Sheryl, the somewhat unlikely center of the drama, is not the nu-bile, bouncy blond cheerleader so coveted in today's sitcoms. She is plain, complex, and vulnerable. Like Elizabeth, she is "redeemed" in part because she too is the victim of a dysfunctional family. Unlike Elizabeth, however, she is further rendered "forgivable" because of her childlike naïveté and her inner suffering when she is separated from her boyfriend, a suffering that leads her to attempt suicide.

Child of My Heart is McDermott's 2002 story of a fifteen-year-old who is visited by her eight-year-old cousin Daisy during a fateful summer in the Hamptons. The novel addresses two potentially melodramatic situations: the deflowering of the protagonist Theresa, a beautiful girl attracted to a seventy-year-old artist, and the wasting away of the cousin Daisy, though no one understands that she has leukemia. While *Child* was greeted with mixed reviews, some finding it mawkish and others brilliantly Jamesian, the novel did forge a different direction for McDermott, for in it she uses an unequivo-cal first-person narrator, Theresa, and not the more ghostlike or vanishing narrators of *Charming Billy* and *At Weddings and Wakes*. Despite its virtues, however, the novel falters in two ways. One is in the tedious similarity of Theresa's memories of relatively uneventful days, as if the narrative itself is mired in the wet sand of the beach the children frequent. The other is in the dichotomous portrait of Theresa. Imaginatively precocious, she has an almost saintlike devotion to the children she watches over and boundless patience with them. While her sweetness and virtue dominate the narrative, she is at the same time impenitently seductive as she, with no apparent mis-givings or moral reflection, offers herself to the elderly artist. If, presumably, Theresa is bored with the routine of her long summer days and seeks the ad-venture of sex as an outlet for her boredom, McDermott never allows her to relate this explanation to the reader. Given the time period and Theresa's Catholic schooling, this seems unrealistic for a writer so conscientious about authentic detail. Still, the reader is inclined to forgive and "redeem" There-sa, knowing the penance that awaits her in the grief of Daisy's death soon after the summer ends. And perhaps the redemption lies precisely there: in the devotion Theresa has to her cousin Daisy and in her ultimate inability to save Daisy from her fate. Theresa, who has often spun stories with her magical imagination to entertain and comfort her charges, does not have sufficient magic, ultimately, to protect Daisy, and she will no doubt have second thoughts about not reporting the telltale bruises which, cumulatively, give her a premonition of what awaits her cousin.

Not all of McDermott's novels are focused on a single character. *At Weddings and Wakes,* for instance, explores the theme of the lack of communication between generations, causing family history to become lost. Lyrical and haunting, the novel recreates memories of childhood that shift fluidly in time and seem told by a ghostly, evanescent narrator. These memories are heavily dominated by regular visits to three aunts and a grandmother and capture disparate events and impressions that only later on, the reader assumes, are understood. The novel is interlaced with delicate insights and observations, such as: "He had the arrested charm of a man who had discovered fairly young that given his looks a little personality went a long way."[26] This describes Uncle John, who asks questions "with a handsome man's license to feign halfhearted interest." At family gatherings, someone almost always vanished for a time "just to prove . . . that like the dead their presence would be all the more inescapable when they were gone." Of the collective narrators' mother, Lucy, a woman disillusioned with marriage, McDermott writes that she "would see that, given the muddle of life, loss following as it did every gain, and death and disappointment so inevitable, anger was the only appropriate emotion."[27] The theme of redemption in this novel is subtle, and perhaps most obviously describes the eventual marriage of affectionate Aunt Mae, the narrator-children's ally and friend, who left the convent years before. Redemption is also found, however, in the interplay of losses and loves, of strength and sorrow and fidelity, that gives this story of family a universal appeal. Families do endure, McDermott suggests, and every sorrow and disappointment can strengthen as well as weaken their bonds. And in this strengthening there is a redemption.

In *After This* (2006), McDermott analyzes a single family's response to the loss of one of its members in World War II. Here the concept of redemption takes on additional theological connotations, though they are implied symbolically rather than imposed. The first chapter begins with Mary, a cen-

---

26. McDermott, *Weddings and Wakes,* 107.
27. Ibid., 109, 112, 109.

tral figure, leaving a church she has visited during her lunch hour. She has lit a candle for those in the service (although the war is over) and for content-ment with her lot if, at thirty, she is destined to remain a spinster, a fate she fears. In the opening paragraphs, McDermott's voice becomes almost incan-tational as she again layers detail upon detail until the passage crescendos dizzyingly. As Mary exits the church, a "bitter April wind" is blowing, bend-ing the lunch-hour crowd into it and blowing their jackets and skirts:

And trailing them, outrunning them, skittering along the gutter and the side-walk and the low gray steps of the church, banging into ankles and knees and one another, scraps of paper, newspapers, candy wrappers, what else?—office memos? shopping lists? The paper detritus that she had somewhere read, or had heard it said, trails armies, or was it (she had seen a photograph) the scraps of letters and wrappers and snapshots that blow across battlefields after all but the dead have fled?[28]

Though Mary does indeed marry, becoming Mrs. John Keane and a mother, life is not as idyllic as she expected. But her low-grade disappointments and the ordinary events of the passing days are treated with a literary virtuosity and grace evoking the style not just of Faulkner but also of F. Scott Fitzger-ald, both of whom McDermott admires. Her deft nuancing, her intricacy of detail, her gentle, decorous qualifications, as if she is under compulsion to leave out no detail, all contribute to her often lyrical and occasionally rhap-sodic tone.

The dramatic events of *After This,* especially the death of one son in the war and the pregnancy of a teenaged daughter still in high school, lead to a provisional redemption of the immense pain of Mary and John as hope and new life salvage disappointment. Through the couple's strong faith and the Church's blessing, the family will survive: in the words of the prayer "Salve Regina," from which McDermott took her title, "after this, our exile," there is the promise of heaven. The final scene of the novel occurs in a church, where daughter Clare will have a small private wedding. The pastor, Mon-signor McShane, is a wise and gentle old man, "pity's fool," and accommo-dates the family with graciousness. In a final redemptive touch, this nec-essary wedding (for Clare is pregnant), filled with painful emotion for the Keanes, occurs on a beautiful evening in which "the sky was that polished blue it sometimes got after a storm, or a long winter."[29] The pianist, a neigh-

---

28. Alice McDermott, *After This* (New York: Farrar, Straus, and Giroux, 2006), 3.
29. Ibid., 276.

bor of the Keanes asked to play for the wedding although he is a Presbyterian, is a student at Juilliard. He comes early to the church to get the feel of the instrument he will play, and Monsignor McShane recognizes immediately the difference between what this young man is able to do on the piano and "what the ordinary Sunday musicians played."[30] The priest listens, caught up in the music of this young virtuoso

who played in a trance, eyes closed, transformed, transported, inspired (that was the word)—not the engine for the instrument but a conduit for some music that was already there, that had always been there, in the air, some music, some pattern, sacred, profound, barely apprehensible, inscrutable, really, something just beyond the shell of earth and sky that had always been there and that needed only this boy, a boy like this, to bring it, briefly, briefly, to his untrained ear.[31]

The final line of the novel, though addressed to the musician, can be read as a counterpoint to the novel's opening phrase, "Leaving the church, she felt the wind rise." Despite the rising wind of disappointments, the tragedy of the war victim Jacob, and the inevitable pain and disillusionment that the novel chronicles in the lives of these "poor banished children of Eve," the priest's final assertion responds to the whole range of events that have led the Keane family into the church at the end of the book, including the small life Clare carries: "'It's a gift then,' the priest said." Shortly before, Sister Marie, the principal of Clare's high school, had told the distraught parents, "Let's remember . . . that there's a new life on the way . . . And life," she added, turning back, "is always a cause for celebration."[32] Significantly, McDermott bookends her rich novel with the dual settings of a church, Mary leaving one at the novel's beginning and entering one at its end. If, then, there is something "dispiriting" about the novel, with its focus on "renunciation . . . while ignoring the possibilities of passion and hope,"[33] still McDermott's message is that all is not lost, and even the inevitable sorrows that keep any life from being "happy ever after," devastating as they are, are nevertheless able to be redeemed through God's transforming grace.

While the theme of redemption, then, occurs with fluctuating meanings throughout McDermott's novels, it is seen most strikingly and addressed most explicitly in *Charming Billy* (1998). Praise for this lyrical and resonant

30. Ibid., 277.   31. Ibid., 278.

32. Ibid., 3, 279, 274.

33. Michiko Kakutani, "One Son Is Lost, and a Family's Ties Are Put to the Test," *New York Times*, Sept. 8, 2006: E34 (L).

tale came from every corner when it won the National Book Award in the same year it was published, with the *New York Times Book Review* calling it "eloquent" and "heartbreaking," the *Miami Herald* "mesmerizing" and "perfectly pitched," and *Publisher's Weekly* "seamlessly told" and "exquisitely nuanced." *Time* magazine critic John Skow even suggested that its "strong, shrewd opening pages should be taught in college writing courses."[34]

As is typical of McDermott, *Charming Billy* is set in a homogeneous Irish Catholic milieu. Its dominant religious theme, however, rippling with both secular and religious significance, is again—and dramatically—that of redemption. Over and over McDermott uses the verb "redeem" in the novel, and in so doing she stirs reflections on the various shades of meaning in this pregnant term. Allusions to redemption move between its purely theological sense, as an action of atonement by God's Son, and a quite secular sense, as when a husband forgets to wish his wife "happy birthday" at breakfast and "redeems himself" by later bringing her roses and chocolate. Somewhere, too, there is a middle ground in which redemption functions as a spiritually purifying action which, though not the great action of the *Redemptor Mundi*, still participates in the ongoing redemptive work of God. With these various levels of redemption McDermott's novel is rich.

Charming Billy is, quite simply, a love story. As young men, Billy and his cousin Dennis meet two young women from Ireland. Billy falls hopelessly and irrevocably in love with Eva, who is visiting her sister, a nursemaid on Long Island. Eva agrees to marry him and accepts his ring, but she must go back to Ireland first to attend to her aging parents. She and Billy write each other often, and Billy is finally able to send her enough money to pay for her passage back to the United States. For several weeks, there is no response. Finally, Dennis gets a call from her sister, whom he had dated, and he brings to Billy the news that Eva has died in Ireland of pneumonia. Five years later Billy marries plain Maeve, the only daughter of an alcoholic widower. While Billy remains both charming and religious, and while he manages to hold onto his job, his habit of drinking becomes more acute. So does his silent devotion to Eva's memory. Years later, increasingly afflicted by alcoholism, Billy accompanies a priest friend to Ireland, where he plans on a retreat to take "the pledge" to stop drinking. While there, he decides to visit Eva's grave, but not before he goes to see her parents. Arriving at her village, he stops

---

34. All of these quotes are taken from the flyleaf of the 1998 Random House edition of the novel.

at a gas station to ask directions, and in the adjoining tea shop, he meets the long-mourned Eva, quite alive and properly shamefaced. She had taken the money he sent her to help her future husband set up his business. Later, back in the States, Dennis apologizes for having lied to Billy. Billy, bleary eyed and totally incurable now, merely mumbles a mild response. Soon, and probably inevitably, Billy drinks himself to death and is found, dark and bloated, in the street. Dennis eventually marries Billy's widow Maeve, possibly redeeming to some extent her long and difficult life of tending two different alcoholics.

In many ways, the elegiac tale of *Charming Billy* is entirely about redemption. Even on page one of the novel, in fact, McDermott moves through three levels of redemption, each more profound than the other. The mourners at Billy's funeral, a scene that begins the novel which then is told largely in flashback, discuss together Billy's life, "redeeming, perhaps, the pleasure of a drink or two . . . from the miserable thing that a drink had become in his life." His friends and relatives converse about Billy as a way of "redeeming the affection they had felt for him" and, most of all, to "redeem Billy's life," for which purpose, of course, they must retell the story of "the Irish girl."[35] Each of these three attempts at redemption represents a different shade of significance. The first may be seen as an attempt to make up for Billy's abuse of alcohol by the mourners' own more responsible and appropriate drinking. Billy's alcoholism does not preclude his friends and relatives downing a few in his memory. On a deeper, more psychological level, Billy's mourners also hope to find in their conversation about Billy's life justification for their own "relentless affection for him." They remember his loveable qualities and recite them like the litany of a saint: "He had the sweetest nature," one cousin begins. "He found a way to like everyone, he really did. He always found something good to say, or something funny." "Everyone loved him," another adds. Still, no matter how they talk around it at first, the mourners find it necessary to bring up Eva, if not to justify Billy's drinking than at least to see in her tragic demise (for all still believe, with the exception of Dennis, that Eva had indeed died) some mitigation of his alcoholism, some further vindication and redemption of their fondness for him, their assertion of his worthiness of their love. "That was a sad thing, wasn't it? That was a blow to him," one comments.[36]

35. Alice McDermott, *Charming Billy* (New York: Random House, 1998), 5.
36. Ibid.

Later, however, the discussion focuses more directly on another issue at first avoided, Billy's drinking. There are two schools of thought among the group. Billy's sister Rosemary, whose comment reflects a quiet but authoritative judgment since she has "done a lot of reading in this regard," says, "Alcoholism isn't a decision, it's a disease, and Billy would have had the disease whether he married the Irish girl or Maeve, whether he'd had kids or not." Immediately, another opinion is expressed. "'Now I don't agree,' Dan Lynch said . . . 'I say it's a matter of will . . . Billy never had the will to stop.'" But Rosemary persists in defending her brother: "That's not fair. When he went to Ireland, when he took the pledge, he was truly determined . . . But the disease had him in its grip."[37] Rosemary attempts to redeem her brother's memory—to redeem Billy himself—by her remarks, but her rationale is never bought entirely by Dan, nor do either of them realize what caused Billy to fall off the wagon in Ireland almost as soon as he had arrived. For neither Dennis nor Billy ever revealed the truth that stunned Billy overseas, a truth that dismantled his determination to stop drinking and an epiphany that seemed to discredit his grand passion, his years of private grieving and persistent loyalty to the memory of his beloved Eva. She was still alive. She had merely jilted him.

Before Billy's jolting revelation in Ireland, however, he had experienced—usually through his drinking—redemptive moments, moments of which he himself was quite aware. For, ironically, alcohol gave Billy's faith force. Sober, his religious conviction sometimes faltered, flaming up only briefly after Communion or perhaps when he entered the dark confessional or when the first scent of incense arose at Benediction. These moments provided Billy "a true redemption—it was a favorite word of his, after a few, Dan Lynch and my father agreed, a favorite topic—a redemption that was not merely a pretty story grown up around a good man but a fact that changed the very fiber of the day, the moment."[38] Like most adults who occasionally question the reality behind the faith they profess, Billy too was plagued at times with religious doubts. But when he'd "had a few" it was different. For, when he was drunk,

Heaven was there, utterly necessary, utterly sensible, the only possible reconciliation of the way he must live day by day and the certainty he'd felt that life meant

37. Ibid., 19.
38. Ibid., 187.

something greater. The only redemption, the only compensation for the disappointment, the cruelty and pain that plagued the living, for love itself, because when he turned his eyes to heaven, heaven was there and Eva was in it.[39]

In this incantational passage the term "redemption" moves in gradations of meaning from suffering to atone for sin, or reparation, to a related but distinct sense of compensation, of receiving back a momentary equivalency of ecstasy to counterbalance Billy's never-ending grief. Further, it offers reinforcement of his faltering faith, reassurance that he *will* see Eva again.

Billy's cousin Dennis, too, is in need of assurance of redemption. After caring tenderly for his wife in her lingering last illness, he also doubts if his devotion to her was sufficient to allow them to achieve "something redemptive" in the endurance of their love. Intensifying his grief were his doubts about the faith, his inability to convince himself "that heaven was any more than a well-intentioned deception meant to ease our own sense of foolishness, to ease pain."[40] Here "redemptive" seems to refer to some enduring value apart from religious faith, some ontological goodness in their love that was independent of faith and a sufficient recompense for the suffering that accompanies the loss of a loved one. Even the elusive narrator of *Charming Billy,* who is Dennis's daughter, finds herself part of a redemptive circumstance when she meets Matt, the man she will marry. He is the son of a couple who rented the cottage Billy and Dennis lived in the summer they met Eva and her sister. Though Matt's parents had had a bitter marriage, and though the cottage itself was shunned by Billy for years since Eva would never be able to come back to it, the narrator sees, in her meeting of her future spouse, an event through which the "whole history of Holtzman's little house" is finally "redeemed."[41]

Despite all the shades of meaning that "redemption" accrues in the course of the novel, it is, finally, Billy himself who echoes McDermott's deepest belief about redemption, and the reader is brought full circle back to the first and most sacred meaning of *the* Redemption, the deliverance of humanity from sin through the saving act of Jesus' death on the cross. Most eloquent when drunk, Billy engages in a late-night theological dispute over the phone with the long-suffering Dennis. He continues to shake his fist at heaven because of Eva's supposed death:

39. Ibid.   40. Ibid., 211.
41. Ibid., 230.

"The injustice of it," Billy said. "The way she was cheated . . ."

"Death is a terrible thing," Billy said . . .

"Our Lord knew it," Billy went on. "Our Lord knew it was terrible. Why would He have shed His own blood if death wasn't terrible? . . ."

"What do we need the Redemption for?" Billy asked. "If death isn't terrible. If we're reconciled? Why do we need heaven or hell? It makes no difference. If death doesn't trouble us, the injustice of it, then we don't need heaven or hell, do we? It might as well be a lie."[42]

In a 2003 article in *Boston College Magazine,* McDermott expands upon these ideas expressed in *Charming Billy.* "The death of the people we love," she writes there, "is unacceptable." Her characters, she continues, "carry on their tongues the tenets of the Church, and yet their spirits rebel against time, against loss, unreconciled, refusing to be resigned."[43] Faced with death her characters "demand, against all reason . . . the return of the loved one in all his or her familiarity."[44] McDermott acknowledges that this is a "mad, unreasonable demand" but also "the primitive impulse that makes faith necessary." In the same article, McDermott recalls the story of the death of Jesus' friend, Lazarus. Jesus, too, refuses to be reconciled to this death. He weeps and is troubled before restoring Lazarus to life and giving him back to his grieving sisters. It is in Jesus' refusal to be reconciled to the death of his friend, McDermott claims, that He makes possible our own "impossible hopes" and "confirms our own primitive rebellion against the terrible thing that is the death of those we love." McDermott concludes the article with a credal statement that her character Billy could no doubt assert with conviction only when in his cups: "At the heart of our faith lies the outrageous conviction that love redeems us, Christ redeems us, even from death."[45] This redemption is as reliable as it is comprehensive, and it includes us as we are, even with all our failings, just as, McDermott suggests, it includes charming Billy.

On several levels, then, the expansive and protean concept of redemption ripples throughout the novels of Alice McDermott. Minimally and somewhat analogically, it describes her clear-eyed sympathy for her characters seen in her comprehensive embrace of each as worthy of her contemplative gaze because endowed with inherent human dignity. It also includes the ex-

---

42. Ibid., 203–4.
44. Ibid., 37.

43. McDermott, "Lunatic," 36.
45. Ibid.

plicit struggle with faith, the persistent determination to find redemption for the inevitable pain, sorrows, and losses of life. McDermott presents the reader with portraits of ordinary persons struggling in various ways to redeem their circumstances, their lives, and the lives of those they love. And in doing so with consummate skill, immense humanity, and persistent faith, she invites her readers into reflection on the great questions of life, a reflection without which we are impoverished and which, undertaken thoughtfully, furthers our own insatiable quest for ultimate redemption.

CHAPTER 2

How Far Can You Go? to *Therapy* ▪ Catholicism and Postmodernism in the Novels of David Lodge

Daniel S. Lenoski

In an article written in 1988, Terry Eagleton, the Marxist critic, pointed out that the novelist David Lodge's Catholicism was ambiguous and "almost wholly unmarked by spiritual passion."[1] Though he continued to go to Mass until 1992, Lodge has confirmed his ambivalence by calling himself an "agnostic Catholic,"[2] writing comic novels about Catholicism, and clearly moving in his criticism and fiction toward post-structuralism and postmodernism. On the other hand, as I have shown in a previous article on *The British Museum Is Falling Down* (1965), to say that Lodge's "Catholicism makes little difference to his conventional liberal wisdom other than providing him with convenient materials for social criticism and comic satire"[3] may be going too far in querying the nature of the Catholicism present in Lodge's writing.[4] As Vatican II was "updating" Catholicism to the twentieth century, Lodge was operating in concert and providing a new way of writing a Catholic novel, one not limited by the realism of the previous generation of Catholic writers such as Graham Greene and Evelyn Waugh. In this essay I examine the proximity of Lodge's work to Catholicism and to the major genres of the novel in the twentieth century with reference to, in particular, *How Far Can You Go?* (1981) and *Therapy* (1995).

Several of Lodge's novels focus on Catholicism. These are *The Picturegoers* (1993), set prior to Vatican II, *The British Museum Is Falling Down*, set during Vatican II and anticipating its outcome, and *How Far Can You Go?*,

---

1. Terry Eagleton, "The Silences of David Lodge," *New Left Review* 172 (1988): 96.
2. Bernard Bergonzi, *David Lodge* (Plymouth, Engl.: Northcote House, 1995), 43.
3. Eagleton, "Silences of David Lodge," 96.
4. Daniel S. Lenoski, "The Catholic Carnival: The Novels of David Lodge," *Ultimate Reality and Meaning* 28, no. 4 (2005): 315–29.

set before, during, and after Vatican II. Many others, like *Small World* (1984) with its mythic and romance antecedents, *Nice Work* (1988), *Paradise News* (1993), *Therapy*, and *Author, Author* (2004) with its comic focus on the after-life, may suggest a Catholic undertext "lurking"—to use Andrew Greeley's word in *The Catholic Imagination*—beneath the surface of the narrative. The result is that in the few novels, such as *Changing Places* (1975), where Catholics don't appear, dedicated Lodge readers tend to wonder which of the characters are closet Catholics. Even *Ginger, You're Barmy* (1962), his novel about the absurdities of compulsory British military service during the cold war, includes three characters, Mike, Percy, and the Protestant narrator, who may possess some of the spiritual passion for which Eagleton is apparently nostalgic. Such characters cling to the cliffs of spiritual agony. They live at the "frontiers of the spiritual life," as Lodge has described characters in the novels of Waugh and Greene.[5]

Ah yes . . . but that was before Vatican II. Bernard Bergonzi is generally correct when he points out that Vatican II has redefined the subject matter of a Catholic novel and that the genre has subsequently focused more on the day-to-day lives of ordinary Catholics.[6] In conversation with Bernard Bergonzi, Lodge himself has commented that "religious language is the symbolic and speculative mode in which we articulate the contradictions and anxieties which are ineradicably part of the human condition."[7] Most of us do not live the desperate and dramatic lives of Catholic characters in so much pre-Vatican II Catholic fiction. Vatican II, particularly that document entitled *Gaudium et Spes* with its spacious, flexible, inclusive imagery and language, transformed the story of Catholicism to include bedrooms, lavatories, kitchens, factories, television studios, cocktail parties, and universities. Though Eagleton has neglected the influence of Vatican II on Lodge's Catholic novels, he has recognized that Catholicism is a cultural phenomenon as well as a religion and that a tension exists within Catholicism between its "two major currents": "a lineage of rigorous doctrinal thought, and a tradition of ethical and social concern."[8]

Following David Tracy's argument in *The Analogical Imagination*,[9] An-

---

5. David Lodge, *The British Museum Is Falling Down* (London: Penguin, 1983), 64.
6. Bernard Bergonzi, "A Conspicuous Absentee: The Decline and Fall of the Catholic Novel," *Encounter* 55, no. 2–3 (1980): 44–57.
7. Bergonzi, "A Religious Romance: David Lodge in Conversation," *The Critic* 47 (Fall 1992): 71.
8. Eagleton, "Silences of David Lodge," 95.
9. David Tracy, *The Analogical Imagination: Christian Theology and the Culture of Pluralism* (New York: Crossroad, 1981).

drew Greeley has argued a similar tradition of tension in *The Catholic Imagination:*

The high tradition is the Catholicism you learned in schools; the popular tradition is the Catholicism you learned in great part before you went to school. The former is contained in the teaching of theologians and the magisterium. It is cognitive, propositional, didactic. It is prosaic Catholicism. The latter is contained in the teaching of parents, family, neighbors and friends. It is imaginative, experiential, narrative. It is poetic Catholicism . . . If the high tradition is to be found in theology books and the documents of the councils, and the papacy . . . , the popular tradition is to be found in the rituals, the art, the music, the architecture, the devotions, the stories of ordinary people. If the former can be stated concisely at any given time in creeds . . . the latter is . . . expressed in stories.[10]

The darkness of what critics call "Greeneland," referring to the atmosphere of many of Graham Greene's novels, and the dramatic situations in which the characters of Greene and Waugh find themselves, reflect the profile of the high tradition before Vatican II. The novels of Lodge, on the other hand, contain the comic, prosaic world of popular Catholicism: diapers, lavatories, bodily functions, underpants, menstruation, and childbirth; too many children and not enough space, money, time, or satisfying emotional and sexual intimacy to sustain tenderness between ordinary men and women. The focus has shifted, in general terms, from the vertical, absolute, and male to the horizontal and relative domestic world of the female. Thus, at the end of *The British Museum Is Falling Down,* having tucked her children in bed while whispering a Hail Mary, Barbara, the archetypal Catholic wife and mother (three children and now the worry of a late period), muses about sex, the rhythm method of birth control, family, and the foibles of men. Parodying James Joyce's novel, Lodge has her correct Molly Bloom's last word at the end of *Ulysses.* A more appropriate word to summarize life for a Catholic woman, and maybe for Catholics in general, is *perhaps.* Despite his attempt to manifest the popular and domestic Catholic tradition in *Ulysses,* Joyce inadvertently betrayed his male bias when he gave Molly the word *yes.* Life is much more relative, conditional, and ambiguous for a Catholic woman than *yes* suggests.

Like *The British Museum Is Falling Down, How Far Can You Go?* moves away from the high tradition of Catholicism toward the popular tradition

---

10. Andrew Greeley, *The Catholic Imagination* (Berkeley: University of California Press, 2001), 76–77.

both in subject matter and form. Nevertheless, it begins in pre–Vatican II 1953 when the high tradition dominates. The Mass in Chapter 1, "How It Was," is Tridentine, and the young priest, Fr. Austin Brierley, is facing the altar. The atmosphere exudes the overall gloom of Greeneland. Our suspicion that Lodge is parodying Greene is confirmed by the knowledge that he did his doctoral thesis on Greene and that his character Michael, one of nine students at Mass, is thinking of doing likewise. Both Michael and Polly, another student at this Mass, draw attention to Michael's similarity to a character in a Greene novel.[11] Later as the inexperienced Michael and Miriam try clumsily to consummate their marriage, Lodge is careful to tell us that they are "suffused with a Greeneian gloom."[12] As Linda Hutcheon has commented, parody can both honor and question.[13] The latter episode certainly makes fun of the pessimism of Greene's world, especially when Miriam comments that she is "awfully sore."[14] Similarly, at the opening Mass the incongruity between the altar's focus on enlightening spiritual darkness and Michael's simultaneous obsession with sex and with the female body is funny. However, both scenes also have serious ramifications. In Lodge's novels sex causes pain as well as pleasure. Barbara's soliloquy at the end of *The British Museum Is Falling Down* summarizes the experience of the major characters in *How Far Can You Go?*, *Therapy*, and many other Lodge novels as well:

It makes you wonder if there's such a thing as a normal sexual relationship . . . it can be wonderful too and there are times when married people have to ought to and it isn't always a safe period either like when Adam was in the army that's how we had Dominic well perhaps the church will change and a good thing too there'll be much less misery . . . but it's silly to think that everything in the garden will be lovely it won't it it never is . . .[15]

The garden metaphor here reminds us not only of the problems in Eden, but also that sexuality and the body are indeed important.

Andrew Greeley has argued that while the high tradition of Catholicism has tended to emphasize the former—the problems in Eden—the popular tradition has been in love with the two latter, sexuality and the body. In Greeley's opinion, "erotic metaphors . . . are part of the Catholic religious sensi-

11. David Lodge, *How Far Can You Go?* (London: Penguin, 1981), 40–41.
12. Ibid., 63.
13. Linda Hutcheon, *A Poetics of Postmodernism: History, Theory, and Fiction* (New York: Routledge, 1988), 126.
14. Lodge, *How Far Can You Go?*, 63.
15. Lodge, *British Museum*, 160.

bility."[16] He recalls Bernini's *St. Theresa in Ecstasy* and the nakedness that Michelangelo's and Raphael's art have disseminated about Rome and Florence. And marriage is, after all, a sacrament. Accordingly, in *How Far Can You Go?* the frequent description of naked bodies and frank dramatization of sexual experience are not at all foreign to Catholicism, the tension between the two traditions with regard to sex perhaps even driving Catholicism forward. However, the novel itself, like its predecessor focusing on birth control, reveals that as the world bore witness to the openness of Vatican II, the popular tradition gained in power and influence.

Following Vatican II and the resultant resurgence of the popular tradition, in *How Far Can You Go?* Lodge deals specifically with the effects of Catholic sexual conservatism on the domestic lives of several Catholic couples. Neglected perhaps in Catholic writing since that out-of-practice Catholic author James Joyce, the messiness of the body makes its graphic tragicomic reappearance here. The romance of love gives way to the soiling of sheets and garments, to sexual flaccidity, to pain, and even to the fear of death, the latter as Michael, worrying about cancer and on his way to the doctor, spends an hour on the hot, crowded London subway discretely carrying a pile of his own feces in an ice cream carton and surrounded by a *cordon sanitaire* of commuters. For the first time in the novel, perhaps the only time, he is not interested in sex. The scene is, of course, hilarious, though we laugh out of the other sides of our mouths.

On the other hand, in opposing the overemphasis on the high tradition and championing the cause of openness, Lodge deals with the former on its own grounds: that is, the more abstract playing field of theology, philosophy, and history. The chapter entitled "How They Lost the Fear of Hell" resembles an essay on sexuality and modern Catholicism. It attributes the sexual revolution of the 1960s to the Church's admission that sex as "mutual love between spouses" is not sinful and to the democratic atmosphere surrounding both Vatican II and its offspring, the encyclical *Humanae Vitae*.[17] The admission that *Humanae Vitae* was not infallible resulted in a great deal of further conscientious democratic debate and, as a result, guilt about sexual activity was largely diminished in both the Catholic world and the world at large and, as the chapter title states, fear of hell began to disappear.

But . . . is this a comic novel or not? Yes indeed, a good many hilarious

---

16. Greeley, *The Catholic Imagination*, 75.
17. Lodge, *How Far Can You Go?*, 116.

things happen, and the domestic settings and informal language suggest a comic vision of life that both celebrates and laughs at human foibles. However, the narrator himself, who bears a remarkable resemblance to both the author David Lodge and to the character Michael, points out that *How Far Can You Go?* isn't *exactly* a comic novel.[18] Some pretty serious and very Catholic religious issues make their appearance, and a good deal of physical and emotional suffering and spiritual passion are indeed present, despite the emphasis on the popular tradition. The novel also contains quite a bit of twentieth-century social, religious, intellectual, political, economic, and even football history as well, often emphasizing low points in human events such as economic cutbacks in Britain, the assassination of President John F. Kennedy, the Russian invasion of Czechoslovakia, the air crash of a jumbo jet in Paris in 1974 and, perhaps most painful and inexplicable of all, the mudslide at Aberfan Wales on October 21, 1966 that killed 144 people, 116 of whom were children. Responding to this latter tragedy and to news that Angela's and Dennis's new baby, Nicole, has Down syndrome, the very pregnant Tessa feels that there has been "some malice in the air" that needed to be sated.[19] Soon we discover that Angela's and Dennis's healthy daughter Anne is killed by a van. Lodge has named her purposefully, for Anne means *grace*, and grace in this novel has a very hard time in the face of evil.

Indeed, like many Catholic novels both before and after Vatican II, *How Far Can You Go?* is very much concerned about the problem of evil and its offspring, death, life's "dirty little secret." In fact, the Book of Job is quoted by Fr. Brierley in his homily as he tries to make sense of the Aberfan tragedy. He wonders how a just God can allow the innocent to suffer meaningless injustice and cruelty.[20] Equally disturbing is that his colleagues, superiors, and most of his congregation refuse to confront the problem. The novel asks hard questions of Catholicism. Why do the ways of the wicked prosper? Why do good people like Angela, Dennis, and their children suffer while guilty and fraudulent parents and husbands like Jeremy and Robin flourish? How far can you go in ignoring or witnessing injustice and attempting to apologize for it before your faith disappears? How far can you go in *aggiornamento* before your religion loses definition and significance? How far can you go in your commitment to the secular world before the sacred is destroyed rather than fostered? And then there are the questions suggested by the Hans

18. Ibid., 112.   19. Ibid., 111.
20. Ibid., 159, 107.

Küng epigraph to the novel: "What can we know? Why is there anything at all? Why not nothing? What ought we to do? Why do what we do? Why and to whom are we finally responsible? What may we hope? Why are we here? What is it all about? What will give us courage for life and what courage for death?" most of which Lodge quotes in the chapter entitled "How They Broke Out, Away, Down, Up, Through, Etc."[21] Later he also adds: "How did it all start, and where is it all going?"[22] *How Far Can You Go?* contains a fair amount of spiritual passion confronting an unfair amount of evil and an unfair number of problems. And this confrontation seems quite Catholic.

Manifesting all of this content are the novel's formal features that foreground it as a fictive act and serve to destabilize the narrative. Just as we are beginning to assume that it is a realist novel proceeding in a linear direction narrated by an omniscient narrator, we discover that what we are reading is actually metafiction. The narrator discusses his storytelling methods with us often, for example, asking questions about the intercourse between our sexual and spiritual lives and explaining the rationale for the names and physical details he has chosen for the characters. As the novel proceeds and as the effects of Vatican II unfold, such interruptions become more intrusive. The narrator becomes more and more familiar until we wonder whether we are reading third- or first-person narration. We also move back and forth between the narrator's attempts to describe and analyze the time period and his stories of individual characters. The result is that though readers approach a sense of security because the narrative is tied together by dates and proceeds chronologically, they never actually achieve it because of the essay-like interruptions and the movement more or less abruptly back and forth from the story of one character to that of another, all of which inevitably results in suspense, uncertainty, and mystery.

The novel's use of parody also disorients and reorients us. I have already spoken of the parody that occurs when, early on, Michael parodies a character out of a Graham Greene novel. Later Michael changes into a parody of Mellors, the gamekeeper in D. H. Lawrence's *Lady Chatterley's Lover,* and the reader is left to consider the extent to which he is like Mellors and Miriam, his wife, is like lady Connie Chatterley, with whom Mellors is having sex. When she douses him with cold water, Miriam's response to Michael tells us a good deal about both of them. Or does it? Shortly thereafter, faced in the

---

21. Ibid., 143.
22. Ibid., 171.

sauna with an accidentally—or purposely—nude Jeremy, Miriam drops her sexual guard for a split second and we are forced to reassess her virtue.[23] In another place, when Michael meets Dennis in a pub to discuss the latter's betrayal of his wife, Angela, by his adultery, Lodge uses the mock heroic as well as parody by comparing Dennis to Kurtz and Michael to Marlow, the characters from Joseph Conrad's *The Heart of Darkness*. We laugh, but we also wonder who or what may be "The horror! The horror!"

Despite the dominance of the more or less third-person omniscient narration, *How Far Can You Go?* also contains a good deal of postmodern variety in its formal structure. We encounter not only the narrator's storytelling and use of parody, but also metawriting, philosophic essays, poems and songs from both the high and popular traditions (for example, from Job, Isaiah, Gerard Manley Hopkins, the Beatles, Simon and Garfunkel), allusions to the literary and scholarly tradition (the Psalms, Greene, Waugh, Conrad, the documents of and language of Vatican II, Hans Küng, Teilhard de Chardin, French literary criticism, Marx, Freud, Masters and Johnson)—even Linda Lovelace. And when much of this eclectic variety appears, irony results. For example, in the context of this novel so much focused on both religion and sex, the reference to the Beatles' *All You Need Is Love* and to a line from Simon and Garfunkel's *Mrs. Robinson* about Jesus' love for the title character develop a strange incongruity.[24]

At least three different types of letters appear. One we might define as part of the high tradition when the superior of Ruth's religious order writes to her to try to retrieve her from the political chaos that was the American experience of Vatican II. Another type is those letters that appear in the popular press regarding advice to those with sexual or romantic difficulty. The novel also contains quotations from at least two love letters and a fan letter from a Czech written in a charmingly overpolite form of what can only be called Czechinglish. The latter raises the question of how we can trust a narrator who would be so self-indulgent.

Another type of formal variety occurs near the end of the novel when the generous, tender-hearted, but emotionally unstable lapsed Catholic, future Sufist, and current Jehovah's Witness, Violet, provides us with a chart titled *Events of History, Past and Present*. We are not certain whether to laugh or cry.

23. Ibid., 216–18.
24. Ibid., 133.

The end of *How Far Can You Go?* also recalls the multiple endings found in a postmodern novel. Chapter 6, "How They Dealt with Love and Death," moves toward what resembles an ending with the reconstruction of the deconstructed marriage of Angela and Dennis, two of the Catholics whose pilgrimage through life the novel has followed since the Mass on the first page. The agent of this renewal is the Vatican II incarnation of Fr. Austin Brierley, the priest that had earlier solemnized their marriage. Lodge calls his intervention both "providential" and "poetic." Furthermore, he appears shortly thereafter at a Paschal festival Mass more in the role of a suitor than that of a priest, holding hands with Dennis's former mistress and clearly moving in a direction opposite to that of his saintly namesake. Though readers here anticipate the end, it does not quite arrive, because the next chapter is the transcript of a video recording of an experimental Paschal festival organized by Catholics for an Open Church, a group inspired by Vatican II. (Can a group with the acronym COC be taken seriously?) The theme of the video is that the Catholic Church is opening, changing, and developing—being updated. The video ends with a frozen frame of film in which three nuns, who are performing a sacred dance, leap into the air while the sun (Son?) shines through their diaphanous robes. We have been told earlier by Ruth that this is supposed to mime the encounter between the two women and Christ at the tomb as well as the Resurrection itself.[25] Such a scene is, recalling a word Gerard Manley Hopkins uses, *fleshbursting* with possibility. But this is not the novel's end either, despite the appearance of the word *ENDS*, because the narrator, rather like a realist writer such as Charles Dickens, now in the next chapter tells us what happens to all the characters. Finally the novel does indeed end, because the narrator bids us *farewell*. However, this finality is undercut not only by the ambiguity caused by the narrator's resemblance to Lodge, but also by the previous paragraph where he informs readers that the diverse background of the new Polish pope embraces both the popular and high tradition of Catholicism, and so the apparent closure is deferred to the future.

According to Wolfgang Iser in *The Implied Reader,* such formal variety in a novel, technical virtuosity, and consequent ambiguity not only foreground a work's fictionality but also reveal a variety of views of life and coexisting "realities."[26] The formal variety of *How Far Can You Go?* appropriately mani-

25. Ibid., 229.
26. Wolfgang Iser, *The Implied Reader* (Baltimore: Johns Hopkins University Press, 1974), 196–233, esp. 201, 203–5, 213, 225.

fests and reflects the disruptive effects of all the questions—existential, philosophic, Catholic—about the nature of reality the book raises. Linda Hutcheon points out that the use of parody and therefore intertextuality, the use of paradox, difference, formal variety, contradiction, and disruption, all serve to avoid closure and a single centralized meaning. The result is ambiguity, possibility, and mystery, an openness that is distinctly postmodern.[27] Lodge apparently agrees. In *The Modes of Modern Writing* (1977), he identifies some defining features of postmodern narrative: multiple and parodic endings, the use of contradiction and paradox, questions about authorship, and moving back and forth between fiction and fact. When the gap between art and life is blurred and arcing takes place, such "short-circuiting," to Lodge, results in the word and the world it represents resisting interpretation.[28] In such a text, readers are challenged to question, to understand and to explain. Of course, this is what *How Far Can You Go?* is all about.

It may be appropriate to mention at this point that both post-structuralist critics (like Derrida for example) and theologians have struggled with the problem of naming the Mystery, of explaining the infinite and numinous using the finite, imperfect language of the world of phenomena.[29] In this light, it is interesting that one of the examples that Lodge uses to explain postmodernism in both *Modernism, Antimodernism and Postmodernism* (1976) and *The Modes of Modern Writing* is a novel by Samuel Beckett called *The Unnameable.* In fact, the Incarnation itself involves paradox and contradiction and inevitably then a redefinition of the gap between the W/word and the world. Like Lodge's novel and postmodernism itself—even perhaps like Vatican II—it calls much into question. Despite their differences about the quest for the Absolute, both Catholicism and postmodernism show a similar affinity for paradox, contradiction, the enlightening short circuit, and unnamable mysteries, and all of this results in an emphasis on the ontological—that is, on different levels of being such as the profane, the sacred, the mythical, the spiritual, the fictional, the historical, and thus the past, present, future, the possible, and even the impossible. For postmodernism, though, some of these are merely what Thomas Pavel calls "theoretical."[30]

27. Hutcheon, *Poetics of Postmodernism,* 126–27.

28. David Lodge, *The Modes of Modern Writing* (Ithaca, N.Y.: Cornell University Press, 1977), 239.

29. Luke Ferreter, *Towards a Christian Literary Theory* (Houndsmills, Basingstoke: Palgrave Macmillan, 2003), 27ff.

30. Thomas Pavel, "Tragedy and the Sacred: Notes towards a Semantic Characterization of a Fictional Genre," *Poetics* 10, no. 2–3 (1981): 234.

It is not surprising, then, that for critics such as Brian McHale in *Post-modernist Fiction*, the "dominant" of postmodernism is the ontological. He is joined in this view by many other critics, including Lodge himself, as well as, for example, a writer like Umberto Eco who, in the "Postscript" to his Catholic and postmodern novel *The Name of the Rose*, comments that writing a novel has less to do with words than with being "a cosmological matter."[31] McHale argues that the form of the postmodern novel is constantly manifesting the ontological questions that Dick Higgins asks: "Which world is this? What is to be done in it? Which of my selves is to do it?"[32] These recall the questions mentioned earlier that are at the heart of *How Far Can You Go?* The violence done to traditional realist methods of telling a story with their linear plot line, orthodox use of language, and consistent and homogeneous formal features, encourages readers to rethink "official" versions of the truth. In a novel like *How Far Can You Go?* this means that the many voices of the popular tradition of Catholicism become stronger.

At the same time, while Lodge uses some of the technical effects associated with postmodernism, his work possesses the nostalgia for unity that Linda Hutcheon identifies with modernism, as opposed to postmodernism's affection for disintegration.[33] *How Far Can You Go?* is underscored by the cultural bric-a-bracolage of Catholicism, its imagery, its names, and its concerns. In addition, the original ten characters at the Mass that begins the novel are all involved in the search for At(one)ment, for the One amid the many. If sex has waylaid some of them on their pilgrimage toward peace, they have also discovered that sex is not enough. Reacting to Michael's illness, the narrator early on comments about those who would replace *the* Good News with the good news about sex: "The good news about sexual satisfaction has little to offer those who are crippled, chronically sick, mad, ugly, impotent, or old, which all of us will be in due course, unless we are dead already. Death, after all, is the overwhelming question to which sex provides no answer."[34]

Nevertheless, the last few pages of the novel contain much that is hopeful and perhaps suggest an answer beyond mere sex. Here, we find a good

---

31. Umberto Eco, *The Name of the Rose* (San Diego: Harcourt Brace, 1994), 512.

32. Brian McHale, *Postmodernist Fiction* (New York: Methuen, 1967), 10.

33. Linda Hutcheon, *The Canadian Postmodern: A Study of Contemporary English Canadian Fiction* (Oxford: Oxford University Press, 1989), 1–2.

34. Lodge, *How Far Can You Go?*, 121.

deal of emphasis on marriage or on other similar family relationships. Adrian and his wife Dorothy are heavily involved in the Catholic Marriage Encounter movement. Angela's brother Tom has left the priesthood and is happily married with two children. Edward and Tessa, and also Dennis and Angela, have renewed their marriages and the latter have a daughter who is in love. Nicole, Edward and Tessa's daughter who has Down syndrome, has become a loving source of happiness and positive growth. Though Polly has divorced the adulterous Jeremy, she is peacefully raising her daughter. Meanwhile, her reaction to her son's conversion to Catholicism indicates she has not left her Catholicism behind. The gay Miles has found in a monastery someone to love. And, fitting hand in glove with all of this are the forward-looking last paragraphs of the novel focused on the new Pope and the future of Catholicism.

It is a scholarly cliché that the end of comedy is marriage. In an essay entitled "The Argument of Comedy," Northrop Frye argues that comedy, whether divine or human, is associated with resurrection, especially when supported by the presence of festivals near the end.[35] Considering the religious imagery present in the Paschal festival that helps end *How Far Can You Go?* and the renewal suggested by marriage, we might say that the novel that previously looked like it wasn't a comedy is a *divine* comedy. As he does in *The British Museum Is Falling Down,* Lodge here suggests that Catholicism, though satirized and questioned, is reaffirmed and renewed.

This implies that Lodge is wary of a simplistic stance, of only moving out toward the margins. In fact, it may be more correct to say that he *recenters* as much as he decenters, both theologically and formally. Despite using formal features that destabilize the narrative and foreground the fictive process, making it self-reflexive and moving it away from life, Lodge also provides readers with formal elements that move in tension in the opposite direction. *How Far Can You Go?*, then, is not a closed system. Indeed, when Nicole is born with Down syndrome, possibly because Dennis and Angela, as good Catholics, have been practicing the rhythm method of birth control, and then their other daughter Anne is killed by a van, the narrator's mask almost disappears. He comments:

I have avoided a direct presentation of this incident because frankly I find it too

---

35. Northrop Frye, "The Argument of Comedy," in *Shakespeare's Comedies,* ed. Laurence Lerner (Harmondsworth, Engl.: Penguin, 1967), 317–25.

painful to contemplate. Of course Dennis and Angela and Anne are fictional characters, they cannot bleed or weep, but they stand here for all the real people to whom such disasters happen with no apparent reason or justice. One does not kill off characters lightly, I assure you, even ones like Anne, evoked solely for that purpose.[36]

The point is that Lodge in his metawriting makes a special effort to emphasize the referentiality of his fiction. He mediates the distance here between art and life so that we understand that though this is not life, such people *do* exist and such things *do* happen.

Lodge's imagery functions in the same way. In *The Modes of Modern Writing,* following Jacobsen in explaining how simile, metonymy, and metaphor function, Lodge suggests that when the reader quickly understands the relationship between the tenor (the thing being described) and the vehicle (the thing to which it is compared) in the metaphor or simile, the story is driven forward and the illusion (or allusion) of the one-thing-after-another real world is maintained. Because metaphor, unlike simile, does not have the help of the words "like" or "as," which orient the reader, and cannot always rely on contiguity and context like metonymy (the part representing the whole), its tenor and vehicle tend toward separation.[37] Thus, abstraction more easily results and, accordingly, so does reflection on the part of the reader. The narrative story line wanes while its meaning waxes. Lodge calls works in which simile and metonymy dominate "realist," while those in which metaphor predominates approach modernism.[38] Holding this in mind when we look at Lodge's fiction helps explain his extraordinary ability to keep the space between tenor and vehicle minimal so that whether we are speaking of the simile that dominates his work or the less frequent metaphor, his imagery is concrete and accessible, and referentiality is encouraged, moving the narrative toward the unity, linearity, and stability of realism. For example, in this brilliant passage from *How Far Can You Go?* Lodge uses a mixture of metaphors and similes to evoke the Catholic worldview prior to Vatican II. While reading this passage we should remember that the ability to evoke the world in which we live and charge it with meaning, as Greeley suggests, is one of the distinguishing features of the Catholic imagination.[39]

36. Lodge, *How Far Can You Go?*, 125.
38. Ibid., 77–91, 200–13.

37. Lodge, *Modes of Modern Writing*, 75.
39. Greeley, *Catholic Imagination*, 1–21, 55–86.

Up there was Heaven; down there was Hell. The name of the game was Salvation, the object to get to Heaven and avoid Hell. It was like Snakes and Ladders:
sin sent you plummeting down towards the Pit; sacraments, good deeds, acts of
mortification, enabled you to climb back towards the light . . . Those who suc-
ceeded in the game eliminated the bad, and converted as much of the indifferent as possible into the good . . . There were two types of sin, venial and mortal.
Venial sins were little sins which only slightly retarded your progress across the
board. Mortal sins were huge snakes that sent you slithering back to square one,
because if you died in a state of mortal sin, you went to Hell. If, however, you
confessed your sins and received absolution through the sacrament of Penance,
you shot up the ladder of Grace . . . Purgatory was a kind of penitential transit
camp on the way to the gates of Heaven.[40]

This passage, with its evocation of Jacob's ladder and use of hellish imagery,
is hilarious, but it also is contextually appropriate to the novel and mimeti-
cally accurate to the period. For many, this board game *is* an image of the
way things worked prior to Vatican II.

Another place in the novel provides an equally immediate and appropriate simile when Michael, with much embarrassment, successfully asks the
hotel clerk for a room with a double bed for his honeymoon: Michael "ran
back to Miriam, grasping the key like a mythical treasure wrested from
a dragon." The sexual connotations of the key and the room, and the use
of the mock heroic in comparing the impatient groom to a dragon-slaying
knight, work wonderfully. In yet another place, Lodge perfectly captures the
way some of us still feel, moving back and forth between the various incar-
nations of the Mass since Vatican II, when the narrator informs us that "Michael . . . felt like a liturgical double agent."[41]

Coming nearly fifteen years after *How Far Can You Go?* Lodge's *Therapy*
is also a novel that contains tension between formal devices that destabilize
and decenter the narrative and those that reveal a nostalgic push toward unity, an underlying realism, and a reaffirmation of more popular post–Vatican
II forms of Catholicism. Lodge understands that the integrity of any narrative
depends on a tension between the formal and the phenomenal. Nor can it be
just monological or dialogical. The voice of the artist and/or narrator is important, but so is deference to other voices. In *Write On: Occasional Essays*,
Lodge "calls for a new kind of literary decorum, a decorum of indecorum, a

---

40. Lodge, *How Far Can You Go?*, 6–7.
41. Ibid., 62, 134.

bursting of the moulds [sic] of obsolete conventions, that yet avoids dissipating its energy in a welter of disconnected and contradictory effects."[42]

The first-person narrator in *Therapy* is Lawrence (Tubby) Passmore, a television writer with money, fame, a faithful wife, successful children, and an expensive car. He is nevertheless filled with dread, inexplicably unhappy, as he describes himself by quoting Kierkegaard: "always absent to himself, never present to himself."[43] These feelings are signaled by a pain in his knee that won't disappear. In an effort to relieve this pain, he tries every known therapy "except chemotherapy"—acupuncture, tennis, aromatherapy, massage therapy, physiotherapy, and cognitive behavior therapy. As a result of the last, Tubby writes a narrative that he calls a "Journal. Diary. Confession," or interior monologue.[44] He also tells us his narrative is a mixture of monologue and autobiography and, significantly, he foregrounds the ontological status of what he is writing when he points out that it combines the present and the past: "The special thing about a journal is that the writer doesn't know where his story is going, he doesn't know how it ends; so it seems to exist in a kind of continuous present, even though the individual events may be described in the past tense."[45] This novel then also involves a fair amount of metawriting, emphasizing the fictive aspect of what we are reading and therefore its lack of reliability with respect to what actually happens in Tubby's life. Tubby is Lodge's creation—but Tubby is also Tubby's creation.

Careful readers learn to be skeptical about what they read. And who wouldn't, when the narrator's nickname is Tubby and his Catholic namesake, Lodge notes, is the martyr St. Lawrence who joked with his executioners while being barbecued alive. Tubby's lack of narrative reliability is underscored when, his marriage to Sally in trouble, he begins an affair with Amy and refuses to admit it.[46] Later Sally's conversation with the marriage counselor, Dr. Marples, reveals that her enthusiasm for sex is not proof of conjugal bliss but rather a desperate attempt to save her marriage. In fact, book II of *Therapy* voices five other monologues, in sequence, switching suddenly from one to another as they describe Tubby's personal and professional life and question his single viewpoint. Each varies in method and style of communication: a court document signed by the tennis pro at Tubby's club; a conversation between Amy and her analyst; a telephone call between Lou-

42. Lodge, *Write On: Occasional Essays 1964–85* (London: Penguin, 1986), 84.
43. Lodge, *Therapy* (London: Penguin, 1995), 100.
44. Ibid., 67, 17, 53.   45. Ibid., 285.
46. Ibid., 28–31.

ise, who Tubby secretly dated, and a friend; a conversation in a restaurant between Ollie, Tubby's producer, and a friend; and a conversation between Samantha, Tubby's script assistant, and a friend. However, all of these are, indeed, monologues, recording the words of only one speaker, and just when we think we have encountered other authoritative views of Tubby's life, we are surprised to discover that Tubby himself has written all of them for his analyst.

Lodge adds to this incongruity the stylistic variations provided by a questionnaire, at least two play scripts, a page from a book called *Quaint Tales of British Rail #167*, the charts Tubby's analyst suggests that he create about his life, and quotations from Kierkegaard's prose, various dictionaries and encyclopedias, and poems and popular songs. Finally, the life Tubby has constructed for himself becomes a kind of parody of Kierkegaard's life. The novel questions, to what extent *is* Tubby like or unlike Kierkegaard? All of this results in a narrative that we can't trust, one that raises the postmodern (and Catholic) ontological questions mentioned earlier in this essay: "Which world is this? What is to be done in it?" And, since the Book of Job also makes its appearance here, how do we deal with injustice and death?

On the other hand, as in *How Far Can You Go?* Lodge provides unifying and stabilizing features in *Therapy* that move in the direction of realism and referentiality. Here we have a single narrator, even if he pretends to be multiple. The novel is ordered by a date-and-time chronology, although there are flashbacks. Lodge also uses simile very often in a manner appropriate to the context, keeping tenor and vehicle close together and therefore moving readers toward the one-after-another concrete world in which we live. Here, for example, is a brilliant series of similes that are immediate to our experience and also charge the scene with Catholic images as Tubby remembers his predatory success involving his lost first love, Maureen's breast (the italics here are mine):

I unbuttoned her blouse and unfastened, with infinite care and delicacy, like a *burglar* picking a lock, the hook and eye that fastened her brassiere . . . She stood there in the dark . . . passive and trembling very slightly, *like a lamb brought to the sacrifice* . . . Holding my breath I gently released a breast . . . It rolled into my palm *like a ripe fruit* . . . I . . . gently squeezed the breast as it lolled in my palm like a naked *cherub* . . . It was *the climax of the ritual, like the priest raising the glittering monstrance aloft at Benediction.*[47]

47. Ibid., 246–47.

The imagery Tubby uses here appears blasphemous, but it also reflects the growing religious judgment that he, reading Kierkegaard, is making on himself for having broken faith with Maureen.[48] Indeed, before the memoir entitled "Maureen" is over, he understands the real therapy for his hollowness is precisely the Catholic process of contrition, confession, penance, and absolution, and he receives it when he follows Maureen on a pilgrimage to Santiago de Compostella. In fact, he speaks of the sacramental nature of the experience even as he does the pilgrimage in his car, a metaphor for the secular world.[49] But significantly, he leaves the car behind and walks the rest of the way to the Cathedral for Mass. As at the end of *How Far Can You Go?*, a kind of "marriage" takes place in close proximity to a festival because Maureen comments that they are making this pilgrimage together and that "it was like a miracle. St. James again."[50]

Lodge takes pains to associate Maureen with the Virgin Mary, who has a special place in the Catholic tradition. Maureen has a son killed by soldiers. Like the Mary of legend she has followed St. James to Spain. The name Maureen is even the Irish form of Mary and, in the Nativity play performed many years ago in the Church of the Immaculate Conception, Maureen played Mary. *Therapy,* then, contains many suggestions of resurrection rooted firmly in the Catholic tradition. And as in the romance tradition, redemption and renewal for the everyman character Tubby arrive through horses (although in this case through horse*power*) and through women (in this case one named Mary). Even the saints such as St. James intercede on behalf of the hero and heroine. Though the Kierkegaard that led him beyond the secular world was a Protestant, Tubby considers that, if he had been Catholic, he too would have made a first-class saint.[51]

It is fully appropriate then to classify *Therapy* and *How Far Can You Go?* as Catholic novels despite the fact that they possess many of the formal features of both modernism and postmodernism, as this essay has noted. What David Lodge has done is to combine the openness, decentering, and questioning that such formal variety suggests with some of the unifying elements of realism and romance, of comedy and Catholicism. This mix provides a direction for the Catholic novel in a world that is both post–Vatican II and postmodern. It manifests the view that neither realism nor the high Catholic

48. Ibid., 279.
50. Ibid., 302.

49. Ibid., 310.
51. Ibid., 311.

tradition alone is enough to tell the Catholic story.[52] What is needed is something that moves back and forth between forms yet with an underlying unity and referentiality that suggests neither a theology of exclusiveness (that is, Catholicism is the absolute truth) nor fulfillment (Catholicism completes the truths of other religions). Rather, Lodge's technique suggests a theology of *sharing* in which Catholicism collaborates with other voices and other views to find the truth.[53]

52. Lodge, *Modes of Modern Writing*, 50.
53. Achiel Peelman, "The Theological Challenge of Religious Pluralism and Aboriginal Spirituality" (Hanley Lecture, St. Paul's College, University of Manitoba, Winnipeg, Canada, October 17, 2005).

CHAPTER 3

"Descending Theology" ▪ The Poetry of Mary Karr

Robert P. Lewis

Mary Karr's most recent volume of poems, *Sinners Welcome* (2006), confirms the depth at which her conversion to Catholicism in 1996 has taken
imaginative root. Karr's first two volumes of poetry, *Abacus* (1987) and *The
Devil's Tour* (1993), assess, even more intimately than her bestselling memoirs of childhood and adolescence in southeast Texas *The Liars' Club* (1995)
and *Cherry* (2000), the emotional toll her volatile family environment took
on her and the imprudent intensities the poet courted to fill the affective
void. Her 1998 collection of poetry, *Viper Rum*, alludes to the alcoholism that
precipitated Karr's resort to prayer and to her subsequent religious conversion. *Sinners Welcome* translates much of the familiar material of Karr's earlier poems into an altogether new key. These later poems express an unwonted joy in the person of Christ, who has claimed the poet in the very depths of
her bodily desiring. Finally, five poetic reflections on Christ's birth, passion,
death, and resurrection, each bearing the title of "Descending Theology"
and each alluding to a deeper moment in Christ's entry into the human condition, make explicit the strategy of *descent* into her own and her contemporaries' lives by which Karr appropriates the Christian mystery.

The *Liars' Club* and *Cherry* recreate the hardscrabble youth of Mary Karr
in Leechfield, Texas, the small town where she was born in 1954. Her mother, Charlie Marie Karr, was beautiful and talented but ill-matched to Pete
Karr, a refinery worker, or to the cultural stultification of Leechfield. In part,
alcohol and pills insulated Karr's mother against this stolid, intolerant, red-

neck world. In even greater part, the stimulants, like the men in her multiple marriages, anaesthetized her guilt at having lost custody of two children in an early marriage. The volatile atmosphere of family life made it difficult for Mary Karr to trust either her world or herself. Two acts of violation haunt her memories of early childhood: a rape by an older neighborhood boy, and her near murder by her knife-wielding, drunk, and deranged mother. "The fact that my house was Not Right," Karr writes, "metastasized into the notion that I myself was Not Right."[1] This primal insecurity expressed itself, during her adolescence and early maturity, in a defensive posture of "undiluted agnosticism."[2]

Cherry details Karr's troubled pilgrimage through the landscape of adolescence in the late 1960s and early 1970s. Like St. Augustine, an inspiration for her own forays into memoir, she found herself enslaved by vacuous pleasure for lack of an adequate "vocabulary for wanting."[3] After graduation from high school, Karr briefly worked in a factory in California before entering Macalester College in St. Paul, Minnesota. She spent two years there majoring in philosophy before succumbing again to wanderlust and departing for travel in England. In a later poem called "The Choice," she describes from this period a serendipitous outing to Wordsworth's cottage after a night of pub drinking, when her callous persona as bohemian and "bimbo" was transformed to "reverence" by the sight of the poet's manuscripts.[4] The experience influenced her return to graduate school for serious literary study, and she completed an M.F.A. program at Goddard College in Vermont. In 1983 Karr, then a member of a writing group in Cambridge, married fellow poet Michael Milburn. Three years later, their son Dev was born. Three years after this, the couple divorced. Without a car or furniture or a steady source of income, and trying to raise a small child while battling the demon of alcoholism, Karr hit bottom. A Whiting writer's grant of $25,000 enabled her to finish *The Devil's Tour,* her second volume of poems.

The prospect of reenacting her mother's dereliction with her children may have lent greater urgency to Karr's search for that missing "vocabulary of wanting." Consequently, she adopted an ex–heroin addict's advice to get down on her knees and pray in thanksgiving every morning and night, de-

---

1. Mary Karr, *The Liars' Club* (New York: Penguin, 1996), 10.
2. Karr, *Sinners Welcome* (New York: HarperCollins, 2006), 69.
3. Karr, *Cherry* (New York: Penguin, 2001), 243.
4. Karr, *Sinners Welcome,* 14.

spite not "having a mystical bone in [her] body."[5] After a month her life did stabilize and, thereafter, prayer became a daily part of her life. So too did the search for a confessional face to this impulse. Karr refers ironically to those years during which she, in the company of her son, searched out the whole gamut of religions as her "God-a-rama."[6] Eventually she found Catholicism most attractive in its consonance with the deep needs of her own nature, and she was baptized into the Church in 1996.

The Liars' Club and Cherry were spectacular popular and critical successes; they redeemed Karr from the poverty and anonymity she had endured for almost twenty years as a poet. But she has also continued to write poetry, publishing Viper Rum and Sinners Welcome after these memoirs. In fact, in a diary entry composed when she was twelve, Karr announced to herself a plan "to write ½ poetry and ½ autobiography."[7] She resumed the course of that prescient forecast with the publication of a third book of memoirs called Lit (2009). Currently, Mary Karr is the Jessie Truesdale Peck Professor of Literature at Syracuse University in New York.

"Serious Talk with My Emptiness": Abacus

The title of Mary Karr's first book, Abacus, captures the tenor of her early poems. They are mordant tallies of unprofitable emotional investments and family estrangements. The speaker in "The Distance" strings on her "abacus of love and hate" a pearl left as a gift by her departed lover.[8] She is numbed by the count of his infidelities, but equally numbed by the mindless regularity of her absolutions and of their reunions. These poems shuttle between the poet's personal past and her present relationships on a rigid frame of inevitability that enforces a strict accounting of inherited temperament and temptations. They parse and package sorrow, fear, and expectancy with ironic detachment. Karr instructs herself in "Courage," for example, to dispassionately calculate loss, to "take this bag of grief, / each little betrayal and pack it small, / roll it like bad wool into a ball."[9]

"The Magnifying Mirror," the first poem in the volume, is a case in point. The speaker recalls manipulating her image in a compact mirror she dis-

5. Karr, "Finding My Religion," interview with David Ian Miler, Mar. 27, 2006, www.sfgate.com.
6. Karr, Sinners Welcome, 85.
7. Karr, Cherry, 23.
8. Karr, Abacus (Pittsburgh: Carnegie Mellon University Press, 2007), 31.
9. Ibid., 12.

covered in her mother's purse as a child. She blithely magnified her "moon-cratered" face, ignorant not just of the "precancerous moles" that may have been a family trait but of those addictive dispositions that would send her years later to a psychiatrist, "to puff me up again."[10] Therapy reveals how she may be trapped in unyielding pattern, "growing into [my mother's] high heels, / her taste for alcohol and men." The terror of such a prospect drives her back compulsively to childhood ritual. Alone, she consults her mirror, fixing at arm's length a momentary image of wholeness. But her bravura dissolves up close as "each flaw and fear" of her psychic inheritance magnifies. The speaker, driven to a corner, discerns a potentially redemptive vector in the unforgiving calculus that rules her life. Purchase on the past may open up "not by looking out, / but by looking in."

The sound of Karr's abacus registering the sad aggregate of human aspiration can be heard in the clicking of the nuns' rosary beads in "Hard Knocks."[11] The nuns pray in vain for their students, who pass with brutal abruptness, in the tedium of a small Texas town, from girlish innocence into premature marriage, multiple pregnancies, and barrenness, if not death, in "an abortionist's garage." The speaker recalls linking arms with those girls, passing with them "into the world of women where all deaths begin." The sound can be heard as well in the "clacking noise" of Louisiana sugar cane in the wind that spins "The Lynched Man," a black man dangling from a tree over the young Mary Karr, his face hooded with a terrifying blank "white cotton shirt."[12] In this finely realized poem, the narrative details—the girl's finger hooked in her uncle's "belt loop" as she watches, and the aroma of "cows and tobacco" off his body, into which she wishes she could retreat—convey another species of violated innocence with admirable indirection and restraint. But the accounting proceeds with stern moral logic beyond the remembered moment into the near present of the poem's conclusion. There the poet, startled by a giant bat she brushes against in a low-hanging tree branch, hurls a stone that drops it at her feet. All at once, her dark fellowship in the long heritage of violence (against herself as well) becomes unsettlingly clear. The "neck-snapped rodent" is her döppelganger, a reflux of unclarified self-hatred, the "little cruelty surge that spread / like an ivory flag unfurling in my chest."[13]

The monitory voice of these early poems is that of Diogenes, a persona

10. Ibid., 3.   11. Ibid., 11.
12. Ibid., 9.   13. Ibid., 10.

Karr adopts in a half-dozen poems strung through the volume. Like the ancient Greek cynic, this whimsical commentator is arch, witty, and irreverent. His cosmopolitan ironies serve both to define and stoically to deflect the full weight of disillusionment that the rural Texas innocent lays herself open to in her romantic relationships. In "Diogenes Tries to Forget" the speaker parries feckless protests of love from her paramour, acknowledging unyielding devotion by one hemisphere of her brain—"the dumb one, which forgets."[14] This antic voice presides throughout the middle section of the volume, which reckons the dispiriting sum of the poet's romantic engagements with wry dispassion. The elegant cynicism of Diogenes can only mute the darker strains of self-doubt that persist beneath Karr's urbane disengagements from romantic betrayal, however. Inherited temperament, not just the vagaries of male egotism, sets the parameters for her all-too-predictable failures in love. She uncovers in "Old Mistakes" this complicit "fascination" with the implacable past, her perverse "eagerness to return to what's been / done."[15]

The final poem in *Abacus,* characteristically titled "Report," tallies the lessons learned from the look inward this volume has initiated. It also points past the suave and urbane dispassion of these early poems toward the more direct, passionate engagement with longing that will fuel Mary Karr's movement further inward, past iron necessity, and ultimately toward a religious answer to her "inner emptiness." Initially, the poet looks out, from the vantage point of a failing marriage (the poem is dedicated to husband Michael Milburn), upon the prospect of a future which is, like the waves of the sea, nothing but *"again again."*[16] She seems fated to reenact, as much because of her own rigidities and insecurities as because of her lover's hardness of heart, the fruitless ritual of mistrust that turned the unitive potential of desire into a "hard red jewel" they merely circled and probed from the outside.[17] The poem concludes by invoking "tenderness" as an alternative to detached, analytic "curiosity" about the beloved, the sort of tenderness with which a fingernail draws "one tiny message . . . / on the palm of someone sleeping."

"Eyeholes / Filled with Sand, Flooded with Dawn": *The Devil's Tour*

Mary Karr's second volume, *The Devil's Tour,* might be called her *Inferno.* Its title, the poems' insistent oracular voice, and the frequent resort to

14. Ibid., 35.
16. Ibid., 52.
15. Ibid., 33.
17. Ibid.

gothic imagery all evoke the Dantesque pilgrimage through the dark forest of the encroaching middle years. It is a point in life when the poet finds herself haunted still by demons she thought she had exorcised in distancing herself physically and professionally from "the brutal limits of that town" that nurtured her.[18] There her intimate friend and "black knight" Coleman, the subject of the very moving opening poem, was cut down by redneck vigilantism. Coleman is the archetypal figure of romance in the mature woman's consciousness, the chivalrous presence who, years before, on summer nights beneath the "chemical-pink sky" created by the local refinery towers, honored "a cracker girl, / preoccupied with books." His is the "missing face" of graciousness toward which she journeys.[19]

The tender gratitude that infuses this otherwise chilling tableau of south Texas life, as well as the poet's more open acknowledgement of her persistent longing for romance, are the new grace notes in *The Devil's Tour*. They mark Karr's spiritual passage beyond the cooler, distancing ironies of *Abacus*. In their more forthright descent into the darker recesses of memory, the poems in her second volume prepare for the definitive entry into the life of faith we see in *Viper Rum* and *Sinners Welcome*.

The haunting "Post-Larkin Triste" achieves this same blend of sharply edged reminiscence of violated innocence with muted, quixotic hopefulness. The poet Philip Larkin is enshrined with Coleman as a tutelary spirit in the poet's descent into her ravaged spirit. Hearing of Larkin's death, the speaker recalls the wintry night years before when she huddled in the shadows outside his house in England, paying shy homage to "the last romantic" as she observed him framed in the window.[20] At this odd moment, as the light of a fire glittered in his eye, the poet glimpsed beneath the mask of Larkin's austere clarity and seemingly militant cynicism (so like Karr's ill-fitting persona as Diogenes) the flames of his suppressed romantic passion. She yearned to salve Larkin's "pent-up hurt," to proclaim some grand cosmic dispensation that would dry up the tears he had once admitted having shed while listening to Wordsworth read on his car radio. Perhaps she might have reassured him that, after all, he was loved by some beneficent cosmic reality. But the authority of Larkin's bitter experience of life eclipses the poet's feeble invocations. Larkin's spectacles reflect a "dread-locked moon," whose face men-

18. Karr, *The Devil's Tour* (New York: New Directions, 1993), 2.
19. Ibid., 1, 2.
20. Ibid., 8.

aces her with a much darker message.[21] In the absence of an equally intense experience of redemptive love, the poet's compassionate gesture remains a pious, ineffectual nostrum.

Karr arms herself, however, with Larkin's wry humor and with his passionate and oddly tender acerbity on her "devil's tour" of brutally betrayed expectations. In "Rounds," a young girl lies in the bed of a mental ward "stalled in herself" and tortured by the dream of romance, a prospect that has been long since extinguished by her father's incestuous attentions. The violation has also undermined any sense of sanctuary in her life, as she seeks "messages / where none were written."[22] In "Memoirs of a Child Evangelist," when the "demon" of lust rises between his legs, a glib rural evangelist violates the trust of another initiate, forcing himself into "her quietest place."[23] This caustic but solicitous Larkinesque voice intercedes again in "The Unweepables" to mourn the procession of "history's lost women," to which such girls belong.[24] Pregnant herself now, the poet "cleave[s] against myself into the birth chamber," her anticipated birth pangs the seal of her communion with all women "wounded by neglect."

Like these poems, the witty "Don Giovanni's Confessor" surveys the carnage wrought by the serpent of male desire. An old priest wearies as the archetypal seducer recites his litany of triumphs, each more proficient and less pleasurable than the preceding, each increasing the Don's loathing for "what he needed most." The priest is driven to recall the grotesquely colorful spectacle of uniformed bodies rotting on a battlefield, on which his eyes had fastened when his mother secured him in a tree trunk years before. The Don's words reawaken that primal scene of evil and so fuse it with the victims of the Don's erotic campaigns that the priest can think of "no fair penance" for the latter.[25]

Karr skirts tendentiousness in these feminine plaints by equal address to her own potential for complicity in the demonic. "Donna Giovanna's Failure," a bravura piece complexly humorous and bawdy and serious, imagines the perverse psychic closure a woman visits on herself in the wake of her lover's ending their ten-year affair. She is so self-absorbed by the hurt that she turns the men she takes to replace him into "stick figures," skeletal images of her resentment, counters on an erotic calculus just as callous as Don Giovan-

21. Ibid., 9.
23. Ibid., 24.
25. Ibid., 3, 4.
22. Ibid., 10, 11.
24. Ibid., 22.

ni's.[26] She cannot summon repentance for the priest who comes to hear her confession, rationalizing that "all she knew / of grace she'd learned in sin." And so she casts away all the tokens of beauty associated with that decade, blurs the borders between romance and masochism, and unleashes from her unconscious erotic demons that "plunge / hard up her rump without ambergris." Ultimately, Donna Giovanna's failure is a failure of faith. Scorched by betrayal, she has banished the possibility of grace. "Untouched and wet to her core," she burns in the "hotter hell" to which she has consigned herself in self-enclosed desiring.

This thematic of self-damnation is echoed in "Sad Rite," where Karr takes on the quasi-autobiographical persona of a barroom habitué, pregnant and contemplating abortion. To fill her emptiness, her body has graced her with a child, but she, hobbled by isolating and paralyzing habits of intellectual self-analysis, decides to "scoop it out, this child," while holding on to the "idea" of it.[27] Thereafter, she retreats nightly to the sad ritual of the barroom, where the bartender neatly stacks her empty glasses, while inside her burns the "bloody flame" of her unborn child and her unquenched desire. "Sad Rite" is a portrait of a possible but not biographically literal stage on the "devil's tour" of Mary Karr's life. Indeed, a fuller treatment of this rich volume would trace how the acceptance of the child that did grow in the poet's womb and then in her heart during the years of an increasingly strained marriage enticed her away from the intellectual arrogance and hatefulness of Donna Giovanna and toward an openness to the possibility of a giftedness in her life. This is certainly the tenor of such poems as "Soft Mask," "Croup," and "The Toddler as Cathedral."

The grace of maternity, as well as her humbling by the sad rituals of addiction, similarly dispose the poet to greater tenderness toward her parents. As she descends into the past in order to exorcize the demons that haunt her, she is able to re-compute their significance in her life on a less rigid calculus than that of *Abacus*. In "Bayou," for example, after committing her father to the grave, the poet rows across one of his favorite haunts, where he taught her how to fish. As her fishing line grows taut, like a harp string "plucked and singing," she feels in herself the tenacity and dogged fidelity to friend and family that was the better part of his legacy to her.[28]

The spiritual passage Mary Karr accomplishes in *The Devil's Tour* is nice-

26. Ibid., 21.   27. Ibid., 26.
28. Ibid., 39.

ly crystallized in "Erectus." A wry anthropological fable, the poem traces our evolution from raw animal barbarity toward refined intellectual arrogance. As claws and nails retreated into the brain, the immediacy and intensity of humans' sensory stimulus and feeling was muted, the poet reasons, as was our capacity for empathy with others and with nature. Erect, we are now "encaged" by the very power of our intellection. All our intellectual acumen leaves us still in "thirsty awe" before the "repetitive gray sea" by which the stubbornly agnostic intellect is mesmerized.[29] We should recapture a more primitive, more ecstatic mode of awareness, the poet sardonically concludes, by burying our departed "atop the earth, skulls tilted back," where the elements can hollow out this proud, insensate brain. Then, as our bones petrify and fossilize, our "eyeholes," once blinded by intellectual presumption, will be "filled with sand, flooded with dawn."

For all its infernal imagery and subject matter, *The Devil's Tour* finally arrives at the foot of Mount Purgatory in its evocation of a redemptive humility that visits a scintillating wit upon those excesses of intellect that blind one to spiritual insight.

"The Dark Meat of Our Bodies": *Viper Rum*

Viper Rum, the title of Mary Karr's third volume, invokes the serpent of alcohol addiction, the python in the gallon jug of rum described in the volume's opening poem that had "choked to death" her marriage and threatened to separate her from her son.[30] The viper is also the dark riot of thought that tempts the poet to suicide in the final poem of the collection; it is the serpentine coil of "garden hose" she had planned to hook to her car's exhaust.[31]

At the same time, the poet's descent into bodily and psychic ignominy turns out, like Dante's infernal spiral, to be the privileged route to purgatorial ascent. The force that rescued her from such self-destruction "can't yet be named," she acknowledges, "but I do reverence to it / every day."[32] And this reverence is not simply notional; it is embodied in the palpable gestures and rhythms of corporate ritual. That is to say, this devotion assumes recognizably Catholic shape. "Chosen Blindness" concludes with the lovely image of Karr and the son she had once been about to orphan sharing a hym-

29. Ibid., 38.
30. Karr, *Viper Rum* (New York: Penguin, 2001), 2.
31. Karr, "Chosen Blindness," in *Viper Rum,* 44.
32. Karr, *Viper Rum,* 2.

nal, his "index finger underlining each word," both attuning their voices to those of their fellow congregants, as if only the translation of thought and desire into disciplined bodily gesture could enable them to "find the pattern emerging."[33]

Viper Rum is very much a book about the humility learned in bodily lowliness; about the gratitude such humility fosters; about those "consolations without a cause," as St. Ignatius called them, which the eye of gratitude alone can discern; and about the prudence that prompts one humbly, gratefully, to trust in the "delivered wisdom" of a mature religious or philosophical tradition to nourish such discernment.[34] But all these interrelated themes are subsumed within, and grounded by, Karr's shock and ecstasy at the experience of the sanctity that dwells at the heart of matter, the light that illumines the heavy "dark meat" that clamors for love and cries out in pain. Essentially, this shock is the surprise of grace—the grace of her growing awareness of the incarnate presence of Christ at one with her joys, but especially with her sufferings. Indeed, for Karr, Christ's divinity intensifies rather than dilutes his humanity: he is a God whose flesh "felt more than ours" because he "saw / beyond each instant into all others."[35] The "poor carcass" he heaved into life's rough and tumble "wept tears of real blood." That humiliatingly vulnerable "carcass"—a willfully unsentimental epithet Karr intones like a mantra throughout the volume—is itself the locus of possible redemption.

In several interviews about her conversion, Mary Karr has remarked on the salutary prominence in Catholic churches of the *corpus* of Christ on the cross. In her poem "The Grand Miracle," she remarks that the ultimate miracle is not the multiplication of loaves and fishes but rather the fact that God fastened animal flesh to himself "to travel our path between birth / and ignominious death." It is also the decisive affront to the "altar of reason" before which enlightened modern consciousness worships. The assimilation of this miracle must be equally palpable. Karr "dumbly" lines up with the members of her two-thousand-year-old "tribe" to receive this God on the "meat" of her tongue.[36] Only such ostensibly blind, crude, atavistic ingestion of God in the Eucharist can free our "poor carcass" from its inertial fear of, indeed even fascination with, death.

33. Ibid., 45.
34. Karr, "Four of the Horsemen," in *Viper Rum*, 8.
35. Karr, "Christ's Passion," in *Viper Rum*, 33.
36. Ibid., 19, 18, 19.

It is also Mary Karr's uncompromising incarnationalism, and not simply feminist *parti pris,* that fuels "The Wife of Jesus Speaks," a brash but remarkable poem bound to test the sympathies of orthodox readers. Karr's persona is Jesus' widow, who recalls their unspeakable ecstasy in that "first inch of time" before "history's / virgin parchment" was sullied by ideological prepossessions;[37] before her lover was petrified into an icon of celestial sacrifice; before the drama of salvation was ripped from its matrix of passionate love and reinserted into a legalistic narrative of atonement; and before more sclerotic ecclesiastical authorities paid her to lie that she never "feasted on his flesh that now feeds / any open mouth."[38] In hell, where she now dwells for having hanged herself in despair, his widow turns her back on the Jesus who extends his "pale hand for rescue." She scorns his agency on behalf of the Father's stern, imperial rule and rejects ascension to such an abstract, remote heaven—much as Dido scorned Aeneas for sacrificing the immediacy of their passion to the hollow futurities of Rome. Instead, Jesus' wife, like Dido, insists upon the self-validating intensity of their union. She will witness in lonely eternity to the salvific experience of Christ's vivid physical and emotional fullness, to that moment when she felt Christ's "hard / stalk of flesh rocking inside me."[39] Christ's unconditional love for her issued in a sexual climax that effected, more importantly, her liberation from all the cultural scripts that had been written for her subjugation. "I was unwrit" at that moment, she exclaims, echoing the intoxicating proclamation of St. Paul in Galatians that in Christ there is "neither slave nor free, male nor female."

We need not equate the speaker's views with the poet's. In comparing Jesus' wife so closely to the embittered, disoriented Dido, Karr leaves ironic space for us to question her impetuous theological simplifications. Nevertheless, Jesus' wife errs on the side of a necessary excess, Karr seems to be implying, in spurning any and all semi-Arian dilutions of Christ's utterly concrete and exigent claim upon the human heart, male or female. Indeed, Karr's ribald figure for this exigency—that "hard stalk"—identifies phallic and chthonic energies which in some fashion, if only by sublimation, fuel spiritual experience. The figure draws theological warrant from St. Paul's own favored metaphor for union with Christ: "Therefore, since Jesus was delivered to you as Christ and Lord, live your lives in union with him. Be root-

---

37. Ibid., 4, 5.   38. Ibid., 4.
39. Ibid., 5.

ed in him; be built in him."[40] Karr has uncovered this "rootedness" of Christ in the very depths of her sexual desiring.

Like "The Wife of Jesus Speaks," Karr's poems on the religious themes identified above—humility, gratitude, prudence, and the discernment of providence—seek the spiritual in the concrete texture of her everyday relationships. In "The Century's Worst Blizzard," for example, the poet narrates the conjunction of two disasters: a crippling snow and ice storm, and a forty-four-year-old friend's incurable cancer.[41] The friend calls to ask advice not about how, but rather why, she should continue to live. Karr has to hang up before she can respond; she feels as trapped by her friend's request as she is by the huge icicles lining her roof. Setting out on foot the next day to mail her friend a note of consolation, she watches an elderly neighbor trying to chop his way out of the ice surrounding his entrance. The hand he pokes through to signal hello precipitates an avalanche from the roof that he barely dodges. He falls unharmed into a snowbank. This unheralded miracle threatens to be eclipsed, however, by the poet's recollection of how the cancer in her friend's body continued to spread with "exponential speed,"[42] and by her doubt about how effectual her homely advice to just "hold on" could have been. Karr's abacus, her erstwhile moral and metaphysical computer, would have ignored the providence of the elderly neighbor's survival as statistically insignificant in comparison with the cancer's unambiguous destructiveness to a younger person. Moreover, that primitive computer could never allow for the inner transformation in the face of death that may have been accomplished in her friend—in part, perhaps, with the assistance of Karr's note. But the more chastened older poet remains in the tension of faith. She recalls, finally, having "plunged dumbly forward" through the snow toward a distant mailbox with that letter, down a serpentine road of "glassy fire," hoping for a mail truck to pass. It does. This final providence would have registered even more faintly on the cynic's abacus of cosmic slights. The poet does not strain to prove otherwise. She does attest, however, that such blessings abound, beyond calculation. Also, she calls into question any jaundiced moral arithmetic that would presume to fix their number and relative value.

Other poems in *Viper Rum*, like the moving "Dead Drunk," about a street beggar whose hands and feet are claimed by frostbite, insist likewise

40. Col. 2:6–7.
41. Karr, *Viper Rum*, 26.
42. Ibid., 27.

on a giftedness incommensurate with rational calculation, accessible only to faith enacted in prayer and ritual. Much as we might have wanted poor Tom's rescued hands and feet intact, "That tale's / unwrit: We cannot make it so."[43] Nevertheless, we have the "chosen blindness" of faith, corporately expressed, which is, at least, far less unwarranted than the unexamined blindness of solitary cynicism. The poet invites us to step beyond wishful second-guessing of Providence and to "stand in company and grieve that fact: / Hail, Tom, asleep under snowflakes, / slack-jawed in burning cold."

Finally, we may note how Karr's imaginative appropriation of her family history and relationships in *Viper Rum* deepens in tandem with her submission to the *telos* of our poor, heavy carcasses, irradiated as she now sees they are by the light of Christ's presence. In "Limbo: Altered States," Karr parallels her plane's descent to earth to her own escape from addiction, the proud limbo where she exercised solitary, godlike tyranny over her body, alternately mixing "the next sickness" for it, and then reviving herself for another cocktail hour.[44] As the plane touches down to earth, she gives thanks for the *"gravitas"* that draws her back to the son awaiting her on the ground.[45] Grace and salvation operate in and through this fleshly leverage.

Karr imaginatively re-inhabits the earthly fount of this grace in the whimsically titled "The Invention of God in a Mouthful of Milk." The sight of her mother drawing closer to death, her soul straining to cast off her "fleshy husk," drives the poet, paradoxically, to search out a primal memory of the birthing of her own soul—at the breast of that now aged, once alcoholic body.[46] The *gravitas* of her maternal bond, once understood as an iron bondage, now unfolds as the locus of pure gift. At that moment when her mother's breast milk streamed down her throat, before the indignities of personal history accumulated (but nevertheless in a moment as historically *real* as those), her own being was conferred and confirmed. In the oceanic wash of her mother's nurture, Karr's infant self was a "god afloat," relishing what time and circumstance subsequently obscured—the fundamental "Rightness" she lost contact with in adolescence. Karr's archeology of infancy, like Augustine's, unearths the operations of divinity in the consummate tasting of self in and through the mother's body. The poet "barely came to sense / an alternate god: Ma and ma and mama." Her redeemed consciousness can "barely" (that is, hardly) distinguish God from its own self-delight or from its

43. Ibid., 30.
45. Ibid., 23.

44. Ibid., 22.
46. Ibid., 36.

own creative urge in language. That consciousness can also "barely" (that is, nakedly, directly) experience God in and through the *gravitas* of bodily connection to redeemed others.

"Facing Altars: Poetry and Prayer": *Sinners Welcome*

Mary Karr's most recent volume of poems, *Sinners Welcome,* features an eloquent and illuminating autobiographical essay on the relationship of her artistic and religious development called "Facing Altars: Poetry and Prayer." The title, as well as the venue in which it was originally published in 2005— the prestigious *Poetry* magazine—herald the greater confidence with which she has integrated her faith commitment with her literary sensibility and with the givens of her temperament and family history.[47]

"Sinners Welcome," the title poem of the volume, refers to a banner stretched across the façade of Karr's church in Syracuse, New York. The banner encapsulates the intoxicating, disorienting, and altogether disproportionate joy to which the poet finds herself admitted after so much torment and heartache, much of it self-induced. The poem that perhaps best communicates this joy unfolds seamlessly, and simultaneously, as a narrative of erotic completion; as an act of thanksgiving to the incarnate God who has claimed her in the Eucharist, her sins notwithstanding; and as a homage to the literary tradition that has empowered her as a poet.

Earlier in the volume, in a poem starkly parallel to this, Karr's comic persona "Miss Flame" had fantasized gyrating before voyeurs across an alley to gratify her "stalled lust."[48] Erotic glamour sputtered into naught when the sun, filling the window, shielded this female Prufrock from sight, and when the men instead took "turns at the pissoir."[49] In "Sinners Welcome," by contrast, Karr's persona is Penelope, who forthrightly opens her blouse to "this man"—a stranger and yet an intimate—and reveals to him the "flaming heart he lit in me."[50] Karr has assimilated the Homeric to the Gospel narrative at a very deep level. Weathering past factitious cultural "clay gods" and spurning the specious allure of meretricious "Sirens" in order to reach and redeem her unimpeachable singularity, this Ulysses/Christ emboldens the demure Penelope to such utterly unself-conscious undress. Her gesture of trust is met with unwonted embrace. The king before whom she should kneel kneels

47. Karr, *Sinners Welcome*, 69.   48. Ibid., 32.
49. Ibid.   50. Ibid., 40.

before her, then carries her off into the "dim warm" of his arms—and to a new depth of self-understanding born out of passionate union with her divine/human lover. This union fractures the old, desiccated self, the one conceived in arrogant self-analysis and lonely fantasy: "He enters me and joy / sprouts from us as from a split seed." Erotic delight suffuses this encounter, but Karr explicitly distinguishes religious joy as a more encompassing ecstasy than pleasure alone and one that unites us to others in greater fruitfulness: as Karr observes in "Facing Altars: Poetry and Prayer," "For me, joy arrives in the body (where else would it find us?), yet doesn't originate there. Nature never drew me into joy as it does others, but my fellow creatures (God's crown of creation) often spark joy in me."[51]

Karr's remarks should alert us to the consonance between the secular idiom of these remarkable later love poems and their sacred resonances. Poems like "The First Step," "Last Love," and "Who the Meek Are Not," mingle profane with sacred delight, fuse *eros* with *caritas,* and revel in a proud, erect animality that nevertheless waits upon the spirit's command. "The First Step" may well be a straightforward love poem in its biographical origins: it is dedicated to Peter Straus, a British literary agent and Mary Karr's second husband. It traces the delicious, measured disorientation of mounting romantic excitement, from her lover's "first step" that swept away her "breezy bravura," to his leaving her athirst for his breath "to come / easing down my lungs."[52] The climax of romantic anticipation comes for the speaker, however, in the beloved's chaste appeal to "browse my face / as if it were page or sacred tome." This emissary of "God's crown of creation" translates into the figures of romance those hieroglyphs that the divine lover had inscribed originally in her concrete physical being. "Last Love" envisions a romantic liaison that effects a deep healing in the speaker through her lover's interventions. For many years, the speaker, like Donna Giovanna, had chosen lovers to suit her moods and fancies, fleeing commitment when any of them threatened to expose to scalding light the primal hurt she guarded. But her "last love" has "slid a palm across / mine eyes," blotting out the spectacle of past mistakes that provokes such defensiveness.[53] Then he "lent me his mouth / (a bitten plum)," both kissing her and implanting in her the sweet/sour fruit of his suffering on her behalf. His head fixed square in her "mid-

51. Ibid., 88.
53. Ibid., 49.
52. Ibid., 41.

dle," he insistently bends her, still guiltily reluctant, toward him. His persistence wins out over her self-mistrust. Their positions are reversed at poem's end, she with her head "on the meadow of his chest," a vibrantly expectant "girl again" by virtue of his (or is it His?) preternaturally skillful ministrations.

"Who the Meek Are Not" begins in the rhetorically grand idiom of Shakespearian verse ("Not marble nor the gilded monuments of time") as it parts ways with servile understandings of Christian love and humility: "Not the bristle-bearded Igors bent / under burlap sacks, not peasants knee-deep / in the rice-paddy muck."[54] Karr illustrates her point in the manner as well as the matter of the poem—in its virile meter and muscular, periodic syntax. Her lifelong apprenticeship to the English and American poetic traditions, now boldly mature, underscores the theological point: Christian humility is heroic, self-affirmative rather than self-deprecatory. It has nothing to do with socially or economically induced passivities, or with the Nietzschean *ressentiment* that typically accompanies self-subjugation. The authentically meek, inspirited by Christ's love, are best conceived as a "stallion at full gallop" who, hearing his master's command, "seizes up to a stunned but instant halt." The horse's obedience to its Master partakes, to begin with, of the Master's own energies of command. That obedience is accomplished not in guilty disparagement of bodily energy and appetite but in their apt deployment. Even as the horse/lover/poet struggles to contain and channel "that great power" bestowed by—and aroused by—the Master, the "muscles" of its "arched neck keep eddying, / and only the velvet ears / prick forward, awaiting the next order." These nimble lines compose, all at once, a figure of lovers keenly attendant on each other's most recondite needs; of the believer disciplining every power of mind and heart in prayer to discern his Master's will; and of the poet fixing her disciplined attention to the shape and fall of syllable and phrase. Prayer and poetry are indeed "facing altars" here.

But joy does not reign serene in *Sinners Welcome*. It salves the wounds of inherited temperament, and it helps the poet to locate, in the mounting deaths of family members and close friends and colleagues, and in the appalling horror of obscure lives, those "pinpoint[s] of light" that the unredeemed heart ignores.[55] But Karr confesses candidly that while she con-

---

54. Ibid., 23.
55. Ibid., 92.

sciously struggles "to accommodate joy as part of my literary enterprise, I still tend to be a gloomy and serotonin-challenged bitch."[56] A number of poems, like "Oratorio for the Unbecoming," "Waiting for God," "At the Sound of the Gunshot, Leave a Message," and "Hurt Hospital's Best Suicide Jokes," reflect this persisting morbidity. Even the bleakest of these is qualified, however, by self-irony. "Metaphysique de Mal" is a kind of imagist tone poem distilling Sartrean nausea. As the eerie "freezerspill / of smoky Arctic twilight" of her refrigerator envelops her during a break from composing still another eulogy for a friend, the poet hears her wristwatch "tapping out *now, now* abruptly fast."[57] The nihilistic litany of the freezer's contents—and of the poet's life—is undercut, however, by the tendentious title. The speaker has once more trapped herself in metaphysical abstractions that are in service more to temperament than to truth. As Karr notes in "Facing Altars," the pessimistic worldview to which she is still prone to succumb at such moments "was never chosen for its basis in truth" but rather as "a focal point around which my tortured inwardness could twist."[58]

Likewise, Mary Karr's religious joy is not a cloying or self-enclosed complacency. It insists on testing religious consolation against the hardest surfaces. In "Delinquent Missive," the poet utters a belated appeal on behalf of a boy she once tutored in ninth grade, a consummate sociopath who subsequently brutally murdered his father and who now, if not executed, languishes in the bowels of a prison or mental institution. She labors to imagine some "organism"—person or plant or insect—that might have solicited his "care" so that "the unbridgable stone / that plugged the tomb hole / in [his] chest could roll back," and so that the divine glory restored to her own face in "The First Step" might "blaze" too from his "slit eyes."[59]

With Christ as companion, Karr harrows the pit of hell again in "Hypertrophied Football Star as Serial Killer," a surreal voyage into the tortured consciousness of another egregious cosmic casualty, ostensibly beyond the pale of redemptive love. She inhabits the brokenness he endured as an exploited high school football star, his compensating fantasies of sexual conquest, his descent into madness and sadism with his female victims, and his ultimate regression to the original torture chamber of childhood, where he imagines himself "a babe again in water wings, paddling toward / the dwin-

---

56. Ibid., 90.
58. Ibid., 83.

57. Ibid., 8.
59. Ibid., 11–12.

dling V of his father's arms."[60] This primal memory, recovered as he sinks into the "darkening jade" of the sea to escape the storm inside his mind, embodies the young man's most urgent unmet need—for a benevolent, welcoming paternity. The poet, however, believes with Simone Weil that "Need is a death's head."[61] It is in the very extremity of suffering that all illusions are stripped away, like the skin from the skulls the demented young man collected. Only then, at the point of naked need, "the mystery finally speaks" to us; only then one "hears the void you've spoken / every longing into, silence articulate."[62] Perhaps, Karr concludes, this would-be football star / serial killer heard that voice in the extremity of his need, telling him to *"Just go out long, I'll find you."*

Karr's *descent* into the heart of Christian joy is signaled explicitly in the five poems scattered throughout *Sinners Welcome* that bear the title "Descending Theology." Each is subtitled with one of the Christian mysteries: "The Nativity," "Being Human" (the Incarnation), "The Garden" (the Agony in the Garden), "The Crucifixion," "The Resurrection." The titles parallel key topics in the schedule of the Ignatian Spiritual Exercises, which Mary Karr completed in the period during which the poems in *Sinners Welcome* were composed. Each poem marks out a deeper movement of God as Christ into the extremity of our neediness. "Descending Theology: The Nativity," concludes—uncharacteristically, for so joyous a mystery—with the image of the infant Jesus imbibing not just his mother's milk but "that first draught / of death, the one he'd wake from / (as we all do) screaming." In "Christ Human" the poet instructs her readers to "feel your cross buried in your flesh." Christ's passion is the very "form embedded" in the skeletal frame we lug through daily life. In "The Garden," Jesus, his face "tear-riven," embraces the bottomless guilt of his betrayer as he kisses his brother Judas. In "The Crucifixion," Christ feels "his soul leak away" as his hung flesh expires and he endures a consummate loneliness.[63]

"Descending Theology: The Resurrection," Karr's final poem in this sequence, locates Christ's rising from the dead at the utmost terminus of his descent into the darkness of the human condition. Resurrection appears at once as the ultimate intensification of, and the inconceivable transforma-

---

60. Ibid., 26.
61. Karr, "Waiting for God; Self-Portrait as Skeleton," in *Sinners Welcome*, 18.
62. Karr, *Sinners Welcome*, 26.
63. Ibid., 10, 31, 38, 52.

tion of, the Crucifixion. As death "inched in" upon him from "the far star points of his pinned extremities," Karr's Christ passes into an emptiness so blankly appalling that he hungers even for the reassurances of bodily torment, to which he had grown numb.[64] The altars of poetry and prayer then point in synchrony beyond the terminus of death, as the poem's form imitates the redemptive action to which it pays loving homage. Although it lacks end rhymes, its strong iambic rhythm, its (mostly) five-stressed lines, its overall length, and most of all its inner structure, infuse this theological reflection with the life and strength of the traditional sonnet. The poem's formal turn occurs in lines eight and nine, as the new life of the Spirit stirs in the "corpse's core," answering to the final beats of the "stone fist" of Christ's heart on his "stiff chest's door." However, it is not Christ's literal risen corpus to which Karr looks for confirmation. Instead, the temporal and grammatical focus of the poem shifts immediately to "now," when it is our "limbs he longs to flow into," and then our "chest," our heart's womb, from which he would issue, flooding the world in a new birth of charity.

The poem brings to a point of contemplative resolution and rest not just the sequence called "Descending Theology" but indeed the entire spiritual quest Mary Karr had initiated in her "serious talk with my emptiness" a generation before, when she launched her "descent" into the darkness of her psychic and cultural inheritance. At the same time, the poet remains poised for fresh intensities of poetic apprehension by virtue of the faith that has energized her. She concludes her essay "Facing Altars" by appealing to "the sense of alert presence prayer can yield," a luminosity of attentiveness to and compassion for one's "brothers and sisters" which she finds especially attractive in the late poetry of Czeslaw Milosz. She knows that "Few poets—in this century or any other—have founded an opus on joy"; yet, like Milosz, she will not relinquish her claim on "the majesty that is every sinner's birthright."[65] Her aesthetic of "Descending Theology" has provided Karr a strategy for savoring the fruit of that bequest within the terms of a committed contemporary consciousness.

64. Ibid., 61.
65. Ibid., 92, 89, 93.

CHAPTER 4

An Irish Catholic Novel? ■ The Example of Brian Moore and John McGahern

Eamon Maher

The issue of Catholicism is a fraught one in Ireland, a nation that only secured autonomy from British colonial rule in 1921 after centuries of strife and rebellion, much of which was the result of the attempts by the Empire to force the indigenous population to abandon their Catholic faith in favor of Anglicanism. One of the strongest elements in Irish nationalism consequently became its close identification with the Catholic religion. Ireland being an island nation, "Catholic Christianity linked Irish identity into a wider, transnational network of authority and belief and community."[1] Links with Catholic countries on the European mainland, especially France, Spain, and, of course, the Vatican, were carefully nurtured by those anxious to overthrow British rule. "Being Catholic" thus became a convenient identity badge to distinguish Irish people from the British (a fact that blandly overlooks the fact that a number of prominent Irish nationalists like Wolfe Tone, Robert Emmet, and Roger Casement were Protestants) and to justify the case the Irish were seeking to make in relation to cultural specificity.

Fintan O'Toole notes, "Catholicism in Ireland has been a matter of public identity more than of private faith. For most of its history, the Republic of Ireland was essentially a Catholic State, one in which the limits of law and of behaviour were set by Church orthodoxy and the beliefs of the Catholic bishops."[2] O'Toole is referring mostly to the twentieth century, when a type of fortress mentality developed wherein the Church and the state attempted to protect the newly formed state from what were considered corrupting

1. Richard English, *Irish Freedom: The History of Nationalism in Ireland* (London: Macmillan, 2006), 495.
2. Fintan O'Toole, *The Ex-Isle of Erin* (Dublin: New Island, 1997), 15.

outside influences. This was in marked contrast to the situation prior to independence. In previous times, a country like France held a special appeal among the Irish for reasons that Brian Fallon summarizes in his work *An Age of Innocence: Irish Culture 1930–1960:*

It was not only admiration for French culture, French political structures and French thought which inclined the Irish intelligentsia towards Francophilia. France offered, in effect, an alternative to English domination or at least a corrective to it. France was republican while Great Britain was monarchist, and the fact that both had colonial empires was often conveniently overlooked in this Irish exaltation of France as the home of liberty, equality and fraternity.[3]

Even more important, as Fallon points out later in the same study, was the fact that France was, or had been, a Catholic country. The Irish tended to look to it as a sister nation, one that shared a common commitment to Catholicism as well as hostility toward British colonial ambitions.

In attempting to assess the way in which there failed to emerge a strong tradition of the Catholic novel in Ireland while the genre flourished in countries like England and France, it is important to note that the two contemporary Catholic writers we will deal with in this essay, Brian Moore (1921–99) and John McGahern (1934–2006), lived out their formative years in an environment in which Catholicism played an integral part. In the case of McGahern, there was a strong collusion between the Catholic Church and the state that ensured that there was little possibility of open hostility to what became in essence an unhealthy theocracy. He expresses it thus in his 1993 essay "The Church and Its Spire":

After Independence, Church and State became inseparable, with unhealthy consequences for both. The Church grew even more powerful and authoritarian: it controlled all of education, and, through its control of the hospitals, practically all of health-care too . . . Faith and obedience were demanded, mostly taking the form of empty outward observances and a busy interest that other people do likewise which cannot be described as other than coercive.[4]

There was limited scope for freedom of expression in such an environment, which is why so many Irish writers from the southern state found the atmosphere stifling and oppressive. While someone like McGahern was attract-

---

3. Brian Fallon, *An Age of Innocence: Irish Culture 1930–1960* (Dublin: Gill and Macmillan, 1998), 124.

4. John McGahern, "The Church and Its Spire," in *Soho Square 6: New Writing from Ireland*, ed. Colm Toibin (London: Bloomsbury, 1993), 26.

ed to the various rituals of the Church, there was also a movement of revolt against the imposition of a belief system that brokered no argument and demanded blind adherence to all its pronouncements. Such a system probably suited a largely rural-based society, poorly educated and thus happy in the main to accept what their local priests and bishops told them. It wasn't until the advent of television, increased access to the motorcar and air travel, free education, and the flowering of the dance halls across the country during the 1960s, that the once all-powerful Catholic Church began to witness some rumblings of discontent from the heretofore submissive lay cohort.

Undoubtedly Vatican II, with its emphasis on the increased involvement of the laity in the running of the Church, also had a profound effect. Thus, the pronouncement of the Archbishop of Dublin, John Charles McQuaid, on his return from Rome after the Council that, "No change will worry the tranquillity of your Christian lives,"[5] can be seen as a failure to accept the radical implications of Vatican II. This same archbishop would subsequently demand the sacking of John McGahern from his position as a primary school teacher for having written a novel, *The Dark* (1965), that was banned by the Censorship Board, a body that operated in Ireland between 1929 and 1989 and whose role was ostensibly to safeguard public morality. Both McGahern and Moore fell foul of this board, and the consequences were particularly injurious for McGahern, who lost his main source of income as a result. "Writers whose books were banned immediately became stigmatized and were regarded as legitimate targets for harassment: however, virtually anyone who published a book was suspect," notes Julia Carlson in her study *Banned in Ireland: Censorship and the Irish Writer.*[6] McGahern, who lived to see a more enlightened attitude toward the arts at the end of the last century and the beginning of the third millennium, found it hard to comprehend the anti-intellectual bias of the Catholic Church in Ireland, a point that is borne out by many commentators.

However, it wasn't just the Church that was anti-intellectual, as Colum Kenny notes: "Throughout the decades following Independence, the new State certainly had among its citizens vibrant artists and interesting writers. However, a stifling blend of nationalism and conservative Catholicism made it increasingly difficult for many to express themselves freely or to work in

5. Cited in Louise Fuller, *Irish Catholicism since 1950: The Undoing of a Culture* (Dublin: Gill and Macmillan, 2004), 112.

6. Julia Carlson, *Banned in Ireland: Censorship and the Irish Writer* (Athens: University of Georgia Press, 1990), 11.

ways that they believed to be moral and necessary."[7] So what does all this tell us when it comes to assessing the reasons for the absence of a Catholic novel in Ireland? The first point I would make is that the earliest Irish novelists writing in English were Protestants (most notably Maria Edgeworth and Lady Morgan, alias Sydney Owenson) from the Anglo-Irish aristocracy. Catholicism became a potent influence on the twentieth-century Irish novel, but in a way that brought out many of the negative aspects of that religion as it was practiced in Ireland at the time. The majority religion, as we have seen, was closely bound up with Irish nationalism, politics, and culture, perhaps too much for the Catholic novel to flourish. But the question that has to be posed is: What is a Catholic novel? It is a term that is sometimes used in a loose manner to cover any novelist who explores issues pertaining to the Catholic faith in his or her work. The big danger, in the opinion of critic Malcolm Scott, is to assume that novelists who are Catholic view their role as necessarily one of defending the Church and its laws: "The term 'Catholic novelist,' which is the only one I can think of to embrace Barbey d'Aurvilly, Bloy, the later Huysmans, Mauriac, Bernanos, and Julien Green, has been blighted by unhelpful assumptions that it must refer to a novelist who puts his art at the service of the orthodox views of the Catholic Church and faith."[8] The French writers Scott mentions here did not accept that they were in fact writing "Catholic literature," if it was meant in this narrow sense. J. C. Whitehouse's collection *Catholics on Literature* (1997) gathers together essays and brief excerpts from a number of important Catholic writers. Thus we hear authors of various backgrounds and writing styles tease out the ways in which their religious faith informs and influences what they write. What is clear is that there is no accepted school of Catholic writers, just as there is no specifically Catholic way of reading and critically assessing literature, which makes the task of defining the phrase "Catholic literature" particularly difficult.

In his opening essay, Whitehouse employs a quote from Jacques Maritain's *Art and Scholasticism* which is revealing: "A Christian work would have the artist, as artist, free."[9] This is a rule that all novelists, irrespective of their religious allegiance, would do well to observe. A work of art is

---

7. Colum Kenny, *Moments That Changed Us* (Dublin: Gill and Macmillan, 2005), 229.

8. Malcolm Scott, *The Struggle for the Soul of the French Novel: French Catholic and Realist Novelists 1850–1970* (London: Macmillan, 1989), 4.

9. J. C. Whitehouse, *Catholics on Literature* (Dublin: Four Courts, 1997), 14.

not about edification or instruction. Whitehouse goes on to draw a distinction between "Catholic writing" and "Catholic literature." The former seeks to persuade and influence, even to convince, whereas the latter "is fundamentally artistic, the fictional expression of idiosyncratic and subjective insights rather than general and analytical ratiocination."[10] His conclusion is insightful: "In short, when we talk of Catholic literature, we are talking of a literature marked by faith, or the tensions of faith, and noticeable as such in the surrounding secularised world."[11]

It seems to me that if we were to apply such a definition to what some Irish novelists achieve, we could possibly claim that they are practitioners of "Catholic literature." Georges Bernanos, whose fictions are populated by wonderfully vivid priests struggling against the forces of secularism in France during the early decades of the last century, sometimes falling victim to despair, at other times gaining access to the illumination of grace, wrote these revealing lines: "The first duty of a writer is to produce good books, in the light of his own ideas of his art and the resources at his disposal, without special consideration for anything or anyone, for every book bears witness and hence must above all be sincere . . . Mediocre art is a scandal, and even more of a scandal when it claims to be edifying."[12] Such sentiments would be largely in line with the view expressed by Cardinal Montini (later to become Pope Paul VI) when, addressing the Third National Congress of Italian Writers in 1957, he stated that, "Art must be a passionate search for ways of translating the invisible into the visible. Literature is a living thing and will survive only if it is vitalized by great ideas."[13] There is no suggestion by Montini here that art should be used in the service of any religious cause. On the contrary, by rendering visible the invisible, the artist is, as Bernanos says above, "bearing witness" to some deep inner truth, being, as he is, someone who is "vitalized by great ideas."

Neither McGahern nor Moore was inimical to the concept of objectivity and fairness when it came to depicting Catholicism. They endeavored, insofar as was possible, to distance themselves from value judgments and social commentary. But they also suffered from an ailment that critic Augustine Martin describes as "inherited dissent." Ever since Joyce abandoned Catholicism to espouse a religion of art, Martin suggests, Irish writers have tended to

---

10. Ibid., 15.   11. Ibid., 17.
12. Ibid., 26.
13. Cited in Thomas Halton, "The Catholic Writer," *Christus Rex* 29, no. 2 (1957): 717.

replace their original faith with blends of the mystical and aesthetic: "They seem to have been needled into apostasy by a Christianity which at that time, in both systems, appeared to be extremely philistine, anti-intellectual, disciplinarian and above all, anti-mystical. It was Christianity smug in the dry complacency of nineteenth century apologetics, suspicious of everything outside devotionalism and observance."[14] Some writers, although quite devout in their religious dispositions, fell victim to an ambient philistinism that made it difficult for them to pursue their writing while remaining within the broad structures of the Church. But Martin would argue that this reality hardened into a cliché that viewed Ireland as "a backward, insanitary, inert, despairing country; a people priest-ridden and superstitious, which despises its artists and intellectuals, treats its autocratic, avaricious and crafty clergy with a sanctimonious servility; a people soaked in dreams and booze."[15]

Like all clichés, the grain of truth contained in this impression conveniently ignores a lot of complex issues and fails to take note of the exceptions that disprove its thesis. I detect this attitude in some of the pronouncements made by the remarkable Seán Ó Faoláin (1900–1991) who, in an article, "The Modern Novel: A Catholic Point of View," stated that the Catholic writer chooses to see man as midway between everything and nothing:

I find in all of them [Catholic novelists] a painful self-consciousness, as if they could not forget they were Catholics, a timidity evident in their fear of the senses, a priggishness and a solemnity which has nothing to do with religion and for which there is no excuse, a lack of humour, and a tendency to underwrite about the emotions as if they feared to raise a storm they could not ride . . . These tendencies, though highly laudable in the writer as a Catholic, are in the writer as a writer the signs of some basic weakness that is, apparently, fatal to his work.[16]

Ó Faoláin displayed sympathy for the Catholic writer who suffered from the fear that art poses some danger to religion—François Mauriac struggled with this throughout his illustrious career—because such a fear deprived him or her of detachment. He continues, "For, the whole human drama is surely the drama of the Seven Deadly Sins, and any novelist who attempts to ignore them is avoiding reality."[17] Irish novelists did not, in fairness, neglect sin,

14. Augustine Martin, "Inherited Dissent," in *Bearing Witness: Essays on Anglo-Irish Literature*, ed. Anthony Roche (Dublin: University College Dublin Press, 1996), 86.

15. Ibid., 89.

16. Seán Ó Faoláin, "The Modern Novel: A Catholic Point of View," *Virginia Quarterly Review* 2 (1935): 345.

17. Ibid., 346.

as they knew that it provided fertile ground for exploration. In fact, I don't think that Georges Bernanos, Graham Greene, or François Mauriac could ever be accused of ignoring the seven deadly sins either. Ó Faoláin was a man who didn't like to mince his words, but the downside is that he sometimes presented a skewed picture of the reality before him. His humanism led him to resent excessive interference by the Church in individual lives because he believed that when you deprive human beings of their freedom to choose, you undermine them.[18] Brian Moore and John McGahern would be sympathetic to this view. While the novels we will discuss were published after 1970, the Ireland they represent retains many of the characteristics and the fortress mentality against which several writers of the early twentieth century, like Ó Faoláin, railed.

If we deal only with a small sample of the later novels by Moore and McGahern, however, the extent to which these authors depicted an Ireland dominated by Catholic principles and dogma is not clear. For example, in Brian Moore's *The Lonely Passion of Judith Hearne* (1955) and *The Feast of Lupercal* (1958), both set in the Belfast of the writer's youth, the characters are prevented from attaining autonomy because of the oppressive religious atmosphere that surrounds them. Similarly, John McGahern's *The Barracks* (1963) and *The Dark* (1965), situated in the northwest Irish midlands, are novels in which the Leitrim writer explores how people in provincial rural Ireland looked to their Catholic faith as a source of both consolation and anxiety. Catholicism is a given in the lives of the characters depicted in these novels, but there is no attempt by any of them to interrogate the philosophical or theological basis of their faith. The "inherited dissent" spoken of by Martin is strongly present here but is replaced in the novelists' subsequent writings by an appreciation of some of the more positive aspects of the Catholic religion. In this regard, perhaps it could be claimed that they were writing a form of the "Catholic novel" as defined by J. C. Whitehouse: "In the Catholic novel, there is a movement away from a picture of human beings working out their own destiny towards a presentation of them in a dialectical and critical relationship to their formative culture, where the old lexis—'faith,' 'grace,' 'sin,' 'salvation,' 'redemption,' 'hope,' 'charity'—is largely meaningless."[19]

18. Maurice Harmon, *Maurice Harmon: Selected Essays*, ed. Barbara Brown (Dublin: Irish Academic Press, 2006), 69.

19. Whitehouse, *Catholics on Literature*, 20.

Brian Moore is one of Belfast's best-known modern writers. He was born into a very Catholic and nationalist family. His father was a doctor, and when Moore was young, the family moved to Clifton Street, a Protestant area, in order to be close to the university hospital where his father worked. Their house was directly opposite the Orange Hall, and the Moores therefore had an excellent view of the statue of King Billie (William of Orange) on his white horse, a symbol of the religious conflict that has bedeviled the island of Ireland for many centuries. In an interview for the BBC in 1997, Moore admitted that from a very early age he "lacked the religious sense." Living in a city and reared in a family where people took their religious allegiance so seriously, such a lack led to a feeling of alienation and a need to escape from the strictures and constraints that met him at every turn. His problems with religion began with confession: he found it difficult to view his natural sexual urges as sinful, and soon he began to invent sins for the priest without experiencing any fear of God's retribution afterwards. But while he was an agnostic, Moore was always fascinated by those who had faith. A discussion of two of his novels, *Catholics* (1972) and *Cold Heaven* (1985), will evaluate the difficulties encountered by characters who find themselves faced with choices that will have serious ramifications in relation to faith and salvation.

Catholics is more a novella than a novel and is set in Muck Abbey, a remote island monastery off the Kerry (southwestern) coast of Ireland, in a period that is deliberately placed in the future: post–Vatican IV to be precise. The monks of Muck have started saying the Latin Mass again in contravention of the ecumenical thrust of Vatican IV. The clash between the traditional and the modern is finely drawn as James Kinsella, a progressive American priest, is sent to Ireland with the task of bringing the monks in line with Rome's new stance. The Abbot, Tomás O'Malley, who has lost his faith, is a man who cares for his community and appreciates how attached the monks are to the Latin Mass. However, he is also realistic enough to know that James Kinsella has come because of the commotion caused by the celebration of the traditional Mass on the mainland: "Most could see the Mass rock and the priest only from a distance, but all heard the Latin, thundering from loudspeakers rigged up by townsfolk. Latin. The communion bell. Monks as altar boys saying the Latin responses. Incense. The old way."[20]

Sadly for the monks, "the old way" is not Rome's way, and this is the

---

20. Brian Moore, *Catholics* (London: Triad/Panther, 1983), 10.

message that James Kinsella carries with him to Muck. He arrives in a he-
licopter and receives this greeting from the Abbot: "You've brought us the
symbol of the century. Just when I thought we'd be able to close the hundred
years out, and say we missed our time."[21] James Kinsella is very much a ste-
reotype of the modern global cleric. He is intelligent and imbued with the
necessary ruthlessness not to allow sentiment and nostalgia to detract him
from what he must do. When one of the monks, Fr. Manus, bemoans the fact
that "this new mass isn't a mystery, it's a singsong," Kinsella doesn't flinch,
emphasizing the importance of orthodoxy and conformity: "We are trying to
create a uniform posture within the Church. If everyone decides to worship
in his own way, well it's obvious, it would create a disunity."[22]

It is significant that Moore wrote this novel at a time in Ireland when
the changes in the liturgy brought about by Vatican II were causing many to
question the abandonment of Latin in favor of the vernacular. Fr. Manus's
comment about the Mass being more of a "singsong" than a true reenactment
of the passion and death of Christ is a sentiment that was often expressed by
Irish people around this time. In her study *Irish Catholicism since 1950*, Louise
Fuller writes, "A recurring theme, echoed by commentators reflecting on the
Irish situation in the post–Vatican II era, was that, despite the updated liturgy, the correlation between life and liturgy, as envisaged by the Council, had
not been achieved."[23] The Abbot of Muck recognizes that the central authority vested in the Pope is designed in such a way as to ensure that the faithful
all over the world worship in a similar fashion and adhere to the same fundamentals in terms of dogma. Nevertheless he feels that there is a case to be
made for granting priests occasionally the right to celebrate the Latin rite.

Abbot O'Malley's loss of faith had occurred years earlier during a visit
to Lourdes. He was appalled by the tawdry religious supermarkets he saw
there, the certification of "miraculous" cures, the lines of stretchers on
which lay the desperate and the ill. It caused him to flee to his room, where
he discovered he had lost the ability to pray. At the end of *Catholics,* when
faced with the possible rebellion of his community after he has announced
that they must conform to Rome's dictate, O'Malley finds somewhere deep
within himself the key that unlocks his unbelief. It does not matter, he tells
the monks, what means you employ to adore God. He is there in the taber-

21. Ibid., 30.   22. Ibid., 55.
23. Fuller, *Irish Catholicism since 1950*, 122.

nacle when you believe in the Real Presence. "Prayer is the only miracle," he says. "We pray. If our words become prayer, God will come."[24] When he then starts mumbling the Our Father, the reader is led to believe that he may have regained his faith.

In Moore's *Cold Heaven*, the main character Marie, on the verge of ending a loveless marriage to her surgeon husband Alex, witnesses what appears to be the fatal collision of his head with a motorboat while swimming in the Mediterranean. Marie and her husband are American, and she has been having an affair for some time with another doctor, Daniel. Both have resolved to leave their respective spouses in order to live together. Marie is an atheist whose mother, a nominal Catholic, had arranged for her to be educated by nuns. When her husband is pronounced dead in the French hospital, Marie wonders if she is in some way responsible for his fate. In addition to her affair with Daniel, Marie has had a strange mystical experience at a place called Carmel, in California, where the Virgin Mary appeared and asked her to tell the priests to build a basilica. By failing to comply with this request, Marie now feels that she has brought punishment down on her husband. The following day, however, when she goes to sign the various forms in connection with the transportation of Alex's body back to the United States, she finds he has mysteriously disappeared. She has the impression that she is being used by some supernatural force, even though she has no belief in such things. The dilemma facing Marie is her knowledge that in order to save her husband, she will have to do as instructed and get in touch with a priest about what she has seen and heard. When she visits Monsignor Cassidy to tell him about her apparition, she can't refrain from announcing that she doesn't believe in the Virgin Mary or in miracles. The Monsignor thinks that his younger cousin, a priest called Ned Niles, would be interested in this story. What happens then is that Niles, an ambitious cleric, takes it on himself to interview Marie. If she is telling the truth, then the possibilities for his professional advancement—he is an investigative reporter of the supernatural with a special interest in Mariology—are immense. Alex shows definite signs of improvement after Marie has visited Cassidy, but she knows that his fate is in her hands: "She saw again the trolley in that hospital room in Nice. She saw the dead face as the French doctor drew back the sheet. *I am the resurrection and the life*. They give and they take away."[25]

---

24. Moore, *Catholics*, 91.
25. Moore, *Cold Heaven* (London: Triad/Panther, 1985), 212.

Niles likens Marie's story to that of Saul of Tarsus, another unbeliever touched by God, and tells her that she still has the right to refuse, to say no to God, that the Church doesn't require anyone to believe in miracles. At the same time, he is busily preparing a case to authenticate the apparition. In the end, a second apparition occurs when Marie is accompanied by two nuns, the saintly Mother St. Jude and Sister Anna, to the site where the Virgin appeared to her. Unusually, the Virgin appears this time, not to Mother St. Jude or Marie, but to Sister Anna, something that will later cause Monsignor Cassidy to observe, "Faith is a form of stupidity. No wonder they call it blind faith."[26] Marie, for her part, feels as though a burden has been taken from her: "It is Sister Anna's miracle now . . . If they are going to make this place a new Lourdes, they need my silence, that must be it. That is why they have released me."[27] Freed from the clutches of a patriarchal Church and the worry that her actions will impact her husband negatively, Marie contemplates a more positive future: "She thought of that life, that ordinary, muddled life of falling in love and leaving her husband . . . The priests were gone. It was over."[28]

In these two novels, Brian Moore delves into the strange workings of grace, the subtleties of faith and loss of faith, and the thin line between the two. Marie, in *Cold Heaven,* abhors what she sees as the superstitious religion of her mother, "with its priests and indulgences and denials of the imperfection of this world for an illusionary life hereafter,"[29] and yet she, an unbeliever, has had a divine revelation. This revelation, however, does not give her faith. Rather, it confirms her determination to steer clear of priests and nuns and to seek happiness in a human relationship built around love. In the case of *Catholics'* Tomás O'Malley, the rediscovery of the power of prayer leads to the prospect of a happiness that he had felt was gone forever. In dealing with such theologically challenging concepts, Moore is certainly placing Catholicism at the center of his preoccupations and is, like Graham Greene, raising questions about how miracles can sometimes happen in the most unlikely scenarios and to people who have few, if any, religious beliefs. (Graham Greene once said, in fact, that Moore was his favorite living author.)

Moore stated in a revealing interview with Joe O'Connor, "Belief is an obsession of mine. I think that everybody wants to believe in something—

26. Ibid., 268. 27. Ibid., 276.
28. Ibid., 286–87. 29. Ibid., 88–89.

politics, religion, something that makes life worthwhile for them. And with most people there's a certain point in their lives . . . when these beliefs are shattered. And it's that point I seize on as a writer."[30] Marie is an example of someone who chooses to put her belief in a system other than the one she encounters in organized religion, as is obvious from what she says to Mother St. Jude: "I don't believe in God. I am your opposite . . . Happiness, for me, is knowing that I am in charge of my own life, that I can do as I choose. Don't you see that you're a victim, as I am a victim? What sort of love is it that's withdrawn from someone as good as you, sending you into despair?"[31] Moore's position in relation to Catholicism is thus quite an ambivalent one. Marie's discovery that her husband has risen, Christ-like, from the dead, links her to Mary Magdalen, the first person to discover the empty tomb after the resurrection. She is an unwilling accomplice in furthering the ambitions of Fr. Niles and, like Moore, is skeptical about faith, even after the mysterious apparition and her husband's miraculous coming back to life. Catholicism is a concern for Moore, and his writings show a marked dislike of hypocrisy (especially evident in the case of Fr. Niles) and the excessive use of authoritarianism by priests anxious to have things on their own terms or not at all (as seen in James Kinsella and Monsignor Cassidy). But his characters for the most part remain at a remove from the Church's teachings and fail to benefit from the healing grace that is the hallmark of novels by Bernanos and Greene, for example. What we have, therefore, is an example of writing that is informed by a Catholic mindset, yet seemingly doubtful of aspects of the faith and, in particular, critical of blind adherence to traditional Catholic practices.

For John McGahern, Catholicism is more closely identified with local traditions and culture than with any issue of faith per se. We have already sketched some of the problems the writer encountered with Church authorities at the time of the banning of his second novel in 1965. His marriage in a registry office in London around the same time didn't do anything to improve his position. The strong, simple faith of his mother, who died from cancer when he was only ten, left an indelible mark on the future writer. On several occasions, he had promised her that he would become a priest. He writes in his *Memoir* (2006), "After the Ordination Mass I would place

---

30. Brian Moore, "An Interview with Brian Moore," by Joe O'Connor. *Dublin Sunday Tribune*, Oct. 1, 1995: 8.
31. Moore, *Cold Heaven*, 199.

my freshly anointed hands on my mother's head. We'd live together in the priest's house and she'd attend each morning Mass and take communion from my hands."[32] As was so often the case in the Ireland of this time, the vocation was more the mother's than the son's, and soon literature replaced the priesthood as McGahern's calling in life: "Instead of being a priest of God, I would be the God of a small, vivid, world."[33] Art fulfilled the role of religion for most of McGahern's adult life. He began to see how writing was his way of working out the complex tissue that constitutes human experience. Through "naming" his world, through bringing it to life in words, he felt himself, in a way, to be performing a divine function. He stated in a 1966 interview that art is "a religious activity which is keeping faith to the sources of one's own being and it is, in the pure sense of the words, a form of praise and prayer."[34] James Whyte's *History, Myth, and Ritual in the Fiction of John McGahern* (2002) traces the writer's fondness for repetition to the influence of religious ceremonies and notes the way in which the language of his fiction "often echoes the rhythms of prayer."[35] In his *Outstaring Nature's Eye: The Fiction of John McGahern* (1993), Denis Sampson goes further, stating that: "[McGahern] is a religious writer in the largest sense because he associates art with a metaphysical quest, with the recovery of traces of mystery and a sense of the sanctity of the person. His fiction is preoccupied with the place of Catholicism in the lives of his characters . . . and with the place of faith in the movements of consciousness."[36]

McGahern's last novel, *That They May Face the Rising Sun* (2002; titled *By the Lake* in the U.S. edition), illustrates the manner in which Catholicism is a fundamental element in the lives of the elderly community that is the central focus of this narrative. One could question the extent to which this book is a novel at all, so absent from it are all signs of traditional plot and character development. The work gives you the impression that you are living as much as reading: days and seasons pass imperceptibly during the calendar year covered by the narrative and you become totally absorbed in the rituals of the people as they go about their daily tasks and repeat the same

32. John McGahern, *Memoir* (London: Faber and Faber, 2006), 62–63.

33. Ibid., 205.

34. Cited in James Whyte, *History, Myth, and Ritual in the Fiction of John McGahern: Strategies of Transcendence* (Lewiston, N.Y.: Edwin Mellen, 2002), 126.

35. Ibid., 132–33.

36. Denis Sampson, *Outstaring Nature's Eye: The Fiction of John McGahern* (Washington, D.C.: The Catholic University of America Press, 1993), 7–8.

formulaic verbal exchanges that they have been doing for years. Most of the action—what there is of it—revolves around the house of Joe and Kate Ruttledge, returned emigrants to Ireland, who settle on a small farm beside a lake, a setting that is strikingly similar to where McGahern and his second wife lived in Leitrim. As was the case with McGahern, with whom he shares a number of traits, Ruttledge's farming methods are viewed with some bemusement by his neighbors and friends. His animals are treated like pets, a fact that is highlighted humorously by the local handyman, Patrick Ryan: "There's an old Shorthorn they milk for the house that would nearly sit in an armchair and put specs on to read the *Observer*."[37]

Although viewed by some as quaint in their habits, the Ruttledges are nevertheless well accepted by the community. They are especially close to Jamesie, a sensitive, good-natured man with a love of gossip. In the opening pages of the novel, Jamesie inquires why the Ruttledges don't attend Mass. When Joe replies that he'd like to go but that he doesn't believe, Jamesie retorts, "None of us believes and we go. That's no bar."[38] This is a revealing statement when one examines the mentality that lies behind it. For Jamesie and the other people living in this area, the Mass is more of a social occasion than a spiritual experience. Joe Ruttledge had spent some years studying for the priesthood but left when he found that he really didn't believe all the fundamentals of Catholicism. He feels that it would be hypocritical for him to attend Mass in such circumstances. Jamesie goes to church, in his own words, "to see the whole performance . . . We go to see all the other hypocrites," which, if we are to believe him, reduces the Mass to a spectacle bereft of any genuinely spiritual dimension. There is indeed a sense in which the characters in this book unthinkingly follow the patterns and traditions that have been passed on to them.

The striking thing about the community is the age profile: there are no children still living in the area. The bachelor Patrick Ryan is conscious that they are the last of their kind: "After us there'll be nothing but the water hen and the swan."[39] Indeed, there is a tone of the elegiac swansong about this and other observations we encounter in the book. In the course of a few months, Patrick loses his brother and then his close friend Johnny, and he sees that when he and his generation pass away there will be nobody to re-

37. John McGahern, *That They May Face the Rising Sun* (London: Faber and Faber, 2002), 76.
38. Ibid., 2.
39. Ibid., 45.

place them. People might be relocated from Dublin to live in this rural setting, but they will not be the same sort of people; they will not share the
same customs and beliefs. Some of these customs are quite pagan in origin.
For example, when they are digging Johnny's grave, they plan it in such a
way that his head lies to the west. When Ruttledge asks why they are doing this, Patrick Ryan tells him: "He sleeps with his head to the west . . . so
that when he wakes he may face the rising sun."[40] Such practices were (and
sometimes still are) commonplace among Irish people who, while outwardly
in conformity with the dictates of the Catholic Church, tend to follow their
own individual belief system. As McGahern observed in his *Memoir:* "Most
people went about their sensible pagan lives as they had done for centuries,
seeing this conformity as just another veneer they had to pretend to wear
like all the others they had worn since the time of the Druids."[41]

The local priest, Fr. Conroy, is portrayed as a sympathetic if marginal
character. The novel, as can be seen from certain references to events such as
the Enniskillen bombing, is set in the 1980s, and already the waning influence of the Catholic Church in rural Ireland is noticeable. Fr. Conroy blends
in with the local community, attends the fairs where he buys and sells live-
stock, and tries not to impose on people. Hence his embarrassment one day
when he goes to visit the Ruttledges on behalf of the bishop, who is anxious
to know why Joe Ruttledge decided to pack in his studies for the priesthood.
The priest tells Joe, "I believe in living and letting live. The man up in Long-
ford [the bishop] is very interested in you and why you left the Church and
has me persecuted about you every time he comes."[42] Joe senses the priest's
discomfort and does his utmost to make him feel at home. He realizes that
Fr. Conroy is essentially a decent man who is fighting a losing battle against
the diminishing levels of belief in his parish. Joe is struck by how few people wear ashes on their forehead on Ash Wednesday, for example, something
that would have been unthinkable a couple of decades previously. The two
men work together to ensure that Bill Evans, given into the care of nuns as
a baby and later sent to work as a "skivvy" on a farm where he lived like a
virtual slave, gets accommodation in the new social housing system that is
being built in the village. Bill is a stark reminder of the harsh treatment that
visited many young Irish men and women who found themselves in the no-

40. Ibid., 282.
41. McGahern, *Memoir*, 211.
42. McGahern, *That They May Face the Rising Sun*, 66.

torious industrial schools or Magdalen laundries during the middle decades of the last century. Bill is fortunate to have found people who were sympathetic to his plight and who gave him food and cigarettes. Although appallingly treated by the family in whose care he was placed at a young age, he remains fiercely loyal to them. When Ruttledge interrogates him on the events of his life, Bill promptly tells him to stop torturing him. This, Ruttledge realizes later, is the only way that Bill can deal with the horrors of his past life: "Bill Evans could no more look forward than he could look back. He existed in a small closed circle of the present. Remembrance of things past and dreams of things to come were instruments of torture."[43]

There is a serenity about *That They May Face the Rising Sun* that was not in evidence in McGahern's earlier fiction. The author seems to have reached the point where he saw that life was but a brief preparation for death. The adolescent narrator of his second novel, *The Dark,* noted in this regard: "The moment of death was the one real moment in life; everything took its proper position there, was fixed for ever, whether to live in joy or hell for all eternity, or had your life been the haphazard flicker between nothingness and nothingness."[44] For both McGahern and Brian Moore, two unbelievers, the issue of Catholicism remained a central concern in their novels. Their characters grapple with issues of faith and dogma, seek answers to the questions of life and death, and wonder if their lives are merely that "haphazard flicker."

Writing in a 2006 edition of *The Tablet,* Mark Lawson states that with the death of Muriel Spark (1918–2006) and John McGahern, it was questionable whether fiction inspired and underpinned by the Catholic faith had a future. Lawson argues that any author who has been for a serious length of time a Catholic carries an almost inescapable tribal and psychological imprint.[45] This was definitely the case with McGahern and Moore. The newest generation of young Irish writers, who live in a society where Catholicism is no longer the central concern it once was and who are largely ignorant of the main tenets of the faith to which most of them adhere only nominally, have other preoccupations and concerns than matters of faith. It might be somewhat premature to declare, as Fintan O'Toole did, "the end of the Catholic Church" in Ireland,[46] but there can be no denying that Irish people's perception of religion has changed substantially in the past couple of decades.

---

43. Ibid., 167.
44. John McGahern, *The Dark* (London: Faber and Faber, 1963), 69.
45. Mark Lawson, "Catholicism's Indelible Mark on the Page," *The Tablet* (April 29, 2006): 16–17.
46. Fintan O'Toole, *The Lie of the Land* (Dublin: New Island, 1998), 65–75.

If we are in fact living in a "post-Catholic" Ireland, it makes the fictions of Moore and McGahern all the more valuable as chronicles of a society that no longer exists. While aware of the abuse of power and the repression wielded by the Catholic Church in Ireland, they were appreciative nevertheless of many of the Church's positive attributes. McGahern, for example, greatly respected his mother's faith, and his attitude to religion was characterized by reverence more than bitterness. As he writes in his *Memoir,* "I have affection still and gratitude for my upbringing in the church: it was the sacred weather of my early life, and I could no more turn against it than I could turn on any deep part of myself."[47]

In conclusion then, for all that distinguishes their work from the traditional Catholic novel, as this genre developed in France and England, Brian Moore and John McGahern nevertheless produced novels informed by a strong Irish Catholic influence. Although the more orthodox tradition that flourished at the beginning of the last century doesn't exist in Ireland, McGahern and Moore offer valuable insights into Ireland's often troubled and complex relationship with the Catholic religion and the manner in which it dominated people's lives. Whereas Bernanos and Mauriac in France and Waugh and Greene in England were acutely aware that they were writing for a public largely estranged from the Catholic project, the Irish writers felt that their public was too much the opposite. I thus subscribe to Brian O'Rourke's summation in *The Conscience of the Race:*

I suspect that the non-emergence, to any notable degree, of an Irish "Catholic novel," may have something to do with statistics and voluntary stance, as well as with imaginative disposition. Several of the French novelists . . . speak of their work as constituting a conscious witness to the faith and this seems to me not unconnected with their consciousness of writing for a de-Christianized public. Conversely, I have the impression that some of the Irish novelists might have been more "Catholic" if more of their compatriots were less so.[48]

47. McGahern, *Memoir,* 222.
48. Brian O'Rourke, *The Conscience of the Race: Sex and Religion in Irish and French Novels 1941–1973* (Dublin: Four Courts, 1980), 62.

CHAPTER 5

The Never-Ending Reformation ▪ Miguel Delibes's *The Heretic*

Salvador A. Oropesa

Together with Graham Greene (1904–91) and Heinrich Böll (1917–85), Spanish author Miguel Delibes (1920–) ranks as one of the most prominent European Catholic writers of the second half of the twentieth century. His work *El hereje,* or *The Heretic* (1998; English translation 2006), is his testament as a novelist and a summary of many issues that preoccupied him throughout his writing career. Indeed, Delibes himself was something of a "heretic" his whole life. During the Spanish Civil War he fought with Francisco Franco's nationalists instead of the progressive Republic in order to defend his Catholic faith, yet after Franco's victory he turned against the Fascist dictatorship to work to bring back democracy to Spain. When Spain returned to democracy, he maintained his independent voice by criticizing the economic growth taking place at the expense of the environment. He consistently resisted any political party, either conservative or liberal, that sought to buy his pen for its cause, and he continued to champion a social Catholicism that could bring justice and peace to a country torn by a fratricidal war.

As an author, Delibes exerted a strong influence on educated Catholics who sought a middle way between Marxist liberation theology and the national Catholicism of Francoism. In *The Heretic,* we encounter a type of never-ending Reformation, the idea that the Christian faith must continually evolve with the movement of society in order to fulfill the spiritual needs of the people. An historical work set in Renaissance Spain, the novel argues for the positive reciprocal influence of *both* sixteenth-century reformations, the Protestant Reformation and the Catholic Counter-Reformation. It examines a crucial moment in Spain's religious past in order to illuminate the deep changes the country endured as it violently confronted the influx of Protestantism and thereby consolidated a national identity based on Catholicism, a process that had already started in the fifteenth century with the gradual elimination of Judaism and Islam. In *The Heretic*, Delibes challenges Catholic readers to confront the Protestant "other" and respect him. In doing so, he points to the fact that the Spain of the new millennium is once again an ethnically and religiously diverse country and that it is imperative for its future not to repeat the errors of the past.

Born in Valladolid, Miguel Delibes studied as a youth with the Catholic Brothers of La Salle. He was sixteen years old when the Spanish Civil War started and nineteen when it finished, and during that time he volunteered as a seaman in Francisco Franco's nationalist navy. As soon as the war ended, he abandoned military service to continue his studies, for he did not want to participate in the repression that the Franco dictatorship imposed after the end of the conflict. He earned degrees in law and economics and became a professor of commerce law at the School of Commerce of Valladolid. Delibes's knowledge of the role of diverse economic forces in society and the way law works allowed him to understand the limits and possibilities of the relationship between economic and political freedom in the context of a conservative dictatorship. Through his contributions to Valladolid's prestigious regional newspaper *El Norte de Castilla*—where he started as a cartoonist— he became a professional writer. At the age of thirty-two, he was named vice director of the paper, and then six years later in 1958, director. He resigned under pressure of the Ministry of Information in 1963 for his refusal to follow official instructions limiting the freedom of the press.

It was his wife, Angeles de Castro, who encouraged Delibes to write fiction, and in 1947 he won Spain's prestigious Nadal award with the novel *La sombra del ciprés es alargada* (Long Is the Cypress's Shadow). In 1944, the Nadal award had revived liberal literature in Spain, first honoring the work *Nada* by Carmen Laforet. Laforet and Delibes represented a group of writers victorious in the Spanish Civil War—they had supported Franco's nationalists—but horrified by the brutality and extent of Franco's repression that killed more than two hundred thousand people,[1] and at its peak in the early 1940s imprisoned more than one million in concentration camps and penitentiaries all over the country. In supporting the Franco regime, the Catholic Church was deeply involved in that repression and as an institution has up to

1. Antony Beevor, *The Spanish Civil War* (New York: Penguin, 2001), 266.

the present day not expressed any public remorse or apology for its actions.

Delibes's lifelong Catholic concerns leading to his culminating work, *The Heretic*, can be seen in several of his earlier novels. His first masterpiece, *El camino* (The Path; 1950), presents an idyllic life in a mountain valley of Cantabria. In the unnamed village, traditional Catholicism resists the entrance of nationalist Catholicism, the Fascist and official religion of the Franco dictatorship with its anachronistic lack of separation between church and state and its lack of regard for the organic religious identity of the village. The novel's title refers to a sermon delivered by the parish priest of the village about the path true Christians have to choose, and the plot involves a young boy who searches for that path.

In 1962 Delibes published the extraordinary novel *Las ratas* (The Rats). The protagonist here is Nini, a poor child and "Christlike figure"[2] who teaches truths about love and nature to the other members of the village. In this novel, one of the key themes in Delibes's writing appears for the first time: the suggestion that the Catholic Church should have intervened to stop the Spanish Civil War instead of being an active party in promoting it. The plot involves a professing Catholic man who kills another man for being an atheist. The victim's son asks his parish priest why a man wearing a big cross on his chest, a Christian who professes to follow the teachings of Jesus on love of neighbor, would kill another man for his beliefs. The priest answers that others, too, are guilty of murder, but the son's sincere rebuttal to this statement is that these others are not Christians.[3] The son is doubly shocked, first because his father was murdered, and second because he was murdered in the name of the Catholic religion. At this time in history, 1962, when censorship was still fierce, Delibes could only suggest this topic without further development. He inserts into the plot an open question about the Church's cooperation with the Franco government that has yet to be answered.

In 1966 Delibes released a novel that had an enormous impact on Spanish society, *Cinco horas con Mario* (1966) (translated as *Five Hours with Mario*, 1988). This novel represented in literature the challenge that the Second Vatican Council (1962–65) presented to Franco's government since it undermined the only real legitimacy the dictatorship had, the one given it by the Catholic Church. When Pope John XXIII published *Pacem in terris* in 1963,

2. Dorothy Ewing, "The Religious Significance of Miguel Delibes's *Las ratas*," *Romance Notes* 11, no. 3 (1970): 497.

3. Miguel Delibes, *Las ratas*, in *Obra completa. Tomo III* (Barcelona: Destino, 1968), 452.

defending the Western values of freedom of speech and democracy, the Franco regime understood that it was as much the target of the encyclical as were Communist countries. Moreover, one of the Council's documents, *Dignitatis humanae*, advocated freedom of religion, a freedom that then did not exist in Spain despite the fact that Catholicism was the country's official religion; and another Council document, *Christus Dominus*, asked civil authorities to renounce their rights in the election of bishops, something Franco refused to do. In 1960, 339 priests, mostly Basque, signed an open letter asking for the separation of the Church from Franco's regime. In 1963, the abbot of Monserrat, the sacred symbol of Catalonia, publicly attacked the regime.[4] Catholic lay organizations followed this lead with a long series of denunciations against a dictatorship that had made Spain the country with the largest number of Catholic priests in prison.[5]

It is in this context that one can best understand *Five Hours with Mario*. The book has been reprinted more than thirty times, and it became, in fact, obligatory reading in secondary education in Spain. A theater adaptation ran from 1979 to 1990, and the play is still staged on a regular basis. Indeed, it seems that the Spanish public cannot get enough of *Five Hours with Mario*. Its success is comparable to the enormous reception of the movie version of *Jesus Christ Superstar* (1973), which was released during the last two years of the dictatorship and was perceived by some as a needed renewal of Catholicism in Spain.

Five Hours with Mario presents a monologue delivered by Carmen Menchu, a traditional Catholic Francoist woman in her forties who, over the course of five hours, speaks to the corpse of her husband Mario who has died of a heart attack. Her reactionary views are evident in her attack on Vatican II: "Nowadays everything's all stirred up with that business about the Council,"[6] she states, adding that the "wretched Council" is "turning everything upside down."[7] According to her, "John XXIII, may he be in glory, placed the Church in a dead-end street . . . [He] has done and said things that are enough to scare anybody."[8] The deceased Mario Díez Collado had been a high school teacher,

---

4. Stanley G. Payne, *Spanish Catholicism: An Historical Overview* (Madison: University of Wisconsin Press, 1984), 197.

5. Ibid., 194–97.

6. Miguel Delibes, *Five Hours with Mario*, trans. Frances M. López-Morillas (New York: Columbia University Press, 1988), 58.

7. Ibid., 59.

8. Ibid., 123.

a humble, honest man and an idealist. He contributed to the local newspaper, was an unsuccessful novelist, and was an engaged and progressive Catholic who found in Vatican II and the thinking of Pope John XXIII the vindication of his social Catholicism and his opposition to the Franco dictatorship. Because Mario refuses to participate in a municipal candidacy and sign the rigged acts of a referendum, he forfeits the possibility of getting a subsidized apartment for government employees, and he is subsequently viewed as a "commie" *(rojo)* by the authorities.

Together, the characters of Mario and Carmen represent the "two Spains," one conservative and one progressive, both affected by the Spanish Civil War and who now, as a married couple with children, must live together under the same roof. Both characters are victims, Carmen of a nefarious education and a reactionary and cold family in which Catholicism was synonymous with class privilege and moral superiority; and Mario of a Civil War that killed his two brothers, one by the nationalists and the other by the Republic. The Catholic Mario is also the victim of the papacy of Pius XI, who blessed the nationalist side during the Civil War, declared the war a crusade, and condemned liberal Catholicism; and of the papacy of Pius XII, who continued this support.[9]

Scholar Fernando Lázaro Carreter has rendered an extraordinary portrayal of the "Marios" of Spain. While specific and overt political gestures were magnified at the time of the transition from the Franco dictatorship to Spain's democracy under the monarchy of King Juan Carlos I, the silent opposition of many ordinary citizens had actually begun with the first signs of tyranny. Lázaro Carreter sees in characters like Delibes's Mario the position of thousands of citizens all over the country who were "suspect" under the Franco regime. These men and women resisted the advances of the dictatorship. They never succumbed to the possibility of climbing socially or receiving privileges if such favors involved any form of tyranny. Such persons were socially and politically ostracized, and they knew that at any moment the whole weight of repression could come down upon them. According to Lázaro Carreter, the quiet opposition over thirty years of these stalwart citizens was more determinant of the success of the transition period than the various political stunts toward the end of the dictatorship.[10] *Five Hours with*

9. Payne, *Spanish Catholicism,* 171–79.

10. Fernando Lázaro Carreter, "Cuarenta y cinco minutos con Mario," in *El autor y su obra: Miguel Delibes,* ed. Ramón García Domínguez and Gonzalo Santonja (Madrid: Actas, 1993), 162.

Mario can indeed be read as a document that helps to illuminate the identity crisis in the recent history of the Catholic Church in Spain.

As is clear from the foregoing analysis of several of his novels, Delibes was concerned all his life with issues of faith and compromise in light of the Catholic Church's position on the Spanish Civil War. He had adopted a nonviolent opposition to the Franco regime, and characters with such beliefs reappear in his literature. As early as 1971, Delibes had expressed in his book of interviews with César Alonso de los Ríos his view on this subject: "And talking about Christ, I think the histories of the Spanish Civil War have undervalued the role of religion, and my own judgment is this factor is key. I have the opinion that if we had had a John XXIII before 1936, the Spanish Civil War would not have started or at least it would have had a different character."[11] At the age of seventy-four, and although sick with cancer, Delibes commenced writing *The Heretic*, an award-winning novel that presents a final exploration of these issues. The story takes place in his native city, Valladolid, and like most historical novels it tells us as much about the present as the past. The protagonist is Cipriano Salcedo, born on October 31, 1517, the same day Martin Luther made public his 95 Theses. Cipriano's mother dies while giving birth to him, and he never becomes close to his father because the father blames his child for his wife's death. First educated by his wet nurse, the youth finds his place in the world when his father decides, against his class and caste, to send him to a school for poor orphan children. Later, at the university, he earns a law degree like his uncle who is a chancery judge, but he chooses not to follow in his footsteps by entering the bureaucracy of the empire. Instead Cipriano becomes a successful merchant in the wool trade. He marries Teodomira, the unsophisticated daughter of a sheep farmer, who succumbs to the consumerism and pomp of the renaissance city. She is an ineffective wife and cannot fulfill the physical and spiritual needs of her husband. To appease his restlessness, Cipriano becomes interested in new forms of spirituality, and he believes he has discovered new truths in listening to Pedro Cazalla and Don Carlos de Seso,[12] members

11. César Alonso de los Ríos, *Conversaciones con Miguel Delibes* (Madrid: Magisterio Español, 1971), 50. This is my translation of de los Ríos: "Y ya que hablamos de Cristo, yo pienso que el factor religioso no se ha valorado lo suficiente en las historias de la guerra civil y, a mi juicio, es clave, hasta el punto de que yo soy de los que creen que si hubiera habido un Juan XXIII antes de 1936, la guerra española no se hubiera desencadenado o hubiese tenido otro carácter."

12. Both are historical characters. See Henry Kamen, *The Spanish Inquisition: A Historical Revision* (New Haven, Conn.: Yale University Press, 1997), 93.

of recently formed Protestant groups in Castile. He converts to Lutheranism, becomes a leader of this illegal "sect," and travels to Germany to buy books and make contacts with other believers. When the Inquisition arrests one member of the group, the whole Protestant conventicle disperses and he is apprehended, judged, and burned alive in an auto-da-fé.[13]

The novel starts with the following quotation, which Delibes attributes to an address Pope John Paul II delivered to the College of Cardinals in 1994:

How can we remain in silence about so many kinds of violence perpetrated in the name of faith? Wars of religion, the courts of the Inquisition, and other mechanisms whereby the rights of individuals were violated . . . It is necessary that the Church, in accord with Vatican Council II, take the initiative in reviewing the darker aspects of its history, judging them in light of the principles emanating from the Gospels.[14]

Delibes, then, begins the novel with an uncontestable strategy: he quotes a source that few would dare challenge and thus sets the tone for a novel that explores in fictional terms the letter and the spirit of the Pope's admonition.

The Heretic is a novel about freedom of conscience and religion and the reciprocal influence between the Protestant Reformation and Catholic Counter-Reformation. In Delibes's view, the Protestant Reformation actually enriched the Catholic Church, but in the end, maximalist national identities trumped the religious debate. Once the precept of "cuius regio eius religio" was adopted in 1555, the religious division of the empire was inevitable, for this ruling meant that all territories were subject to the religion of their respective governors, whether Catholic or Protestant. As a result, as critic Diarmaid MacCulloch points out in his study, *The Reformation: A History*, religious freedom suffered in all Christian kingdoms.[15] According to MacCulloch's analysis, although a violent process, the Reformation was primarily a debate about words and ideas, which served to shape in significant ways the future of European identities. There was a real window of opportunity in 1541–42 to solve the differences between Catholics and Protestants, but it unfortunately failed, leading to what MacCulloch calls confessionalization or "the creation of fixed identities and systems of belief."[16] All these elements are present in Delibes's

13. For an historical account of Lutheranism in Castile during the sixteenth century with special emphasis on the Valladolid autos-da-fé, see Jesús Alonso Burgos, *El luteranismo en Castilla durante el siglo XVI. Autos de fe deValladolid de 21de mayo y 8 de octubre de 1559* (El Escorial: Swan, 1983).

14. Miguel Delibes, *The Heretic*, trans. Alfred MacAdam (New York: Overlook, 2006), 13.

15. Diarmaid MacCulloch, *The Reformation: A History* (New York: Viking, 2004), 266.

16. Ibid., xviii–xxii.

novel. *The Heretic* is an honest attempt to respect Protestantism from a Catholic point of view and revisit the origin of the schism among Christians. Delibes wishes to make his readers comprehend how Protestantism at the time challenged Catholic soteriology and how this challenge radically changed Spain. He presents a paradox: while the reaffirmation of Catholic identity through Castilian Spain's Counter-Reformation caused orthodoxy to gain a preeminence that it did not have before, resulting in an increase in the quality of the spiritual lives and Christian instruction of most people, Catholicism also became much more narrow and less accommodating. According to MacCulloch, there was now "only one way to be a Spaniard, and . . . this was to be a traditionalist Catholic untainted by unsupervised contact with alien thought. Protestantism was added to the list of un-Spanish traits that already included Islam and Judaism."[17] Delibes's protagonist Cipriano represents the influx of new spirituality in sixteenth-century Europe and its challenges: the birth of a new era of religious freedom and the test for tolerance.

The Heretic begins with a prelude in which Cipriano is aboard a *galleass*, or a cargo ship, traveling from Germany to Spain. It is October 1557, and he is returning home after meeting Protestant leader Philipp Melanchton at Wittenberg in Germany and buying books abroad following the orders of the Valladolid Protestant conventicle to which he belongs. Cipriano asserts, "I've accepted the doctrine of justification by faith, as has the entire Valladolid group, because I think faith is the essential thing and that Christ's sacrifice has a greater value as far as my redemption is concerned than my good works, no matter how altruistic they may be."[18] With Cipriano, the other clandestine traveler on the ship is Isidoro Tellería, a Calvinist from Seville. By this Delibes shows that the small Protestant groups in Spain at the time were as divided as in the rest of Europe between evangelical and reformed.

Following the prelude, the novel proper restarts from Cipriano's birth. It is divided into three books: "The Early Years," "The Heresy," and the "Auto-da-Fé." In the first section, we learn that with the exception of his wet nurse, Minervina's, love and care, the majority of Cipriano's childhood is lonely and uneventful. Minervina is in charge of the intelligent boy's religious education. She is from Santovenia, a small village with a group of the heretical religious sect the "illuminati" *(alumbrados)*, and she defends their right to religious freedom. But even while expressing this liberal stance, Minervina

17. Ibid., 291.
18. Delibes, *Heretic*, 23.

passes on to Cipriano traditional Catholic teaching and prayers: "The first thing she taught him was to cross himself at his head, mouth and heart."[19] In the context of her faith there is no doubt whatsoever of the existence of heaven and hell and her ineludible responsibility to teach her ward the basic truths of the Catholic religion. When Cipriano's father, Don Bernardo, realizes Minervina cannot educate his son further, he decides to send the boy to a foundling hospital, or orphanage. The detailed description of the prayers and basic beliefs that Minervina teaches Cipriano plus the description of the life in this institution and the indoctrination of the students there create the redundancy necessary to explain the deep set of core beliefs that shaped Catholic Castile and gave the region its strong religious identity. Scholar Carlos Eire's comment on the pervasive power of such deep beliefs in sixteenth-century Spain applies here: "Religious ritual is not simply a cultural construct: it is a form of cognition that constructs models of reality and paradigms of behavior."[20]

The foundling hospital that Cipriano attends is "managed by the Guild of Saint Joseph and Our Lady of O,[21] dedicated to educating abandoned children."[22] Delibes's word *cofradía* here is translated into English as "guild," but it can also be translated as "confraternity."[23] One of the main reasons for the existence of confraternities was—and still is—the charitable act of burying the dead, ensuring that the brother or sister conferee receives proper burial. Confraternities existed in Castilian Spain because it was firmly believed that a person's last hours in earthly life and first hours in the afterworld were crucial for salvation. A dying person was about to confront the particular judgment, and he or she needed all the help that could be gleaned from the prayers of the members of the confraternity as well as from priests, orphan children, the poor, and the saints. One sees this concept illustrated, for example, in the 1586 El Greco painting, *The Burial of Count Orgaz*, in the church of Santo Tomé in Toledo. This work is an iconographic representation

19. Ibid., 107.

20. Carlos M. N. Eire, *From Madrid to Purgatory: The Art and Craft of Dying in Sixteenth-Century Spain* (Cambridge: Cambridge University Press, 2002), 90.

21. Nuestra Señora de la O is short for Nuestra Señora de la Expectación o Esperanza del Parto—Our Lady of the Expectation. The typical medieval representation of this devotion was the Virgin Mary in an advanced stage of pregnancy with a transparent belly that reveals a tabernacle. The "O" comes from the "O" antiphons recited between the day of this devotion, December 18, and Christmas Eve: "O Sapientia, O Adonai, O Radix Jesse, O Oriens Splendor, O Rex Gentium, O Emmanuel."

22. Delibes, *Heretic*, 113.

23. See Eire, *Madrid to Purgatory*, 134–48.

of the particular judgment in orthodox Catholic teaching of the time. Two saints, Augustine and Stephen, help the soul of an aristocrat who is being taken by an angel into the presence of Christ. We see the count's friends and relatives, a Franciscan, a Dominican, and a little child praying for him. The Virgin Mary and the saints are in heaven waiting for the soul and ready to intercede for him. If the soul dies in a state of grace but still needs purification, it will be cleansed in purgatory.

One of the most striking scenes from the first part of *The Heretic* occurs when Cipriano and two of the orphans at the school are charged with burying the bodies of the poor and of those who have been executed. At dawn the children prepare a donkey cart and go to the morgue of Mercy Hospital. They load the corpses into the cart and are told which church to bring them to. As they travel with the corpses through the streets, the orphans recite litanies for the dead. If hired, they also will also sing the *Dies Irae* and *Litany of the Saints* at the funeral Mass, the first as a remembrance of the harsh judgment the soul can expect after death and the second to ask the saints to intercede for the soul. Because the main mission of the confraternity is to give Christian burial to its members, in charity it also undertakes the burial of the less fortunate of society. Those who support the orphanage with alms not only help the foundlings but also aid the deceased poor because they ensure that someone will intercede in prayer for them. To bury the dead and pray for their souls are corporal and spiritual acts of mercy, so the benefactors also help themselves spiritually through their funding of the orphanage. So evolved in this Catholic society a circle of charity and an effective system of reciprocal aid.

In his study of sixteenth-century Madrid, Eire has established that the presence of confraternities at deaths were requested in a high percentage of wills, more than 60 percent in the 1560s and more than 50 percent in the 1570s and 1580s.[24] The same can be said of orphan children. While in the 1550s they were requested at only ten percent of funerals, this percentage jumped to 48 percent in the 1560s and then to 75 percent in the 1570s.[25] The increase of the presence of confraternity members and orphan children in Madrid's funerals show a reaffirmation of, but also a certain anxiety about, Catholic beliefs at a time when orthodoxy was being challenged all over

24. Eire, *Madrid to Purgatory,* 136.
25. Ibid., 146–47.

Europe. In this first section of the novel, Delibes carefully details how Catholicism was lived in the Valladolid of the Renaissance. By illustrating the strength of orthodox belief, he enables the reader to understand how upsetting the challenge to such belief was and how Christians became so sharply divided. While *The Heretic* ultimately defends freedom of conscience in terms of religion, Delibes also demands respect for the traditional beliefs of Catholic Castile.

It is around this time, however, that Cipriano's Catholic faith becomes more problematic because of his scrupulous conscience. He finds that he cannot repent of his sin against the Fourth Commandment: he feels no love for his father, whom he believes has abandoned him at the orphanage, and he decides therefore that he must stop going to confession and receiving communion.[26] In addition, the human injustice he witnesses around him torments him. He cannot understand the poverty of the many and the privilege of the few.

The Heretic interweaves this crisis in Cipriano's spiritual life with a major event in Valladolid's religious history. During the summer of 1527, Valladolid became the center of theological discussion in Spain as the Spanish Inquisition convened a conference in the city to discuss complaints from various Catholic religious orders about the works of the monk Erasmus. Thirty-three distinguished theologians, bishops, teachers, and members of monastic orders from Spain and Portugal gathered to discuss apparent problems of doctrine, including issues concerning the Trinity, the veneration of the saints, and the legitimacy of relics and pilgrimages. The conference lasted six and a half weeks but was then suspended because of the arrival of the plague and did not reconvene. In an article on the theological discussions of the conference, Lu Ann Homza explains that the traditional simplification of scholars like Marcel Bataillon in his work *Érasme et l'Espagne: Recherches sur l'histoire spirituelle du XVI siècle* (1937) that divided the conference into pro-Erasmists and anti-Erasmists, reformers and non-reformers, does not correspond with the twenty-nine responses from the proceedings that have been preserved. Far from merely having a two-sided argument, the theologians worked as professionals, carefully discussing Erasmus's points one by one and using various scholarly methods to do their evaluations. As Homza puts it, their opinions "illustrate the complexity of Spanish intellectual prac-

26. Delibes, *The Heretic*, 126.

tice, such as the relative balance between authority and philology, hagiography and historicism, and scholastic method and humanist technique."[27] The theologians criticized the monastic orders who originally lodged the complaints because the orders decontextualized Erasmus's quotations in their dossiers and created paragraphs using sentences from very different writings, thus producing texts that Erasmus never composed. Most of the theologians were familiar with and even experts on Erasmus's books, and they proved that they could not be manipulated by such skewed documents. Spain's emperor Charles I attended the conference and sympathized with Erasmus, as did the young Dominican Bartolomé de Carranza. Carranza, later the Archbishop of Toledo and confessor to Queen Mary I, Mary Tudor, of England, was eventually to become the most famous victim of the Inquisition.

Delibes presents this actual historic conference from the point of view of the orphans. According to these young witnesses, Valladolid's citizens were divided on the conference's issues, and during the weeks of the convention these issues were the single topic of conversation in the school and in the city. Public opinion was, in fact, very important to the development of the conference, and homilies were regularly delivered to advance certain positions. Crowds of people moved from church to church to hear orators on both sides.

Delibes includes these episodes because he is most interested in the Catholic Erasmus as a champion of free will. Erasmus tried to avoid a confrontation with Luther, but he ended up using the topic of free will to attack Luther in 1524, publishing *A Diatribe on Free Will.* Luther's answer, *Of the Slavery of the Will* (1525), presents an essentially dismal picture of human nature, for he "set out the full pitiless message that human beings could expect nothing but condemnation, and had nothing to offer that would merit salvation."[28] Erasmus could not accept this conclusion because it diminished the role of human responsibility on the path to salvation and hence the importance of human reason. Cipriano is instinctively sympathetic to Erasmus's insistence on free will even as he moves toward Luther's position on justification by faith alone,[29] a doctrine Delibes clearly finds distasteful, for it undermines the relevance of a life committed to growth in virtue through grace. In fact, it

---

27. Lu Ann Homza, "Erasmus as Hero, or Heretic? Spanish Humanism and the Valladolid Assembly of 1527," *Renaissance Quarterly* 50, no. 1 (1997): 82.

28. MacCulloch, *Reformation*, 147.

29. Delibes, *Heretic*, 131.

is obvious here that the relationship between the author and his protagonist grows problematic. Indeed, Delibes's creation of Cipriano in *The Heretic* is a tour of force. He is the "other" for the author and for the majority of Spanish readers who consider themselves either practicing or cultural Catholics: people for whom Catholic rituals and sacraments are ingrained in daily life and who share an unwavering belief that good deeds are necessary for salvation. Delibes confronts his readers with a protagonist who does not elicit empathy. It is never fully clear why Cipriano becomes a Protestant: for him, it is far less an intellectual process than a vague feeling of unease with conventional religious tradition. In the secret Protestant conventicle with its improvised readings from the Scriptures and singing of hymns, Cipriano states he feels the presence of Jesus in a way he cannot achieve in Catholic services. For the Spanish reader, the challenge is to accept without judgment Cipriano's personal journey away from traditional—and national—Catholicism.

In twentieth-century Spanish literature, Castile often stands for the timeless and intrahistoric land described by fin-de-siècle writers,[30] but Delibes is more interested in detailing the rise of capitalism and noting its impact on religious change in Renaissance Valladolid. *The Heretic* thus goes against the grain of modernist literature and returns to nineteenth-century realism in its minute account of monetary issues. As he matures into a successful wool merchant, Cipriano's business partakes of the new global economy, for it depends on foreign markets: the wool from southern Castile is gathered in Burgos on its way to the port of Bilbao to be manufactured in Northern Europe. Cipriano understands that progress is not in producing raw materials but in manufacturing them, and he develops a new fur overcoat that is sold in Castile but is also exported to Antwerp. The novel explains in detail the source of the skins needed, the people involved in the hunting of the rabbits, and the new techniques of mass production.

Cipriano's wife, Teodomira, is a *mestiza* with little education. The cou-

---

30. "Intrahistory" is a term coined by the most important Catholic writer of twentieth-century Spain, Miguel de Unamuno (1864–1936). Unamuno created the term while writing *Paz en la Guerra* (1897; *Peace in War*) about the last Carlist War (1872–76). This was a late religious war between traditionalist Carlists, who wanted to implement a nationalist and Catholic society, and a liberal government. Intrahistory is the metaphysical fantasy that a culture can exist outside of history. Unamuno wanted to believe in a Basque country untouched by modernity. His fellow fin-de-siècle writers like Antonio Machado moved this fantasy to Castile and created an immutable region of shepherds and snowy moors without trains, telegraphs, or private property. In contrast, Delibes situates the action of his novel in a mercantilist Castile integrated into the European wool markets, with flourishing stores, elite consumerism, and a new bourgeoisie immersed in urban life and its comforts.

ple cannot conceive children, and after a few years of relative happiness, the marriage sours due to this fact. As Cipriano becomes a pioneer in Castile's evolving capitalist system, so Teodomira completes the capitalist equation by becoming a consumer of the luxurious goods then flowing into Spain. As Europe becomes a single market, Teodomira can now purchase products made of walnut, mahogany, ebony, ivory, leather, damask, brocade, and other fine materials from such places as Venice, Flanders, Germany, Holland, and Bohemia. Fine goods such as a *cassone* (wedding chest), a canopied bed, tapestries, and a candelabra embellish the house.[31] The same forces that are opening Spain to trade also open it to the influx of new ideas. Cipriano can now purchase books from all over Europe and establish business and religious contacts outside of Spain. Delibes makes clear that these elements belong to the same process: the incoming new commercial, religious, and political freedoms cannot be separated, and they serve to strengthen and influence each other. For instance by 1570, after the end of the so-called Protestant crisis in Spain and through treaties with England, France, and Germany, Protestant merchants could no longer be prosecuted by the Inquisition while doing business in Spain because such trade was considered more important than any theoretical danger the new religion might bring.[32] Even books circulated almost freely. Most books sold in Spain during this time were published outside the country, and in some bookstores these constituted more than 80 percent of the items for sale. Booksellers did not own individual copies of the *Index of Forbidden Books,* drawn up by the Inquisition in 1557, because such copies were very expensive and rare. Therefore, by 1570, "total freedom of movement between the Peninsula and France and Italy guaranteed an unimpeded circulation of people, books and—at one remove—ideas."[33] But this newfound freedom came about only after the violent events described in *The Heretic.*

The final part of *The Heretic,* "Auto-da-Fé," is dedicated to the apprehension of Cipriano and the rest of his coventicle by the Inquisition. After Teodomira's death, Cipriano becomes an oxymoronic "Catholic Protestant." He deepens his belief in Protestant tenets such as salvation by faith alone, denial of purgatory, and the irrelevance of the Virgin Mary, but his behavior seems more like that of a mystic Spanish Catholic, with its strong influence

31. Delibes, *Heretic,* 210.
33. Ibid., 133.

32. Kamen, *The Spanish Inquisition,* 277.

of Jewish and Muslim mysticism. He takes two traditional monastic vows, chastity and poverty, and distributes half his wealth among his employees and associates. His conversations with Agustín Cazalla, the religious leader of the Protestant group to which he adheres, are similar to Catholic confession, although there is, of course, no absolution. Cipriano believes that he has had a vision of Jesus, which greatly disturbs Cazalla, and he continues to uphold the concept of free will in contrast to Cazalla's belief in predestination. While finding freedom of conscience in the Protestant reform, Cipriano also comes to represent the new Christian Renaissance man, one who studies the Scriptures and its commentators for himself, an act discouraged by the Catholic Church which has, according to Delibes, failed to anticipate the needs of the rising educated merchant class. At the end, Cipriano forges his own spiritual path, however unorthodox. For Delibes's Spanish readers, the difficulty lies in accepting that the right to religious freedom of dissidents like Cipriano trumps the need to maintain at all costs traditional spiritual and cultural values.

When Cipriano realizes that the Inquisition is after him because of his Protestant leanings, he flees but is caught with others in France. As the prisoners are marched through the kingdoms of Navarre, Rioja, León, and Castile, the villagers turn out to burn bales of hay in their sight, reminding them of their fate. They arrive in Valladolid on August 5, 1558. During the first four months in prison, Cipriano's eyes become infected and he is close to blindness; his feet are also badly wounded because of the shackles. His uncle, Ignacio, is allowed to visit Cipriano only briefly, although he is president of the Chancery, one of the two main civil courts in Spain. Ignacio represents one of the model Catholics often found in Delibes's novels, and his words reflect what, to Delibes, the Catholic Church should be instead of what it had become. Religion, Ignacio tells Cipriano, "That's the most intimate corner of our soul. Live according to the dictates of your conscience, and don't worry about the rest. We shall all be judged according to that measure."[34] Indeed, this is the main point of the novel. It is more important to be the kind of Christian who lives according to Christ's teaching than ascribe to orthodoxy outwardly (whether Catholic, reformed, or evangelical) but use religion for personal gain or for the imposition of a false moral superiority on others. When Cipriano is judged, he uses similar words in his defense. When

---

34. Delibes, *Heretic*, 304.

asked why he embraced the new doctrines of Protestantism, he responds, "I didn't accept them out of pride, greed, or vanity, sir. I simply found myself in them. But I would not hesitate to give them up if you were to convince me of my error. By the same token, I will never give them up just to save my life."[35] Almost fifty years later, we see Delibes repeating the same thesis of his first major novel *El camino:* the Christian life is a path, a quest, and each individual has the obligation to follow the truth wherever it leads.

Under trial, Cipriano does not reveal the names of the persons who helped him to convert to Lutheranism, even though the tribunal already knows of them because other members of the conventicle have confessed. Cipriano swore loyalty to his group, and he keeps his word. He endures the barbaric torture of the pulley but is disjointed and badly injured on the rack. At the same time, Archbishop Carranza of Toledo, the head of the Spanish Catholic Church and supporter of Erasmus during the Valladolid convention, is arraigned. The historic Carranza spent eight years in the Inquisition prison before being absolved and released. Delibes thus contrasts the Valladolid of 1527, when the best of Iberian theologians discussed the works of Erasmus and free discussion triumphed, and the Valladolid of 1558, when all discussions ceased and the only reality was an obsession with orthodoxy and the destruction of dissidence.

Uncle Ignacio is allowed to visit Cipriano again before the auto-da-fé. He consoles his nephew once more: "Some day . . . these things will be considered a violation of the freedom Christ brought us. Pray for me, my son."[36] There seems to be no doubt in the mind of Ignacio, a devout Catholic, that his nephew is going straight to heaven. Cipriano confesses his sins for the last time to a Dominican friar: among them, hatred for his father and disaffection toward his wife. He is remorseful for these sins, but because he refuses to abjure his Protestant leanings, he does not receive absolution. On May 21, 1559, wearing his *sambenito,* blind and barely able to walk, in the presence of the king, two archbishops, and one of the largest crowds ever assembled in Castile, twenty-one people are sentenced to death in the auto-da-fé, with five, including Cipriano, to be burned at the stake.

■ ■ ■

The opening words of *The Heretic* from Pope John Paul II represent Delibes's final testament. Christians must revisit their history, especially the

35. Ibid., 309.
36. Ibid., 325.

most violent episodes, with honest eyes and objective analysis so as to learn from the past and not repeat errors in the future. Repentance is crucial, but more important is the act of contrition and amendment of life. As Delibes's novel suggests, the common denominator between the violent sixteenth century and the equally bloody twentieth century was ideological confusion. The Church's part in the violence of the Spanish Inquisition as well as its complicity in the repressive Franco regime are dark spots on its record that cry out for redress, not least because they have strongly shaped the cultural and spiritual heritage of today's Spain. Catholicism in particular, and Christianity in general, are always in need of an ongoing reformation—the self-scrutiny, clarification, and reorientation necessary to better conform to the teachings of Christ.

When Dan Brown's *The Da Vinci Code* came out a few years ago, some were puzzled at the novel's immense appeal to Catholics as well as non-Catholics. The reason, however, is clear: such works of popular culture, even if purely fictional, fill a gap for many in their thirst for knowledge about the Church. Much better researched and more thought-provoking than Brown's work, *The Heretic* essentially responds to the same longing. The book leads believers and nonbelievers alike to consider the complex intersection of faith, intolerance, identity, and nationalism. Delibes presents the devastating consequences of religious confrontation in Reformation Spain to help contemporary readers understand the necessity for religious tolerance in the future. By doing so, he challenges Christians to realize that during times of such intense religious conflict, their extremely difficult role may be to tread patiently a middle path rather than too hastily jump to one or the other of the aggressors' parties. In the last analysis, it seems, the Catholic Delibes would opt for the role of martyr instead of that of inquisitor, even if the martyr is incorrect and the inquisitor is correct in their religious conviction.

CHAPTER 6

Some Contexts for Current Catholic Women's Memoir

Patricia Hampl and Her Contemporaries

Nan Metzger and Wendy A. Weaver

"The memoir," Patricia Hampl tells us, "once considered a marginal literary form, has emerged in the past decade as the signature genre of the age."[1] Of course, this news is brought to us in a memoir about memoir, Hampl's signature genre. Nevertheless, the recent proliferation of the memoir and fiction disguised as memoir (for example, *Memoirs of a Geisha; Confessions of a Wall Street Shoeshine Boy; A Million Little Pieces*), support Hampl's claim and that of a recent *New York Times* cover story aptly titled "The Age of the Literary Memoir."[2] Marginalized though it has been in certain periods, this literary form has a long history, one inextricably entwined with the Catholic Church. From saints Augustine, Teresa of Avila, and Edith Stein, to the multiplicity of contemporary women memoirists we read today, spiritual journeys figure significantly. This essay examines a number of these recent memoirs in the contexts of their literary predecessors, themes in relation to Catholicism, and types of narrative plotting.

Since at least the time of Augustine and perhaps even earlier, the West has been enamored of the autobiographical impulse. In her preface to a 1998 Vintage Books edition of Augustine's *Confessions*, Hampl suggests that the fact that Christianity itself is "founded on the narrative of a single life—that of Jesus of Nazareth—may help to explain the appeal of the life stories in Christian literary culture."[3] Augustine's innovation was to record his own life story of conversion to that same Christ nearly four hundred years later.

1. Patricia Hampl, *I Could Tell You Stories: Sojourns in the Land of Memory* (New York: Norton, 1999), 19.
2. Ibid.
3. Hampl, Preface to St. Augustine, *The Confessions*, trans. Maria Boulding, OSB (Toronto: Vintage, 1998), xvi.

Calling him the "first and greatest autobiographer,"[4] Hampl ascribes Augustine's enduring allure to the "intimacy" of the *Confessions*. His is an individual soul's expedition in pursuit of communion with the Almighty, his Creator, the lover of his soul. Indeed, the first and most prominent of Augustine's several audiences is God himself. It is God to whom Augustine confesses, although his work also has the dual purpose of preaching the Gospel to others. Alluding to Romans 10:14, Augustine asks, "But how can people call upon someone in whom they do not yet believe? And how can they believe without a preacher?"[5] So his purpose is here established: he will make God known so that others can believe. Yet even while he preaches, he continues his own search, and his sermon, his *Confessions,* is simultaneously a part of his search and the record of that search: "Let me seek you, then, Lord, even while I am calling upon you, and call upon you even as I believe in you."[6] And this search, as contemporary autobiographers also attest, takes a lifetime.

The Confessions is not merely a record of the outward events of Augustine's life, such as dates, places, or activities. Rather, Augustine continues to "startle" his first-time readers, according to Hampl, because he "found a way to reveal the profound intimacy of a mind thinking."[7] This complex narrative style lends a modern tone to contemporary readers. Hampl writes: "Augustine makes of himself that searching figure, alone but companioned by his own questing mind, objectified by his own questing mind, objectified by the act of writing. 'I have become an enigma to myself,' he says, 'and herein lies my sickness.' Saying this, he becomes the West's first existential hero, both protagonist and narrator of his own inner struggle."[8] From Augustine's time on, the questing protagonist facing an existential crisis becomes a theme that unifies Catholic memoir.

Later, some female Catholic autobiographers also serve as both protagonists and narrators of their own inner struggles. Teresa of Avila is notable here. Although the impetus to write her autobiography did not originate with Teresa herself, her writing also demonstrates a mind at work. However, in yet another layer of complication, she struggles not only with her writing but also with those who commissioned it. Her autobiography is produced at the

---

4. Hampl, *Blue Arabesque: A Search for the Sublime* (Orlando, Fla.: Harcourt, 2006), 28.
5. Augustine, *Confessions*, trans. Boulding, 3.
6. Ibid., 3.   7. Hampl, preface to *Confessions*, xvii.
8. Ibid.

"command of her confessor" and is to be edited by that same confessor. In her Preparatory Note to her *Life*, Teresa encapsulates the conflict: "Having been commanded and left at full liberty to describe my way of prayer and the favours which the Lord has granted me, I wish that I had been allowed to describe also . . . my grave sins and the wickedness of my life. This would have been a great comfort to me, but I may not do so. In fact, I have been put under severe restrictions in the matter."[9] As for many memoirists, including Augustine, her desire to record certain matters—here, her "wickedness"—is curtailed by the looming prospect of both propriety and censorship. Teresa had somewhat more control over her second book, *The Interior Castle*, which is, according to Hampl's foreword to a 2004 HarperCollins edition, an "anti-memoir" because it concentrates too much on telling and not enough on showing,[10] whereas Hampl defines "memoir" elsewhere as a proportioned combination of showing and telling.[11]

Like Teresa of Avila, Sr. Teresa Benedicta of the Cross (Edith Stein), a Carmelite nun, was urged by a priest friend "to write down what I, child of a Jewish family, had learned about the Jewish people since such knowledge is so rarely found in outsiders."[12] Although she denies that her autobiography, *Life in a Jewish Family*, is "meant to be an apologia for Judaism," it clearly *is* an apologia for the Jewish people.[13] In response to the "horrendous caricature" of the Jews prevalent in 1930s Germany, Stein asserts that there are many people who would dispute this faulty depiction because they have found in Jewish friends and acquaintances, "such goodness of heart, understanding, warm empathy, and so consistently helpful an attitude" as to be outraged by the condemnation of Jews in Germany.[14] Stein not only successfully portrays these qualities in her Jewish family and friends but also illustrates her own capacity for them in her self-portrayal, especially the quality of empathy. Perhaps it was her own strong sense of empathy that made her reading of Teresa of Avila's *Life* the turning point in her own life. Stein's editors write, "In

9. Teresa of Avila, *The Life of Saint Teresa of Avila by Herself*, trans. and ed. J. M. Cohen (New York: Penguin, 1957), 21.

10. Patricia Hampl, foreword to *Teresa of Avila: Selections from the Interior Castle*, ed. Emilie Griffin, trans. Kieran Kavanaugh and Otilio Rodriguez (San Francisco: HarperSanFrancisco, 2004), viii.

11. Shelle Barton, Sheyene Foster Heller, and Jennifer Henderson, "'We Were Such a Generation'—Memoir, Truthfulness, and History: An Interview with Patricia Hampl," *River Teeth* 5, no. 2 (2004): 134.

12. Edith Stein, *Life in a Jewish Family*, in *The Collected Works of Edith Stein: Sister Teresa Benedicta of the Cross Discalced Carmelite*, vol. 1, ed. L. Gelber and Romaeus Leuven, trans. Josephine Koeppel (Washington, D.C.: ICS, 1986), 23.

13. Ibid., 24.

14. Ibid.

Teresa's response to Christ's love, Edith found the answer she had sought" and that "from that moment on, Edith was strongly aware that an attraction to live out her baptismal commitment as a member of the Discalced Carmelite Order . . . was inseparable from her resolve to enter the church."[15] Just as Teresa of Avila looked to Augustine, as she acknowledges in her autobiography, and Stein looked to Teresa, contemporary Catholic memoirists regard Stein as both a writing predecessor and a spiritual mentor.

There is thus a clear "tradition" of the Catholic memoir, and Hampl views Augustine, Teresa of Avila, and Edith Stein as significant forerunners to contemporary manifestations of this genre. In describing these works as forming a "fascinating linked chain of conversions,"[16] Hampl refers to Stein's biographer, Waltraud Herbstrith, to explain how each of these authors had a different "shadow" over him or her, from which the liberation—conversion or, in the case of Teresa of Avila, a deeper commitment to the Church—was the same. As Hampl summarizes, "These three figures are cameos of Western civilization's history of spiritual dilemmas," culminating in Stein's "existential burden."[17] What Herbstrith identifies as "shadows" over their individual lives (Augustine's "unbridled sensuality," Teresa's "surface pleasures of 'society,'" and Stein's "materialist worldview") we may see as ongoing spiritual concerns in current Catholic memoir.[18] Capturing the spirit of a culture, as Stein does, is one project a memoirist may embark on; capturing the nature of an internal spiritual struggle, as all three, Augustine, Teresa of Avila, and Edith Stein, do, provides the arena for many contemporary Catholic memoirists to explore how a particular culture can be the crucible for a spiritual conversion.

While it is commonly recognized that Jewishness is a culture as well as a religion, what is less recognized is that Catholicism, likewise, embraces a cultural milieu and not only a religious belief. As Hampl notes, we often hear people today identify themselves as having been "raised Catholic," implying that they have imbibed the culture but no longer practice the faith.[19] But what is it specifically about being "raised Catholic" that makes such an indelible impression, even when the practice of the faith or belief itself laps-

---

15. L. Gelber and Romaeus Leuven, "Chronology 1916–1942," in Gelber and Leuven, *Collected Works of Edith Stein,* 1:420.

16. Hampl, *I Could Tell You Stories,* 115.   17. Ibid.

18. Ibid.

19. Hampl, *Virgin Time: In Search of the Contemplative Life* (New York: North Point, 1992), 50.

es? Some Catholic memoirs by contemporary women writers explore this question. Debra Campbell, collecting narratives of "graceful exits" from the Catholic Church (and a few graceful returns as well), quotes author Antonia White's diary from 1940: "The pull of the Church is very strong. It is like one's native language and, though one may have become denationalized, one cannot help reverting to it, and even thinking in its terms."[20] The deep hold of the Church on the psyche, often the result of the strictures of formal Catholic education, informs many Catholic memoirs, whether their narrator's stance on the Church is rebellious or rejecting, fond or nostalgic, longing and seeking, or departing and then returning to the fold.

Perhaps those Catholic life writings garnering the most notoriety today are those that rebel against and reject a Catholic upbringing. Railing against every offense, real or imagined, from patriarchy to misogyny, these memoirists may classify themselves as "recovering Catholics," or, in a different view, may be seen by others as "bitter ex-Catholics." Elizabeth Evasdaughter, a former Dominican nun raised a Protestant, collected details on many of these types of autobiographies for her *Catholic Girlhood Narratives: The Church and Self-Denial* (1996). The intent of her study seems to be to substantiate the claim that the Church has damaged women over the years and to show how some have resisted that damage. Describing the path she took in preparing her study, Evasdaughter writes that "the first set of autobiographies I read dismayed me with what seemed to be an ersatz sunniness," which drove Evasdaughter to the next set of autobiographies, which were "frank about both negative and positive experiences."[21] In response to these, she "could not understand why parents, priests, nuns, and other Catholic teachers would impose the prohibitions and frustrations that were leveled at these girls."[22] It should be noted, however, that although Evasdaughter's study contains a wide breadth of autobiographies covering several continents, many of the better-known texts she concentrates on are from an earlier generation, a time when such restrictions were more common. That being said, however, Evasdaughter does identify a trend, in that "what seems to link girlhood narratives by twentieth-century Catholic women is their de-

20. Debra Campbell, *Graceful Exits: Catholic Women and the Art of Departure* (Bloomington: Indiana University Press, 2003), 153.

21. Elizabeth N. Evasdaughter, *Catholic Girlhood Narratives: The Church and Self-Denial* (Boston: Northeastern University Press, 1996), x.

22. Ibid.

sire to discuss what it was like to grow up under the pressure of Catholic gender training."[23] Treating the same subject with more sensitivity, perhaps, to faithful Catholics is Debra Campbell's *Graceful Exits: Catholic Women and the Art of Departure* (2003). Her full-length study also includes chapters on women who have returned to the faith with titles such as "A Nun Forever" and "Coming Home." Whether the tone is resentful or reconciled, issues of Catholicism's intersection with feminism usually surface in the life writings of contemporary Catholic and ex-Catholic women—or, indeed, even in some non-Catholic women's memoirs as well. For example, Kathleen Norris, both a practicing Presbyterian and a Benedictine oblate, writes from the vantage point of not having yet resolved her relationship to the Catholic Church, of an appreciative outsider looking in. Rather than bracing herself against Church practice, she embraces it for the new insights it brings to her feminist leanings. As she puts it in her 1998 memoir *Amazing Grace:*

In learning to interpret the Bible more skeptically, I found that I also needed some balance; I soon realized that reading with suspicion worked best when I also read with trust, with belief enough to nourish my developing faith. Here, the Benedictine practice of lectio, the meditative reading of scripture, was a great help to me, as was the communal worship with my monastic friends . . . Gradually, I learned to be as suspicious of easy feminist assumptions as I had earlier learned, starting in college, to be suspicious of misogynist ones.[24]

Other women memoirists never arrive at a détente between their early Catholicism and their later feminism, and the rift becomes bitter and permanent.

On the other hand, a more recent trend in Catholic memoir is to look back on Catholic upbringing, and particularly Catholic school education, with varying degrees of nostalgia. Some writers balance such nostalgia with comedy and still others with irony, now viewing the traditions of their Catholic schooling with an adult sophistication that either laughs at their own naïveté or questions what they had been subjected to. This current trend can be witnessed by the popularity of comic stage performances such as the recent *Late Night Catechism* or, earlier, *Do Black Patent Leather Shoes Really Reflect Up?* (1975). Gina Cascone, author of *Pagan Babies and Other Catholic Memories* (1982), offers another example of such fond but broadly comic nos-

23. Ibid., 4.
24. Kathleen Norris, *Amazing Grace: A Vocabulary of Faith* (New York: Riverhead, 1998), 133.

talgia. In relating past tales of Christmas pageants, Cascone writes with her characteristic humor, "The Christmas pageant in an all-girl school was an experience. There is, after all, only one desirable part."[25] The humorous exaggeration with which she recounts her Catholic education produces a sense of warm sentiment. Rather than criticizing the patriarchal structure of the Nativity scene, for example, she basks in the memory of her good fortune at getting the minor stage role as the innkeeper.

Patricia Hampl, however, takes a more nuanced ironic approach to her Catholic past. Describing funny scenes that illustrate prototypically Catholic situations involving, for example, nuns and students, is more difficult for her because her humor typically doesn't work in an exaggerated vein. Whereas writers like Cascone seek to portray stereotypical moments that many Catholics can relate to because of their universal appeal, Hampl dwells instead on highly personal moments that are distinct in detail but universal in effect. For example, when Hampl relates a story of a past Christmas in *The Florist's Daughter* (2007), it is of working in her parents' florist's shop with the ladies Ollie and Mrs. Butler on Christmas Eve. A young teenager, she tries to take last-minute orders with the same sophistication that she admires in them. However, instead she is duped by a fraudulent customer who places a substantial order and then reneges on payment. Confronted after the holiday rush by her father with the evidence that she's been taken in and that her family may be burdened by the cost, Hampl recalls feeling the pangs of self-revelation and pricks to her pride. Hampl portrays individual characters and events unique to her own childhood, but the loss of innocence, of youthful naïveté in the face of adult duplicity, universalizes the story. Because she includes so many details of the specific situation, the overall result creates a layering of epiphanies. As she reflects back to this moment while sitting beside her dying mother in the hospital, she sifts through these epiphanies:

But did I understand then or is it only possible now, in the middle of the night of the last day of this life, to see in the great framed panels of memory how my father struggled, how trapped he was as he explained the situation to me? There he is, sitting miserably at his desk with the lavish orders before him. I've been an idiot, naïve, so easily taken in. But he can say none of that. He, the great believer in the teaching moment, can use this experience to teach me nothing.[26]

25. Gina Cascone, *Pagan Babies and Other Catholic Memories* (New York: Washington Square, 1982), 99.

26. Patricia Hampl, *The Florist's Daughter* (New York: Harcourt, 2007), 107.

The loss of innocence, combined with the situation of working for her own family and with the realization of the suffering her error may cause her family, further complicated by the suffering she recognizes in her father at not being able to use this teaching moment—all these epiphanies are specific to Hampl's life but at the same time form part of the universal experience of growing up, one that readers readily recognize. This is Hampl's signature technique as she quests within past events for their spiritual significance.

Some memoirists who write from a spiritual perspective adopt the role of seekers. Their life stories demonstrate a longing for something more, which is often later identified as a closer relationship with God through more formal religious structures. Although Kathleen Norris fell away from her childhood religious belief, her memoir *The Cloister Walk* (1996) exemplifies the return to more orthodox religious practice of many of her generation:

I hear many stories these days from people who are exiled from their religious traditions . . . Many, like me, are members of the baby-boom generation who dropped religious observance after high school or college, and are now experiencing an enormous hunger for spiritual grounding. One woman wrote to me to say that she felt a great longing for ritual and community . . . She'd joined some political organizations and a women's service club but found that it wasn't enough . . . Since what she's seeking is salvation, and not therapy, not political or social relevance, I suspect that she might eventually find what she is looking for in the practice of prayer and in communal worship.[27]

Often what those who have departed from religious practice, or have never known it, find upon their return is that both the "practice of prayer" and "communal worship" are essential; communing with God and communing with others serve as the balm that heals the rift between the individual and her religious tradition, the re-enfranchising of the disenfranchised.

Indeed, the practice of prayer and communal worship are often resisted, even as they are desperately needed for spiritual maturity. This is as much the case for those who never had a formal practice of religion as it is for those who have. The former resist seeking fulfillment in a place that they have rejected *a priori*. In *Amazing Grace*, Norris confesses to her readers that the first of these vital practices, prayer, was "impossible" for her for many years because she felt "alienated" from her religious heritage and thought that her prayers would cause "more harm than good."[28] However, when a

27. Kathleen Norris, *The Cloister Walk* (New York: Riverhead, 1996), 65.
28. Norris, *Amazing Grace*, 58.

Catholic priest asked Norris to pray for him, she was "shocked" that he would "trust" her with the practice.[29] Earlier, in *The Cloister Walk*, Norris addresses the common experience of hostility toward communal worship. She writes, "I was asked by a college student how I could stand to go to church, how I could stand the hypocrisy of Christians. I had one of my rare inspirations, when I know the right thing to say, and I replied, 'The only hypocrite I have to worry about on Sunday morning is myself.'"[30] To counter her own resistance to churchgoing—the inevitable weariness and boredom—she tells herself that "I am there because I need to be reminded that love can be at the center of all things, if we will only keep it there. The worship service will most likely not offer an aesthetically pleasing experience, great theological insight, or emotional release, although all of those things are possible."[31] To Norris, traditional forms of prayer and communal worship are essential to the spiritual life—the very vehicle through which grace may be given.

Like Kathleen Norris, contemporary author Anne Lamott has also written a number of spiritually oriented memoirs. While not Catholic, Lamott converted from a bohemian agnostic background to a liturgically based Protestant faith, Episcopalianism, and she often comments on her conversations with her Roman Catholic mentors. Like Augustine she is vivid in recalling the details of the life from which she converted. In her 1999 memoir, *Traveling Mercies: Some Thoughts on Faith*, she reverses some aspects of the "seeking" narrative tradition with a striking image. While many conversion narratives show the narrator as a penitent seeking redemption, for Lamott redemption seeks the not-yet repentant. In Lamott's image, the Holy Spirit is like a stray cat that nobody wants, scrounging around the neighborhood, looking for a home. This characterization, while not flattering, perhaps, to the Holy Spirit, illustrates the stubbornness of human resistance to God and the stubbornness of God's persistence in return. As she writes:

> I felt him just sitting there on his haunches in the corner of my sleeping loft, watching me with patience and love, and I squinched my eyes shut, but that didn't help because that's not what I was seeing him with.
>
> Finally I fell asleep, and in the morning, he was gone.
>
> . . . But then everywhere I went, I had the feeling that a little cat was following me, wanting me to reach down and pick it up, wanting me to open the door and let it in. But I knew what would happen: you let a cat in one time, give it a

---

29. Ibid.
31. Ibid., 346–47.

30. Norris, *Cloister Walk*, 346.

little milk, and then it stays forever. So I tried to keep one step ahead of it, slamming my houseboat door when I entered or left.[32]

Enduring a week of this tense resistance, she eventually capitulates: "'Fuck it: I quit.' I took a long deep breath and said out loud, 'All right. You can come in.' So this was my beautiful moment of conversion."[33] In the end, as in many narratives of religious seeking since Augustine's prototype, God's persistence triumphs.

Similarly, we see Hampl in a posture of spiritual seeking from an early age. But there is also evidence of Hampl making other moves in her spiritual quest, including rebelling against the Church and expressing nostalgia toward it. Debra Campbell might categorize her work as that of "departure and return" to the Catholic faith. In his full-length study *Circuitous Journeys: Modern Spiritual Autobiography* (2000), critic David J. Leigh discusses what he sees as the "circular structure" of spiritual autobiographies since Augustine. Like other Catholic life writers, Hampl follows the "general three-stage narrative pattern" that Leigh outlines, "in which childhood events (stage one) raise questions that drive the author on a negative journey of wandering in a desert of illusory answers (stage two) before he or she discovers a transforming world in which the original questions can be resolved (stage three)."[34] However, Hampl's stages are not quite so clearly drawn, and they span several book-length memoirs. In fact, we see this multiplicity of life stories in the works of many memoirists. While some of their narratives may have a particular focus in terms of chronological time or theme, often we find that across a series of memoirs the writer returns to particular scenes multiple times, offering "re-visions" of the same incident from different vantage points.

In the vein of rebellion against Catholicism that precedes her return to faith, Hampl provides two poignant scenes that she relates in several of her memoirs. The first example is that of her initial teenage rejection of attending church. On a Sunday in 1968, when her father, who is standing on top of the dining room table to replace a light bulb, asks her the familiar question, "What Mass you going to?," she responds, "I'm not going . . . I'm not going to Mass anymore."[35] Revisited in *I Could Tell You Stories*, Hampl sets this in-

32. Anne Lamott, *Traveling Mercies: Some Thoughts of Faith* (New York: Pantheon, 1999), 49–50.
33. Ibid., 50.
34. David J. Leigh, *Circuitous Journeys: Modern Spiritual Autobiography* (New York: Fordham University Press, 2000), 5.
35. Hampl, *Virgin Time*, 16–17.

cident within the broader context of recalling numerous arguments waged over the same dining table (regarding the Vietnam War and other explosive contemporary issues), and her rebellion is now rendered with a more humble and mature understanding when she writes compassionately of her father, "He said nothing ... no matter what rebellion I visited upon him with my gnatlike persistence, my protests, and arch refusals and ardent avowals."[36] Given the larger context in the second telling of this incident, Hampl's rejection of Catholicism is placed within a broader generational rebellion rather than a strictly religious rejection. Here, then, it is plainly marked as merely one scene in a developing spiritual Bildungsroman, with the narrator-protagonist viewing herself as not yet mature enough to grasp an adult faith. What can't be forecast in the immediacy of the scene is the speaker's ultimate return to the practice of the faith she learned from her parents.

A second example that Hampl records of her rejection of the Church, this time as a young adult, is when she twice tells the story of taking her first prescription for the birth control pill. In *I Could Tell You Stories,* she describes how, after seeing her physician, she takes herself to lunch to celebrate, in a quasi-ceremony, her taking the first pill.[37] This symbolic feminist gesture not only portrays a struggle common to many women who question Church teaching on sexual mores but also signals the author's conscious rejection of that teaching (even as, ironically, the "ceremony" she enacts around the occasion parodies aspects of the Catholic liturgy, including the act of breaking bread). In her earlier memoir, *Virgin Time,* Hampl relates this same incident in a briefer manner and within the broader context preceding her wedding day.[38] With this backdrop, we see her assertion of independence as a young woman as but one step along the path to maturity. In recounting this incident, Hampl's tone apparently dismisses the staunch righteousness of her youthful self, particularly as she relates the scene within the context of her attempts to reconnect with her religious tradition. The context thus also shows the incident as a step in the developing spiritual Bildungsroman as it begins to shift the narrative ground from her rejection of the Church to her eventual return to it.

Another contemporary Catholic memoirist, Beverly Donofrio, makes a similar if more striking move from rebellion to return between her memoirs. In *Riding in Cars with Boys* (1990), Donofrio chronicles her youthful high jinks,

36. Hampl, *I Could Tell You Stories,* 48.   37. Ibid., 38–40.
38. Hampl, *Virgin Time,* 13.

resistance to the discipline of her police officer father, and early marriage and motherhood. In a later memoir, however, *Looking for Mary: Or, The Blessed Mother and Me* (2000), she illustrates herself as a protagonist taking her first steps toward rediscovering the Church she has earlier renounced. This return originates seemingly by chance when, in the course of scavenging for furniture at a yard sale, she is captivated by a picture of Our Lady of Fatima in a framed postcard. She scoops it up, and thus begins a collection of images of the Virgin Mary. Her growing obsession with Mary evolves into a creative endeavor when she travels the country to research material for a radio documentary on supposed apparition sites. Through this work she meets many devotees of Mary who encourage her to pray the rosary. These events further lead her to travel to another purported apparition site, Medjugorje, a trip that includes a silent fasting retreat in Bosnia. While she states that she has "come as a writer and have been going to chapel and lectures and church every day as part of the job," Donofrio also admits that she has "been praying to Mary, hundreds of Hail Marys, which is not part of the job."[39] While the inconveniences of the overseas trip and her irritation at her fellow travelers are related with the acerbic wit for which she is known, Donofrio's drollness comes mixed in this memoir with a sincere earnestness and humility in regard to her own failings, a tone that was absent from *Riding in Cars with Boys*. Ultimately, through a variety of experiences all linked in some way to traditional forms of Church practice—for example, veneration of the Virgin and going on pilgrimages—Donofrio begins to return to the practice of the faith.

Similar to Hampl's revisiting of particular scenes across memoirs, Donofrio's second autobiography retells significant earlier moments in her life in new, more mature contexts. Thus, scenes that appear in *Riding in Cars with Boys* as those indicating rejection of Catholicism reappear in *Looking for Mary* as moments to be understood and reconciled in a new light. In the later memoir, Donofrio describes her failings, especially as a mother, and she promises to reform, enacting a type of confession in both the religious and literary sense. Her acknowledgement of her faults is steeped in regret, especially at failing to protect her son from her abusive boyfriend. In portraying herself as taking serious steps to reconcile with her adult son, Donofrio shows that she, too, is molding her successive memoirs into a kind of overall spiritual Bildungsroman. She observes herself coming to maturity in other

39. Beverly Donofrio, *Looking for Mary: Or, the Blessed Mother and Me* (New York: Penguin Compass, 2000), 1.

ways, too. If one of the assumptions of her youth was that having a romantic partner was a primary need, she now understands that this need is no longer urgent. For example, when she describes how her father and son come to help her move, she recalls, "I looked at them gratefully, the two men in my life. There were no others."[40] If in the past she rejected the authority of her father, now she is able, as a parent herself, to respect that authority and be truly grateful for his ongoing love and aid. If she earlier disdained Church teaching regarding sexuality, marriage, and motherhood, it is through her investment in traditional Catholic practices that she comes to regret that attitude. In fact, it is feeling the Virgin Mary's unconditional love that helps her to reconcile with her own failings and try to be a better mother to her son, using Mary as a model.[41] Thus, viewed together, Donofrio's two memoirs present the pattern of departure from and later return to the Catholic Church.

Unlike the parameters of its strictly secular counterpart, a spiritual Bildungsroman is never ending. It covers an entire life span and revisits events in life to view them in different lights. Literary critics who deal with the genre often too easily try to separate out religious issues from autobiography, distinguishing between religious conversion or confession narratives on the one hand and most "secular" narratives on the other. In Sidonie Smith and Julia Watson's critical study *Reading Autobiography* (2001), for example, the authors delineate a number of types of "narrative plotting" in autobiographies separate from confession or conversion narratives,[42] including "the Bildungsroman or narrative of social development, the Künstlerroman or narrative of artistic growth . . . testimonio, and quest for lost identity or a lost homeland or family."[43] While useful on some level, this list of "types" doesn't take into account that most autobiographies are hybrids, interweaving multiple forms. Many memoirs, of course, may be seen through a spiritual—or at least quasi-spiritual—lens. But as we have noted, it is Patricia Hampl's work that has set the foundation for the current popularity of the spiritual Bildungsroman. Whether discussing an explicitly religious matter or not, Hampl tends to present everything she describes from a spiritual point of view, and her frequent use of Christian-inflected language indicates this. For example, when traversing the hills of Italy as part of a pilgrimage, she writes, "We

40. Ibid., 8.
41. Ibid., 230–33.
42. Sidonie Smith and Julia Watson, *Reading Autobiography: A Guide for Interpreting Life Narratives* (Minneapolis: University of Minnesota Press, 2001), 169.
43. Ibid., 70.

walked long hours every day . . . moving in and out, back and forth across the Umbrian antiphon of light and shade."[44] Here she adapts a term from liturgical music to capture the deeply spiritual nature of the setting. In *The Florist's Daughter,* she uses more explicit Christian imagery to describe what she considers the three major themes of her writing: "the Trinity I held sacred—beauty, the idea of elsewhere, and the holy ghost of history."[45]

Although such images and language mark her style across her memoirs, creating an ongoing spiritual Bildungsroman, Hampl's *Virgin Time,* with its subtitle *In Search of the Contemplative Life,* is her most explicit narrative of religious development. Smith and Watson describe the Bildungsroman plot pattern as "unfold[ing] as a narrative of education through encounters with mentors, apprenticeship, renunciation of youthful folly, and eventual integration into society."[46] Early in *Virgin Time,* Hampl introduces us to her *spiritual* mentor, Donnie, a contemplative nun in the convent of San Damiano in Minneapolis. In like manner, her visits to Donnie constitute a type of *spiritual* apprenticeship, and her joining other believers, or at least fellow wrestlers with the faith, on a pilgrimage to Assisi shows her *spiritual* integration into a community. As Hampl reverses here her youthful rebuff of Church teaching, she fulfills yet another archetypal move in the classic Bildungsroman plot, namely "the renunciation of some ideal or passion and the embrace of heteronormative social arrangements,"[47] but she does so in a manner consistent with her spiritual intent.

In a similar vein, Hampl's *Blue Arabesque: A Search for the Sublime* (2006) may be seen as a type of spiritually infused Künstlerroman, a narrative of an artist's growth. In this recent memoir, Hampl weaves the story of the development of Henri Matisse as an artist into her ongoing "trinitarian" themes of "beauty, the idea of elsewhere, and the holy ghost of history." In doing so, she also traces the development of her own thoughts on the intersection of religion and art, and thus *Blue Arabesque* instantiates a Künstlerroman for Hampl as well as one for Matisse.

Two other types of Smith and Watson's "narrative plots" are the testimonio, "the act of testifying or bearing witness,"[48] and the quest for lost identity, homeland, or family. Throughout her memoirs, it is clear that Hampl is

44. Hampl, *Virgin Time,* 23.
45. Hampl, *The Florist's Daughter,* 186.
46. Smith and Watson, *Reading Autobiography,* 70.
47. Ibid., 190.
48. Ibid., 206.

intent on giving a spiritual testimonio of her age: as she states, she identifies herself primarily as the product and representative of a certain generation, the baby boomer generation of the 1960s, rather than of a particular church, family, or nation.[49] In seeing herself so intimately bound to the thought of an era, Hampl comes to realize later, as an adult, that her ties to her particular family heritage were never fully developed. This set her on a quest for this lost part of her identity, a quest that took her abroad in search of her Czech origins as her first memoir, *A Romantic Education* (1981), recounts. While soaking up the cultural atmosphere of Prague, she views her travel to that city as primarily a means of reconnecting with her heritage on a spiritual level. "My original intention in going to Prague was simple," she states, "to see the place my grandparents had come from, to hear the language they had spoken."[50] But once she is there, she realizes there is more to find: "Perhaps, if you go to the old country seeking, as third- or fourth-generation Americans often do, a strictly personal history based on bloodlines, then, the less intimate history of the nation cannot impose itself upon you very strongly. History is reduced to genealogy, which is supposed to satisfy a hunger that is clearly much larger."[51] What she finds in Prague is the deeper contemplation of the three elements that will comprise her lifelong "trinity" of themes: the city's intrinsic beauty (even through its drab Iron Curtain visage), the city as "elsewhere" (away from the stultifying Midwestern environment of her hometown, St. Paul, Minnesota), and the "holy ghost" of the layers of history and culture of the region that indelibly stamped itself on her own family heritage. Hampl's inspiration in Prague, her connection with beauty, history, culture, art, and family, begins her lifelong quest for spiritual identity, which culminates in her re-embracing of that other family heritage, the Catholic faith. Across her memoirs, Hampl shows her signature ability to blur and merge the distinctions between the narrative plot lines that Smith and Watson delineate and inflect them at each step with spiritual insight.

If the prototype of the Catholic conversion story may be figured as St. Paul's blinding moment on the road to Damascus, Augustine's dramatic throwing of himself under the fig tree, or even Edith Stein's declaration, "This is the truth!" upon reading Teresa of Avila's *Life*, then none of the contemporary women spiritual writers we have examined here achieve this type

49. Hampl, *I Could Tell You Stories*, 48.
50. Hampl, *A Romantic Education* (New York: Norton, 1999), 146.
51. Ibid., 148.

of convicting moment. Rather, in a postmodern world, they are consciously suspicious of their own motives and cautious about both what they seek and what they find. When visiting a church near Medjugorje, Donofrio writes, "As soon as I enter the church, I smell roses. I don't believe it at first, but the scent is strong and does not go away . . . I want to believe that the roses are Mary's way of letting me know she's here, of giving me support."[52] In her phrasing, "I want to believe," Donofrio simultaneously acknowledges her belief and her unbelief—her desire to believe yet the strong pull of reason and education that suspend the possibility of unquestioned belief. On the other hand, Patricia Hampl, in *Blue Arabesque*, meditates on one of the few things we still can believe in in today's skeptical world:

It's strange that we still believe in inspiration . . . Inspiration may be the one bit of God we haven't managed to kill off. The big bearded Primary Cause and his timepiece may have stopped ticking for us, Jesus may have become "historical," but the Holy Ghost is still aloft . . . And while many people are careful to make clear that they have no time for "organized religion," they attest fervently to the importance of their "spiritual life."[53]

With inspiration—the "breathing in" of spirit—as her guide, Hampl returns to her Catholic religious roots. Other Catholic memoirists find the God of their ancestors, the Ancient of Days, in rediscovering the vigor inherent in such ancient Church practices as monastic contemplation, pilgrimages, and praying to the saints. In the final analysis, contemporary Catholic women's memoirs reveal their significant connection with earlier Catholic autobiographical works through the use of similar themes and narrative plotting. Where these memoirs differ from those of their predecessors, however, is in the blurring of distinctions in traditional Catholic themes and plot lines, situating the contemporary memoir in a more liminal space that suits postmodern resistance to formal strictures of definition. The writings of Patricia Hampl not only bridge such traditional categories but transcend their proscriptions in a more sophisticated manner than the works of many of her contemporaries. Her delicate interweaving of her trinity of themes—beauty, the idea of elsewhere, and history—throughout her memoirs is one marker of her finesse. As a representative of her generation, she testifies to the integral and universal longing for God as well as the power of accepting traditional sacred practices as one way to make present the Holy Presence.

52. Donofrio, *Looking for Mary*, 151.
53. Hampl, *Blue Arabesque*, 151.

CHAPTER 7

"A Ransom of Cholers" ▪ Catastrophe, Consolation, and Catholicism in Jon Hassler's *Staggerford, North of Hope,* and *The Life and Death of Nancy Clancy's Nephew*

Ed Block

> Problems should always become more luminous in the light of the great mystery in which we live and move and have our being. A sense of mystery is a Catholic sense.
> —Hans Urs von Balthasar, *The Grain of Wheat*

As they have about Graham Greene, Flannery O'Connor, and André Dubus, critics disagree about whether to call Minnesota author Jon Hassler a "Catholic novelist." In this essay I skirt that formulation of the question, proposing that, whatever his conscious (or unconscious) intentions, Hassler's worldview—as we can infer it from his work—is decidedly Catholic. I address this question by considering three works from different times in his career: *Staggerford* (1977), his first novel; *North of Hope* (1996), the supreme achievement of his work in the 1990s; and *The Life and Death of Nancy Clancy's Nephew,* the second of two novellas that comprise *The Staggerford Murders* (2004).

More Chaucerian in tone and style than Dantean, Hassler's work falls clearly in the mode of comedy, but it is the type of comedy that can include a substantial amount of trouble, sorrow, and even tragedy. Stylistically, his work falls between the satire of Evelyn Waugh and the existential realism of Graham Greene. There is also enough of the macabre in some of his works to remind one of Flannery O'Connor. But the best of his novels, like *North of Hope,* transcend all reductive categories. Like New England novelist John

Excerpts in this essay are from "The Small," copyright 1956 by Theodore Roethke, from *Collected Poems of Theodore Roethke* by Theodore Roethke. Used by permission of Doubleday, a division of Random House, Inc.

Cheever, whose work he admired and from whose style he learned, Hassler delights in creating unique characters, rich in oddity and mystery. Not all are morally admirable, but all celebrate, by their very being, the wonder and mystery of creation. To pursue the Chaucerian analogy: Hassler's characters are more properly seen as pilgrims on the journey of life. For most, it is a journey toward some good, some fulfillment that they more or less clearly intuit and more or less actively seek. But, as the epigraph to *Staggerford* (from which I take part of my title) notes, many also experience "a ransom of cholers" along the way. This is true of the protagonists in all three narratives I shall discuss. The protagonist of the final story experiences perhaps the most "cholers" on his pilgrimage, dying after having achieved at most a moment's emotional and spiritual release. How the individual characters' ordeals and achievements can be seen as part of a Catholic worldview is the subject of this chapter.

Jon Hassler was born on March 30, 1933, in Minneapolis and was raised in the small towns of Staples, and then Plainview, Minnesota. He attended Catholic grade school and public high school, then St. John's University in Collegeville, Minnesota. After graduation in 1955, he began teaching in high schools and junior colleges in northern Minnesota. In 1960 he earned a master's degree from the University of North Dakota, and in 1980 he returned to St. John's University where he taught English and creative writing until his retirement in 1997 as emeritus professor. He moved to Minneapolis where he lived with his second wife, Gretchen. Though afflicted with supranuclear palsy since 1995, Hassler continued to write. On March 20, 2008, having finished the manuscript of a final novel, *Jay O'Malley*, he died in Minneapolis from complications of the disease. Hassler dated his mature writing career from September 1970, when he determined to write a short story every two weeks for a year. At the end of the year he had over twenty short stories, numerous rejection slips, and half a dozen published stories. An agent read and liked some of those stories, and on that basis Hassler was, by 1977, able to publish his first novel, *Staggerford*.

Before discussing the Catholic worldview manifest in *Staggerford, North of Hope*, and *The Life and Death of Nancy Clancy's Nephew*, I will first lay out what I consider some principle features of this view.

First, a Catholic worldview includes a capacity for wonder and a belief in mystery. A writer with a Catholic perspective understands that God loves each one of us, although it is true that we are so often plunged in grief and trouble that we can't always see that love at work. Nevertheless God's loving presence, with us here and now, is an overwhelming reality. This is in contrast to the prevailing secular/Protestant view that often perceives God as infinitely aloof, distant, if not totally absent. The Catholic belief in God's loving presence manifests itself in the writer's treatment of the everyday, the particular. The Catholic writer says, with philosopher Simone Weil, "I shall 'attend' carefully to this world and to the individual human beings in it." Moreover, the writer says, "I will attend to *you* and to your sufferings." Almost every word, every sentence of such a writer's work is, therefore, suffused with the sense that each person is valuable and lovable; each instance of suffering is worthy of attention. At its most heightened, this attitude can become an "analogical" sign of how God is, in some mysterious way, present in each character, each object, each event, each moment of our everyday lives. A corollary to this belief is that a Catholic perspective is at least subliminally attuned to the seasons. A writer with a Catholic worldview will have learned such "attunement" from the rhythms of the liturgical year with which he or she grew up. The natural rhythm of the seasons is, therefore, often a significant backdrop for the action of a Catholic-inspired work of literature.

Second, a Catholic perspective distinguishes between good and evil. It acknowledges mitigating circumstances in actions and decisions and the effect of people's backgrounds and individual weaknesses on those actions and decisions. But it does not exonerate individuals of responsibility for their actions. "Hate the sin but love the sinner" is the guiding principle for someone with a Catholic worldview. Because of this distinction, a writer with a Catholic perspective shows compassion and love for his or her characters. But the writer will also feel free to criticize, even satirize, the evil, narrowness, and bigotry of individuals and groups. A Catholic worldview accepts human responsibility, but it does not, in the manner of the Gnostics and the prevailing secular/Protestant viewpoint, expect that human beings alone can solve all problems or save themselves by their own power. A Catholic worldview opposes evil and works to alleviate suffering. But it also acknowledges the key role of grace, and it lives in hope. Even when "bad things happen to good people," as the old cliché goes, a Catholic perspective seeks to discover meaning and significance in suffering. A writer with a Catholic sensibility shows this attitude in the way he or she celebrates uniqueness, in the way he or she values the detail, the particular. As Jesuit poet Gerard Manley

Hopkins put it in "Pied Beauty," such a writer says, "Glory be to God for dappled things." And these dappled things can include not only the unique and variegated characters who appear in a story but also events and phenomenal details that are—in Hopkins's words—"counter, original, spare, strange." And, often, the way they are unique and variegated is precisely the way they mix the evil with the good.

Finally, a Catholic worldview sees life whole and recognizes—and at least tries to intimate—a sense of the *pleroma,* that fullness of the Godhead that is Christ and toward which this world can only point.[1] We often find this wholeness in the little-noticed detail. Though Hassler stated that the poets referred to in his work were only the ones he happened to be reading at the time,[2] it seems clear that the work of Theodore Roethke in particular had a more pervasive impact. Even before Hassler used a passage from Roethke's short lyric, "The Small," in his novel *A Green Journey* (1985), his work was imbued with something of the "awed" sensibility manifested therein. The poem begins:

> The small birds swirl around;
> The high cicadas chirr;
> A towhee pecks the ground;
> I look at the first star:
> My heart held to its joy,
> This whole September day.[3]

I won't argue that Hassler imitates Roethke's style, though he may in places. Nor will I point to the significance of the images: of birds and insects, moon and wind, and sodden ground. These too may be part of Hassler's attraction to Roethke, part of that "attunement" to the seasons referred to earlier. Rather, it is the spirit of Roethke's poem that one finds in Hassler's work. The poem goes on to record another half-dozen impressions of a day in September with an almost breathless awe, an awe simply at their "being." To recognize the "being" of the things of this world without immediate, particularly self-interested, judgment: this is how a Catholic sensibility acknowledges the wholeness, the connectedness of all creation and its manifold mysteries.

1. St. Paul refers to Christ in Colossians 2:9 as *pleroma tes theotetos.*
2. Jon Hassler, "A Conversation with Jon Hassler," *Image: A Journal of the Arts and Religion* 19 (Summer 1998): 54, 55.
3. Theodore Roethke, "The Small," in *Words for the Wind* (Bloomington: Indiana University Press, 1961), 178.

The couplet that concludes the poem is perhaps as much metaphysics as Roethke—or Hassler—allows to creep in: "Things throw light on things, / And all the stones have wings." At almost every turn Hassler's fiction shows how "things throw light on things," yielding visions of a world that is loved by God. The protagonists in the first two works I will discuss are attentive observers of these visions. The protagonist of the third is not, and—as we shall see—that poses a particular challenge to the writer's skills and his evocation of a Catholic perspective.

Staggerford

Full of narrative dislocation yet tightly focused on a week in the life of thirty-five-year-old high school teacher Miles Pruitt, *Staggerford* has the makings of a classic. Basing it on a real-life incident that he heard about when he was teaching, Hassler sets the story sometime in the early 1970s, as we learn by way of various allusions to political and cultural events of the period. The novel explores the meaning and significance of a man's life against a backdrop of pettiness, regret, loss, and futility. The events are, for the most part, the ordinary ones of high school life in a small Minnesota town in fall: a Halloween party, a retirement gathering, and student misbehavior. One student's misbehavior leads to an "uprising" of local Native Americans after a fight in school. Central to the plot is Miles Pruitt's efforts to help a part–Native American student, Beverly Bingham, the first of many "hardscrabble girls" in Hassler's novels, young women whose dysfunctional families or unpromising social circumstances leave them vulnerable and unable to cope with life.

A number of puzzling features in the novel resolve themselves if one considers Miles's story a segment of the archetypal hero's journey as analyzed by anthropologists and critics such as Joseph Campbell and Northrop Frye. One of the most prominent features in the hero's journey is the seasonal background—in this case fall, the time of dying and decay—as well as the hero's encounter with a number of archetypal situations and characters. Hassler complicates the structure by employing a wandering point of view that will become a trademark of his work. The narrator's consistent tone, despite the shifting viewpoint, contributes to the sense of connectedness among the characters and actions.

The casual reader of *Staggerford* might identify it as a "Catholic novel" based on the prominence of Agatha McGee, the pre–Vatican II minded grade school teacher who is, without question, one of the novel's most memorable characters. But calling it a Catholic novel on that basis alone would likely reflect a superficial understanding of the work's intent. Of course there are also references to Mass, to the pastor Fr. Finn, and the school's principal, Sister Rosie. In addition, there are set "Catholic" pieces, including a survey of Agatha's library of Catholic "classics." But the Catholic worldview of *Staggerford* is much more subtle and pervasive than a catalogue of such external details can convey.

The novel begins with Miles Pruitt's sense of futility. Like some ancient hero doomed to bear the weight of the world, Miles carries around 114 student papers describing "What I Wish" in his briefcase, pulling them out one by one, when he can, to grade them. In time we come to see these papers as expressions—perhaps symbols—of his students' sense of hopelessness, confusion, and entrapment. In the course of the novel, we learn some of the reasons for Miles's own sense of futility. In high school he was betrayed by his brother Dale, and his girlfriend, Carla Carpenter, who dumped Miles for Dale. Thereafter, Miles goes through life wounded and without "the ability to see life as simple and cohesive." He now understands that "everything in life was subject to change—without notice,"[4] and he struggles, as it were, to see how "things throw light on things." After his betrayal, which may be seen indeed as a version of the Fall, Miles is cautious, even timid, at least where women are involved. Another symptom of—if not reason for—Miles's sense of hopelessness, the narrator tells us, is that Miles has lost his Catholic faith as well. Only one time do we see him uncharacteristically attending Sunday Mass, where "for an unguarded moment Miles was his former self, believing what the priest held in his hands had ceased to be bread and wine."[5] But such a moment does not last.

Against this background, then, *Staggerford* is a bit like *Pilgrim's Progress*, a story about striving to avoid the slough of despondency. Referring to his 114 student papers, Miles acknowledges the struggle: "It wasn't the poor penmanship after all that made reading these papers so difficult. Nor was it the futility of trying to teach English grammar. It was the way these papers teased him off the road of hope into the gulch of despair."[6] One of Miles's

---

4. Jon Hassler, *Staggerford* (New York: Ballantine, 1993), 129.
5. Ibid., 96.
6. Ibid., 229.

ways of resisting despair is a combination of humor and imagination. Despite an abiding sense of regret and burnout, he takes life as it comes, quietly acknowledging its beauties and incongruities even as he responds both imaginatively and actively in helping others, particularly his student Beverly.

Miles still has a capacity for almost childlike, unreflective wonder. This wonder is most evident in his observations of nature and in his interpersonal exchanges, particularly with Beverly. A single example combines the two. On a weekend walk, Miles heads down the Bad Battle River toward the gulch where Beverly and her mother live on a chicken farm. He watches a flock of grosbeaks and is taken with the sight: "One of the birds turned and looked directly into Miles's line of vision. It was a male, with bright yellow chevrons on his wings and bright yellow eyebrows." He is so absorbed that he is startled when Beverly appears. When he tells her what he was looking at, her indifferent answer, "I never notice birds," indicates her immersion in her own troubles.[7] This comes out when she says the only birds she notices are chickens, and that her rundown farm is "overrun" with those chickens. At this point, Beverly's mother, Corrine Bingham, suddenly appears, a woman known as "the bonewoman" because she scavenges the bones of chickens she has sold to Staggerford citizens. Miles observes her appearance closely as she passes by. Then, as he starts home, "He heard the mournful call of geese, but light was dying in the sky and he could not see them."[8] Coming as the final event in an afternoon fraught with meaning, this brief description carries an ominous tone, suggesting that Miles's ability to look attentively can be threatened—if not destroyed—by events or people such as the cynical Binghams who, embittered by their hard lives, have no capacity for wonder or beauty left in their souls.

In a kind of archetypal lead-up to the novel's climax, Miles's students finally recognize his leadership. Although he tries to remain on the sidelines during the Native American "uprising," he is dragged into the fray and there achieves at least a calming effect with his usual quiet though mischievous humor. In the case of Beverly, Miles perceives a vast discrepancy between how she thinks he helps her and the way he perceives his own feeble efforts in doing so. At the very least he persuades her—as much by being attentive to the lonely girl as by anything else he says or does—that she can succeed in college, if she only tries. He gives her hope in the midst of potential despair.

7. Ibid., 69.
8. Ibid., 72.

Staggerford remains memorable because of its characters, particularly Miles Pruitt. Unassuming and thus largely unaware of the positive effects that he has on others, Miles *is* the glue that connects the otherwise scattered characters and events. It is *he* who "throws light on things" and—with the help of the narrator—leaves the reader with a dark but searching sense of the mysteries of life that are integral to a Catholic worldview.

North of Hope

In *North of Hope,* Hassler blends the sensitive portrayal of character in a rural northern Minnesota context with an intricate yet powerful story line. Fr. Frank Healy is one of the most fully realized protagonists Hassler has created, and Libby Girard is the most completely depicted and memorable example of the "hardscrabble girl." Postmodern in many of its themes and details—spiritual and vocational burnout, dysfunctional families, drug dealing, alcohol, and psychosis—it also contains Hassler's fullest and most sympathetic portrayal of Native Americans since *Staggerford.* It is, finally, a novel thoroughly Catholic in not only its larger perspective but also in its characters and events as well. A kind of discontinuous life chronicle, *North of Hope* resembles Larry Woiwode's *Beyond the Bedroom Wall,* an acclaimed family chronicle of the 1970s with which it shares a number of themes and incidents as well as a pervasive Catholic sensibility.

I will highlight three events from the latter part of the novel that illustrate its Catholic nature. Stretching from the 1950s into the late 1970s, *North of Hope* begins in Frank Healy's junior year of high school. Frank is suffering through a typically painful adolescence. Since his mother's death, his father has become more and more uncommunicative. Like Miles Pruitt, Frank suffers a broken heart. He allows his friendship with Libby Girard—which had promised to become love—to falter, and in the end both he and Libby share responsibility for Libby marrying an ill-tempered high school football star.

Obeying his mother's purported dying wish, Frank becomes a priest and spends more than two decades as a teacher and a coach at Aquinas Academy. When, after twenty-three years, Frank meets her again, Libby is now in her third marriage, this time to Dr. Tom Pearsall. Trying to minister to the Native Americans of the Basswood Indian Reservation, where Tom Pearsall is doing community service for a drug conviction, Frank finds himself increasingly involved with the family as he offers to help Libby's mentally unstable daughter, Verna, the child of her first marriage. Verna has been sexually abused and herself abuses drugs and alcohol. Other shocking secrets of the family and reservation life come to light as Frank himself struggles to overcome depression and a sense of burnout in his work. But by the end of the novel, his relationship with Libby and Verna appears to be not only a consolation to them but also a way back for Frank to a deeper sense of his priestly vocation.

When Frank and Libby first meet again, Frank has had two work assignments since the closing of Aquinas Academy. While he suffers from depression and is drinking too much, he has matured in a number of ways. Like Miles Pruitt, he is a close observer of northern Minnesota nature, attentive to the things around him. And he has become a close observer of human beings and of his own spiritual and emotional state as well. Though flawed, his perceptions and conscience are likewise "attuned" to recognize the evil that threatens him and those around him.

Frank and Libby's reunion begins in the dead of a northern Minnesota winter, with the season underscoring the mood of the action. But even amid this time of physical, emotional, and spiritual "chill," Frank finds himself delivering a heartfelt homily at Mass one Sunday morning on the reservation: "He spoke of the healing power of the Sacraments, and as he concluded with the story of Fr. Zell [an early Minnesota missionary] . . . he felt once again the same old priestly zeal that had carried him through the seminary to ordination." Feeling confident for the first time in a long while, he concludes that his Basswood ministry "was exactly where he belonged." In a prescient way, he even believes that something at Basswood will help him "justify his life as a priest."[9] But almost immediately this confident mood changes: "Frank's experience with a murky spirit had taught him not to trust this ray of light . . . by Communion time he was asking himself cynical questions about his desire to imitate Fr. Zell."[10] He even darkly considers that this desire to emulate Fr. Zell might be a death wish. This subtle inner view of Frank's suffering shows it worthy of attention. Here is a mystery, an almost immediate and incomprehensible change of spirit from optimism to cynicism. And it is a change that Frank intends to fight.

Like Miles Pruitt, Frank tries to help victims of evil, such as Verna, but

9. Hassler, *North of Hope* (New York: Ballantine, 1990), 119.
10. Ibid.

he often feels that he is doing little good. He feels the same futility as Miles. Yet it is his very weakness and interior suffering that make him particularly sensitive, attentive to the weaknesses and suffering of others. In spite of his apprehensions and feelings of inadequacy, Frank is more or less properly disposed to grace, and even as he struggles with his own inner turmoil, grace is indeed given.

The second event I would like to focus on involves Frank and Verna. While she is in the appropriately (or ironically) named "Hope" psychiatric unit of the Berrington Hospital following the death of her boyfriend, Roger Upward, Frank visits her and tries to comfort and calm her. They walk outside in the cold wind to a snow-covered tennis court, where Verna slumps against a wire fence and calls out to the dead Roger. In response, Frank lays his hand on her shoulder and says, "You loved him." Then he patiently gets Verna to acknowledge that love: "Suddenly her knees buckled and she hung for a moment by her outstretched hands locked in the fence; then, losing her grip, she sagged further and Frank caught her under the arms."[11] Though Verna is no Christ figure, this scene recalls the crucifixion, with Frank in the role of the Blessed Virgin in her "pieta." Verna keeps repeating, "I loved Roger and I treated him like shit." Empathetically taking up her language, Frank tries to explain: "When you love people, you want to take them into your soul. You want them to know what you're like. So you make them feel like shit because then they'll understand how you feel." But then he adds, "You've got to stop feeling like shit, Verna, otherwise you'll never be decent to people you love."[12] Speaking from his own depression, Frank's attentiveness to Verna starts to have positive effects on both her and on himself.

A final event to consider is part of the long climax of the novel. Grief stricken over the loss of her husband, Libby is on her own and feels both loneliness and futility. But she has also grown dependent on Frank and wants a closer relationship. When Frank visits her in her apartment in Berrington, she asks him to sleep with her. When he answers, "I can't," she retreats to the bedroom. After a few minutes, she calls to him, and when Frank goes to the door he sees that she is naked. Refusing again her request for sex, he instead helps her into her bathrobe:

As he drew the lapels together over her breasts he reflected not with regret so much as wonder on the superhuman perversity expected of the priest, the con-

11. Ibid., 269.
12. Ibid., 270.

trariness of covering the sublime nakedness of a woman other men—normal men—would naturally disrobe. And yet this did not feel like perversity to Frank. Not tonight. Not with Libby so distracted, so desperate, so vulnerable. It felt like common sense.[13]

This scene verges on being melodramatic cliché. Yet the close observation and the reflection, measured out in a careful crescendo and decrescendo of short and long and short again sentences, holds it in emotional balance. And in this way the narrator confirms the sense of Frank's attentiveness and his sensitivity to the person of Libby, an empathy that does not need, perhaps even positively precludes, the sexual act itself.

North of Hope ends with Frank and Libby's friendship, as well as Frank's commitment to his priestly vocation, growing stronger. Verna, too, has started on the slow road to recovery. Though nothing is absolutely resolved—including the exact nature of Libby and Frank's future relationship—the novel leaves the reader with an unexpected sense of hope. In considering the novel as a whole, one could say, reductively, that Libby is a pessimist and Frank an optimist. But that oversimplifies, even falsifies the matter. For Frank, the world *is* good. He lost his mother, yes. He also lost his first love, the young Libby. He lost a job he'd loved and only clings in hope to his sense of religious vocation. But he is still able to affirm, through his close observation of and sensitivity to the things and people around him, such hope and its concomitant disposition to receiving grace. For Frank as for Miles Pruitt, "things throw light on things," and if all the stones do not yet have wings, he still is ready to wait, patiently and attentively, for that miracle, that mystery, to occur.

The Life and Death of Nancy Clancy's Nephew

In his writings about rural upper Midwest life, Hassler has depicted the occasional farmer. Sometimes, as in his novel, *The New Woman* (2006), they are brother-farmers, men worn out and often broken from working the land alone or nearly alone. In strong contrast to the loquacious Agatha McGee, they are taciturn and of dry, laconic humor. As such they resemble the parody of Scandinavian Minnesota farmers that Garrison Keillor has popularized on his radio show "A Prairie Home Companion."

13. Ibid., 409.

The novella *The Life and Death of Nancy Clancy's Nephew* is a close study of one such farmer. It is a complex, subtly ironic, but moving story of a man who grows old without having come to a sense of self-understanding commensurate with his age. While sympathetically told, it is also without doubt one of the sharpest critiques Hassler has applied to any character in his fiction. *The Life and Death of Nancy Clancy's Nephew* is the portrait of an emotionally and spiritually crippled old man who experiences but one moment of deeply felt humanity before he dies. As with my previous two examples of Hassler's fiction, I focus here on just a few incidents, primarily from the end of the novella, that illustrate the way in which this late work manifests a Catholic worldview.

The challenge for a writer whose work, for decades, has embodied the Roethkean principle that "things throw light on things" is to maintain that perspective as he seeks to depict a life and a community whose chief attributes are disconnection, alienation, and isolation. The characters in this work have few relations, in both senses of the word: few near family members and few lasting ties to others in the community. Nevertheless, Hassler's careful depiction of protagonist W. D. (Warren) Nestor emerges as key to the story's overall Catholic sensibility. In the unveiling of the portrait of W. D.—a man who finds the little he has been given taken away—the Catholic worldview is not readily apparent but rather something caught, as if out of the corner of one's eye. Unlike Miles Pruitt and Fr. Frank Healy, who are attentive observers of the world and their own lives, W. D. becomes increasingly insensitive to much that occurs around him. It is, rather, the narrator who "attends" to things, even as W. D. sees less and less. The narrator, however, seldom ventures far beneath the surface of W. D.'s mind. Our view of his inner life is, therefore, oblique, fragmented, and conjectural. The effect is a flat, unreflective portrayal that gives a somber sense of rural life around the fictional town of Bartlett, Minnesota, somewhere along the South Dakota line. Our "sense of the whole" and how "things throw light on things" is only there obliquely, by negation or implication, until the last few pages of the story.

It is primarily through W. D.'s memories—sparse, specific but muted, bleak, and just slightly out of focus—that Hassler is able to depict the pervading sense of disconnection and loss. The novella's title character provides an example of this. Until the last chapter, Nancy Clancy is just a distant relative, referred to only once when W. D. and Lucille Schuler elope to be married in Abernathy, South Dakota. Though Nancy is said to keep track of "half a dozen branches of her family,"[14] this single early reference merely serves to underline the actual aloofness and disconnectedness of the family's relationships.

The characterization of W. D. Nestor provides readers, perhaps, with the ultimate test of Hassler's understated Catholic perspective. If W. D. is a believer, we know little of it. The novella's only references to religion—Protestant and evangelical—are incidental and satiric. W. D. is a stoical, undemonstrative individual, and with good reason. He has had a difficult life, and we learn of the difficulties only indirectly, through flashbacks. He grew up on a farm, one of two sons. At nineteen, his older brother was shot one hunting season by a hunter who was never found. W. D.'s mother thinks he killed his brother, and for a brief time fears he may shoot her too. W. D. does not cry over his brother's death: "He shed no tears that day or at any time afterward—not until the final weeks of his life, over sixty years later."[15] This utter emotional repression, born of tragedy, determines the story's tone and gives it a strangeness bordering on the macabre. Even when his only son, Sonny, runs away as a teenager, and W. D. loses his wife to Alzheimer's disease, his response remains impassive.

When he is seventy-two (where the story begins), W. D.'s farm has shrunk to a turkey lot run by his daughter Viola and her husband Kermit and leased to the local poultry processor. The one routine to which W. D. clings is his mile-a-day jog around the turkey yard. He began the habit years before, after he and wife Lucille had watched a newsreel clip together about the Finnish runner, Paavo Nurmi. At the start of one day's run W. D. passes the sick turkey pen. The narrator's careful and attentive recounting of W. D.'s observations and memories here is almost clinical in detail. As W. D. passes by the pen, he notes that one of the sick turkeys staggers over as if to peck him but then stops and hangs his head. Immediately, a memory of his wife, Lucille, surfaces: "He kept a picture of Lucille taped to the wall in his bedroom . . . It showed Lucille sitting up in bed and staring emptily straight ahead—her typical Alzheimer's look . . . Her head hung forward, it seemed, in exhaustion." At the end of this description—certainly one, as Hopkins would put it, "counter, original, strange"—the narrator records: "Sometimes in his dreams,

14. Jon Hassler, *The Life and Death of Nancy Clancy's Nephew*, in *The Staggerford Murders* (New York: Penguin/Plume, 2004), 141.

15. Ibid., 114.

since Lucille died, life was a mile and he could not run."[16] W. D.'s whole relation to his wife is filled with such a painful and unexpressed sense of loss.

A single positive turning point in the midst of the story is W. D.'s meeting with Kevin Luya. W. D. meets Kevin for the first time when the boy is about ten years old and W. D. is seventy-four. Coming into Barlett to run on the high school track, W. D. watches a Little League baseball game and observes Kevin, the weakest member of the team. The son of a minister who is too wrapped up in his profession to pay attention to his son, Kevin turns up again later in the fall when W. D. visits the library to watch videos, as he and Lucille had often done together. A latchkey child, Kevin is alone in the library, spending time after school before returning to his empty home. W. D. invites Kevin to watch videos with him so that, as with Lucille, he has someone to whom he can explain or comment on them. Thus begins the unlikely friendship of an aging man and a young boy, both lonely and without family support. Over the next eight years W. D. and Kevin play pool and watch videos together every week, and W. D. is surprised at how fond he becomes of the boy. The narrator notes, "The boy was on his mind day and night the way Lucille used to be." When, at the age of eighteen, Kevin joins the army, W. D. misses him and sends several postcards. Kevin writes a few letters back, but "after that he wrote nothing."[17] This characteristically flat, uninflected narrative report conveys a deep sense of loneliness and implies a deeper sense of loss. It also helps explain, as we come to find out later, Kevin's seemingly callous behavior when W. D. dies. Yet, importantly, such reportage does not leave the reader with an impression of either disgust or pain. Rather, however quiet and laconic, the attentive narrative voice makes even such sadness luminous. The simply reported fact that "the boy was on his mind" the way his wife had been, is a brief revelation of what lies deeper in W. D.'s heart than even he might realize.

On the last day of his life—a fact to which the narrator alerts us—W. D. gets a sudden urge to visit his Aunt Nancy Clancy, about whom we've heard nothing since the story's start. It is March, just before the start of (archetypal) spring—but we don't learn that immediately, because W. D. has lost track of months as well as days. W. D. is now eighty-two years old. Kevin has returned from the army and is caring for W. D. while Viola and Kermit are win-

---

16. Ibid., 116–17, 118.
17. Ibid., 173.

tering in Florida. Kevin notes how rapidly W. D. is failing in health. On the ride to town, W. D. thinks about his son, and this awakens a memory of the last day that he, Lucille, and Viola had seen Sonny. Arriving at the apartment where Nancy lives, Kevin and W. D. encounter a small boy bundled up for winter. As they begin to climb the stairs in the building, which has no elevator, W. D. begins to feel ill: "A fountain seemed to be rising up his spine and bubbling in his brain . . . He felt as though he had outdistanced some vital part of himself—his lungs, his soul—and he was waiting for it to catch up."[18] When Nancy answers the door, W. D. mistakenly introduces Kevin as Sonny. Nancy invites them in, and Nancy and her nephew start to reminisce. They argue gently over things in their past that they remember differently, and a tone of pathos grows. One recollection causes W. D. to laugh silently, "but [the laugh] grew until it shook him like a convulsion and caused tears to spring into his eyes. Kevin had never seen W. D. laugh before." The pathos rises as W. D.'s mixture of laughter and tears even causes the old man to wet his pants.[19]

After tea Aunt Nancy brings out a photograph album. W. D. misreads the pictures but won't admit his vision is failing. Kevin, growing bored, looks out the living room window. Imperceptibly, the tone moves from pathos to uncanniness as Kevin observes the little boy they had met earlier looking at a kite in a tree, and he goes downstairs while Nancy and W. D. continue to look at the photo album. A question posed by Nancy about Sonny brings back the thoughts that had occupied W. D. on the trip to town. W. D. recalls that from the time Sonny was eleven they couldn't sign up for the annual father-and-son dinner at church because Sonny refused to go. At the memory, W. D. tries to hide the tears that begin to overflow his eyes.

Outside, Kevin tries to help the little boy fly his kite, and their conversation is a study in miscommunication. It seems clear that the little boy is where Kevin was eight or ten years before, left on his own by a father who builds him a kite but is not around to help him fly it. After two attempts, Kevin manages to get the kite in the air, and then the level of uncanniness rises again as the narrator explains how odd the kite appears, heavy rather than fragile, "as though something earthbound had taken flight." Suddenly the boy shouts for Kevin to bring it down, informing him, incongruously only

18. Ibid., 183.
19. Ibid., 187, 188.

now, that his father told him not to fly the kite because its string was too weak and would break. Kevin tries to bring the kite down, but it "spun in the sky and the string snapped."[20]

In this continued series of discrete impressions from which the reader must construct the whole, the narrator recounts how Kevin, turning back to the apartment, sees W. D. lying in a snowbank. As he tries to help the old man, he hears what he thinks is the ringing of a bell but it is, he realizes, Nancy in the apartment window beating W. D.'s pipe on a brass bowl. "He's dead, I know he's dead," she said. "Looking at old pictures up here, he cried like a baby. And when he left, I came to the window to tell him he forgot his pipe, and I saw him fall."[21] Kevin looks up past Nancy's window, sees a star in the sky, realizes it's getting dark, and walks to his car. For a moment, narrative time jumps back, and we are now with the little boy, as he too hears the "bell." He goes to investigate the sound and he sees an old lady shouting from her window and an old man lying in the snow. He tries to raise W. D.'s arm, "but the old man, scowling, seemed determined to stay where he was." The improbable and strange here become grotesque in a way reminiscent of Flannery O'Connor's work. From his car, Kevin calls to the boy to come and get in so they can look for his kite. When the boy asks whether Kevin knew a man was lying on the ground, Kevin responds, "'Yeah, what a bummer' . . . He felt terrible. He knew now why he disliked old people. He hated the way they died."[22]

With this epitaph *The Life and Death of Nancy Clancy's Nephew* ends. The flat, mostly external account of the final events in W. D. Nestor's life do little to create a sense of hope, redemption, or forgiveness. Regret, heartache, and incomprehension seem the burden of the tale. Yet something in the style and focus of the story lends not just a sense of mystery but also a sense of enduring value unacknowledged by the characters. W. D's life has obviously not been a happy one. It has been a series of continual losses and surrender: loss of a brother, a son, a wife, a farm, his own powers, and those things he has come to appreciate, too late and perhaps too little. Ultimately it is gradual surrender to the forces of life that attack us all. Yet despite the narrator's implicit and explicit criticism of W. D. along with that of his relatives and the community in the alienated and alienating world of rural Minnesota, *The Life and Death of Nancy Clancy's Nephew* pays respectful attention to

20. Ibid., 194.
21. Ibid., 195.
22. Ibid., 197, 198.

and affirms the essential mystery of human life, of suffering, of moments of clarity and focus when startling images break through our consciousness. A kite broken free and whipping in the wind, the sudden appearance of a single star or a mysterious child, a banging pipe sounding like a tolling bell. These are hardly unequivocal signs of hope—let alone harbingers of meaning and salvation. Yet these distinct images, like those in Roethke's poem, "The Small," bear witness to a sense of grace and presence in this world. If "things throw light on things," these images point to the *pleroma* by the heightened sense that the words bestow upon details closely attended to. And, in a way, the possibility of grace and redemption suffuse the scene of W. D.'s death through the evoking of such images, as indeed the signs in nature did the day that Jesus died.

Abandoned by his only friend in death, while just one woman tolls a bell, W. D. Nestor is like the bereft, tragic protagonists at the end of Graham Greene's *The Power and the Glory* or Georges Bernanos's *The Diary of a Country Priest*. Like Miles Pruitt and Fr. Frank Healy, W. D. Nestor experienced much of his life as "a ransom of cholers." But in each work the narrator's voice has sought to show how "things throw light on things." Even in the midst of sometimes satiric criticism, the reader can also find strangely consoling the narrator's perspective on these characters' fates. Thus, the reader comes to view these often anguished lives with the same attentive, loving gaze the narrator has lavished on them. In this way, we as readers may also experience that luminous sense of mystery that is, in the words of Hans Urs von Balthasar, "a Catholic sense."

CHAPTER 8

Our Litany ▪ The Varied Voices and Common Vision of Three Contemporary Catholic Poets

Gary M. Bouchard

There was a time not very long ago when Catholic poets, novelists, and playwrights were as much a part of the American and English literary landscape as writers of any other stripe; a time when one would not have to go searching to find a prominent Catholic author, and that writer would not have to blush when found. Consider the literary presence and prominence of but a few of the Catholic authors from the decades of the mid-twentieth century. In the United States: Flannery O'Connor, Katherine Anne Porter, Walker Percy, Allen Tate, Robert Lowell, John Berryman, Mary McCarthy, Tennessee Williams, John Fredrick Nims, and Thomas Merton. In Britain: Graham Greene, David Lodge, Evelyn Waugh, Edith Sitwell, J. R. R. Tolkien, and Anthony Burgess. It is not that there was a renaissance in Catholic literary production during these years, but that within the culture and for many significantly successful authors, literature and Catholic belief were synchronistic rather than contradictory. We can hardly say the same today.

One could spend time considering the many reasons for this. I leave that to others better suited to understand such things. My modest purpose in this essay is to hold up the poetic work and thought of three award-winning contemporary poets, each with a strong, established literary reputation, each with a different cultural background, each different in style, form, and technique, and each Catholic. I hope to offer some assurance and accompanying evidence that something called Catholic poetry not only exists today but endures with a particular strength that can be evidenced in the works of these three poets. Dana Gioia, Desmond Egan, and Sherman Alexie have such distinctive biographical origins and poetic voices that the only thing they may share, apart from the excellence of their verse, is something of a common Catholic vision. Seeing that vision, like discovering or recovering Catholic poetry, requires not so much knowing where to look but how to read.

Learning how to read, of course, is what we teachers of poetry spend our lives doing, and as the majority of mine has been spent in the sixteenth and seventeenth centuries, and most recently among the dark alleyways and secret hiding places of Catholic recusant poets, I bring a rather unusual aperture through which to contemplate the poetry of these three contemporary Catholic authors. Through that aperture I am witness to a curious paradox. The poet Robert Southwell, SJ (1561–95), did everything possible to conceal his Catholic identity lest he be arrested, tortured, and executed. On the other hand, the Catholic aspects of the poetry written by this sixteenth-century Jesuit posing as a gentleman were anything but covert. Its entire purpose was to use the familiar forms and techniques of Elizabethan poetry to foster the Catholic mission. The worst of this poetry is so overtly catechetic as to be clumsily didactic to contemporary ears. The best of it reflects an apt blend of allegorical and metaphorical imagery, poetic form, and scriptural meditation. The publication and distribution of this poetry was accomplished with great stealth, but the poetry itself was a veritable trove of Roman Catholic meditation, prayer, and teaching.

Fast forward to our present century. Gone from the Western world, thankfully, are the macabre instruments of torture and execution by which religion was enforced upon individuals. And yet, to consider matters honestly, instruments, primarily economic, remain in place that govern what gets printed for a wide audience of readers. University presses and major publishing houses do not conspire against religious literary works, but they do function, like all of us, in a devoutly secular society. In a world where tolerance is the highest value, we share as well a quiet discomfort with overt religious expression, especially within the confines of the campus and in the intellectual world more generally. Whether or not the late Patrick Moynihan was right in observing that "anti-Catholicism remains the one respectable form of intellectual bigotry," I will not argue here. The kind of bigotry of which he spoke, I suspect, extends toward many people beyond the bounds of the Catholic Church. The point is, and I think it is not such a controversial one, that in our society one's ideas and art are more likely to be taken more seriously by more people if they sound secular.

Thus I arrive, and I hope not too circuitously, at the present paradox. Whereas Southwell and his secret band of supporters had to physically conceal their Catholic identity, their literary art revealed and promoted Catholicism in every word, phrase, and theme. Today, poets like Gioia, Egan, and Alexie need make no secret of their Catholic identity, and while they may speak of it with varying degrees of openness, none of them makes any effort to hide it. In their poetry, however, we more often discover Catholic belief and thought abiding in secret. In fact, for someone coming from the world of the sixteenth-century underground, some of their poems can appear like an unsuspecting Jesuit garbed in a gentleman's silks. As in the case of the costumed priests, the presentation of these poems should be seen, I believe, as a kind of pragmatism. That is, unlike hunted Catholics of the sixteenth century, these poets of our secular age are not deliberately concealing their religious identities in order to preserve their lives or careers. Rather, their art is appropriately dressed in the ironic, objectified fashion of the day. What fabric of belief or unbelief is visible beneath depends, as I say, on our learning how to read.

Dana Gioia

Dana Gioia (b. 1950), the chair of the National Endowment for the Arts from 2004–8 and one of America's leading poets and literary critics, came to the public's attention with his 1991 *Atlantic Monthly* essay entitled "Can Poetry Matter?" The question became the title of a significantly influential book of criticism in 1992, provoked an ongoing discussion about poetry's relevance in contemporary culture, and brought enough attention to his own poetry and criticism to allow him to leave a lucrative business career and devote himself to writing full time. His first two volumes of poetry, *Daily Horoscope* (1986) and *The Gods of Winter* (1991), received critical acclaim, and his volume *Interrogations at Noon* (2001) won the 2002 American Book Award. Among other things, Gioia is credited with helping to revive the use of rhyme, meter, and narrative in contemporary poetry. As chair of the National Endowment for the Arts, he implemented innovative programs to encourage the reading of poetry in public.

The son of Italian and Mexican immigrants, Gioia is a faithful Catholic and yet neither his admirers nor his critics would describe him as a "religious poet." The designation or withholding of such a moniker would, from his point of view, miss the point. "I believe very deeply," he says, "that a poem can be Catholic without being explicitly religious. Catholics look at the world differently from agnostics, from Protestants or other people, and that worldview pervades everything they see or describe."[1] It's hard, often impossible, as Yeats reminds us, to "tell the dancer from the dance" or the poem from the poet. From Gioia's point of view, the dancer is always and inevitably in the dance. "It's not a matter of sitting down and writing a Catholic poem," he says. "Real poetry comes out of at least three things: technique, inspiration, and who you really are—authenticity—who you are and who you aren't. If you are a Catholic, it's in your art."

Gioia notes that many readers are looking for rather superficial markers in searching out religious or Catholic ingredients in a poem. It isn't, he says, a matter of finding crucifixes or other conventional Catholic images. Rather, it is the inevitable and substantial expression of a particular vision. "Catholics, whether practicing or lapsed, are rooted in a common worldview" that includes, he thinks, some basic concerns: a sense of moral and spiritual journey, a sense of human imperfection, a relationship between the material and the nonmaterial world, and a sacramental sense of the world. Sin and redemption are not unique to Catholics, but their prevalence and pervasiveness may be. For Gioia, it mainly comes down to grace. "Original sin is an essential tenant of the Catholic worldview. Catholic writers have a sense of their own sinfulness, their own inability to measure up to their goals without the avenue of grace." "In fact," he observes, "when Catholic writers say they're Catholic, they are really admitting their own deficiency." Our contemporary culture calls it inadequacy. Old-time religion called it depravity. By any name, it is that profound loss at the center of one's life, health, marriage, job, education, family, art, or very existence that cannot be ignored and that, from the Catholic point of view, provokes us to seek redemption in the form of God's grace.

Anyone who has studied poetry, or read serious literature for that matter, comes to recognize that nearly all of it is more or less born out of loss. That this loss can and must be redeemed is not a uniquely Catholic belief, but layer in the sacramental manner in how that redemption takes place, the pro-

---

1. Personal interview with Dana Gioia conducted by the author, June 21, 2007. All prose quotations from Dana Gioia in this essay are from this interview.

found physical reality of the Incarnation and the paschal mystery, the relational intimacy of the Trinitarian God, and the emphasis on the paradoxical mystery of the Eucharist, and one is approaching the kind of Catholic worldview that Gioia describes. The poets of the devotional tradition—Constable, Southwell, Herbert, the mature Donne, Hopkins, or Rossetti—create explicitly religious poems by writing about these things. Rarely has any major poet since Eliot done so. Or have they?

To say that loss is a central theme in Gioia's poetry is actually to understate the number of his poems that are unexpectedly and even matter-of-factly elegiac. The speaker does not typically lament a personal loss in bold emotional language, seek to invoke the listener's pity, or even offer conventional memorial praise for that which is no longer so. Rather, many of Gioia's poems calmly invite the unsuspecting reader to contemplate the extraordinary loss inherent in our everyday lives. Consider as examples four of the poems in his most recent collection, *Interrogations at Noon*.

The poem "Summer Storm"[2] is a meditation upon memory and the human propensity to re-imagine not only what was but what might have been. The recollection of "a memory" from an evening two decades earlier when the speaker stood as a wedding guest with a woman he did not know on a "rented patio" and watched a summer storm is by itself a lovely piece of lyrical nostalgia, the depicting of an *ekphrastic* moment which, like Keats's "Ode on a Grecian Urn," is all the more enticing for the possibilities that this spontaneous, innocent, and curiously sensual moment holds. Or rather, held. A storm arises and then subsides, and the woman is called inside and "merge[s] into the group." What-might-have-been is often a more treasured part of our imagination than what actually was. The poet could legitimately have ended this recollection after the first six quatrains, noting without any judgment that the two of them "didn't speak another word / Except to say good-night." Instead, for three more stanzas he contemplates not the existential dead end of what-might-have-been, but a far more ponderous problem:

> Why does that evening's memory
> Return with this night's storm—
> A party twenty years ago,
> Its disappointments warm?

It is not a Catholic moralist who concludes that our memory "insists on pining / For places it never went, / As if life would be happier / Just by being dif-

2. Dana Gioia, "Summer Storm," in *Interrogations at Noon* (St. Paul, Minn.: Graywolf, 2001), 66–67.

ferent." Robert Frost might have, and often did, come to such wry resolve in his poems. But we learn something about Gioia the poet in the very fact that he keeps writing after these lines. Having identified the problem of why such memories won't stay buried, he offers two possible answers: the first existentially and romantically modern, namely, our lives are full of *what-ifs;* and the second old-fashionedly moral in its grown-up wisdom: *"As if* life would be happier."

In "Pentecost,"[3] comprised of four brief stanzas that follow the stark inscription *"after the death of our son,"* the indescribable sorrow and persecution of this loss is paradoxically aligned with the "implacable tongues of fire" that transformed the apostles. But in this case, the repetition of the apostles' declaration "We are not as we were" is deeply and excruciatingly ironic. No "prayers / Improvised to an unknowable god / Can extinguish the flame." Readers who are either desirous or concerned that religious platitudes might afford the poet consolation, hear instead the voice of a lamenting psalmist speaking to his spouse: "Comfort me with stones. Quench my thirst with sand. / I offer you this scarred and guilty hand / Until others mix our ashes." If the poem requires commentary, I leave it to others, only presenting it here as evidence that loss for Dana Gioia is not an intellectual abstraction or playful poetic trope.

In the title poem of this collection, "Interrogations at Noon,"[4] the poem's speaker becomes a pained listener by confessing that often "just before noon" he hears the "whispering in [his] head" of "the better man I might have been." Bewildered and disgusted at the "grim mistake" that granted the speaker life "but left him still unborn," this superior version of the speaker does not "disguise his scorn." Most of us keep at a safer distance this banished alter ego of our conscience who asks, "'Who is the person you pretend to be?'" and who reminds us, even if our friends won't, that we are a "failed saint" and a "simpering bore." The poet of these four quatrains endures, like Prufrock, the self-conscious revelation that our greatest loss lies in our failure, our inability to be the better person we might have been: "Extravagant and empty, that is you."

Reading Gioia's poems we are reminded that, like our first parents in the garden, knowledge is its own punishment: knowledge in the form of warm memories, acute grief, and the daily knowledge of the chasm between who we seek to be and who we actually are. Present, if not spoken, in these po-

---

3. Gioia, "Pentecost," in *Interrogations at Noon*, 18.
4. Gioia, "Interrogations at Noon," in *Interrogations at Noon*, 5.

ems is the Christian paradox central to the paschal mystery celebrated in the Catholic liturgy. Loss—physical, spiritual, cosmic—is not something that is then redeemed. Rather, redemption, paradoxically and mysteriously, resides within loss. This is the central truth contained in Christ's crucifixion. From Adam's *"felix culpa"* forward, sorrow and joy reside in simultaneity. Gioia celebrates this paradox in "The Litany,"[5] a poem whose first line might serve as the catalogue description for this collection of poems: "This is a litany of lost things." The vocabulary of the poem, beginning with the title, is familiarly and unapologetically Catholic, even while it is ironically counterbalanced by the more recognizably acceptable language of contemporary skepticism. How else to arrive at declarations like "This is a prayer to unbelief," or "This is a litany to earth and ashes"? In fact, the genius as well as the beauty of the poem is the manner in which it retains the tone and appeal of a contemporary meditation—which one of our lives does not contain "a canon of possessions dispossessed, / a photograph, an old address, a key"?—and is simultaneously as sacramental as any poem Gerard Manley Hopkins ever wrote. The smile on the Madonna may be of stone, the incense may be "drifting into emptiness," but that does not undermine "the silent fury of the consecrated wine, / a benediction on the death of a young god, / brave and beautiful, rotting on a tree."

In this poem's final stanzas, the speaker addresses his unfinished prayer to "my love, my loss, my lesion" and begins separating "time's illusions" from the "pure paradox" of the mist rising from a gorge, "the shattered river rising as it falls—." He declares in the stanza's opening two lines ". . . at last it is our litany, *mon vieux*, / my reader, my voyeur . . ." Since it is all couched in a safely ironic "as if," the pure paradox of the *simultaneity* of loss and redemption is left to the onlooking reader, beholding this "rosary of words," to decide what he or she sees. Nobody has been preached to here, but outward signs of inward grace crowd the poem—crowd the earth and crowd our lives, Gioia would say. And they invite, if not demand, our response. "I can live unformed experience," Gioia says of his life and art: "I can experience loss, but I cannot ignore the problem of who to blame or who to cry to if there is no such thing as sin, or the problem of where to go to if there is no place to which we can transcend."

---

5. Gioia, "The Litany," in *Interrogations at Noon,* 10.

Desmond Egan

One of Ireland's most prolific and innovative poets, Desmond Egan (b. 1936) lives in his beloved Irish Midlands between frequent plane flights to the U.S., Asia, Europe, and the Middle East and is paradoxically, therefore, one of his country's most Irish as well as one of its most international poets. He has published a dozen books of poetry since his first collection in 1972, and his *Collected Poems* was awarded the U.S. National Poetry Award in 1983. His work has been reviewed by critics on nearly every continent and championed most notably by the modernist scholar Hugh Kenner. Apart from working for many years as a teacher, Egan's enterprises include the founding of his own press in 1972 as well as founding and directing for nearly two decades a highly successful international conference on Gerard Manley Hopkins in Monastervin, the one place in Ireland where Hopkins found some solace.

In Ireland, of course, "Catholic" is as much a political as religious designation, and Egan's poetry inevitably reflects the view of a "southern [Irish] Catholic at home in his state, its majority church, its landscape."[6] Only in his volume of poems called *Seige!* does he confront the politics of Ireland with sustained directness, and the frustration and indignation contained in those poems, we may say, is quite ecumenical. Apart from the politics of his country, Egan is a Catholic poet whose yearning for peace in his world and his life is often made even more evident by the modernist angst and syntactical complexities of his verse. "The religious impulse," he writes in *The Death of Metaphor,* "will always reveal itself as a search for wholeness, as a search for one's roots, a longing for psychological and cultural individuality." "Such preoccupations," he observes, are "never far away in modern writing" and "are the most obvious expression of the religious instinct in this turbulent century."[7] The twenty-first century, certainly, has not diminished in turbulence, nor has Egan's longing for wholeness in a fractured world. It is present in every poem he has ever written.

The late Patrick Rafroidi, commenting on what he perceived to be a lack of explicit religious expression in Egan's poetry, noted that the speaker's repetition of "God Bless" at the end of "Echo's Bones," in response to Samuel Beckett's use of that same formulaic farewell, "was one of the rare instances of the

---

6. Brian Arkins, *Desmond Egan: A Critical Study* (Little Rock, Ark.: Milestone, 1992), 16.
7. Desmond Egan, *The Death of Metaphor* (Newbridge, Ire.: Kavanagh, 1990), 133.

naming of his Creator in the works of that Catholic poet."[8] "But Sweet Christ!" Egan might well respond to Rafroidi's observation. For this three-word epithet and prayer is the hinge upon which his popular poem "Peace"[9] turns from personal yearning to a lament for "the globe still plaited in its own / crown of thorns." Counting the number of times Egan names his Creator in his poems is a curious way to misapprehend the spiritual substance, the yearning for wholeness, that is evoked in his poetry. Placing Egan among those Catholic writers who apparently "take their faith for granted," Rafroidi says that in Egan's poems "there is no theorizing, no moralizing, no preaching, perhaps not even any real questioning."[10] The first three of these rhetorical activities, Egan would insist, and I would agree, are not the function of poetry. As for questioning, Egan's poems, it seems to me, do so with a feverishly modernist voice, while standing banished outside of Eden, or shuffling his feet at the foot of the cross, or making his lonely way down a familiar street, or shaking his head in front of the news on the television; while holding an undusted memory up to the light, mourning a friend, or selling an old car.

Certainty is always elusive. Thus Egan creates a collection of poems about the people and places of his hometown, and then includes in the very title of the book a question mark, *Athlone?* If not asked outright, as they frequently are, the poet's questions are implicit in the observations that he makes, the things that, like any skillful poet, he plants between the lines. Egan is a master of the indigenous Irish trait of saying much, but not too much. If the tone of Gioia's poems is often casually and even elegantly elegiac, the tone of Egan's often erupts with impatience in the face of loss. The pervasive question in his poems, it seems to me, is "How can this be so?" or rather "Sweet Christ, how can this be so?" Common to the works of both poets is the recognition of human depravity, the yearning for grace and its momentary discovery in the ordinary things and people that fill their days and their memories.

To be sure, still stinging four hundred years later from the imperialist, genocidal vision and the particular crimes against the Irish by the likes of Lord Grey and Edmund Spenser, Desmond Egan is decidedly not a man who takes his Catholicism or his God for granted. Counting the number of times

---

8. Patrick Rafroidi, "Pilgrim's Progress," in *Desmond Egan: The Poet and His Work*, ed. Hugh Kenner (Orono, Maine: Northern Lights, 1990), 138.

9. Desmond Egan, "Peace," in *Selected Poems* (Newbridge, Ire.: Kavanagh, 1992), 143–44.

10. Rafroidi, "Pilgrim's Progress," 139.

he calls God by name is, like the search for conventional religious subject matter and imagery to which Gioia refers, a superficial manner of reading what is really there. Like Gioia, Egan describes the Catholicity in his poems as a kind of anthropological inevitability that affects not only one's thoughts but, quite literally, the shape those thoughts take: "If you are a believer, it will affect your sense of form; it will influence the very sentence you write as much as its content, and how could it not? Your native place determines your accent, even the way you walk."[11]

At the end of his collection *Selected Poems* (1992), Egan includes a lyrical meditation, "Epilogue,"[12] in which the speaker finds himself looking out of the window of his study on "a leaden March morning." For no reason, he says, he remembers the town of Kerry and "the long road of stillness." No sooner does the remembrance ripen to a few particulars than it fades to "somebody's voice coming a long way / life draining from a hill / landscape of tragic faces / where time fades to eternity / that great grey movement / over us all." The somberness of the tone notwithstanding, Egan's reflections do not lead him or us to an existential bleakness. Time does not dissolve to nothingness. It "fades to eternity." And as it does so, Egan makes his way through memory down the hauntingly familiar streets of his hometown, or along a path in the landscape from his past, or into conversations with people now gone. "All life / becomes goodbye," he writes as the concluding lines of the poem "For All We Know,"[13] a brief memoriam for Billie Holiday. And in his meditation upon the death of John Berryman he recalls the poet's sad, suicidal plunge: "one last breath / pluming—like Gabriel's message—out of his lips . . . *Ha ha alas* so long Berryman / Christ—who knew the fall the jerk— / save us all."[14]

In a poem entitled "For Father Romano on His 45th Birthday,"[15] Egan speaks directly to a Filipino priest who dedicated himself to organizing poor laborers and seeking, as Egan states in a note to the poem, "living wages and tolerable work-contracts." Romano disappeared during the last months of President Marcos's regime, last seen "being forced into an army jeep." The poem begins as a tribute to the priest and his work and steadily unveils the indignation and outrage that such violence and injustice provoke in those

11. Egan, *The Death of Metaphor*, 132.
12. Egan, "Epilogue," in *Selected Poems*, 176.
13. Egan, "For All We Know," in *Selected Poems*, 28.
14. Egan, "For John Berryman," in *Selected Poems*, 33–34.
15. Egan, "For Father Romano on His 45th Birthday," in *Selected Poems*, 139–40.

who care to pay attention. It is always, I think, an artistically delicate if not dangerous maneuver to write the social justice poem, to rail against the system, any system, in verse. Topical complaint is the life of much folk music and, more recently, the force driving many rap and hip-hop lyrics. But the lyrical or narrative poem with lasting qualities will need to lift the reader beyond cursing the inevitable oppression of the latest rogue government or unjust policy. "For Father Romano" does so, transcending the topical with striking sacramental imagery from the very beginning:

> in you Romano I salute the few
> who hand out like bread to others
> their ordinary life
> and build up block by block
> anonymous in the loneliest villages
> their chapel to the spirit.

The speaker salutes those "who make their flesh and blood an angelus / pealing across huts and plots" and then confesses "when I hear that such as they as you / have ended up in prisons or ditches / I feel as well as rage a fierce pride a / joy of sorts." The joy at such horrific news originates from the only place it could, the "reminder / that the resurrection continues." It is in a vivid religious vision that the poem moves from rage to redemption:

> Romano your persecutors will only succeed
> in squeezing from your body the blood of Christ
> and though they dump you in one compound or another
> your soul flies with ease up over
> their pathetic cement their money sentries
> their rusting barbed wire.

Following this, the poet's bold concluding line, "no one can stop our march," is itself a metaphorical proclamation of the spiritual strength and determination gained from martyrs like Romano whose very lives—"bread for others . . . blood of Christ"—become Eucharist.

"On the long road of stillness" that Egan walks in his search for wholeness, all loss reveals itself with a stated or implied sacramental quality, whether in the remembered landscapes and conversations of "Eugene Watters" or in the sale of an old car. It is worth considering one other quality of Egan's work that is part, I think, of his Catholicity. For all the emphatic seriousness in many of his poems, Egan possesses an irrepressible comic sense, evident in his public readings, memorable to anyone who has ever rushed to get him from one place to another, and quite on display in poems like "Goodbye Old Fiat,"[16] a tribute to the rusting car the poet is selling. He begins to catalogue its many quirks and flaws, from the "leak puddles each side of the floor," to "the visor that slowly comes down as one drives." As he does so, he recalls the many rambunctious and chaotic years during which this old car has been the repository of the "typewriter coat case books letters / on top of everything else in your back seat." It has been the vessel for a life lived, and the speaker recognizes that he

> will never be sad
> delighted hopeful annoyed browned-off thoughtful
> again inside you
> who loitered at the background of my life
> bringing together like a symbol those last few
> so suddenly finished years.

The poem evokes a nostalgic sentimentality that might be unforgivable if not, on the one hand, so comic, and on the other, part of an absolutely sincere belief in the sacredness of things. The poet wonders if the next owner of this old car will discover odds and ends of his life and "realise that he has bought a haunted car."

This blend of the sacred and the comic is never more successfully on display than in Egan's use of the Catholic formula of *kyrie eleison* to comment upon the more strenuous and pitiable aspects of a poet's life. "Have Mercy on the Poet"[17] lists thirteen images followed by the alternating liturgical refrains of "Lord, Have Mercy," "Christ, Have Mercy": "—the poet waiting his turn at the Bank Manager's confessional . . . the poet filling-in his Tax life . . . the poet haranguing an audience of 17 . . . the poet *holding down a steady job*," and so on. The sympathetic listener delights in the comic litany of common circumstances. As a device of self-pity and deprecation, the liturgical refrains are richly ironic in their very employment and repetition. Simultaneously these familiar prayers *are* prayers and as sincere as anything Egan has ever written, poignant especially in the final line: "—the poet scrounging down the jeweled road *Lord, Have Mercy / Christ, Have Mercy.*" Our snickering suddenly ceases. This poet means it. His poems are all a kind of prayer, and most

16. Egan, "Goodbye Old Fiat," in *Selected Poems*, 107–8.
17. Egan, "Have Mercy on the Poet," in *Selected Poems*, 145.

are a prayer for and of forgiveness. How else can that atrocity or this loss be so? How else amidst the brokenness of this world is wholeness possible?

Sherman Alexie

"How did I become this / Catholic and catholic, wanting to get to Heaven / as painfully and quickly as everyone else?" asks the nervous airline passenger in Sherman Alexie's poem "Airplane."[18] It is no rhetorical question. Born in October 1966 into the Spokane / Coeur d'Alene Indian tribe, Alexie grew up on a Spokane Indian Reservation about fifty miles northwest of Spokane, Washington. An early and avid reader with several health complications, Alexie became prey to the humor of other kids on the reservation. His insatiable appetite for learning and reading would eventually lead beyond reservation schools to Gonzaga University and then Washington State University, where his talents as a writer were recognized and encouraged. Today Alexie is a prolific, prize-winning poet, novelist, and short-story writer with eighteen books and two films to his credit, including nine books of poetry. His novel, *The Absolute True Diary of a Part-Time Indian,* won the National Book Award in Juvenile Fiction in 2007. He has been dubbed by one *New York Times* reviewer "the most lyrical voice of his generation," and few in or out of the Native American literary community can deny the thematic versatility and often shocking strength of that voice, which ranges in tone from deeply ironic and angry to outright comic to suddenly delicate and reverent. Alexie is, as he says in one poem, "an Indian / who knows the difference / between Monet and Manet,"[19] and his poetry contains all the stuff that the various worlds that he has inhabited has deposited there, from James Dean and Janis Joplin to the intricacies of his tribal mythology, to canonical American and English literature, to the dismal socioeconomic realities of contemporary reservation and urban life.

To treat Alexie as a Catholic poet is, perhaps, a presumption. Catholicism is not something outside of a handful of poems of which he speaks, and in his prolific collection of works there are but one or two poems in which Alexie's Indian heritage is not on display explicitly, passionately, proudly, angrily, and often ironically. Desmond Egan's Irishness is at the heart or the

18. Sherman Alexie, "Airplane," in *The Summer of Black Widows* (Brooklyn, N.Y.: Hanging Loose, 1996), 81–83.
19. Alexie, "Things (for an Indian) to Do in New York (City)," in *Summer of Black Widows,* 128.

fringe of much of his poetry, but Alexie's Indian identity saturates his every verse. Furthermore, while Egan speaks and champions the indigenous Gaelic language that predates the coming of Catholicism to Ireland some fifteen hundred years ago, his racial and national identity is by now inseparably intertwined with his Catholicism. For Alexie, Catholicism is a much more recent and controversial import of the notorious fifteenth-century Columbian exchange, another piece of imperial Anglo-culture displacing the Spokane beliefs and life that centered both practically and mythically on the salmon. In his prosaic poem "The Powwow at the End of the World,"[20] Alexie's refrain is "I am told by many of you that I must forgive and so I shall." He shall, he says, only after the mythical salmon swims upstream and comes to his people to tell them three stories: one to teach them to pray, one to make them laugh, and one to make them dance. He shall forgive only "when [he is] dancing / with [his] tribe during the powwow at the end of the world." This, without irony, is the essence of Alexie's vision and the hope that permeates his many painful observations of contemporary reservation life and the poverty, alcoholism, violence, confusion, and loss that infect so many of the individual lives there.

So "how did" Alexie "become this crazy / Catholic who steals the navigational flags / and races down the runway, waving at them all, all / those planes . . . frantic, wanting to know how I became like this, / just like this, wanting to bring everybody back home"?[21] "Wanting to bring everybody back home" is, in one way or the other, the spiritual yearning in everything Alexie has written. Like Egan, he understands that "All life / becomes goodbye," and his poetry, like Gioia's, offers the reader "a litany of lost things." But Catholicism is one of the "White" elements that has caused much of this loss, so why does it persist in his poetry at all, and why is it not simply emblematic of White imperial abuse of the Indian? Partly because belief, and religious belief in particular, is so much more complicated than any of us would like to admit. And partly because from whatever complex blending of beliefs and mythology Alexie speaks, he shares the common anthropological ingredients common to the Catholic vision: a sense of moral and spiritual journey, of human imperfection, of the relationship between the material and the nonmaterial world, and of the sacramental nature of things.

In his 2003 collection of short stories, *Ten Little Indians* (2003), Alexie de-

---

20. Alexie, "The Powwow at the End of the World," in *Summer of Black Widows*, 98.
21. Alexie, "Airplane," 82–83.

scribes a Native American college student named Corliss who is likely similar to himself at that age. She is "contradictory and young and confused and smart and ambitious,"[22] and in her insatiable quest to experience all things poetic, she is a reader of Gerard Manley Hopkins. One day, while trying to sneak past a couch sagging with the weight of her not-so-literary family, Corliss is stopped and interrogated by her elders: "I bet you're reading one of those white books again, enit?"[23] To answer their immediate concern that this Hopkins guy was an Indian killer, Corliss informs them that he was a Jesuit priest, causing the men to curse "with shock and disgust." Soon enough they have snatched the book away from her and are enjoying a collective mocking of the lines of poetry to which they happen to have turned: "'Glory be to God for dappled things— / For skies of couple-colour as a brindled cow.' All of the men laughed . . . 'What the hell does that mean?'" asks one of her uncles.

In the internal response of this young student to her family's ridicule, Alexie reveals the complexity of poetic response, spiritual yearning, religious belief, and the desire "to bring everybody back home":

How could she tell her father and uncles she read Hopkins precisely because he was a white man and precisely because he was a Jesuit priest? Maybe Hopkins had been an Indian killer, or a supporter of Indian killers, but he'd also been a sad and lonely and lovely man who screamed to God for comfort, answers, sleep, and peace. Since Corliss rarely found comfort from her family and friends, and never found it in God, but continued to want it and never stopped asking for it, then maybe she was also a Jesuit priest who found it in poetry . . . How could she tell her Indian family she sometimes felt like a white Jesuit priest? Who would ever believe such a thing?[24]

Who indeed? Who would believe that the Indian racing down the runway with the navigational flags is doing so, among other reasons, because he is a "crazy Catholic" longing "to bring everybody back home?"

I offer here two other Alexie poems in which his Catholic voice speaks, the first in characteristic humor and irony and the second in sacramental subtlety. Like "Airplane," both are from his 1996 collection *The Summer of Black Widows*. "How to Remodel the Interior of a Catholic Church"[25] is, as its

22. Alexie, *Ten Little Indians* (New York: Grove, 2003), 4.
23. Ibid., 13.
24. Ibid.
25. Alexie, "How to Remodel the Interior of a Catholic Church," in *Summer of Black Widows*, 85.

title says, a list of instructions that suggest what is good and what is lacking in a Catholic church. The average parish council is likely to abide only by the first recommendation that "the mute carpet must be replaced with mute carpet." Painting the walls a dark blue and leaving shoes at the door likewise seems reasonable enough perhaps, but the poet's next recommendations call for a church where the people's lives are part of rather than remote from what happens there. Face half the pews east and half of them west, he suggests: "The parishioners will be performers." No adjustment is needed in how a Catholic or a Spokane Indian reveres his elders: "Keep your favorite saint like a coin in your pocket. / Keep your favorite saint like a ringing in your ears." A mirror should be hung for "the Mohawk saint Tekakwitha" whose "smallpox scars disappeared as she died." Building nests in the rafters for the birds and sculpting candles like beautiful men and women are suggestions that are likely to raise the eyebrows and objections of the local ladies' guild, but the essence of the poet's proposals is contained in his radical idea that "The stained glass should be filled with home movies: / Junior imagines a sin, commits the sin, and then is forgiven." If we look to stained-glass windows to be inspired by God's presence among us, the suggestion is perhaps not so peculiar as it initially sounds. The sacred in the everyday, the holy imbedded within the profane, is as central to Alexie's thinking as it is Egan's and Gioia's.

This is nowhere more evident than in the sparse three stanza poem entitled "Diabetes,"[26] in which the poet reflects on the dietary caution required by his medical condition and arrives by indirection at a surprising meditation upon the Eucharist. "Having learned sugar kills me / piece by piece, I have to eat / with more sense / than taste," the poet states simply in stanza one, punning as he does so upon the various meanings of the word *sense*. Taste, of course, is one of the five senses, but surviving with diabetes requires good common sense. Since what is unseen in foods is potentially fatal, one needs to sense where the poisonous sugar might reside. Stanza two speaks to the isolation of this condition: "so I travel alone in this / limited feast, choosing / the right place / and plate." Life as a diabetic is a limited feast. So too, though, as the poems of Gioia and Egan both declare, are all of our lives. Fullness lies behind us in our elusive and embellished memories or before us in our hopes, but in the present, whether we move with

26. Alexie, "Diabetes," in *Summer of Black Widows*, 44.

caution or with recklessness, we share a common unfulfilled spiritual hunger, satiated for Catholics in the sacrament of the Eucharist. Hence, Alexie's startling final stanza: "and take the hard bread exactly / in my teeth, knowing what / the bread contains is / what contains me." The poem may remain a poem about diabetes and the hidden sugar contained in bread. However, hard bread taken exactly in the teeth suggests something more sacramental and specific, and the reader familiar with Thomas Aquinas's metaphysical explanation of the Eucharist, "Receive what you are, become what you receive," recognizes its profound paraphrase in the last eight words of this poem, where, I believe, Alexie has even improved upon the original. It is hard to say with "an Indian / who knows the difference / between Monet and Manet," whether such thought comes of reading Hopkins, whose singular preoccupation was with Christ incarnate. But it may be that, in the remodeling of Alexie's Catholic church, we are, like Corliss, all white Jesuit priests. Who would believe such a thing?

It is unlikely that Dana Gioia, Desmond Egan, and Sherman Alexie, whose poetry I have treated here, will ever have their names joined together elsewhere for the sake of literary or cultural analysis. Their lives, their works, their worlds, their very geographies are so different that one has difficulty imagining the common cultural elevator on which they might find themselves standing together, or just what they might say to each other if they did. And yet, here I have sat them down together, as it were, in the same church pew, sharing this uncomfortable but somehow still consoling confinement with the devout blue-haired church lady, the bored conscripted teenager, the restless obnoxious toddler, the angst-ridden mother, the daydreaming doubter, the well-coifed late arrival—a sacramental assemblage of human imperfections of the kind that pervade the poetry of these three men. A row of humanity. The broken body of Christ: their sins original, and yet not so much so; their lives redeemed and yet who can be certain? Filled with and yet still yearning for that elusive grace that arrives in the most ordinary and everyday occurrences. They are Catholic. They belong to a religion that Pope Benedict XVI, in a recent dialogue with priests, said has "always been considered the religion of the great *et et* [that is, both/and]: not for great forms of exclusivism, but of synthesis."[27] When theologians construct a list

---

27. Pope Benedict XVI, words spoken at a meeting of Pope Benedict XVI with the clergy of the Dioceses of Belluno-Feltre and Treviso, Church of St. Justin Martyr, Auronzo di Cadore, July 24, 2007, www .vatican.va.

of the apparent paradoxes embraced by Catholicism, it resembles the works of the poets sampled above: both physical and metaphysical, both temporal and transcendent, both broken and whole, both having and seeking, both full of joy and full of sorrow, both comprehending and resigned to everyday and eternal mysteries, both *other* and catholic, both Mexican-Italian, Gaelic, Spokane—and Catholic. "Sweet Christ!" our three poets might declare. And then ask, "Who would believe such a thing?" Then resolve, perhaps, "It is our litany, *mon vieux,* / my reader, my voyeur."

CHAPTER 9

Graham Greene's *Monsignor Quixote* ▪ A Pilgrimage of Doubt and Reason toward Faith and Belief

Michael G. Brennan

> "It was only by tilting at windmills that Don Quixote found the truth on his deathbed."
>
> —Graham Greene, *Monsignor Quixote*

The 1978 Christmas issue of the British Catholic journal *The Tablet* included a short story, "How Father Quixote Became a Monsignor," subsequently revised to become the first chapter of Graham Greene's last major novel, *Monsignor Quixote*, published in 1982. Set in post-Franco Spain, both short story and novel mischievously play with their readers' expectations of the traditional distinctions between fiction and reality by making the monsignor a direct descendant of his renowned fictional namesake in Cervantes' *Don Quixote*. A sense of amiable comedy pervades Greene's novel, which derives much of its scenic descriptions, theological discussions, and incidental details from his own leisurely summer peregrinations, replete with hampers of cheese and choice Galician wines, through the Spanish countryside with a close friend of his later years, Father Leopoldo Durán, a Catholic priest and former lecturer in English literature at the University of Madrid.[1]

In Greene's novel the unworldly Father Quixote of El Toboso is unexpectedly elevated to the rank of monsignor through the good offices of a visiting curial bishop from Rome, whose favor he gains by rescuing him from a car breakdown. Quixote hospitably shares his lunch with him (horsemeat masquerading as steak) and easily fixes his car (by filling the empty gas tank). Unimpressed by what he regards as an undeserved promotion, his local bish-

---

1. See *The Tablet*, 23/30 (Dec. 1978): 1238–41; Norman Sherry, *The Life of Graham Greene*, vol. 3: *1955–1991* (London: Jonathan Cape, 2004), 661–81; and Leopoldo Durán, *Graham Greene: Friend and Brother*, trans. Euan Cameron (London: HarperCollins, 1995), 212–30.

op pressures him into taking some leave from his parish. Quixote sets out in the company of the communist ex-mayor of the town, Enrique Zancas, whom he affectionately calls Sancho, the only other man in the village who has read Cervantes' novel. They travel around the Spanish countryside in Quixote's battered old Seat 600 car, fondly known to both of them as Rocinante after the trusty steed of Don Quixote. Drawing upon his still vibrant comedic narrative skills—honed over the preceding decades in such works as *Our Man in Havana* (1958), *Travels with My Aunt* (1969), and numerous wry short stories—Greene constructs a lively picaresque narrative based upon the traditional comic device of the innocent abroad. Replete in its dialogues with intellectual tilting at windmills, the narrative regularly leads the monsignor into potentially threatening situations, involving farcical events in a brothel and a pornographic film, hearing a confession in a public toilet, and even a police chase in which they help an escaping criminal. But, simultaneously, Quixote is protected from any detrimental moral consequences by his unwavering innocence and his firm trust in the essential decency of humanity.

Published when Greene was in his late seventies, *Monsignor Quixote* puzzled several of its earliest critics who could readily applaud its gently elegiac sense of incidental comedy and its endearing central characters but at the same time suspected that it was the work of a once great writer no longer able to grapple with the sustained intellectual and physical demands of novel writing. Given that its central protagonist is a Catholic priest, the intense skeptical questioning of issues relating to religious doubt and belief—so prominent in earlier novels such as *The Power and the Glory* (1940), *The Heart of the Matter* (1948), and *The End of the Affair* (1951)—seems almost entirely absent in *Monsignor Quixote*. Certainly, its plot continually touches upon matters of ecclesiastical authority, theological problems, and Catholic religious practices, but always, it seems, in a lighthearted tone. Yet, this essay argues, it is misleading to overlook the culminating personal and spiritual significance of this late novel to Greene's longstanding reputation as a writer fascinated by issues of Catholic doctrine and liturgy in favor of simply enjoying its picaresque narrative and likeable characters. Such a narrow perspective effectively strips away elements that seem to have steadily grown in their creator's mind to become one of the novel's most potent levels of significance. Developing, ultimately, into a meditation upon his own impending mortality, *Monsignor Quixote* marks Greene's final shift from a writer noted for his rational skepticism over faith and belief toward a more resigned and hopeful attitude, linked specifically with the Tridentine liturgy (since the monsignor dies as he enacts fragments of the Latin Mass) and an acknowledgement of the possibility of divine redemption.

Before exploring these aspects of the novel in more detail, it is important to note the remarkable contrast between the apparently carefree comic tone of the novel and the highly stressful and debilitating personal circumstances during the years (1976–82) of its composition. At this period Greene was comfortably based in his flat in Antibes but was still an indefatigable traveler and an outspoken commentator on international politics. In addition to trips to Belize, Costa Rica, and Cuba, as well as twice acting as an intermediary in political kidnappings in El Salvador, he became heavily embroiled in Panamanian politics through his friendship with its dictator, General Omar Torrijos Herrera. He even agreed to be a member of the official Panamanian delegation to Washington in 1977, when a treaty was ratified between President Carter and Torrijos in the presence of such controversial figures as Generals Pinochet of Chile, Stroessner of Paraguay, and Videla of Argentina. Greene's personal admiration for Torrijos, who was killed in a suspicious plane crash in August 1981, was loyally recorded in his *Getting to Know the General* (1984), which bravely voices the unsubstantiated rumor that the CIA had planted a bomb in his aircraft. He was also sympathetic to the cause of the Sandinista guerrillas in Nicaragua, not only visiting the country but later splitting the Spanish royalties of *Monsignor Quixote* between the Sandinistas and the monastery at Osera that features climactically in the novel as the location of the monsignor's death.[2]

The greatest strain on Greene's physical and mental state during this period, however, came from much closer to home. Yvonne Cloetta, whom he had first met in 1959, lived nearby in Antibes and became his close companion for the last twenty-five years of his life. Greene was especially fond of her eldest daughter, Martine, but from 1978 until 1984 he was drawn into increasingly acrimonious disputes with Martine's husband, Daniel Guy, from whom she was seeking a divorce and custody of their daughter, Alexandra. Convinced that Guy, who had served various prison sentences and had a deserved reputation for violence, was heavily involved in the Nice mafia and was seeking to manipulate the courts, Greene wrote impassioned letters of denunciation to the authorities and the English press. He even sought to re-

2. See Sherry, *Life of Graham Greene*, 561–97; Cedric Watts, *A Preface to Greene* (Harlow: Longman, Pearson Education, 1997), 74–81; and Durán, *Graham Greene*, 53–74.

nounce his appointment as a Chevalier of the Legion of Honour, awarded to him in 1969, when he felt that the French government was not taking prompt enough action over the matter. His defense of Yvonne Cloetta's daughter culminated in his bilingual pamphlet, *J'Accuse* (grandiosely borrowing its title from Emile Zola's intervention in the Dreyfus case), claiming the thuggish Guy was being protected by corrupt officials. Lawsuits followed, with Guy being awarded damages against Greene and his publishers. Greene had already received death threats, which he took seriously, and Father Durán, who had sought to offer him support throughout this ordeal, commented:

I knew two Grahams: one belonged to the period before 1979 and the battle with the mafia; the other, to the period afterwards. The struggle against the wretched mafia affected his nerves and his sleep more than ever . . . one had to bear in mind the colossal mental and psychological pressure on the man during those ghastly years. He was very tired and he would get upset much more easily.[3]

While, as both a novelist and an individual, Greene had usually been highly adept at compartmentalizing various aspects of his life and writings, the idea that *Monsignor Quixote* became at first an indirect and then an increasingly personal response to his own wearying trials and tribulations between 1976 and 1982 grows more feasible and understandable. The novel steadily gnaws away at the supposed potency of human rationality and skepticism in favor of a more resigned acceptance of the mysteries of divine authority and compassion. Having previously depicted in its preceding chapters the quixotic monsignor tilting at so many minor intellectual and theological windmills, the novel concludes triumphantly with him celebrating a fragmentary but deeply moving rendition of parts of the Tridentine Latin Mass. But, before considering in more detail the culminating significance of this scene, it is interesting to trace exactly how Greene manages to place his hero in such a position.

Monsignor Quixote's Second Journey

After various innocently motivated but increasingly scandalous escapades during his first period of travels, Monsignor Quixote is kidnapped at the behest of his local bishop and his secretary, Father Herrera, and forcibly brought back home. But, with the help of his trusty Sancho—the communist

3. Durán, *Graham Greene*, 83–84; see also 247–59 for a fuller account of these problems.

ex-mayor Zancas—he manages to escape in Rocinante and they head off to-gether to Galicia. Echoing Cervantes' original, this second itinerary is of a distinctly different tone than the first—not so much a picaresque excursion as an increasingly testing and dolorous pilgrimage. To avoid the attention of the Guardia, even Rocinante has been disguised by Sancho with a new set of license plates and its color changed from rusty red to bright blue. As Quixote says farewell to his loyal housekeeper, Teresa, he answers her inquiry as to where he is going with the prophetic words, "I'm going, God willing, to take a long rest in a quiet place." His concluding thoughts, however, become dis-tinctly Greeneian when he tries to assure her that, for a Christian, goodbye can never be forever: "How is it that when I speak of belief, I become aware always of a shadow, the shadow of disbelief haunting my belief?" As this last stage of the novel develops, it becomes clear that "disbelief" or doubt is an unavoidable attribute of human reason ("Doubt is human"), while the route to "belief," at least for the monsignor, is rooted in the familiar gestures and words of Catholic ceremony and liturgy.[4] This becomes especially im-portant to him when he finally reads a letter from his local bishop, which he had stuffed into his pocket and forgotten about when fleeing with the may-or. In this pompous missive, the bishop formally suspends Quixote from his priestly duties, *Suspensión a Divinis*, thereby forbidding him from saying Mass either in public or in private.[5]

The monsignor and his Sancho head into Galicia, where they visit a vine-yard to stock up on their supplies. The owner, Señor Diego, tells them of his grandson, a priest who has been driven from his parish because he would not charge the peasants a thousand pesetas for saying the Responses over the dead. This sense of the pervasive veniality of the established church es-calates when they are told of a nearby town where on that day a highly com-mercialized festival in honor of Our Lady is taking place. According to Señor Diego, the priest habitually auctions the honor of carrying her statue in the procession to the four highest bidders. Horrified by this exploitation, Quixote hurries there, only to find that this year the priest has become even greed-ier, now offering six places for auction. This traditional Catholic ceremony is so debased that the crowd is expected to plaster the statue with large-denomination banknotes and the stunned Quixote thinks, "Was it for this she saw her son die in agony? To collect money? To make a priest rich?"[6] En-

---

4. Graham Greene, *Monsignor Quixote* (Harmondsworth: Penguin, 1983), 196, 197, 205.
5. Ibid., 208.   6. Ibid., 227.

raged by this blasphemy, he is accidentally struck on the side of his head by the processional censer just as he is about to rip some of the notes from the statue. Inevitably, the statue soon comes crashing to the ground, and the procession ends in total chaos. Denounced by one of those who had paid to carry the statue as a thief, blasphemer, imposter, and communist, the bleeding and dazed Quixote is dragged away by Sancho, who drives him off toward the Trappist monastery at Osera where they hope to take sanctuary.

This fracas at the procession of the Virgin Mary, both farcical and poignant, effectively marks the end of the narrative realism of the novel. The final chapter of part two, "How Monsignor Quixote Rejoined His Ancestor," is divided into four distinct sections and shifts between a more dreamlike and elegiac mode and the concluding dramatic action of the monsignor's final picaresque journey toward his own demise. In the brief opening section, Greene provides both a literal and impressionistic description of a first glimpse of the Osera monastery. He describes its geographical location, solitary in a trough in the Galician hills with a small shop and a bar at the entrance to its grounds. The carved exterior dates from the sixteenth century and is decorated with wooden images of the popes and the knights by whose order the monastery was originally founded. As he contemplates these ancient and battered statues, the author's imagination takes flight: "They take on the appearance of life, as sad memories do, when the dark has fallen." He likens the scene to "an abandoned island" undergoing colonization by a small group of new arrivals "who are now trying to make a home in the ruins of a past civilization."[7]

The second section of this final chapter begins with the mundane concerns of a Father Leopoldo (the real name of Greene's regular traveling companion). He has just cooked an unappetizing meal for the monastery's only current guest, whose plates have been brought back virtually untouched to the kitchen by a lay brother. Through this unlikely trinity of characters, the novel's formerly rich sense of comedy briefly flickers into life once more. The unnamed lay brother is a master of transcending the Trappists' vow of silence through eloquent winks, and Father Leopoldo reveals himself as a frustrated Descartian rationalist who has somehow found himself in a monastery. Surveying the inedible remnants of the guest's meal, he ruminates that Descartes—an eminently practical man who worked on spectacles to

---

7. Ibid., 233.

assist the blind and wheelchairs for the infirm—would have known exactly how much salt to put into the soup and would not have overgrilled the
fish. More sharply satirical is the depiction of the American visiting scholar called Pilbeam, a professor of Hispanic Studies at Notre Dame University,
who is described as the greatest living authority on the life and works of the
Jesuit saint Ignatius Loyola. In reality, Pilbeam is an unimaginative, Dicken-
sonian Gradgrind-like figure ("Facts are what I like") who has no time for the
likes of Cervantes ("too fanciful for my taste").[8] He also cares little for Saint
Ignatius's spirituality and admits that he dreams only of unearthing hitherto
undiscovered factual documents about his chosen saint's life.

As Father Leopoldo and Professor Pilbeam idly discuss the difficulties
of distinguishing between fact and fiction and how each of them has come
somewhat idiosyncratically to be defined as "Catholic" (Leopoldo by way of
Descartes and Pilbeam simply because he has not bothered "to change the
label" he was born with), they hear the sounds of gunshots and a crash outside the monastery.[9] Pursued by the Guardia after their debacle at the procession of the Virgin, Monsignor Quixote and the mayor are almost at their
sanctuary when the police shoot out their tires. This causes Rocinante to
crash into the wall of the church, leaving Sancho bloodied and the semicon-
scious Quixote having to be carried into the monastery on a mattress. He is
brought into the church and up the nave on his way to a guest room, asking
expectantly if he might say a Mass, before he is given a strong sedative.

In the third section, Monsignor Quixote awakens at one o'clock in the
morning and is clearly delirious, making fantastical references to Cervantes'
characters and half-communicating with those around him. He makes his
way, followed by the mayor, Leopoldo, and Pilbeam, into the moonlit church
and then steps up to the altar to initiate a truncated version of the Tridentine Latin Mass. Through its reassuring sounds and gestures, in which his
trusty *compañero*, the communist mayor, passively receives an imaginary
communion host, Monsignor Quixote finally achieves "truth on his deathbed."[10] Greene self-consciously creates a divine comedic closure to his novel
by ending his character's priestly and earthly life within the security of the
sonorous echoes of the Tridentine liturgy (just as the author's own requiem
Mass at Westminster Cathedral after his death in 1991 was also celebrated in
Latin, according to the *Novus Ordo*). The fourth and final section of the chap-

---

8. Ibid., 237. 9. Ibid.
10. Ibid., 24.

ter concludes with Sancho and Father Leopoldo discussing whether Monsignor Quixote had really celebrated the Mass and how his petty-minded bishop had telephoned the abbot just before Quixote's death, still insisting that he was not allowed to say Mass even in private. As he leaves the monastery, Sancho wonders at the mystery of how hate for an individual (even one as grand as Franco) tends to die with their death, while love seems to live on and grow "in spite of the final separation and the final silence."[11]

"Fact and Fiction—They Are Not Always Easy to Distinguish"

While discovering traces of an author's personal beliefs and doubts within his own fictional creations is virtually inevitable, critical specificity over such matters is usually a much more elusive issue.[12] But throughout his career, Graham Greene was a writer who relished a delicately self-reflective form of writing, in which his readers seem to be challenged to spot echoes and shadows of the author's own preoccupations and previous writings. *Monsignor Quixote* is certainly no exception to this mode of composition and may even be regarded as one of the most substantial examples of how Greene used his fiction as a means of interrogating not only his own doubts and beliefs but also his earlier writings. Cloaked beneath this gentle comedy of an elderly priest's journey toward his own mortality is, it seems, the lightly disguised figure of an elderly author coming to terms with the approaching finality of both his own literary creativity and physical vigor. In spiritual terms the novel seems to suggest that this most skeptical and questioning of writers is now willing to ponder the sheer impotence of doubt itself, regarding it merely as a persistent aspect of finite human rationality.

Greene's own presence persistently haunts the action, dialogue, and thoughts of this novel. After all, if an author creates a fictional character (Monsignor Quixote) who is supposedly descended from another fictional character (Don Quixote), why cannot he himself occasionally slip in and out of the fictive narrative? Intriguingly, Roger Sharrock has suggested that the figure of the Italian curial Bishop of Motopo whose car breaks down at the beginning of the story, thereby setting in motion Monsignor Quixote's adventures, may be interpreted as that of the author himself.[13] Clearly pos-

11. Ibid., 256.
12. The quote in the heading is from ibid., 237.
13. Roger Sharrock, *Saints, Sinners and Comedians: The Novels of Graham Greene* (Tunbridge Wells: Burns and Oates, 1984), 270.

sessing Greene's own physique as a strikingly "tall man" who has to stoop down to enter Quixote's humble parlor, as well as the author's distinctively smooth facial features, the bishop also shares Greene's indulgent partiality (during his trips with Father Leopoldo Durán) to Spanish wines, cognac, and cheeses.[14] Furthermore, a curial bishop traditionally does not preside over a real see but, instead, is endowed with one of a fictional name, usually drawn from either ancient or imaginary locations in Asia Minor, while assuming whatever duties are allocated to him by the Holy Father. But Greene's choice of "Motopo" is a somewhat sly one since at least some of his well-heeled readers of the early 1980s would have readily recognized it as the Motopo region in Africa, now a national park in modern day Zimbabwe, so renowned among wealthy North American and Western European travelers for its stunning landscapes that even the arch-colonialist Cecil Rhodes himself hoped to be buried there.

If, then, this sequence of tentative hypotheses is at all feasible—and given they are prompted by the comedic pen of the game-playing Greene it is possible to doubt or accept them—the opening of the novel may be summarized as follows. Hiding behind the figure of a Mercedes-driving curial bishop, whose imaginary see is named after an Eden-like tourist venue in Africa, Greene the author briefly steps into his own fiction to visit the village of El Toboso. But even though there is a real village of this name in Spain, its choice may be yet another subtle Greeneian blending of fiction and reality. In Cervantes' version, the Don's beloved is known as Dulcinea del Toboso, although she never appears in person and seems more likely to be an idealized fiction of Don Quixote's imagination than a real woman. Greene drives home this point of comparison by noting in his own novel that Father Quixote's remarkably plain and forthright housekeeper, Teresa, had never been compared by any of the villagers to Dulcinea.[15] And, most pointedly, what does Greene gain by making his own fictional padre supposedly the actual descendant of another fictional character? While Father Quixote's obnoxious local bishop merely scoffs at this fantastical genealogical line of descent, the visiting curial bishop (perhaps disguising Greene himself), who clearly admires the imagination and vision of Cervantes, immediately enters into the sheer fun of the idea, graciously thanking his host for the honor of being a guest in Don Quixote's house.[16] As he continues to discuss Don Quix-

14. Greene, *Monsignor Quixote*, 14–15.
15. Ibid., 15.   16. Ibid.

ote with Father Quixote, who humbly reminds him that the local bishop has dismissed Cervantes' immortal creation as a mere fiction, the curial bishop wisely concludes, "Perhaps we are all fictions, father, in the mind of God."[17]

The more closely the text of *Monsignor Quixote* is scrutinized, the more self-referential Greene's narrative seems to become. Some passing references to his own writings will be obvious for most readers of his literary canon. For example, when Quixote replies to Sancho's offer of another glass of wine, "I fear if I'm not careful I shall become what I've heard called a whisky priest," any keen reader of Greene recalls the central character of *The Power and the Glory* and also, of course, notes just how innocently unlike the original "whisky priest" Monsignor Quixote really is.[18] Other indications in the novel of Greene's own reading at the time, including not only Cervantes but also St. Francis de Sales, St. Augustine, various progressive post–Vatican II theologians, and controversial responses to Pope Paul VI's *Humane Vitae* (1968) on sex and birth control by Edward Schillebeeckx and Hans Küng, merely require brief reference for clarification to standard biographical sources. But another, more discreet level of reference takes the informed reader to the very heart of Greene's spiritual and theological preoccupations while writing *Monsignor Quixote*.

"'A Girl Called Martin.' / 'She Was Your Dulcinea?'"

Three examples of this third kind of embedded referencing lie in Greene's keen awareness in this novel of the lives and writings of the mystic and originator of the austere Carmelite reform, St. Teresa of Avila (1515–82); the simple Carmelite nun, St. Teresa of Lisieux (1873–97), known as "The Little Flower"; and the Spanish philosopher and writer Miguel de Unamuno (1864–1936).[19] In each case, their influences are delicately handled, and Greene ensures that his readers do not necessarily have to be aware of their personal significance to the author to continue enjoying the picaresque progression of his characters. However, their respective impact on the culminating spiritual preoccupations of the novel is considerable. Also, they are all the more interesting in that they usefully exemplify how Greene was able to combine both lifelong (the two St. Teresas) and more recent (Unamuno) influences in his compositional processes during the final decade of his literary career.

17. Ibid., 24.   18. Ibid., 90.
19. The quote in the heading is from ibid., 104.

When an eager young priest, Father Herrera, is sent to El Toboso by the local bishop to take over Father Quixote's parish, they briefly discuss their favored religious reading. As a recent seminarian, Herrera prefers the encyclopedic authority of *Moral Theology* by the renowned German theologian Father Heribert Jone, which he views as an essential easy reference handbook for busy parish priests. In contrast, Quixote finds a far greater depth of meaning in the emotional appeal of St. John of the Cross, St. Teresa, St. Francis de Sales, and the Gospels, all of which, it may be assumed, correspond in a manner to Don Quixote's beloved volumes of chivalry.[20] The St. Teresa mentioned at this point in the novel is Teresa of Avila, since she was a friend of the young Carmelite priest, Juan de Yepes (St. John of the Cross) who instigated in 1568 the Carmelite reform for men. Later, when driving in Rocinante and stopped by the Guardia, the mayor mischievously confuses the policeman by claiming that they are on the way to Avila especially to say prayers for the Generalísimo (Franco) addressed to the ring finger of St. Teresa, which, he explains, is kept in a convent outside the city walls.[21] But once on the road again, they decide to pass by Avila since the Guardia will probably have been warned to keep an eye on them there. Instead, Quixote's mind turns to the other St. Teresa, admitting to Sancho his personal devotion to a girl called "Martin" (the family name of St. Teresa of Lisieux), whose letters had proved a great comfort to him during his struggles with the local bishop.[22] As evening draws on, they pull into the ancient city of Segovia and find a small *albergue* near the Church of St. Martin, a name that again reminds him of her. Quixote much prefers always to think of her as "Señorita Martin," rather than formally as St. Teresa or even as the Little Flower. He even chooses to pray to her under her family name, fancifully imagining that this ploy might help to catch her ear amid all the other incantations addressed to her by legions of other earnest devotees.[23]

These references to the two St. Teresas, of Avila and of Lisieux, implicitly take the author back to his earliest years as a writer during the 1920s. Greene's youthful interest in Catholicism as a student at Oxford University was prompted by meeting in the spring of 1925 his future wife, Vivienne

20. Ibid., 40.

21. Ibid., 95. Durán, *Graham Greene*, 134–35 recounts their visit in July 1976 to the Convent of the Incarnation, where the relic of St. Teresa's ring finger is preserved: "the finger with which she wrote her wonderful books." Franco, a pious Roman Catholic, kept Teresa's hand as a holy relic by his bedside until his death in 1975.

22. Greene, *Monsignor Quixote*, 104.

23. Ibid., 105.

(usually shortened to Vivien) Dayrell-Browning, herself a recent convert to the Catholic faith. After a secret engagement in September of that year, he took instruction and became a communicant of the Roman Catholic Church in February 1926. Graham and Vivien were married on October 15, 1927, at St. Mary's Catholic Church, Hampstead. As their marriage invitation specified, "The Mass is that appointed for the Feast of Saint Teresa, Carmelite (Oct. 15)," namely the sixteenth-century St. Teresa of Avila and the saint to whom Sancho proposed to offer prayers for Franco.[24] Vivien was a devout Roman Catholic, as Graham himself also aspired to be during the early years of their union, and she would certainly have honored the saint on whose feast her own marriage had been celebrated. But perhaps of even more spiritual importance to their early married years was a shared interest in the life and canonization of that other Carmelite nun of exceptional devotional zeal and spiritual purity, St. Teresa of Lisieux.

The life of this St. Teresa was already well known in England through a collection of her epistolary essays, written at the order of her prioress and first published in 1898 under the title *Histoire d'une âme* (in English, *Story of a Soul*). These are the letters that Father Quixote read with such devotion during his persecution by his own local bishop. The most popular English translation by Ronald Knox was published by the Harvill Press in 1958 as the *Autobiography of a Saint: Thérèse of Lisieux*. Vivien Greene's own copy of this publication has survived, and inside she carefully preserved until her death in September 2003 various newspaper clippings about St. Teresa, including a copy of the photograph taken (probably by one of Teresa's sisters) in 1886 and the widely known one taken by Teresa's sister Céline in June 1897, four months before the saint's death.[25] Graham had first met Vivien a few weeks prior to the saint's canonization in May 1925, and he was fascinated by the processes of hagiography promulgating the cult of, as Father Quixote habitually refers to her, "Señorita Martin of Lisieux."[26] In particular, his imagination was caught by the ceremony at St. Peter's in Rome in May 1925 celebrating her canonization. The Carmelites of her own convent at Lisieux produced for this event an immense painted banner—reputedly designed by Teresa's sister, Céline (Soeur Geneviève)—depicting the apotheo-

24. This wedding invitation is reproduced in Norman Sherry, *The Life of Graham Greene*, vol. 1: *1904–1939* (London and Toronto: Jonathan Cape and Lester and Orpen Denys, 1989), 353.

25. *Waterfield's Vivien and Graham Greene Centenary Catalogue* (Oxford: Waterfield's Antiquarian Booksellers, 2004, lot 971); in possession of the author.

26. Greene, *Monsignor Quixote*, 244.

sis of the saint surrounded by a semicircle of angels *(putti)*. As I have argued elsewhere, Greene used this image as inspiration for the depiction of his impregnably virtuous heroine, Elizabeth, in his first published novel, *The Man Within* (1929). In this novel, the angels are converted into doves (which were also associated with the cult of St. Teresa of Lisieux), and his hero, Andrews, fondly recalls a childhood memory of "a pictured saint, a young girl with a pale, set face, round whose head a flock of doves turned and twisted."[27]

At this point, it might be reasonably asked how closely Greene's spiritual interests in the late 1920s may be linked to those of the late 1970s when he begin writing *Monsignor Quixote*. Is it really possible that his fascination with the cult of a young French saint could have still preoccupied him almost forty years later? Fortunately, due to Greene's self-referential literary habits as a writer, it can be readily demonstrated that not only the image of St. Teresa but also the central plot and characterization of *The Man Within* were all very much in his mind during his late seventies and eighties. His last novel-length work to be published during his lifetime was *The Captain and the Enemy* (1988), which was partly set in the Panama of General Torrijos. The young hero of the novel falls into the company of an older man, a slippery trickster type of character who eventually dies in an unsuccessful attempt (betrayed by the CIA) to bomb President Somoza of Nicaragua. As already noted, Greene's interests in the dangerous world of South American politics, leading to much of the plot of *The Captain and the Enemy*, ran alongside the genesis of the apparently gentle comedy of *Monsignor Quixote*. Furthermore, a comparison of the hero and heroine of both *The Man Within* and *The Captain and the Enemy* reveals just how powerfully the preoccupations of his first published novel were lingering in his mind as he composed the last of his novels to appear in print before his death in 1991.

In a striking act of self-reflective circularity and authorial closure, Greene's last work is rich in echoes of his first published novel. The hero of *The Man Within*, Andrews, escapes from a hated school life and meets a mercurial seafaring smuggler, Carlyon. In *The Captain and the Enemy*, the young hero Jim Baxter also falls into the company of a mysteriously attractive figure, known as the Captain, who takes him away from his uncongenial school life. (Both incidents implicitly refer to Greene's own discontent at Berkham-

---

27. Graham Greene, *The Man Within* (London: William Heinemann, 1929), 142. See my "Graham Greene's Catholic Conversion: The Early Writings (1923–29) and *The Man Within*," *Logos* 9, no. 3 (2006): 134–57.

sted School where his father, Charles Greene, was headmaster.) Carlyon and the Captain have much in common in the admiring eyes of their respective young companions, even if the former operates as a smuggler along the familiar Sussex shoreline during the early 1800s while the latter is drawn into the world of espionage and political conspiracies of the Sandinista guerrillas of Nicaragua during the late 1970s and 1980s.

Two mysteriously iconic young women dominate the emotional and spiritual sensibilities of Andrews and Baxter. In the early novel, Elizabeth pointedly lacks a solidly fleshed out character and seems intended more to embody a sense of unwavering moral certainty and virtuous self-sufficiency. As a resolute and clear-thinking young woman of unassailable and apparently almost saint-like purity, Elizabeth overtly recalls the potent innocence of St. Teresa of Lisieux, as she lives a nun-like existence in a small cottage set within the pastoral isolation of the Sussex Downs. In *The Captain and the Enemy,* this inspirational role is taken by Liza (a pointed modernization of her counterpart's name from the 1929 novel), who also lives a solitary, nun-like existence, but this time, as befits the 1980s context, in an urban basement flat in Camden Town. The figure of St. Teresa of Lisieux seems to stand visibly behind both young women who are placed, both metaphorically and spiritually, above the adventure-story narratives of their respective novels. It seems as though in seeking to create an idealized female figure for his last published novel, Greene instinctively turned back to the ideal of female virtue upon which his first St. Teresa–like heroine had been based in the late 1920s. Hence, Father Quixote's personal devotion to "Señorita Martin of Lisieux"[28] becomes not only an echo of Greene's own two novels of 1929 and 1988 but also perhaps a poignant remembrance of his courtship of his wife Vivien and their shared interest in the canonization of St. Teresa of Lisieux.

"There Was One Professor with a Half-Belief"

One last major source for the philosophical and spiritual contexts of *Monsignor Quixote* may be briefly examined to confirm the richness and diversity of Greene's Catholic imagination during this final period of his creative literary life.[29] As a boy, Father Quixote had dreamt of studying at the University of Salamanca although, as he discusses with the visiting curial bishop at the

---

28. Greene, *Monsignor Quixote,* 244.   29. Quote in heading is from ibid., 110.

opening of the novel, its entry standards then seemed well beyond him.[30] Naturally, he is very pleased when on his travels in Rocinante with Sancho they leave Segovia to pay a visit to Salamanca, although as Quixote arrives there he is still not aware of the true purpose of their "pilgrimage."[31] The emphasis here upon an unintended "pilgrimage" is an interesting one in that it is motivated by Sancho, his communist traveling companion. Quixote eagerly looks forward to visiting the university lecture room in which St. John of the Cross listened to the teachings of Fray Luis de León. Once again happily blending reality with fiction, Quixote amuses himself to think that Fray Luis might have even personally known Don Quixote, if the knightly travels of Cervantes' hero had ever taken him to Salamanca.

The real reason for their visit becomes clear when the mayor admits that he had himself once studied there and attended the lectures of Miguel de Unamuno y Jugo, the renowned Spanish author and philosopher who was professor of Greek at the University of Salamanca and became its rector in 1901, serving in this post intermittently until his death in 1936. Like Greene, Unamuno was preoccupied in his writings with the tensions between reason and the Christian faith and, in his most famous work *The Tragic Sense of Life* (included on the *Index Librorum Prohibitorum* until the Second Vatican Council), with the finality of human mortality, a tragedy that cannot be fully justified or comprehended by reason alone. Similarly, just as Greene involved himself in struggles with the Nice mafia and with supporting the Sandinista guerrillas in Nicaragua, so Unamuno never hesitated to compromise his own safety and public position in the cause of his political beliefs. He first lost his post as rector of the university in 1914 for political reasons and again in 1924, when he was exiled to Fuerteventura in the Canary Islands for publicly opposing the military dictatorship of General Primo de Rivera. He lived as a political exile in Paris and the French Basque town of Hendaye until Rivera's death in 1930. Returning to Salamanca, he was reappointed as rector in 1931 and took up a chair in the history of the Spanish language. But once again, in 1936, he was denounced and removed from his post, this time because of his unwavering opposition to Franco's Falangists. He was placed under house arrest but died on December 31 of that year in Salamanca, soon after the outbreak of the Spanish Civil War.

Based upon his own visit with Father Durán, Greene takes his readers of *Monsignor Quixote* to visit the little house in an obscure square at Sala-

---

30. Ibid., 23.   31. Ibid., 109.

manca where Unamuno died, now fronted by a commemorative stone bust of the philosopher, "the hooded eyes expressing the fierceness and the arrogance of individual thought."[32] Quixote and Sancho also visit Unamuno's grave in the cemetery on the extreme edge of the city. Unlike Franco's grandiose mausoleum in the so-called Valley of the Fallen, which they had previously visited with some distaste, Unamuno's final resting place turns out, much to the monsignor's approval, to be a simple box, denoted only by the "number 340," in a long white wall of modest burial caskets.[33] In his semiautobiographical work *Ways of Escape* (1980), Greene recorded that he had read one of Unamuno's most imaginative and stimulating works, *The Life of Don Quixote and Sancho* (1905), in which comparisons are made between the life of the founder of the Jesuit order, Ignatius of Loyola, and Cervantes' heroic knight, who seems in Unamuno's version to be endowed with almost Christlike qualities. The readers of *Monsignor Quixote* are pointedly reminded of this connection at the end of the novel when Father Leopoldo tells Professor Pilbeam at the monastery of Osera that "one of our great modern philosophers compared Saint Ignatius to Don Quixote. They had a lot in common."[34]

Graham Greene also had much in common with Miguel Unamuno.[35] Both men consistently questioned the ultimately irreconcilable tension between reason and faith, and they both considered that doubt was an essential tool in the pursuit of belief. Like Greene, Unamuno argued for the centrality of suffering to both the human condition and the pursuit of a restorative belief in the workings of an absolute God. In *The Tragic Sense of Life,* he argued for a faith in a suffering God in terms that seem entirely applicable to Greene's own personal preoccupations during the late 1970s. Furthermore, Unamuno's thoughts are relevant not only to a late work such as *Monsignor Quixote* but also to several key novels from earlier periods of Greene's career, all of which highlight the tension between doubt and belief, including *The Power and the Glory, The Heart of the Matter,* and *The End of the Affair.* As Unamuno explains:

Suffering tells us we exist; suffering tells us those who love exist; suffering tells us the world we live in exists; and suffering tells us that God exists and suffers;

---

32. Ibid., 111.   33. Ibid., 86–87.
34. Ibid., 237.
35. See Mark Bosco, SJ, *Graham Greene's Catholic Imagination* (Oxford: Oxford University Press, 2005), 141–43. Greene refers to his reading of Unamuno in *Ways of Escape* (London: Bodley Head, 1980), 257–58. See also Durán, *Graham Greene,* 47 and 136 for Greene's keen rereading of Unamuno and their discussion of his theory that Cervantes had derived his inspiration for Don Quixote from St. Ignatius Loyola. Durán, *Graham Greene,* 126–28, 212, and 300 also provides informative accounts of their visits to Unamuno's tomb.

and this is the suffering of anguish, the anguish to survive and be eternal. It is anguish which reveals God to us and makes us place our love in Him. To believe in God means to love Him, and to love Him is to sense His suffering and have compassion for Him.[36]

Viewed in this light, Monsignor Quixote's travels with his friend the communist ex-mayor of El Toboso ultimately become an allegory of a personal pilgrimage toward death, gently tinged with a nascent hope in the possibility of another life. Typically with Greene, however, there is no absolutely firm and comfortably reassuring conclusion to the novel's spiritual questionings. As Quixote, still dazed from his car accident and heavily drugged, struggles to offer a truncated echo of the Tridentine Mass, he oscillates wildly between gobbets of Latin and his own tongue. He tries to repeat for one last time his garbled mantra: "By this hopping you can recognize love,"[37] a phrase in which, poignantly, the spiritual efficacy of "hoping" is confused with farcical "hopping."[38] In fact, much of his speech in his native tongue now slips into Babel-like confusion ("Lamb of God, but the goats, the goats"),[39] but in contrast, key phrases from the liturgy of the Latin Mass remain crystal clear in his mind (*"Hoc est enim corpus meum," "Hic est enim calix sanguinis mei," "Agnus Dei qui tollis peccata mundi,"* etc.). With Quixote's last coherent words, Greene allows his humble parish priest and comically unwilling monsignor to enact the central moment of the sacrament of communion, intoning the words *"Corpus Domini nostri"* before taking the invisible host on his tongue and raising the invisible chalice to drink some of the invisible wine. In his last few moments of life, Quixote places another invisible communion host on the tongue of his *compañero* the mayor and, with his priestly duties complete, his heart stops beating as he is gently eased to the floor in the arms of his beloved Sancho. However each reader chooses to interpret this final scene, it seems that its author has finally decided to allow the invisible power of a sacramentalized drama to supersede the illusory potency of human reason and doubt.

36. Miguel Unamuno, *The Tragic Sense of Life in Men and Nation*, trans. Anthony Kerrigan (Princeton, N.J.: Princeton University Press, 1972), 226–27; quoted in Bosco, *Graham Greene's Catholic Imagination*, 141.

37. Greene, *Monsignor Quixote*, 246, 250.

38. Greene may also be echoing here Unamuno's emphasis on the importance of hope in *The Tragic Sense of Life:* "We do not hope because we believe, but rather we believe because we hope" (quoted in Bosco, *Graham Greene's Catholic Imagination*, 129).

39. Greene, *Monsignor Quixote*, 249.

CHAPTER 10

Contemporary British Catholic Writers ▪ Alice Thomas Ellis, Piers Paul Read, William Brodrick, and Jonathan Tulloch

J. C. Whitehouse

Despite an ongoing and widespread distrust of Catholicism, Britain in the mid–eighteen hundreds was no longer the Protestant police state it had been in the worst penal years. The second half of the eighteenth century and the early decades of the nineteenth saw the growth of a more tolerant climate of opinion and the consequent introduction of certain reforms. Against a background of significant if not total political and social reform epitomized by the Catholic Emancipation Act of 1829, and as a result of a religion strengthened by the restoration of the Catholic hierarchy in 1851 and the consolidating and unifying effects of the First Vatican Council (1869–70), Catholics in Britain acquired a new confidence and were inclined to make their presence felt more forcefully. In these circumstances the new and vigorous phenomenon of a specifically Catholic literature began to appear. Increased confidence and newer ways of picturing Catholic thoughts, feelings, motives, aspirations, fears, and anxieties became apparent in English literature as in English life. The growth of a specifically Catholic English literature has been chronicled systematically and in-depth in Ian Ker's *The Catholic Revival in English Literature, 1845–1961* (2003) and in a wider ranging and more general fashion in Thomas Woodman's *Faithful Fictions: The Catholic Novel in British Literature* (1991) and Joseph Pearce's survey, *Literary Giants, Literary Catholics* (2005). From John Henry Newman onward (despite what he said about the impossibility of a specifically Catholic English literature), such writing was to blossom for over a century, moving gradually back into the mainstream of English literary life. In the first half of the twentieth century in particular, Chesterton, Belloc, Greene, Waugh, and their Catholic contemporaries have been dominant figures, widely read and discussed by

Catholics and non-Catholics alike. The Second Spring for the Church Newman had spoken of had arrived, to be followed by the high summer of the middle years of the twentieth century. There are some signs, however, that in the fiction of the last decades of the twentieth and the early years of the twenty-first centuries, Catholic writing has undergone a marked change in approach and tone, moving, as Catholicism itself has moved, toward a new, outward-looking, more accommodating and less exclusively monolithic position.

It is not easy to say whether the Second Vatican Council (1962–65) was the cause or the consequence of such a shift, but at least it put it sharply into focus at both the lay and clerical levels. The ideas and sensibilities of many contemporary Catholics are not the same as those of an earlier generation. There has been, for example, a movement away from the idea of man as an individual in a unique relationship with his Creator to a new appreciation of existential freedom and, ultimately, to an image of the human being as a nexus of social relationships. Catholics are often no longer readily distinguishable from their neighbors, and their Church appears not so very unlike other socially active institutions. Moreover, the emphasis of what that Church teaches has also shifted. In earlier generations, the most important element of Catholic teaching was a stress on the individual seeking his own salvation and the importance of the Four Last Things, namely Death, Judgment, Heaven, and Hell. Over the last few decades, that emphasis has weakened, and the idea of personal sin and the necessity of contrition and a serious purpose of amendment no longer dominate the Catholic mind. In their place, it seems, is a common assumption among Catholics that on the whole they are not too bad and might well all go to heaven. What all this means in terms of literature is a new view of human living and a Catholic literature that, as Newman said it would, "resembles the literature of the day."[1] At one level, some contemporary Catholic literature is not an improving literature. Self-control, the search for purity, and ascetic practice are not overtly praised or preached (see, for example, Andrew O'Hagan's *Be Near Me* (2006) or David Lodge's fiction as a whole, where such concerns seem irrelevant). In addition, after Vatican II, in literature as in life, there has been in the Catholic mindset a marked incidence of what we might call the "desacralization" of places (church buildings, which are often no longer places of silence, med-

1. John Henry Newman, *The Idea of a University* (New York: Holt, Rinehart and Winston, 1960), 246.

itation, and prayer), and persons (the priest, who is at best nowadays often more of a "regular guy" than the separate and special figure he once was, and at worst a rather unrepentant sinner).

But the outlook is not altogether gloomy. There are still Catholic novelists whose work is marked by Catholic insights and faith, whose compensatory hallmark remains a rich and profound exploration of the complexities of the interior life in its individuality beyond the simplistic abstraction of official formulations and moral treatises. This insight gained through literature is to be welcomed, said Pope Paul VI in a 1967 allocution to writers: "We are not asking of you that you should play the part of moralists. We are only asking you to have confidence in your mysterious power of opening up the glorious regions of light that lie behind the mystery of man's life."[2] Illuminating the mystery of human life and the light that can lie behind it is still the hallmark of the true Catholic novelist. In fact, several recent British Catholic writers have not sacrificed the older and more visible orthodoxy in its depth and rigor and have thus to some degree swum against the contemporary tide. Two of these, Alice Thomas Ellis (1932–2005) and Piers Paul Read (1941–), are well worth considering as a real link between what we might call "classical" Catholic fiction and its later developments in the works of the younger generation of authors like William Brodrick (1960–) and Jonathan Tulloch (1968–).

There are several ways of defining Catholic writers. In simple, but not simplistic, terms, we could say that they are believing and practicing Catholics whose faith to a varying but recognizable degree informs and shapes their work thematically, imaginatively, aesthetically, and perhaps to some degree ideologically. Such authors are Catholic writers in a way in which non-Catholics writing about Catholic people, places, events, beliefs, and attitudes, or Catholics whose work is not noticeably informed by their beliefs, are not. Believing and practicing Catholics imbued with a Catholic worldview are the subject of this chapter. But since the four authors explored here are Catholics writing for the contemporary world, they are in some ways different from their predecessors. A new openness to the world and the consequent reflection on modern thinking have produced changes, or at least a marked difference of emphasis, in Catholic attitudes, anthropology, catechetics, and practices.

2. Quoted in Austin Flannery, OP, ed., *Vatican Council II: The Conciliar and Post-Conciliar Documents* (Wilmington, Del.: Scholarly Resources, 1975), 312.

■ ■ ■

Alice Thomas Ellis (whose real name was Anna Margaret Haycraft) was born in Liverpool in 1932 and educated in Bangor, Wales. The daughter of humanist parents, members of the Church of Humanity founded by Auguste Comte, she decided in her late teens that she could no longer disbelieve in God and promptly became a Catholic, remaining an ardently practicing one of the pre–Vatican II variety until her death in 2005. Her career as a writer of fiction began in 1977 with the publication of her first novel, *The Sin Eater,* which marked the arrival of a new and often disturbing talent and set the pattern and atmosphere of her subsequent work, a characteristic blend of psychological perception, tightly controlled and very felicitously effective language, satire, a rather baleful examination of human foibles, an intransigent, if sometimes no more than implied, and to varying degrees pervading, Catholicism, and moments of impressive and illuminating insight.

The Sin Eater is an appropriate starting point for readers of Ellis's fiction. It is a gem. In the big house, near what was once a pleasant, decorous, middle-class Welsh holiday resort but which now serves a new and resolutely plebeian clientele, its head, the old Captain, lies upstairs waiting to die. When he does, his loathsome housekeeper Phyllis will, it is said, serve the funeral baked meats on his chest and then eat the crumbs, together with his sins, according to what is allegedly the old Welsh custom. The family consists of Henry, the Captain's eldest son, whose misanthropic wife Rose, a lapsed Catholic of Irish descent, scorns the whole of humanity except her adored twins; a second son, Michael, an idle and feckless homosexual with a snobbish and lecherous wife, Angela; and Ermyn, the youngest child and only daughter, vapid, fearful and retiring, and sickened by human evil. There is also a visitor, a drunken journalist called Edward, and the housekeeper's spoiled, slovenly, and slothful son, Gomer. The acerbic Rose, whose sharp and ruthless observations provide a pitiless gloss on the people and events of the book, is the dominant character. Rootless and set somewhat apart because of her slightly disreputable background, she is further marginalized by her status as a Catholic, but also as a Catholic who feels betrayed and abandoned by her Church, which, she believes, has stopped being what it once was and seems to have renounced its mission. She lives in a world where there is nothing to do on Sundays since the pope went mad.

Paradoxically, the author's hard and brilliant pessimism is a joy. Rose's stoical and sharp lucidity both ridicule the crassness and boredom of existence and make it more bearable. Wit, scorn, and caustic comment may be all she offers, but she presents them with the grace and beauty of a keen and subtle intelligence and a refined and chiseled prose. Perhaps her elegant stream of full and witty consciousness achieves what Freud claimed for psychoanalysis, namely that it changes an irrational melancholia into a rational unhappiness. In both cases, the method is the same. The distress perturbing us is exteriorized, examined, and named, and thus to some extent controlled. The wit and style of the novel fortify the reader. The great pleasure it gives stems from the recognition of an honest and perceptive mind overcoming the howling desert of the world with the power of controlled, precise, and evocative language.

The linguistic vigor often shakes us, sometimes by leading us along a familiar and easy path toward the expected and comforting cliché, and then, suddenly and economically, perhaps with a single word, shattering the mood. It is usually when Rose is at her most curious and active that she is particularly prone to making barbed comments, but they are always in the air, spoken, thought, or hinted at. And she is generous with them, extending her malice even-handedly to all her assembled kin, to their relationships with each other, their tastes, prejudices, and preferences. Characters are summed up in neat sentences combining sharp observation and intriguing malice. Conversation is initiated, engineered, and sustained by Rose to annoy, disturb, and humiliate her relatives. There are tart little sketches of the wet-lipped Angela cooingly approving Edward's every drunken pronouncement or action and occasionally giving him a not very successful come-on.

Class and the less endearing cultural foibles of the English, Welsh, and Irish are similarly given short shrift. The seaside town is now full of moronic proletarian yobs, with a smaller number of depressingly respectable artisans. The English are castigated, the Welsh are assigned derogatory nicknames, and unseemly things are thought about the Irish. Rose is also an outstanding coat-trailer, producing a lively parody of Edward's more arcane and contradictory pontifications (on Freud, Fraud, Freudulent conversion, psycho-Semitic problems, and the primal scene). At its conclusion, she irritates Angela by remarking upon how little the latter had been taught at Roedean, when both of them are fully aware that she had never darkened the doors of that august institution. Yet Rose's angriest, longest (three pages), and most telling outburst in the novel is not directed against individuals but against her Church, which in other circumstances might have been the pivot of her life, but has, she maintains, abandoned her. Here, as has been the case with many disturbed Catholics, we may be at the heart of her problem. And so the jaundiced, bilious eye travels all round its field of vision. The opening dreamlike sequences of the novel contrast starkly with the waking reality, captured in intense, vivid pictures of the new housing estate, the housekeeper's ugly modern bungalow, and the building site, which is the self-expression of a mediocre architect. Together they form a setting for an inner landscape of disappointment and deep dislike, in which we can have no lasting abode, and to which, in immediate human terms, a savage humor is the only possible riposte.

That first fine and careless rapture, the sensibility, malice, and wit encapsulated in an intellectually lucid and emotionally persuasive prose, is stimulating and challenging, both aesthetically and religiously. Ellis's subsequent novels also incorporate a cool and often merciless look at the social, sexual, and ideological environment her characters inhabit, the most lucid and perceptive of whom find it alienating. Somewhere, they sense, there must be another place, another world, where things would be similar but better, more meaningful and satisfying. Ellis's second novel, *The Birds of the Air* (1980), a bleak look at the dark places of a Christmas gathering, is to some degree a picture of purgatory, enlightened only by the grace, polish, and aesthetic distinction of her language. From time to time in her writing, however, as in *The Inn at the Edge of the World* (1990), Ellis provides a glimpse, despite the usual cast of misfits, self-deceivers, fools, and hopeless incompetents, of an attempt to shape life, in Sartrian jargon, into meaningful being rather than simply to exist, formlessly and futilely. The existentialist sage and the deeply traditionalist Catholic may have little in common, but they are both acutely aware of the shapelessness that characterizes unredeemed life.

All of Ellis's fiction is similar in the sense that she is preoccupied with certain themes, and her novels often contain a suggestion of the macabre and the supernatural. Works like *The 27th Kingdom* (1982), *The Other Side of the Fire* (1983), and *Unexplained Laughter* (1985) all leave the reader with an indefinable but tangible sense of a divine presence behind the rather dreary everyday reality. Her important series *The Summerhouse Trilogy*, comprising the three novels *The Wardrobe* (1987), *The Skeleton in the Cupboard* (1988), and *The Fly in the Ointment* (1989), is deeply concerned with infidelity, betrayal, the search for the wholeness of a bruised, wounded, and almost destroyed psyche, and the falsity of some self-concepts. In Britain, the trilogy was successfully filmed for BBC television. To the end of her career as a writer of fiction, Ellis maintained, in such works as *The Inn at the Edge of the World* and *Pillars of Gold* (1992), her satirical look at the desperately feckless lives of women in an anonymous and deeply unsatisfactory urban world. These works, her collection of stories *The Evening of Adam* (1944), and a novel about the unexplained appearance of a strange newborn baby, *Fairy Tale* (1996), all perpetuate the strange, fearsome, and yet oddly bracing and deeply compelling fictional world she had so brilliantly created in *The Sin Eater.*

Alice Thomas Ellis is certainly no apologist for contemporary Catholicism and no creator of (in the narrow sense) improving tracts. Nevertheless, her work is marked to varying degrees by Catholic insights, beliefs, and practices (or in some cases refusals to practice). Throughout her fiction we hear intermittently of characters whose families have been Catholic since the earliest times and still have traces of that inheritance. We also see those who have lost their faith by lapsing from it or rejecting it altogether. Perhaps, as a disheartened, disappointed, old-fashioned Catholic, she is simply presenting a jaundiced view of the world to suggest its more meaningful and satisfying opposite. After all, there are many ways of being a Catholic. Using a critical mind can be one of them and may be a better basis for faith than an uncritical total acceptance. Rose's scolding of the Church is clearly infinitely more faithful than the passive and very dubious hook, line, and sinker assent epitomized, for example, by Rex Mottram in Evelyn Waugh's *Brideshead Revisited.*

What is more of a problem is the conflict between, on the one hand, Ellis's attitudes toward her fellow human beings and the dreary society they both create and inhabit and, on the other hand, the charity we are all called upon to practice. That her novels work admirably in that they are witty, amusing, and provocative is clear. What is more puzzling is her hard-heartedness. Like many intelligent, aesthetically and critically minded people, she is at her best when she is at her worst. Satire—and she is certainly often a satirist—exaggerates what it ridicules in order to evoke something that is missing. Ellis is not simply a misanthropist, for her descriptions of human life in the here and now represent an awareness of the fact that it is impossible to create a sinless literature about sinful human beings. Wit can be deeply enjoyable for its own sake, an end in itself as all great pleasures are, and a useful correction for illusion, self-deception, sentimentality, and bland self-satisfaction.

Ellis's hard-hitting and often intolerant nonfictional work offers an insight into her fiction. No one could accuse her of appealing niceness, modernism, or wishy-washy liberalism. It is worth reading her highly polemical *Serpent on the Rock: A Personal View of Christianity* (1994), a scathing attack on the more foolishly applied reforms introduced by Vatican II and their effects on subsequent generations of Catholics. In both her fiction and her polemical writing, Ellis was always intelligent, unafraid, unwilling to suffer fools, a scourge of sentimentality and self-deception, and of course totally intolerant. In all her works, she wrote like an angel, even if the polished grace and wit in her novels are perhaps more attractive than her incandescent polemics.

A second older-generation Catholic writer is Piers Paul Read, born in Beaconsfield, Buckinghamshire, in 1941, who describes himself as a believing and practicing Catholic coming from a not-particularly-Catholic background.[3] He sees himself as Catholic writer, and not simply as a Catholic who writes, since in his opinion his Catholic beliefs have affected almost everything he has written. Catholicism, he suggests, can provide illumination and color in writing. It can be more than merely a literary device that enables confrontation and conflict; rather, it may pave a way toward knowledge and understanding. In Read's view, Catholic novels should not be polemical or even apologetic, but the insights they provide may change the reader and can be both a mirror to life and a means of changing society, since the overriding objective is to tell the truth. His collection of essays, *Hell and Other Destinations* (2006), which raises such matters, includes a reflection on the dilemma of the Catholic novelist.

Read's fiction is varied and the list long and impressive, including *The Junkers* (1968; winner of the Sir Geoffrey Faber Memorial Prize), *Monk Dawson* (1969; winner of the Hawthornden Prize and the Somerset Maugham Award; filmed 1997), *The Upstart* (1973), *A Married Man* (1979; televised 1983), *The Free Frenchman* (1986; televised 1989), *A Season in the West* (1988; winner of the James Tait Black Memorial Prize), *A Patriot in Berlin* (1995), *Knights of the Cross* (1997), *Alice in Exile* (2001), and *The Death of a Pope* (2009). He has also written several television plays and a radio play. His nonfictional output is equally impressive, including investigative journalism in such works as *Alive* (1974; filmed 1992), *Quo Vadis: The Subversion of the Catholic Church* (1991), *Ablaze: The Story of Chernobyl* (1991), and a biography, *Alec*

---

3. Personal e-mail from Piers Paul Read to the author, dated February 21, 2007.

Guiness (2003), the authorized life of the English Catholic actor. *Quo Vadis* provides a clear idea of the sort of Catholic Read is and a hard-hitting analysis of what he sees as the failings of the institutional Church.

All of Read's fiction has received favorable attention in the British press, with reviews ranging from the respectful to the enthusiastic, and the televised versions of several novels have been competent and faithful. Critics like his fellow (non-Catholic) novelist Malcolm Bradbury have spoken highly of his intelligence and his ability to disturb his readers, an ability that arises from what Marion E. Crowe calls his "psychomachia," by which she means his depiction of the human psyche as the battleground of the eternal struggle with the world, the flesh, and the devil, where the clash of corrupt human desires and the demands of an unyielding God are in perpetual conflict.[4] Read uses his considerable skills to create a kind of fiction both appealing to contemporary tastes and dramatically challenging to Christian readers. His writing is strongly traditional, with a clear and readily comprehensible plot, well-drawn and often extremely interesting characters, and a strong dose of lively and convincing realism. His settings vary widely—England, France, Poland, the United States, Israel, Russia—and the physical world, in all its quiddity and charm, is beautifully rendered. This world may not be our lasting abode, but it has its attractions. It is, however, full of temptations, offering again and again the occasions of sin, usually sexual sin. Disordered sexuality and the concomitant disordering of the human psyche feature largely in Read's fiction, creating squalor, dissension and, in purely human terms, irreparable devastation. Yet there is often also a movement toward God, initiated by a deep sense of shame and disgust. What marks all Read's work is a very traditional Catholic viewpoint, Augustinian to a certain extent, a way of seeing human life tinged by a faith and a morality that together deeply permeate a carefully created mental and imaginative world, whether the characters are faithful Catholics or somewhere between faith and unbelief.

Unfashionably, Read's fiction is concerned, however indirectly, and however immersed in the everyday world the characters may be, with the spiritual development of the protagonists. His work includes plenty of occasionally striking but never pornographic sex, and compelling pictures of the ways in which the world tempts various kinds of people. The three novels that have

---

4. Marion E. Crowe, "A Modern Psychomachia: The Catholic Fiction of Piers Paul Read," *Christianity and Literature* 47, no. 3 (1998): 309ff.

received most attention are *Monk Dawson, The Upstart,* and *A Married Man,* dealing respectively with the laicization and subsequent debauchery of a young priest (and his ultimate redemption), the deep and rancorous class hatred of a hypersensitive man of humble birth who uses depravity as a release but is ultimately drawn to conversion by self-loathing, and the potential breakdown and hence dangerously provocative nature of a stable but boring marriage. In all three, the existential mess that the characters make of their lives is the beginning of a long, tortuous, and painful road to salvation.

The setting of *A Season in the West,* which Read has described as his most Catholic take on life, is largely the London of the 1980s. Josef Birek, a young dissident Czech writer and a Catholic, has crossed through Yugoslavia into Austria, asking the British embassy there to allow him to go to England. His British admirers support his application, and his English translator, Laura Morton, who has also written an essay on his work and has a job at the Comenius Foundation, a London foundation for Czech exiles, meets him when he arrives at Heathrow. A nice but rather innocent thirty-nine-year-old with three children, married to a merchant banker, Laura is immediately struck by Birek's combination of naïveté and certainty. In the Mortons' rather freewheeling circle of friends, one particular serial seducer, Charlie Eldon, is making an unhurried, deliberate, and calculated play for the rather guileless Laura. The two of them manage to obtain political asylum for Birek. Eventually, Laura persuades her husband to allow Birek to stay at their house, where a liaison soon develops between Laura and Birek. Laura's husband gathers what is going on, as does Charlie Eldon, as Laura half-delightedly knows. Meanwhile, Birek becomes deeply appalled by smart London society and, as the affair inevitably begins to cool, the loneliness he has always felt becomes more intense. Sex between the lovers becomes rapid and almost casual. The final breaking point comes when Laura's Mercedes is vandalized outside the cheap apartment she has found for Birek. In a fury, she stops paying his rent and writes to say that the affair is over. He tries to contact her only to find that she has left the country. Dunned for his rent, Birek sinks into despair, wretched and penniless. His not-very-robust Catholicism fails, and he finds prayer impossible. In his deep distress, he tries to commit suicide on the Underground, but is saved by a compatriot who recognizes him. He attacks the West at a press conference and returns to Czechoslovakia as a useless and unhappy party hack. Laura, back in England after a holiday abroad and piqued by the dull and virtuous role she has been obliged to resume after Birek's departure, tries in vain to renew Charlie Eldon's interest. She grows abrupt with her husband, who sadly realizes that human affection within their family will disappear once his youngest child is a few years older.

Both structurally and thematically, *A Season in the West* is a straightforward work. An interesting narrative carries the reader along and into the minds and emotions of the characters. With a sharply achieved setting, a deft depiction of social markers, and an adept use of dialogue and authorial comment, Read offers a clear understanding of the situation and the personalities involved, putting them in a specific and well-delineated geographic, social, economic, and cultural background. That setting does not, however, hide or entirely explain their individual destinies but rather heightens and illuminates them. What it does add is an element of the fable, that is, of a tale that conveys a lesson through a fictional narrative.

All of Read's writing is concerned with moral themes and perspectives. His novels are explorations of the moral lives of his characters and the results of their choices. Here, it is Laura's husband and her lover who both reflect, increasingly critically and self-questioningly, on their personal morality and change as a result, whereas the rather superficial Laura seems merely peeved by the situation her actions have led her into. It is important to remember, however, that *A Season in the West*'s focus is on the young Eastern Bloc dissident rather than on Laura, and in the novel the importance of their affair is its effect on Birek, notably his decline and the ultimate loss of the autonomy and freedom he had hoped to find in the West. The main matter is a reflection on the moral life in terms of a specific individual destiny. A moral concern does not, of course, necessarily entail showing meritorious characters coming to impeccably correct conclusions and leading exemplary lives. It can involve something very different from preaching or edifying by pious exhortation. The still, sad music we hear in compelling literature is perhaps more moving in those novels involving failure than in those concentrating on success. Read gradually removes the false glamour from Laura's affair and provides a sharp criticism of the ideologies of both East and West. A bonfire of the vanities need not be a dull matter. It can, as Read's does, provide a sharp and stimulating edge that is more effective than an overtly uplifting message.

In the West that Birek discovers, there is little evidence of faith, hope, or charity, and no powerful aspirations beyond a love of wealth and posses-

sions and the preservation of a satisfactory status quo. The higher apparat-
chik echelons of the dying Marxist system seem no better. The picture of the
beginning, ripening, and decline of desire of two rather disparate people is
set against a largely amoral "civilized" background of uncaring materialism, and the author distances himself from the main characters. Yet all is not
bleak, and *A Season in the West* is by no means a cynical novel. The cuckold-
ed husband, Francis, has enough of a conscience to be troubled about the
unethical activities of his merchant bank, and he certainly has a desire to
see his wife happy. Though Laura has only the faintest and rarest glimmers
of self-knowledge, Birek, weak, young, and isolated, who returns to Prague
and joins the system he despises, is at least aware of his failure and humbled
by it.

A Season in the West is critical in its delivery and could no doubt be read
as sharp, serious, and ironical modern literature. But Read is a Catholic author, one whose mind and imagination are informed by a Catholic understanding of human life in all its aspects, and he portrays his characters in
this light. At the same time, the novel is catholic with a lowercase "c," in the
sense of universal, for it includes much that is not Catholic in a doctrinally
or ecclesiastically defined sense. It is the duty of the Church to show us how
to live, but it may be the duty of the Catholic novelist to show us how deep
and almost invincible our ignorance may be and to help us understand the
pathos and anguish of life without faith and without the sacraments. Above
all, Read's work illustrates Augustine's famous dictum in his *Confessions:
Fecisti nos ad Te et inquietum est cor nostrum donec requiescat in Te* ("Thou
hast created us for Thyself and our heart is not quiet until it rests in Thee").
It seems clear why Read has written of the Augustinian influence in all his
work.

Finally, it is worth pointing out that like most serious Catholic writers,
Read asks of himself intelligence, imagination, profundity, aesthetic competence, and truth. He presents his own view of the world with honesty and
compassion. Aesthetic competence and the desire for truth do not call for
pornography or titillation, and his work, profound and sensitive to human
sexuality as it is, is not cheapened by them.

■ ■ ■

As we move toward the younger end of the age range of contemporary
British Catholic writers, two striking figures come into view, both of whom are
still at an early stage of their career and, like their older contemporaries, writ-

ing as orthodox, declared, committed, and practicing Catholics. The main difference between them and their older colleagues is quantitative rather than qualitative, in that they cannot yet match the output the former have achieved over a working lifetime. The first is William Brodrick, born in Bolton, Lancashire, in 1960, who has so far published three profound, interesting, and well-received novels, *The Sixth Lamentation* (2003), *The Gardens of the Dead* (2006), and *A Whispered Name* (2008).[5]

Brodrick describes himself as a practicing Catholic from a Catholic family, where his father's faith was that of the Chesterton-Belloc type and his mother, a Dutch convert from nominal Lutheranism, was nourished more by piety rather than apologetics. Both these "polarities of thoughts and feelings, resistance and submission, the rather loud and the very quiet," he says, were the soil in which his faith was rooted.[6] He is a Catholic writer, he says, in the sense that all that he writes has its origin in his Catholic identity and in every experience of life and death that he has had in the context of a lived faith. His religious identity is apparent in the language he uses, a way of seeing and interpreting the world. In Brodrick's view Catholicism can provide richness of color and insight, a language and a ritual that give meaning to human experience. He has an interest in mirroring life and society for the sake of authenticity, and he sees his novels as simultaneously operating on two planes: "ordinary" life in society, where the plot's crisis is located, and the monastery, where it is ultimately resolved. Brodrick's own career has been interesting. Reversing the path of Fr. Anselm, the barrister-turned-priest protagonist in his first two novels, he himself moved from the clerical to the legal sphere. After some years in religious life, including university studies, he left the Augustinian order amicably before taking his final vows, worked for a time with the homeless in London, and then trained for the bar. Thus, he writes knowledgably about both worlds.

In *The Sixth Lamentation,* which is loosely based on the wartime experiences of Brodrick's own mother, Anselm is sent to meet an old man, Edward Schwermann, a low-ranking SS officer who had sent thousands of Jews to their deaths. The old man asks what he should do when the whole world turns against him, and he is told to seek sanctuary from the Church. This could, of course, entail serious risks if the action is discovered, ranging from

---

5. Brodrick's *A Whispered Name* (London: Little, Brown 2008) was published after this essay was completed; hence, the discussion that follows deals with his first two novels only.
6. Personal letter from William Brodrick to the author dated May 1, 2007.

scandal and public outcry to accusations of criminal conspiracy. But if he is refused sanctuary, he will be tried for crimes he insists he did not commit. In the weeks leading up to Schwermann's trial, Anselm is given the task of investigating his story and finding out why the Church had apparently given Schwermann sanctuary fifty years earlier and helped him to escape from France and assume a new identity in Britain. While Anselm is attempting to find out the truth of the matter, others are furthering their own investigation into the Holocaust and trying to uncover their own complicated histories. In a parallel strand of the story, an elderly expatriate French woman now living in England, Agnes Aubret, who is suffering from a progressive motor neuron disease and whose death is imminent, tells her granddaughter of her work in Paris during the German occupation as a member of a Church-supported resistance group, the Round Table, which had smuggled Jewish children out of France and into safety. The group had ultimately been betrayed, its members captured by the Nazis and either killed or sent to concentration camps. No one knew who had betrayed them. At the end of her life, Agnes wants to bring Schwermann to justice, but she must reveal her own startling past to do so. The two apparently unconnected strands of the narrative ultimately come together. False identities, secret relationships, sickening deeds and motivations, and all the complex ramifications of events that had taken place decades earlier reemerge in the lives of the participants in those events and their descendants. The language of the novel is subtle and dense as the complexity of the story and the troubling and disturbing switch from past to present time dictates. As a search for the truth hidden behind lies and an investigation of the mysteries of human motivation and feelings, this combination of thriller and philosophical meditation is well worth the serious effort it calls for from the reader.

A search for truth and understanding marks all of Brodrick's fiction, and he has pointed out that he writes from his own history both of faith and "in the world," with Anselm as his vehicle.[7] This effort he has called "faith seeking understanding" and it marks his second novel as deeply as his first. Even more than in *The Sixth Lamentation*, the reader of *The Gardens of the Dead* is required to make an effort to find out what exactly is happening. That knowledge is acquired slowly and as hesitatingly and gradually as it is by the characters themselves. Elizabeth Glendinning, an eminent QC (a rather superior

7. Ibid.

kind of English lawyer), has lost faith in the legal system she has served all her life. In order to restore that faith, she has secretly worked out a way of bringing a guilty man, Graham Riley, whom she had defended and who had been acquitted, back to court. In order to ensure a contingency plan should things go wrong, she leaves Anselm the key to a safe deposit box to be opened in the event of her death. A few weeks later, she is found dead in the East End of London. When Anselm opens the box, a chain of events is put in motion, and he sets out to complete the dead woman's efforts. The story, which has all the power and rigor of a serious thriller, is another search for authenticity. Like Brodrick's first novel, *The Gardens of the Dead* is a Catholic novel in a specific sense, namely because it is imbued with the author's Catholic way of seeing and presenting the world. That way is not hortatory, didactic, or even directly explanatory. Like Read's novels, Brodrick's make the reader aware of two important presences. On the one hand, there is a Catholic vision of life, a particular way of understanding what we may still call the soul and mean by that the inner reality of his characters. On the other hand, we have, perhaps semiconsciously and grudgingly, a sense of the presence of God in and behind the existential situation. At most, both presences can only be sensed, and it is virtually impossible to explain, quantify, or define them. They do not need to be bolstered by external Catholic paraphernalia, and in their mystery may even be the most powerful religious experience encountered in Catholic literature. As I have tried to suggest, Brodrick's world is one in which mystery and partial knowledge and understanding are components of the matter and manner of the fiction. The insights and information gradually and sometimes confusingly discovered are steps toward a truth beyond the apparent nonsense of our lives, an intimation of the meaning behind the formulas that express the truth of Catholic teachings about our nature. It is in this sense that Brodrick is a deeply Catholic writer in both *The Sixth Lamentation* and *The Gardens of the Dead*.

A second younger-generation contemporary Catholic writer is Jonathan Tulloch, born in Kendal, Cumbria, in 1968, who describes himself as a practicing Catholic married to a Catholic and, for better or worse, immersed in Catholicism.[8] He is William Brodrick's junior (and, in fact, was once taught in school by "Bro Bill"). A formative experience of Tulloch's life was a stint

---

8. These and the following comments and quotations are from a personal e-mail from Jonathan Tulloch to the author, dated March 12, 2007.

of voluntary work in Johannesburg in a school run by Assumptionist nuns, working with children from the various townships and with Rwandan refugees, some of whom had escaped the genocide, "finding a path through the forest of machetes." On his return from Africa, he published his first novel, and he has written four to date: *The Season Ticket* (2000; filmed as *Purely Belter*), *The Bonny Lad* (2001), *The Lottery* (2003), and the powerful *Give Us This Day* (2005). All these are set in the postindustrial northeast of England among the decay and toxic waste of a landscape disfigured and largely destroyed by heavy industry, including shipbuilding and chemicals. They often incorporate as characters the now largely lapsed descendants of a nineteenth-century Irish Catholic immigrant labor force, the very place and community where the author has lived and worked. *Give Us This Day* especially embraces a theological dimension while also set in the same ugly, harsh, and apparently godforsaken area, exploring, Tulloch says, "the notion that Jesus was God because he was fully man." With his wife Shirley Tulloch, a former lay missionary in Africa, he has also cowritten a children's book, *I Am a Cloud, I Can Blow Anywhere*, based on their experiences in Africa and telling the story of a girl from the Tonga tribe on whose thin shoulders falls the responsibility for the survival of her whole family. A priest smuggles the girl over the border at great risk to himself, a reflection on the fact that the Church-based Justice and Peace group in Zimbabwe has for years been one of the very few voices of opposition to the corrupt Mugabe presidency. Based on his writings, there seems little doubt about the honesty and fervor of Tulloch's position as a Catholic writer.

In *The Season Ticket,* Tulloch's characters have little sense of belonging to the Catholic community beyond their Irish surnames or scattered religious souvenirs. The plot involves a young thief who kills a man, and it also concerns his sister, whom we see examining the souvenirs of her first Holy Communion that her father had rummaged through in the hope of finding some beer money. In *The Bonny Lad,* such characters are epitomized by Joe O'Brien, the cantankerous retired miner who is suddenly forced to look after the grandson he has never met, a drug mule and a so-called rat boy (or child criminal), and refuses to see him as a gift from God (although he later experiences a growth of mutual tenderness and acceptance). In Tulloch's third novel *The Lottery,* lottery winner Audrey McPhee is baptized by her friend in sweet cider, using the local dialect: "I baptize ye the Queen of Gateshead. Wor Lady of the tower blocks, Patron Saint of every bugger what's ever bought a lottery ticket with her last poond coin."[9] The marginalized yet resilient immigrant poor, even if their faith is little understood and poorly practiced, says Tulloch, have always been for him the basis of attraction to Catholicism.

A more theologically based novel, *Give Us This Day* presents a variation on and enlargement of some of these themes. Its major character is a priest, Fr. Tom Carey, who has arrived at a crisis in his faith and what Tulloch calls an unlikely meeting with God. The world has gone bad, the Church staggers from scandal to scandal, and abandoning his comfortable parish for the post of port chaplain on a busy estuary, Carey finds himself caught up in the shady world of people involved in smuggling and beset by all kinds of trials and scandals. The priest's life, like those of his parishioners, is harsh in many ways and deprives him of many things, including self-respect. It does, however, make him more human, stripping away a facile pride and eventually bringing him closer to God. The novel also contains echoes of liberation theology, since the old presbytery becomes a kind of base community in which Fr. Carey, a disgraced fellow priest, a prostitute, and a down-and-out man must function together. It is worth noting that the novel came into being through Tulloch's research into the terrible conditions experienced by seafarers, carried out by actually going on a series of voyages with a Filipino crew and published as an article in the *Guardian* newspaper. He found, however, that the article could not begin to say what he needed to say, so the germ of the novel was born.

If many of Tulloch's characters seem to be degraded and brutalized people, it is because he has seen and lived life in raw conditions. But, as he has stated, he believes that the Crucifixion will always be at the heart of Christianity, "with a weak, defeated, bloodied God being laughed at by spiritual and temporal powers," in a world where "the laughter of a murdering meathead might have been the last thing Christ heard." This from a writer who often feels, he says, that the promise of paradise to the repentant thief is "the finest moment in the literature of the world." *Give Us This Day* is a compelling reflection on that insight. We can see Fr. Carey's case as parallel to it. Weak but helped with a sense of humor and a real ability to pity and love, he moves through the pain, horror, and squalor of his local world toward a strengthened and calmer faith. There is, however, no easy conclusion to the

9. Jonathan Tulloch, *The Lottery* (London: Vintage, 2003), 142.

story. All we know is that the effort is immense and demanding and that Tom Carey struggles to exercise his priesthood as best he can. Graham Greene's alcoholic priest would understand him and welcome him as another repentant thief trying to overcome his weakness and move via hope and charity ever closer to faith.

■ ■ ■

Clearly, the Catholic novel, defined here as fiction marked by the faith and understanding of believing Catholic authors, still survives in Britain. Alongside those not-so-rare semidetached, sporadic, former, unbelieving, emancipated, and all other varieties of near misses as Catholics and Catholic writers, there are those novelists among both the older and newer generations of contemporary Catholic authors who in their differing ways keep the genre alive, well, and deeply interesting. While notably different than its mid-twentieth-century predecessors, for the changes of Vatican II and the passage of time have produced altered ways of looking at the world, Catholic writing, like the Church itself, remains faithful to its vocation and has survived contemporary modifications. It is still recognizable, still makes us think, reflect, and imagine—and perhaps even become a little wiser and more human. It does so by reminding us of our world, giving us pictures of ourselves and others, and by suggesting too that there is, as Pope Paul VI maintained, a deeper dimension to our being, regions of light lying behind the mystery of man's life.

CHAPTER 11

The Contemporary Catholic Bildungsroman

Passionate Conviction in Shūsaku Endō's *The Samurai* and

Mary Gordon's *Men and Angels*

Nancy Ann Watanabe

"Our every good act is a response to grace."

—Edward William Clark, *Five Great Catholic Ideas*

My aim in this chapter is to use a traditional genre approach to shed light on aspects of two novels published during the same decade, the 1980s, by Catholic authors who are separated by geographical, national, and linguistic boundaries. Born in Tokyo in 1923, the Japanese author Shūsaku Endō was baptized into the Catholic faith as a boy by his mother, who had converted to Roman Catholicism. He was given the Christian name Paul in honor of St. Paul, the apostle whose name was changed from Saul to Paul when he converted to Christianity. American Mary Gordon was raised in an Irish Catholic family and is a New Yorker. Both of these authors portray character in ways that illuminate important Catholic themes that emerge as an underlying cultural and spiritual motif common to both novels. This motif, or unifying idea, is the role of the Christian man and the Christian woman in a non-Christian society. Endō's historical masterpiece *The Samurai* (1982; *Samurai*, 1980) joins his critically acclaimed *Silence* (1972; *Chimmoku*, 1969) as an exploration of the triumph of faith in an era of anti-Christian sentiment in Asia. Gordon's award-winning feminist novel *Men and Angels* (1985) radically moves to a poeticized role the sacramental, the scriptural, and the ritual of Catholicism, which played a more central role in her earlier works, *Final Payments* (1978) and *The Company of Women* (1980). Critic Don Brophy, who wrote *The Story of Catholics in America* and served for many years as an editor at Paulist Press, bestows recognition upon Endō's *Silence* and

Gordon's *Final Payments* in his *One Hundred Great Catholic Books: From the Early Centuries to the Present*.[1] Both *The Samurai* and *Men and Angels* are much more than mere sequels. Endō and Gordon in these novels of their maturity demonstrate an even greater craftsmanship in coping artistically with the complexities and complications connected with contemporary life in a worldly culture. In *The Samurai* and *Men and Angels,* artistic compressions of the fundamentals of the Christian faith give rise to remarkably similar types of psychological symbolism that appear to render problematic the spiritual integrity of the protagonists. Vividly, Endō and Gordon depict the struggles of a religious individual within a social and political milieu that is predominantly nonreligious, resulting in a revolutionary sort of universalism that parallels the ecumenical movement in the Roman Catholic Church. In the quest to assert selfhood through attempting to vanquish opposition, the Christian individual acquires greater understanding of self and society. While the Christian individual moves from ignorance of the truth to knowledge of the truth, the success of this interior learning process is undermined by anti-Christian forces of adversity in the exterior world of reality. Endō's *The Samurai* portrays Catholic themes directly by entering the minds of characters whose faith deepens. Gordon's *Men and Angels* renders the minds of characters whose divided selves and alienation from one another underscore the importance of true Christian love in a utilitarian society.

As contemporary Catholic novelists, Endō and Gordon confer new meaning upon the Bildungsroman literary genre. Their works perpetuate the traditional novel of education, a genre that rose to prominence during the eighteenth and nineteenth centuries. With craftsmanship and intellectual verve, Endō and Gordon elevate the Bildungsroman from a straightforward depiction of manners, mores, and cultural milieus to a more subtle and sophisticated probing of the religious fabric of modern society as an outgrowth of Renaissance globalization, commercialism, and secularization. By virtue of the pervasive limning of interior consciousness with respect to matters of religious belief and moral responsibility, the contemporary Catholic Bildungsroman as written by these artists may be viewed as belonging to the theological novel genre. Literary theorists often equate the Bildungsroman with a related genre, the Erziehungsroman, which portrays a central character who is acquiring familiarity with a social and cultural milieu through

---

1. Don Brophy, *One Hundred Great Catholic Books: From the Early Centuries to the Present* (New York: Blue Bridge, 2007).

personal experience. The Bildungsroman places emphasis on certain episodes or stages in the development of the central character's imagination,
perhaps because the root German word *das Bild* means "image," and the
German word *die Bildung* denotes "formation." The Erziehungsroman shows
the movement from ignorance to knowledge in the education of the novel's
protagonist, since the root German verb *erziehungen* connotes progressive
familial and societal acculturation. The contemporary Catholic Bildungsroman, which accords importance to the inner life of the spirit in the context
of moral and spiritual issues within modern society, encompasses the Erziehungsroman in a special way.

As post–Vatican II novels, *The Samurai* and *Men and Angels* extend their
reach to embrace the global family of the ecumenical Catholic Church. Ecumenical efforts in the Church date back to the two Ecumenical Councils of
449 and 451 that attempted to unite the churches of the East (Greek) and West
(Latin). Later attempts to heal the Eastern Schism of 1054 galvanized the ecumenical movement on an international scale during the Vatican Council in
1439 at Florence. In modern times, the Second Vatican Council, convened in
1962, examined compelling issues in an increasingly global and secular society such as atheism, the treatment of marriage and the family, and the role
of the Church in carrying its message to the modern world. Pope John XXIII
held that the Catholic Church was obligated to "submit to a renewal of its own
inner reality so that it would be more credible in the eyes and judgment of
the separated brothers."[2] *The Samurai* and *Men and Angels* examine how the
faith is tested in light of modern society's values and how, in turn, it serves to
challenge secular and materialistic norms.

Even a basic analytical study of character portrayal and themes in these
contemporary Catholic novels reveals salient theological features that over-
ride neat categorizations of *The Samurai* as a historical novel or *Men and
Angels* as a feminist novel. Ideally, observes Mary R. Reichardt, Catholic literature invites consideration of the "gray areas of paradox, ambiguity, and
moral dilemma."[3] Indeed, in the complexly drawn *The Samurai*, Endō tells
two intersecting stories, both of which are replete with such gray areas. An
unassuming samurai named Rokuemon Hasekura, a deposed nobleman

2. G. C. Berkouwer, *The Second Vatican Council and the New Catholicism,* trans. Lewis B. Smedes
(Grand Rapids, Mich.: Eerdmans, 1965), 14.

3. Mary R. Reichardt, "Literature and the Catholic Perspective," in *Ethics, Literature, Theory: An
Introductory Reader,* ed. Stephen K. George (Lanham, Md.: Rowman and Littlefield/Sheed and Ward,
2005), 175.

of the powerful military caste in medieval Japan, along with several other handpicked samurai delegates and their retinues, is asked to undertake a voyage to New Spain in order to open negotiations that will result in possibilities for trade. He agrees to lead the delegation, as success may reinstate the right of his family—his wife Riku, their two sons, and his aged uncle—to reside on their glorious ancestral estate, which had been confiscated by regional officials. The novel allegorizes the dangerous sea voyage as an exterior image that closely reflects the interior spiritual journey of Hasekura and his manservant Yozō. It radiates spiritual energy from its theological core, which is Hasekura's baptism into the Catholic faith during the course of the voyage and the consequences of that sacrament that lead to martyrdom instead of apostasy. Parallel to the realistic representation of Hasekura's struggles with his role as a political delegate and his acceptance of faith is the story of the Spanish Catholic missionary priest Velasco, a proud man who aspires to be named bishop of Japan as his reward for strengthening the religious bond between Japan and the Church, which was inaugurated in 1569 with the founding of the Roman Catholic Church in Nagasaki. The religious conflict in the novel between the Franciscans and Jesuits suggests a spiritual allegory in which the Franciscans' Pauline evangelism and humble lifestyle coalesces with the Jesuits' ecumenical agenda to build Japanese churches in the spirit of Peter. For Christ gave Simon the name Peter (Latin *petra* means rock), saying: "Thou art Peter, and upon this rock, I will build my church."[4] A Franciscan, Velasco is fiercely competitive in his desire to win more conversions to the Catholic faith in Japan than other Catholic orders, especially the Jesuits, who have established colonies and appointed tax collectors and whom he therefore resents. He accompanies the voyage ostensibly as the Japanese envoys' translator yet ambitious to see his own desires carried out. In the end, he undergoes a change of heart that subdues his pride and allows him, among other signs of inner conversion, to administer sacramental last rites to a suicide despite his fellow priests' opposition and to feel comradeship with a Jesuit when both are imprisoned. While *The Samurai* is largely based on fact, historically the martyrdom of missionary Father Luis Sorelo (1574–1624), the biographical model for Father Velasco, actually occurred two years after Hasekura's execution in 1622. Altering the historical record, Endō narrates in juxtaposed texts the struggles of Hasekura and Velasco in their shared search for an authentic Christian faith.

4. Matt. 16:18.

After the Council of Elders informs him that he is appointed as an envoy to New Spain and charged to deliver important letters to Spanish authorities, Hasekura is shocked and fearful, but he learns to take this high-level order to embark on a transoceanic voyage for the incredible adventure it is. Endō uses "narrated monologue,"[5] or indirect discourse, extensively to portray his characters by narrating their consciousness in the third-person instead of the first-person point of view. He employs this type of narration to reveal the great wonder of Hasekura as he continually muses, "But why had he been chosen as one of the emissaries?"[6] Examining his past life of obedience, endurance, and perseverance, he knows that he has done nothing to deserve the honor. In his naïveté, throughout the novel he remains largely unaware of the complex political machinations that determine this unexpected turn in his life and that will serve to alter his destiny in a definitive way. He is indeed, as is slowly revealed to the reader, an instrument in a much larger political and religious concatenation of circumstances. Yet his traits of character as a samurai who humbly cares for his family, retainers, and the peasant workers in his charge endow him with an inner strength to meet the challenges imposed on him by the political intrigue unfolding around him.

Informed in New Spain that no decisions could be made to open trade routes without first consulting with authorities in Spain, the delegation sails on to Europe. During the long voyage, Velasco has repeatedly told the Japanese that they will have success in their mission only if they convert to Christianity. Without any knowledge that a fierce nationwide persecution of Christianity has begun in Japan with the Edict of 1614, Hasekura, along with his fellow envoys, accepts baptism in Madrid. Initially, Hasekura becomes a Christian because he is deeply loyal to his role as a delegate. He has also been told that if he completes his assigned task successfully, confiscated lands will be returned to his family, and thus his family honor will be restored. But later his motives are no longer tainted by self-interest, as his code of fealty to his superior, Lord Ishida, a wealthy northern Japan *daimyō*, or military warlord, is gradually replaced by his fealty to the Christian Lord God. Although the sincerity of his new Catholic religion seems undermined by his claim that his decision to convert is merely based on the exigencies of his mission, he nevertheless subtly affirms the growing genuineness of his faith. He begins to move from skepticism about the life of Jesus toward belief

5. Dorrit Cohn, *Transparent Minds: Narrative Modes for Presenting Consciousness in Fiction* (Princeton, N.J.: Princeton University Press, 1978), 105.
6. Shūsaku Endō, *The Samurai*, trans. Van C. Gessel (New York: New Directions, 1982), 39.

when Velasco helps him understand the Christian notion of heaven as similar to the Buddhist notion of the Pure Land. Velasco tells Hasekura, "Christians believe that they can go to the true Pure Land only with the help of
Jesus. For Jesus took upon Himself our irredeemable sins and willingly sub-
mitted Himself to tribulation and agony."[7] Velasco demonstrates his knowledge of the Japanese converts' point of departure in Buddhist-Shinto belief,
which enables him to help Hasekura acquire cognitive understanding of
Christianity's claims.

During the course of the voyage on the ship, aptly named the *San Juan
Baptista* because it will lead the protagonists to Christ as John the Baptist led
his disciples to Christ, Hasekura and his fellow travelers must contend with
the threats of another envoy, Matsuki, a political opportunist who aborts the
mission, returning to Japan where he spearheads the anti-Christian purge.
Matsuki views the envoys as sacrificial pawns who were "chosen" to go on
"this miserable journey," and he is convinced that when they fail to complete their impossible mission they will be punished as a "warning" to dis-
contented samurai vassals angry over governmental reapportionment of
their fiefdoms.[8] Since Hasekura accepts his mission as a samurai envoy as
a matter of faith, he remains impervious to Matsuki's ominous predictions.
Rather, he envisions his task as a battle, but one in which he erroneously
sees the Japanese Council of Elders as rear admirals directing the "combined
forces" toward a single goal.[9] His naïve political faith in a unified Japanese
government, though, begins to give way to a growing religious awareness
that the Mass celebrated daily on the ship, the glorious cathedrals of Europe,
and the pope in Rome are all part and parcel of the larger entity of the Catholic Church and, ultimately, the unified mystical Body of Christ. Paradoxically, the Catholic priest is taught this lesson, too. When Velasco insists on his
own course of action, his uncle, Don Diego Caballero Molina, a prominent
churchman and courtier, reprimands him for ignoring the Church's hierarchy in decision making: "The Archbishop can't just step in and arrange an
audience for the Japanese without considering the opinions of the bishops,"
he informs Velasco.[10]

As a missionary, Father Velasco looks to St. Paul as a model of ecumenical leadership. As an integral part of the novel's structural design, this Pau-

---

7. Ibid., 173–74.   8. Ibid., 64.
9. Ibid., 65.   10. Ibid., 154.

line faith in the Triune God oscillates with the rise and fall of Velasco's emotions. At one point, Velasco muses,

I thought then of Paul, who was pitted against the Apostles of Jerusalem because he took the gospel to the Gentiles. Even Paul was hindered, reviled and abused by other Christians. The Christians at the Church headquarters in Jerusalem gave it out that Paul was unqualified to carry the word of the Lord beyond national borders and without respect to race. In the same manner the Jesuits consider me a priest unworthy to proselytize in Japan.[11]

Velasco views his soul's struggle as a battle: "O Lord, command me to fight. I am alone . . . I must conquer with the power of Thy gospel."[12] Significantly, his struggle with faith occurs when officials treat him as a subordinate, merely as an interpreter whose value is limited to his bilingualism. But although his pride clouds his conscience, his sincerity to the dogma of the faith and his passion for conversions, like that of St. Paul, is clear. For instance, in Spain he accuses his interrogator, Father Valente, of "belittling" the "many Japanese saints whom he baptized with his own hands," and he shouts with the force of conviction: "The sacrament of baptism transcends the will of man and bestows the grace of God upon the recipient."[13] Somewhat ironically, this turns out to be true. Although all the Japanese merchants, envoys, and their retinue on board the *San Juan Baptista* accept baptism at Father Velasco's cajoling only to ensure successful trade negotiations with the Spanish, the power of the sacrament does indeed, Endō implies, eventually bring salvific grace to at least three of those who receive it, Hasekura, Nishi, and Yozō.

While in Mexico, Hasekura and Nishi accept from a poor village monk living among the Indians a "life of the Saviour," which he wrote.[14] A pivotal figure in the novel, this Japanese monk is key to the two samurais' sacramental conversion. In 1978, Shūsaku Endō received the International Dag Hammarskjöld Prize for his *A Life of Jesus* (1979; *Iesu no shōgai*, 1973), and in the same year he published another prose narrative, *Kirisuto no tanjō* (*The Birth of Christ*, 1978). The knowledge Endō acquired in researching these two religious monographs, which were written to present Christianity to the Japanese people, informs his Catholic themes in *The Samurai*, in particular the universal appeal of Christ as the "man of sorrows," the God who endures

---

11. Ibid., 139.   12. Ibid., 144.
13. Ibid., 168.   14. Ibid., 122.

pain for and with his people. The novel is replete with Christian symbolism pointing to this face of Christ. For example, in an early chapter, the description of the Japanese carpenters hammering nails into the planks of timber transported from across Japan for the building of the great ship evokes the cross on which Christ was crucified. The new ship's framework resembles the "weathered skeleton of a wild beast,"[15] which suggests that the sea symbolizes the political upheaval, moral confusion, and spiritual uncertainty that led to the Crucifixion at Golgatha, "the place of skulls." According to the *Catechism of the Catholic Church,* the "water of the sea" can even be a "symbol of death" and, therefore, can "represent the mystery of the cross."[16] Both Hasekura and Velasco come to identify with the forsaken, crucified one. And this identification leads both to martyrdom for the faith.

After being baptized as a boy, Endō remained a devout Catholic all his life. As Sumie Okada observes in *Japanese Writers and the West,* Endō "tried faithfully to spread Catholic beliefs in Japan," "was well known for his missionary-like or even evangelical activities, persistently advocating to his secular friends that they should be baptized," and "did convert a number of Japanese novelists successfully to Catholicism."[17] Endō studied French Catholic literature at Keio University, focusing on the works of François Mauriac and Georges Bernanos, and he then did postgraduate work at the University of Lyon in France, where he continued his reading of Catholic authors. His masterful writing of *The Samurai* is directly attributable to his religious fervor, to his specialization in Catholic literature, and to his lifelong interest in East-West relationships stemming from his experience as an Asian in Western Europe. In particular, Endō was fascinated by the challenge of showing how it was that Japanese Christians, numbering 750,000 when the persecutions began, withstood cruel and repressive treatment and grew to more than a million at the end of the 250-year Tokugawa hegemony when a democratic government was formed in 1868. What was it in the sensibility of the Japanese that allowed them to accept the Christian God and, perhaps more pointedly, what qualities of personality and character empowered the missionaries to bring the light of Christ to Japan? In light of the latter concern, Endō depicts the missionary priest in *The Samurai* more richly and densely than he does the samurai Hasekura. A Renaissance man, educated, world-

---

15. Ibid., 40.
16. *Catechism of the Catholic Church* (New York: Doubleday, 1995), 344.
17. Sumie Okada, *Japanese Writers and the West* (New York: Palgrave Macmillan, 2003), 82.

ly, and ambitious, Father Velasco epitomizes the type of altruistic Catholic missionary that the Japanese admire. A proud nation that believes in human perfectibility, especially in its leaders, the Japanese can empathize with a robust and energetic but embattled missionary priest who atones for his sins in ritually suffering bodily punishment, this penance culminating in a torturous death that is imbued with spiritual and moral significance. Ecumenism forms the crux of Endō's Bildungsroman, for Father Velasco's attainment of a morally right relationship to Christ coincides with the spiritual courage of Japanese converts like Hasekura and Nishi who decline to renounce their faith in Christ by apostatizing. Before he learns the error of his ways, Velasco rejoices when he is released from prison, mostly because he can pursue his lusty bid for glory. But the gradual defeat of his plans for self-glory as the ship travels to first New Spain, then Spain, and finally on to Rome parallels the growth of his moral conscience. His decision to return to Japan, knowing he will be executed in the anticlerical purge, is an act of penance, as shown in his meek request of Father Lenegro, a Jesuit, to serve as his confessor so that he may confess his sins and receive extreme unction in his death cell. His last confession is revealing: "I have even denied God. Because God ignored my wishes," he states.[18] The confession is important in the way it implicates the breach between God and man in a materialistic and humanist post-Renaissance world: "I was not aware of my own pride and my lust for conquest," Velasco concludes.[19] At the beginning of the novel, Velasco thinks, "I am willing to die if it be Thy will," but now he understands, in his newfound humility, that he "confused [his] own will with the will of God."[20]

At each point, the obedient samurai Hasekura complements Velasco's self-pride and craving for independent action. Hasekura is a Christian samurai who represents the best of two worlds. His loyalty to his growing understanding of Christ emanates from his fealty to the samurai code of honor. Yet, he rebels against his former life in Japan, and he begins to understand that the Christian God, that emaciated dying man on the cross that has seemed to him both strange and shameful, transcends race and nation when he and young Nishi visit the monk whose penitent rebelliousness teaches Hasekura to see not a Japanese outcast but Christ's ecumenical mission to teach all nations about universal love. When he learns that he is to be burned at the stake for pledging his faith to Christianity, he suffers because he feels forsak-

18. Endō, *Samurai*, 265. 19. Ibid.
20. Ibid., 17, 264.

en by his motherland, just as Christ momentarily felt forsaken by His heavenly Father when the sins of man crucified Him. When Lord Ishida fails to see that he is a "changed" man,[21] Hasekura understands that the Japanese, like the Romans who crucified Christ, did not know what they were doing. In his final moments, Hasekura confirms his faith in Jesus to Yozō, who blesses him, saying, "From now on He will be beside you," and then, realizing Christ has always accompanied them, adds, "He will attend you."[22] Endō's Bildungsroman envisions Hasekura moving at long last to his spiritual destination and true home with the Lord Jesus: "The samurai stopped, looked back, and nodded his head emphatically. Then he set off down the cold, glistening corridor towards the end of his journey."[23] This penultimate moment in his sacral pilgrimage unites him with Yozō, a servant, and Nishi, a subordinate, who, as he has always known by the Holy Spirit, are his equals in the eyes of their Father.

While *The Samurai* portrays the dynamism of the ecumenical movement as an outreach of Christianity through the establishment of Roman Catholic Churches in non-Christian nations, Mary Gordon's *Men and Angels* suggests that ecumenical outreach refers not only to proselytization abroad in Third World nations but also encompasses contemporary domestic life. Ordinarily, ecumenism aims to bring unity to all of the churches of the world. But these are extraordinary times. While the setting in *Men and Angels* is contemporary America, the novel harkens back to the earliest epoch when the Apostolic Church was born. Through symbolism and other poetic devices, the novel thematically explores religious rebirth, pointing to a crying need for an ecumenical movement in America. The lifelong ambivalence of Mary Gordon, who was born in Far Rockaway, New York, on December 8, 1949, to her strict Catholic upbringing makes *Men and Angels* much more than the feminist novel she intended it to be. Some of the religious elements in *Men and Angels* may be traced to facts drawn from her life. Gordon received a Catholic education through high school, but her father, David Gordon, exerted the most influence on her religious sensibility. A Lithuanian Jew who converted to Roman Catholicism in 1937, David Gordon taught Mary the Latin used in Catholic Mass when she was five, and he said a Jewish blessing on her bowed head each night. Mary was born when David was fifty-five, and their intense father-daughter relationship was made more precious by his prema-

21. Ibid., 122. 22. Ibid., 262.
23. Ibid.

ture death from a massive heart attack in a library while he was researching an essay on Catholic writer Paul Claudel. As a sensitive and impressionable Catholic girl, Gordon was strongly affected by the way her father devoted his life to intellectual pursuits that pitted his Catholic beliefs against the modernist movement in literature and art. Resisting the stifling pre–Vatican II atmosphere of her upbringing, Gordon joined the growing women's movement of the times, which catapulted her toward higher education unbounded by religious regulations. She won a four-year scholarship to attend secular Barnard College, where, influenced by Virginia Woolf's stream-of-consciousness novels, she shifted from writing poetry to fiction. Contrary to the novel's apparent secularism, Gordon returns to her Catholic roots in an artistically refined way in *Men and Angels*. "The metaphors of Catholicism, the Catholic way of looking at the world, these are in my bones," she has explained. "It is my framework of language."[24]

The novel's interplay of appearance and reality centers on the theme of authentic Christian love, a theme Gordon suggests in her epigraph from St. Paul: "Though I speak with the tongues of men and angels, and have not charity, I am become as sounding brass, or a tinkling symbol."[25] The novel's title *Men and Angels* is also compelling in calling attention to the way feminist themes coalesce with religious beliefs. The coupling of the secularized anthropocentrism and theological religiosity in the words *Men* and *Angels* is reflective of the strong influence of David Gordon on Mary during her formative years. Notwithstanding Gordon's overriding concern for feminist issues, the novel thematically couples maternal love with religious fervor and parental negligence with religious fanaticism, casting into sharp relief its underlying exploration of the strident demands imposed by the secular world vying against traditional Christian values. In penetrating to the ontological core of faith as experienced by Anne Foster, an East Coast upper-class wife, mother, and art historian, and by Laura Post, a homeless twenty-two-year-old nanny, *Men and Angels* rises to a sublime art commensurate with the theological novel genre.

Gordon's contemporary Catholic Bildungsroman is a multilayered palimpsest in which the characters' lives, which are seemingly bereft of any conscious regard for Catholic values, form only the surface layer. As the story unfolds, a poetical pattern gradually emerges, evoking Christian concepts. Char-

24. Mary Gordon, interview by Barbara A. Bannon, *Publishers Weekly* (Feb. 6, 1981): 274.
25. I Cor. 13:1.

acterization is strategically designed to suggest symbolic correlations between the secular characters and their spiritual namesakes. Neo-impressionist pointillist scaffolding connects the novel's contemporary secular figures to traditional Catholic authority figures. For example, Anne's namesake is St. Anne, the mother of the Virgin Mary. Anne's husband Michael resembles St. Michael the Archangel, who calls souls to Judgment Day. Anne's intellectually gifted nine-year-old son Peter is a scion of St. Peter, who was the first person to enter the risen Christ's empty tomb. Anne's art historian friend and sponsor Benedict Hardy is an avatar of St. Benedict, a Roman nobleman of the sixth century whose *Rule* organized monastic life according to the virtues of hard work, obedience, and humility. Most poetically, *Men and Angels* invokes the power of the Holy Spirit as an indwelling presence. As a Catholic writer, Gordon provides the novel with ghostlike figures that hover at a distance from the two feminine protagonists. The pivotal figures in this partly secular, partly spiritual corps of secondary characters are, significantly, a neglected early-twentieth-century artist named Caroline Watson and her son, Stephen, who preceded her in death. A Hellenistic Jew, St. Stephen was the first Christian martyr. Ostensibly, Anne rises above the significant other people in her life. Inspired and encouraged by Ben Hardy, she holds her beloved son, daughter, and friends at a distance while she sequesters herself in Michael's private study. The novel's backdrop creates an allegorically nuanced cultural milieu, seemingly of demons and angels floating in an etherealized atmosphere that fuels Anne's intellectual journey as an art historian.

Similar to *The Samurai*, *Men and Angels* pursues two divergent storylines that thematically explore conflicts between materialism and spirituality. Laura and Anne are set at cross-purposes, but the story of these two women is really about the need for ecumenism in an America separated from the Body of Christ. For example, the alienation of both Laura and Anne from their biological mothers is a feminist theme that gives rise to the theological Virgin Mary/Holy Mother motif in the novel. The absence of maternal love symbolizes women's unfulfilled yearning for a spiritual relationship with Mary the Mother of God. Broaching this Marian religious motif through a feminist perspective, the novel invokes spiritual hunger for the religious succor of "Our Lady of Sorrows." This feminist theological motif, in turn, evokes a compelling demand for meeting society's need for the Church to help women find spiritual sources of inner peace and moral integrity. Patricia Cox Miller observes, "Although St. Paul had called the church the 'body of Christ' (1 Corinthians 12:17), from the second century onward it became conventional to speak about the church as a 'female' entity as well."[26] Clement of Alexandria, in *The Pedagogue* (2 A.D.), eulogizes the "Father," and the "Word," and the "Holy Spirit," which is "one and the same for all"; and the "virgin Mother," whom he calls the "Church."[27] The narrative of Laura's and Anne's scintillating inner lives exposes socioeconomic forces that rive the roots of the Catholic Church in a materialistic culture marching to perdition. As does Dante in *The Divine Comedy, Men and Angels* traces the inner workings of souls in a state of moral decay and spiritual angst.

Men and Angels' first chapter is devoted exclusively to probing the mind of Laura Post, an uncompromising young woman who personifies the polarization of religiosity and atheism, for she is absolutely certain that she is one of God's favorites and, at the same time, has a total lack of confidence in "unbelievers." Gordon's theologically sophisticated depiction of Laura Post may be inspired by the biography of St. Laura Evangelista (1875–1967), born out of wedlock, who fasted for ten years as penance and dedicated herself to "nursing the sick poor."[28] In trying to rationalize a recent rejection of her services as a babysitter, Laura cannot recall the exact reason; thus she concludes that the couple who fired her is sinful, that they do not possess the "Spirit" as she does. Similar to Endō, Gordon uses the modernist technique of indirect discourse to narrate the thoughts of her protagonists. Laura is portrayed sympathetically in a veiled appeal that awakens readers to the novel's underlying ecumenical theme. Her internal mantra is a poetic refrain borrowed from Matthew 10:16: "Behold, I send you forth as sheep in the midst of wolves: be ye therefore wise as serpents, and harmless as doves." The novel links Laura to the notion of a universal Apostolic Church that is ecumenical and not exclusionary of her as a fundamentalist Christian. She determines to teach the children she cares for that the "human love" withheld from them by their parents is "not important" and that the "suffering" inflicted by parents "would end" in the same way her suffering "had ended."[29] Her unhappy thoughts reveal that she still suffers unspeakable anguish, because she remembers how she tried hard to be "a good child," though her mother did not

26. Patricia Cox Miller, ed., *Women in Early Christianity: Translations from Greek Texts* (Washington, D.C.: The Catholic University of America Press, 2005), 312.

27. Ibid., 313.

28. Sarah Gallick, *The Big Book of Women Saints* (San Francisco: HarperCollins, 2007), 104.

29. Mary Gordon, *Men and Angels* (New York: Random House, 1985), 4.

love her, and her father rejected her because he wanted a son instead of a daughter. Laura has found solace in religion, particularly in the idea that she is "chosen of the Lord," something her parents "had not known." Her secret thoughts conflate predestination, the Garden of Eden, and Christ's mission. She is sure that the Lord came to her in a vision when she was seventeen and gave her the understanding that "the way of the Lord was beauty, was the Spirit in the garden. It was also fire. And it also was the sword."[30] Her logic is inspired by Genesis 3:24 ("So he drove out the man, and he placed at the east of the garden of Eden Cherubims, and a flaming sword which turned every way, to keep the way of the tree of life"), which is reinforced in Christ's warning, "Think not that I came to send peace on earth: I came not to send peace but a sword."[31] Thus, her epiphany of joy at being chosen by God is closely tied to her belief that her life necessarily entails "the sword" of hardship and suffering and that she brings this "sword" to others for their own salvation. Her chosen role is that of an avenging angel sent by Christ.

Laura becomes convinced that Christ has "sent" her to "save" Anne because of her collaboration with a straitlaced French Catholic woman, who debriefs her about Anne and creates from the novel's beginning an ambiguous ecumenical atmosphere.[32] On a transatlantic jet to New York, Laura meets Hélène, a French exchange teacher. Hélène suggests a bifurcation in Laura's mental life when she inquires if Laura reads her Bible because she has "a religious life" or because she enjoys "the poetry." Perceptive and accommodating, Laura immediately seizes on the phrase: instead of avowing that she is chosen of the Lord, which she now realizes alienates adults, she can say that she has a "religious life." She regards her chance meeting with Hélène as a direct message from God to help her, but she also warns herself to be "wise as serpents" in her dealing with Hélène. Laura feigns empathy when Hélène confides that she, too, has a religious life. She wants Hélène to help her, so she appears to listen "with love."[33] But when Hélène expresses sadness over leaving behind her friends, some worker priests and a missionary nun, Laura's mind wanders. Adept at wearing a social mask, Laura conceals her satirical acuity so well that Hélène invites her to live with her during her job hunt and entrusts her with the keys to her house in Selby, Massachusetts. Through Hélène's influence, Laura secures the position as nanny to Anne Foster's children.

30. Ibid., 4, 5.   31. Matt. 10:34.
32. Gordon, *Men and Angels*, 30.   33. Ibid., 7.

In the novel's first few pages, Laura's interior monologue reveals a woman whose mind is suspended between angelic faith and demonic zeal. Just when it seems most plausible for readers to conclude that she is mentally ill, however, the narrative shifts perspective and the situation becomes more ambiguous. Laura relaxes her inward defensive posture in her conversation with Hélène, whose kindness makes her desire to be "wise as serpents" productive, not self-protective. Hélène disarms Laura's defense mechanisms when she speaks condescendingly of Anne, the wife of the exchange teacher who will be teaching her classes in Toulouse while she takes his place at Selby College. Because Laura keeps her pent-up passionately held religious beliefs to herself, Hélène takes Laura under her wing. Hélène symbolizes nonecclesial aspects of the Church as an ecumenical structure that magisterially exerts influence, for she mediates between "Men" and "Angels" in a gray area between heaven and earth. Hélène's visits to Catholic acquaintances in New Jersey, Georgia, Illinois, and California are reminiscent of Constantine's mother St. Helen, who advocated ecumenism, erecting Christian churches in Rome, Bethlehem, Jerusalem, and Palestine. Although Laura and Anne, the two protagonists in *Men and Angels,* are not Catholic *per se,* Gordon's novel of moral revelation resonates deeply with Catholic thought.

Obliquely, in the consummate artistry of its structural design, *Men and Angels* argues the relevancy of Christian values in contemporary society. Ecclesiastical ecumenism mediates the gray areas between "created things" and "the divine,"[34] such that the concept of ecumenical outreach within the Catholic Church would embrace "orthodoxy" which, as Thomas Hopko defines the word, affirms "in all religions and philosophies and in all human thoughts and actions—what is positively true and good in them."[35] Hopko insists that such orthodoxy, which defends "anything worthy of praise,"[36] is needed to reform the Catholic Church. When Anne, an emblem of this orthodoxy, is asked to research and write a brochure on the artist Caroline Watson, she accepts the commission because she badly wants to fit into the college-town milieu. Absorbed in Caroline's life and art, which are, the novel suggests, not particularly estimable, Anne grows aware of the artist's tragic neglect of her son Stephen, which erects a "barrier" that is "as profound as one of language"

34. Mary R. Reichardt, ed., *Catholic Women Writers: A Bio-Bibliographical Sourcebook* (Westport, Conn.: Greenwood, 2001), xv.

35. Thomas Hopko, *All the Fullness of God: Essays on Orthodoxy, Ecumenism and Modern Society* (Crestwood, N.Y.: St. Vladimir's Seminary Press, 1982), 100.

36. Ibid., 102; cf. Phil. 4:8.

and precipitates Anne's righteous indignation: "You have done wrong, she always wanted to tell Caroline. Caroline the ghost who had taken over her life, hovering, accepting worship."[37] Ironically, she remains unaware, until after Laura's death, that whenever she ignores Laura, who becomes, in a sense, her surrogate child, she hypocritically reincarnates Caroline, whom she despises. In Gordon's dualistic vision, Anne is shaped by the decision of her mother Susan Elliott, who left a Catholic convent school after she spent twelve years in residency. Susan's defection from Catholicism symbolizes a larger scheme in which the absence of sacraments, Scripture, and religious ritual seems symptomatic of moral laxity, uncertainty, and indeed, even intellectual and cultural degradation. Nevertheless, the research work that Anne performs is fruitful in helping her begin to probe her predicament as a woman who seems to be a happily married wife and mother yet who feels unfulfilled and insecure.

Laura is a perfect housekeeper and indeed very good with the children, but Anne, increasingly paranoid, feels ominously that "a religious disposition" is "something powerful and incomprehensible" that makes people "behave extraordinarily" and turns them into "monsters of persecution, angels of self-sacrifice."[38] She wavers between treating Laura too familiarly as a member of the family, buying her gifts and making her a birthday cake, and viewing her disparagingly as hired help. Increasingly, Laura retreats into her imaginary world of spiritual fervor in which her image of Anne is reified like a Catholic frieze of the Virgin Mary/Holy Mother. Paradoxically, the more unloved Laura feels, the greater grows the flame of her adoration of Anne. The more remote Anne, the "ideal" wife and mother, makes herself, the more she rises to an esoteric realm that Laura equates with her image of the exalted Mother of God. Although she is the antithesis of Laura in that she evinces no spiritual leanings, Anne has qualms that develop into scruples as a result of Laura's silent and ubiquitous presence. Anne, a woman who outwardly has everything—a healthy husband, two lively children, and an advanced academic degree—develops a gnawing sense of inadequacy because her innate perspicacity detects the downside of depending on an uneducated nanny to fill her shoes while she leads a monkish life as an art historian. Reminiscent of Flannery O'Connor's technique, the novel thus begins to shift our judgment about the character we at first considered "normal." Perhaps the

37. Gordon, *Men and Angels*, 68.
38. Ibid., 162.

novel's moral center resides in Ed Corcoran, a character who makes only a cameo appearance in the novel yet is important in underscoring Anne's spiritual bankruptcy. Ed has a life filled with misfortune. Rose, his wife, is gravely ill, and he is thousands of dollars in debt, which means he has to bring his little son on his electrician's rounds. When Anne tries to seduce him, he gently rejects her offer, reminding her that they are both married and telling her sincerely that he still values her friendship. Anne is deeply humiliated, because she sees his goodness and integrity in light of her own fawning insecurity and emptiness. Ed seems to possess true charity, but when Anne fails to conquer her dislike of Laura Post, she simply aborts the relationship with Laura, and her shaky sense of self-worth is restored.

Critic Mariella Gable notes, "Often the good can be truly appreciated only through a negative treatment," which makes the "good more manifest."[39] Finally and harshly rejected by Anne, Laura commits suicide by cutting her wrists in Anne's bathtub, where first Peter and then Anne find her lifeless body. Although the police will not "name" her as "the criminal," Anne knows that she "closed her heart to Laura" and "had driven her to death."[40] Ironically, Anne reveals her potential for true compassion when she affords Laura a measure of dignity after her death. Obliquely, the novel portrays vestiges of Catholic religious worship in Anne's ritual-like clothing of the body, summoning of a Catholic priest to give last rites, and scattering of Laura's ashes by the river where Anne and her family had previously celebrated Laura's birthday. Thus, we may perceive Laura's death as an image of spiritual death and resurrection. In this sense, the bathtub is a maternal womb in which Laura submerses her body in life-giving water commingled with the blood of passionate suffering. Flowing blood and water point to Christ's merciful love, which cleanses sinners from the failure to love as He has loved us, the love of *caritas*.

Men and Angels' climactic episode reconfigures Matthew 14:27–32, which depicts "Peter the braggart panicking as he tries to walk on water like his Lord."[41] When Anne succumbs to temptations, she denies the Holy Spirit in her, which is redolent of Peter's denials. Twinges of conscience on learning

39. Mariella Gable, "The Novel," in *The Catholic Booksman's Guide: A Critical Evaluation of Catholic Literature*, ed. Sister M. Regis (New York: Hawthorn, 1962), 417.

40. Gordon, *Men and Angels*, 216.

41. Gordon, "Appetite for the Absolute," in *The Best American Spiritual Writing 2005*, ed. Philip Zaleski (Boston: Houghton Mifflin, 2005), 95.

of her revered collaborator Jane Watson's "love affair" with her mentor Ben at the moment when her children's lives are in danger prompt Anne to vent her anger at Laura, who is calmly reading her Bible while Peter and Sarah walk on the pond's icy surface. The ice symbolizes the barrier that finally causes Anne to denounce Laura. Her firing Laura for reading Sacred Scripture reflects her slowness in consciously accepting Christ's love. Christ rebukes Peter for savoring "not the things that be of God, but those that be of *men*."[42] In the miracle of God's grace, the Apostolic Church gathers Peter into the fold, like Anne gathers Sarah and Peter into her arms. Ultimately, Anne learns moral responsibility through Laura, who becomes a cross for Anne to bear. After putting in place sacramental rites for Laura's burial, Anne realizes, "[Laura] did this because she wanted to bring me to God."[43] Anne accepts her culpability for Laura's premature death: "and Anne knew that she had helped the whip descend." Anne comes closest to repentance during the Catholic sacrament of the last rites when, "listening to the priest," she wishes she had recognized and reciprocated Laura's *caritas*.[44]

The spiritual Bildungsroman genre imaginatively portrays ecumenism as a progressive undertaking whereby the Church emulates the fullness of created and divine being as part of the Universal Church, demonstrating the mystical power of God's grace, Christ's love, and the Holy Spirit to transform lives at home and abroad. Rejuvenating Christian narratives of spiritual journeys like John Bunyan's *The Pilgrim's Progress*, Shūsaku Endō's *The Samurai* yokes together Velasco's Catholic idealism and Christ's Crucifixion as symbolized in Hasekura's martyrdom. Hasekura is a secular father whose death redeems the life of his sons, thus allegorically invoking Christ's *caritas*, which Hasekura emulates as a child of God. Mary Gordon's *Men and Angels* inscribes in its protagonists' fluctuating consciousness Gordon's insightful critique of Catholicism's ecumenical mission in the homes and on the streets of America, suggesting that ecumenical birthing and nurturing of the Church as a community of believers united in love is as relevant to our contemporary world as it was for the first Christians.

---

42. Matt. 16:23, my emphasis.
44. Ibid., 232, 233.

43. Gordon, *Men and Angels*, 230.

CHAPTER 12

"Art with Its Largesse and Its Own Restraint"

The Sacramental Poetics of Elizabeth Jennings and Les Murray

Stephen McInerney

In the peroration to his *Lectures on Poetry*, delivered in the first half of the nineteenth century, John Keble, the Anglican poet and priest, declared, "Poetry lends religion her wealth of symbols and similes; religion restores them again to poetry, clothed with so splendid a radiance that they appear to be no longer symbols, but to partake (I might almost say) of the nature of sacraments."[1] Almost fifty years later, Matthew Arnold argued that since the "fact" had failed it, the strongest part of religion was the "unconscious poetry" of its rites and rituals.[2] A hundred years later still, the English novelist and philosopher Iris Murdoch declared that art and poetry fill the void left by sacraments and prayer in an "unreligious age."[3] While Murdoch was paradoxically equating art and sacrament at the very same time as she was sounding the death knell of religion, the Catholic painter and poet David Jones was coming to the end of a career that had been devoted to reconnecting art with its ancient roots in sacramental practice. Persuaded by Jacques Maritain's extraordinary claim that "the Eucharistic sacrifice [is] at the heart of poetry,"[4] Jones related art to the sacramental life with a sophistication and

For permission to quote from Elizabeth Jennings's "Grapes" and "Towards a Religious Poem," I am grateful to David Higham Associates Limited. For permission to quote from Les Murray's "Poetry and Religion," "Once in a Lifetime, Snow," "Blood," "The Abomination," "The Broad Bean Sermon," and *The Boys Who Stole the Funeral,* I am grateful to Mr. Les Murray. Part of my discussion of Elizabeth Jennings has appeared in a different version in the online *Literary Encyclopedia* (www.litencyc.com), to whose chief editor, Robert Clark, I am grateful for permission to reuse material essential to the cohesion of this essay.

1. John Keble, *Lectures on Poetry: 1832–1841* (Bristol: Thoemmes, 2003), 481.

2. Matthew Arnold, *Essays in Criticism* (Second Series) (London: Macmillan, 1903), 1.

3. Iris Murdoch, *The Fire and the Sun* (Oxford: Clarendon, 1977), 76.

4. Jacques Maritain, *Art and Scholasticism* and *The Frontiers of Poetry*, trans. Joseph W. Evans (Notre Dame, Ind.: University of Notre Dame Press, 1974), 132.

depth that exceeded any before him. For Jones, the sacraments themselves were a form of craftsmanship by which the work of human hands became an incarnation of the divine. As the body and blood of Christ are said to exist under the "species" of bread and wine respectively, so a painted object or scene really exists "under the species of paint," and "as through and by the Son, all creation came into existence and is by that same agency redeemed, so we, who are co-heirs with the Son, extend, in a way, creative and redeeming influences upon the dead works of nature, when we fashion material to our heart's desire."[5]

Contemporary literary criticism has also borne witness to the increased awareness of the relationship between poetry and the sacraments, giving rise to something of a minor genre in critical discourse.[6] This is particularly noticeable in Hopkins scholarship, where some extraordinary claims have been made about Hopkins's intentions for his poetry. Maria Lichtmann, for example, has argued, "The poem, for Hopkins, is the Body of Christ. It is the Eucharist in the sense of bearing the motionless, lifeless Real Presence of Christ, of acting with sacramental, transforming instress on the reader as Hopkins has himself instressed nature."[7] Eleanor McNees is equally daring (and equally vague) in her claim that Hopkins "crafts a poem as a kind of Mass in which all words work to voice the one Word—Christ. The successful poem enacts the Eucharistic process . . . The moment of sacrifice is the culmination of real presence in the reader."[8] Margaret R. Ellsberg, meanwhile, has argued that, for Hopkins, poetry "is the sacrament of flesh, word and spirit charged by their interpenetration with each other."[9]

More recently, connections between art and sacrament have been brought to a new point of fusion in the poetry of two modern Catholic poets, Elizabeth Jennings (1926–2001) and Les Murray (1938–). "Poetry," Jennings writes, is

5. David Jones, *The Dying Gaul and Other Writings* (London: Faber and Faber, 1978), 287.

6. See, for example, David Brown and Ann Loades, eds., *Christ: The Sacramental Word—Incarnation, Sacrament and Poetry* (London: Society for Promoting Christian Knowledge, 1996); Theresa DiPasquale, *Literature and Sacrament: The Sacred and the Secular in John Donne* (Cambridge: James Clarke, 2001); Eleanor McNees, *Eucharistic Poetry* (Lewisburg, Pa.: Bucknell University Press, 1992); Kathleen Norris, "A Word Made Flesh: Incarnational Language and the Writer," in *The Incarnation: An Interdisciplinary Symposium on the Incarnation of the Son of God*, ed. Stephen T. Davis, Daniel Kendall, and Gerald O'Collins. (Oxford: Oxford University Press, 2002), 303–12.

7. Maria Lichtmann, "The Incarnational Aesthetic of Gerard Manley Hopkins," *Religion and Literature* 23, no. 1 (1991): 44.

8. Eleanor McNees, *Eucharistic Poetry: The Search for Presence in the Writings of John Donne, Gerard Manley Hopkins, Dylan Thomas and Geoffrey Hill* (Lewisburg, Pa.: Bucknell University Press, 1992), 77.

9. Margaret R. Ellsberg, *Created to Praise: The Language of Gerard Manley Hopkins* (Oxford: Oxford University Press, 1987), 45.

"a kind of secular sacrament, a true grace, something altogether deeper than a mere blessing."[10] Murray goes even further, arguing that the "sacramental is the body, it's the mystery of embodiment [and] words form a body called a poem."[11] This essay explores the sacramental dimensions of the work of these two writers, the most significant "sacramental" poets since David Jones.

Elizabeth Jennings

Elizabeth Jennings was born in Boston, Lincolnshire, in 1926, and lived there for six years before her family moved to Oxford. She read English at St. Anne's College, Oxford, and resided in the city for most of her adult life, working variously at the Oxford City Library and as a publisher's reader before finally abandoning formal employment. This decision, which freed her to write, condemned her to relative poverty for most of her life, and she was purportedly mistaken for a "bag lady" from time to time.[12] Her editor, Michael Schmidt, has recorded that on one such occasion he needed to explain to a restaurant proprietor that Miss Jennings was, despite appearances to contrary, one of the country's most acclaimed poets.[13]

Jennings's childhood was essentially a happy one, and many of her poems celebrate the innocence of the nursery in contrast to the "bad dreams," "haunted memories," and "talk of sin or pain" that troubled her throughout adolescence and adulthood.[14] A cradle Catholic, her faith intensified when, as a young girl, she felt the wonder of the natural world:

I had a very strange experience when I was about ten years old. I remember going out one night into our front garden in Oxford which was full of small trees and shrubs. The sky was crowded with stars and I felt an exaltation such as I had never known before and have never known since so fully and richly. The arrival of self-consciousness as I experienced it at the age of 15 had the very opposite effect on me.[15]

Religion, as such, was a paradoxically consoling and painful part of her life, combining an awareness of innocent freedom and joy in God's presence (the

10. Elizabeth Jennings, "Saved by Poetry," *The Tablet* (May 15, 1993): 613.

11. William Scammell, "Les Murray in Conversation," *PN Review* 25, no. 2 (1998): 31.

12. For these and the other details of Jennings's life described in this essay, I am indebted to Michael Schmidt's preface to Jennings's *New Collected Poems* (Manchester: Carcanet, 2002).

13. Schmidt, preface to Jennings, *New Collected Poems*, xxiii.

14. Jennings, *New Collected Poems*, 210–11.

15. Jennings, "Saved by Poetry," 613.

Easter liturgy, for instance, is "like childhood once again") with a sense of sin and guilt ("cries of love are cries of fear"). She was filled with wonder at the thought of God's existence, yet she was simultaneously frightened by the troubling questions such wonder often induces. This tension between wonder and fear left an indelible impression on her work, and in some sense it characterizes her whole approach to questions of faith: "Take my unlove and despair / And what they lack let faith repair."[16]

The rituals of the Church were always a source of poetic inspiration for Jennings. Many of her poems explore the joys and consolations of the sacramental life, particularly the Mass. "Nothing matters but this Holy Meal," she writes in "At Mass (II)," which seems to respond antiphonally to "At Mass (I)," where she asks, "Why are we not amazed? . . . A bell is rung and the bread wraps / Christ thinly in it." In these poems, Jennings typically strives to stress the love that motivated Christ to give his life and feed us with His flesh and blood. Her voice is urgent at times, as she begs the world to "live abundantly and by our Faith / Accept what all the Godhead longed to give."[17] These frequent reiterations of God's love for the world are made all the more poignant precisely because of the difficulty Jennings experienced in accepting that she was herself the object of this love. She seems to have suffered from excessive scrupulosity. This meant that the sacrament of penance, for example, was especially difficult for her to frequent. "This healing sacrament / Was hurting for me," she writes in "First Confession," where she also describes how her childhood "ceased / Upon that day."[18] In "A Childhood Horror," she recalls going to confession as a fifteen-year-old. Rebuked by the priest for expressing uncertainty about "my faith's tenets," the teenage girl was told not to take communion, an experience that wounded her for "five harsh years."[19] In a revealing article, "Saved by Poetry," which appeared in the *Tablet* in 1993, Jennings explains that she "was terribly muddled about my faith in relation to sex . . . This, together with all my theological and philosophical doubts, made my middle to late teens very unhappy."[20] She would be dogged by depression throughout her adult life and, like some of her more famous female contemporaries (for example, Anne Sexton and Sylvia Plath), she suffered a number of crippling breakdowns.

In the context of twentieth-century poetry, Jennings appears as a some-

16. Jennings, *New Collected Poems*, 131.
18. Ibid., 250.
20. Jennings, "Saved by Poetry," 613.
17. Ibid., 301, 302.
19. Ibid., 243.

what paradoxical figure. Her greatest influences were Eliot and Hopkins, yet her work avoids the stylistic and syntactical complexities of both these figures. Her typical utterance is plain, direct, and classical, while her religious poems are characterized by a conventional range of symbolic reference, which she nonetheless redeems from any hint of cliché or triteness. She was often associated with the group of writers collectively known as "the Movement," which included Philip Larkin and Thom Gunn, yet she was anything but typical of this generally agnostic group whose work is notable for its ironic reserve and melancholic resignation. "Nothing, like something, happens anywhere," Larkin once said, in a line that captures the despondency of so many writers linked to the Movement. Jennings's real affinities with the group are less ideological than stylistic. The Movement poets were consciously middle-class and sought to look at the world of teapots, frayed curtains, and seaside holidays unsentimentally. Artistic conservatives, they rejected the obscurantism of the modernists on the one hand, and on the other, the emotional outpourings of confessional poets like Robert Lowell and neo-romantics like Dylan Thomas. Jennings, for example, although she wrote explicitly about her depression, did so cautiously. Her work has none of the nervous tension of confessional poetry nor, despite her celebrations of the natural world, does she mythologize it in the manner of Dylan Thomas or, later, Ted Hughes. At the same time, however, J. D. Scott's suggestions that the Movement was characterized by skepticism, robustness, and irony does not adequately describe Jennings's own work,[21] which is rarely ironic and is permeated by Christian hope.

Jennings believed, moreover, that poetry could "save." Poetry could transform the world, if not in the manner that Arnold or Murdoch envisioned, yet humbly and discreetly. As Schmidt has said, "Enactment in language, a function of rhythm, word-order, [and] diction can impart a spiritual dimension to work of secular writers; poems can mean more than a poet intends, as if touched by a grace the poet inadvertently accesses and cannot deny."[22] The Movement may have been, according to Scott, "prepared to be as comfortable as possible in a wicked, commercial, threatened world which didn't look, anyway, as if it's going to be changed much by a couple of handfuls of young English writers,"[23] but Jennings never lost faith—despite peri-

21. Andrew Motion, *Philip Larkin: A Writer's Life* (London: Faber and Faber, 1993), 242–43.
22. Schmidt, preface to Jennings, *New Collected Poems*, xxi.
23. Motion, *Philip Larkin*, 242.

ods of intense doubt and depression—in the ability of art to point to the numinous.

Jennings's first collection, *Poems,* appeared in 1953. It is preoccupied with the problem of identity, which is linked for Jennings to the question of how we order experience and make sense of reality. Identity, as the poem of that name argues, is something that we "assemble" and "shape" (an important word in her lexicon). Fishermen learn "themselves in this uncertainty" of waiting to catch a fish;[24] "Every man / Tied to the rope constructs himself alone";[25] and the poet, in whittling "A pattern from the shapeless stony stuff / That now confuses,"[26] finds the pattern and shape of her own being. The influence of David Jones's aesthetics is evident here, perhaps surprisingly given the considerable stylistic differences between the two writers. Jones refers frequently in his poetry and essays to the relationship between sacrament and "shaping." Mankind, according to Jones, was a "maker" of "significant" shapes. In his epic *Anathemata,* he describes how the "groping syntax" of the priest in the Canon of the Mass "already shapes" the Eucharist;[27] and the *Anathemata* was itself described by Jones as a "shape in words." Yet Jennings's frequent references to "shape" and "shaping" can be traced through Jones back to Hopkins. In a recent article, James Finn Cotter has explored the possibility (first noted by V. de S. Pinto, as Cotter points out) that Hopkins may have in part derived his term "inscape" from Phillipe de Mornay's *De la Verite de la Religion Chrestienne.*[28] There, "in*shape*" implies God's creative patterning of the universe, that God is the "togetherbeer," "the shaper, the giver and former of shape."[29] Hopkins similarly uses "inscape" "as a synonym for pattern." "Inscape" was a sacramentally loaded word in Hopkins's nomenclature. Although it is not a connection Cotter makes, he quotes a passage from the translation of de Mornay's work whose cadence and theme is almost identical to a passage in one of Hopkins's letters in which he discusses the Blessed Sacrament. Referring to the incarnate Christ as the mediator between God and man, de Mornay writes, "This marke is so of the very substance and inshape of Religion, that Religion without that should be utterly

---

24. Jennings, "Fishermen," in *New Collected Poems,* 6.

25. Jennings, "The Climbers," in *New Collected Poems,* 5.

26. Jennings, "Reminiscence," in *New Collected Poems,* 1.

27. David Jones, *The Anathemata* (London: Faber and Faber, 1952), 49.

28. Translated by Sir Philip Sidney and Arthur Golding as *Worke Concerning the Trewnesse of the Christian Religion.* 1578 (Delmar, N.Y.: Scholars' Facsimiles and Reprints, 1976).

29. James Finn Cotter, "The Inshape of Inscape," *Victorian Poetry* 42, no. 2 (2004): 197.

unavailable and vayne."[30] Explaining to E. H. Coleridge the importance of the doctrine of the Real Presence, Hopkins writes, "Religion without that is sombre, dangerous, illogical."[31]

For Jennings, "shape" has a similar connection with the Eucharist as it had for Jones and as its etymological cognate "inscape" had for Hopkins, as is evident not only from her poems but also from her criticism. By the time she had begun writing the poems that would make up *Song for a Birth or a Death* (1961), she had started to investigate systematically the relationship between poetry, mysticism, and the sacramental life. *Every Changing Shape* (1961), the first of her two major literary critical studies (the other being *Seven Men of Vision*, 1976), was the result. It explores the writings of over fifteen authors, from St. Augustine through St. John of the Cross, to Simone Weil, T. S. Eliot, and Hart Crane. The connection Jennings felt with the mystics about whom she wrote—many of whom, including St. Augustine, St. Teresa of Avila, and St. John of the Cross, had chosen the religious life—was profound. Contemplative rather than ecstatic, her own writing is characterized by the restraint of its utterance, a restraint she recognized in the writings of St. Teresa of Avila, who (as Jennings argued *contra* the famously ecstatic image of the saint by Bernini) eschewed the dramatic in favor of "homely, natural and precise imagery"[32]—a phrase that could well serve as a description of Jennings's own approach.

The homely, the natural, and the precise were qualities Jennings also discerned in the sacraments of the Church, which use ordinary materials to make the divine present. *Song for a Birth or a Death,* like several of her later collections (in particular *Growing Points,* 1975), contains a number of poems on the sacramental and liturgical life. Writing on the Eucharist in her tribute to David Jones, Jennings compares art, "with its largesse and its own restraint,"[33] to the Eucharist; and again in "Harvest and Consecration" (addressed to a priest), her view of the Eucharist reflects both her aesthetics and the understanding of mysticism she had discovered in her prose treatment of the subject: "I see / The wine and bread protect our ecstasy."[34]

Growing Points must surely stand as one of the most significant collec-

30. Ibid., 198, 199.

31. Claude Colleer Abbott, ed., *Further Letters of Gerard Manley Hopkins* (Oxford: Oxford University Press, 1956), 17.

32. Elizabeth Jennings, *Every Changing Shape* (London: Andre Deutsch, 1961), 59.

33. Jennings, "Visit to an Artist," in *New Collected Poems,* 45.

34. Jennings, *New Collected Poems,* 39.

tions of religious poetry in the twentieth century, containing as it does a dazzling array of prayers, meditations, and reflections on sacramental practice. Jennings manages to treat subjects that would, in the hands of writers of lesser skill, be overwhelmed by the echo of the conventional treatments in various pious works and hymns. Her modest lyrics manage to restore something of an original freshness to the recurring images of bread, wine, wheat, and grapes:

> Those grapes, ready for picking, are the sign
> Of harvest and of Sacrament. Do not
> Touch them; wait for the ones who tread the vine,
> See Southern air surround that bunch . . .
>
> Intense small globes of purple till the hour
> Of expert clipping comes. There is a pang
> In seeing so much fullness change its power.[35]

Beneath the overtly sacramental imagery there is, as well, a more subtle range of religious allusion. "Do not / Touch them," for instance, recalls the words of the resurrected Christ to Mary Magdelene: *Noli me tangere.* The "clipping" of the vine, meanwhile, locates the poem within a scriptural frame in which Christ refers to Himself as both the vine and the vine keeper who prunes his branches to bring them to perfection. And the "pang" induced by "seeing so much fullness change its power," must surely result from an awareness of the Passion that makes the miracle of transubstantiation both possible and efficacious. "Seeing" is an odd word here, however, for strictly speaking this miracle is not "seen." That gerund, though, does two things simultaneously, shifting the poem in two apparently opposite directions: toward a mystical "seeing" on the one hand, and on the other a natural "seeing." The supernatural by definition transcends the natural, and yet the implication is that Christ's Passion is somehow already inscribed into the processes of the natural world.

Presented in Jennings's typically accessible sonnet form, the simplicity of "Grapes"—like so many of Jennings's poems—belies the profundity of her vision and the daring of her approach in the contemporary context. It was this context that she described so forcefully in "Towards a Religious Poem," also from *Growing Points:*

35. Ibid., 95.

Christ in this age you are nameless,
Your praises and slanders have sunk
To oaths. Love has somehow slipped by
What once throbbed in an occupied sky.

In my stanzas I'll only allow
The silence of a tripped tongue,
The concerns and cries of creation
To hold you.[36]

Jennings was wrestling with the problem of finding a place for Christ in a milieu increasingly hostile to His message. Yet her struggle was not merely grounded in the problem of naming Christ in a modern setting. The modern predicament simply heightened her awareness of the more general problem of naming and representing God in the first place. In other words, her struggle was a mystical one. It was Jennings's passionate interest in the mystical life, in all its dimensions, that enabled her to make sense of her depression and the breakdown she suffered in 1961. Jennings stated that her depressive episodes "were too earthbound and commonplace" to be compared with the "Dark Night of the Soul" of the mystics,[37] yet she was able to see parallels between her own trials and those of the writers she admired, including St. John of the Cross and, perhaps most of all, Hopkins.

Jennings's later major collections, especially *Consequently I Rejoice* (1977), *Extending the Territory* (1985), *Tributes* (1989), *Praises* (1998), and *Timely Issues* (2001), extend her thematic and technical range, particularly in the direction of memoir and reminiscence, while retaining a sturdy commitment to the poet's sense of her own "religious" vocation. In her final work she dedicates a poem to George Herbert. "Prayer: Homage to George Herbert" is also an homage to the power of poetry and the role Jennings believed it plays in service of the Word: "Christ needs words to show / He's dying . . . But I shall need the words that rise also."[38] Throughout her career she searched for the words "that rise" as she explored the paradox that although God is present to humankind through His incarnational extension in the sacraments, these nonetheless point beyond the "now" to the kingdom yet to come, when all anxieties will be dispelled. Her poetry shares in this hope, yet it is faithful to the reality of her anxieties and the complexities of

36. Ibid., 99.
37. Jennings, "Saved by Poetry," 613.
38. Jennings, *New Collected Poems*, 345.

215

the world that generated them. As such, Jennings is both a frank realist and a poet full of supernatural joy, who shows the sorrow of life and its tragedy while pointing to the One who, by embracing both, offers redemption to all who seek Him.

Les Murray

Where Jennings's work is marked by the restraint of its utterance and its indebtedness to the "provinciality" that characterized much of postwar British poetry, Les Murray's poetry is notable for its "largesse" and Whitman-like scale, placing Australian poetry on the map. His place at the forefront of contemporary poetry in English has been generally acknowledged since he was first feted by two Nobel laureates. The late Joseph Brodsky described him as "the one by whom the language lives";[39] while Derek Walcott has said: "There is no poetry in the English language now so rooted in its sacredness, so broad-leafed in its pleasures, and yet so intimate and so conversational."[40] In 1983 Murray dedicated his sixth collection of verse, *The People's Otherworld*, "to the glory of God." Each of his subsequent collections has carried this dedication. This astonishing gesture reflects Murray's position as one of the most avowedly Catholic poets of the twentieth century. Certainly the sense of the sacred has been a feature of his poetry from the beginning.

Murray's view of poetry as sacred differs slightly from Jennings's, not in its essence but in its extent. Like Jennings, he reifies into sacramental shapes the ordinary, mundane details of day-to-day life and experience while also stressing the mystical similarities between poetry and religion:

> Religions are poems. They concert
> our daylight and dreaming mind, our
> emotions, instinct, breath and native gesture
>
> into the only whole thinking: poetry.[41]

Yet Murray goes farther than Jennings in advancing an idea of the poet as a priest, an offerer of sacrifice, and this is his most distinctive contribution to

---

39. Quoted in Les Murray, *The People's Otherworld* (Sydney: Angus and Robertson, 1983), back cover.

40. Derek Walcott, "*Crocodile Dandy:* Les Murray," in *What the Twilight Says: Essays* (London: Faber and Faber, 1998), 184.

41. Les Murray, "Poetry and Religion," in *Collected Poems: 1961–2002* (Potts Point: Duffy and Snellgrove, 2002), 265.

the notion of a sacramental poetic. His view of the poet as priest links him with Jones. Unlike Jones, however, Murray does not stress the relationship between the "re-presentation" of Christ's sacrifice in the Mass as the *representation* of a "thing" under another "species" (paint, clay, or language). For Murray, the poet is rather a hierophant, a speaker for the tribe who offers "unbloody" sacrifices. With respect to his own work, he has spoken in specifically Christological terms: "This quasi-priestly work of poetry is Christ, for me; it's His life as I can live it by my efforts."[42]

Born in 1938, Murray grew up in a dairy farming district in Bunyah on the North Coast of New South Wales, an area notable for its natural beauty and the toughness of its farming inhabitants. His mother died when he was nine due to complications resulting from his own birth, and her absence haunts his work: "I didn't mean to harm you / I was a baby."[43] A lonely child who ominously took his rifle on long walks in the bush, Murray was victimized at school for being overweight, an experience that informed his lifelong suspicion of bullying in all its forms. Leaving the North Coast in 1957—he would not return to live there permanently again until 1987—he commenced a bachelor of arts degree at the University of Sydney. There he met his future wife, Valerie Morelli, a young Catholic of Hungarian-Swiss descent. They were married in 1962. Murray, who had grown up in a strongly Presbyterian community, followed her into the Catholic Church in 1964.

Like both Hopkins and Jones before him, each of whom also converted to Catholicism in his early twenties, the young poet was spiritually and intellectually riveted by the Church's principal ritual:[44] "I identified with the Eucharist. I thought, yes, yes, the absolute transformation of ordinary elements into the divine. I know about that. It didn't strike me as unlikely, and it opened such illimitable prospects of life. Most secular mythologies seem to be anxious to close the possibilities of life down and delimit them. This one opened out."[45] The tenor of this statement closely resembles that of another Murray made in an interview in 1998, where he addressed a more ideological reason for his conversion. As though in response to the critic who once aligned a dimension of his work (and, by implication, his religion and pol-

---

42. Quoted in Peter F. Alexander, *Les Murray: A Life in Progress* (Melbourne: Oxford University Press, 2000), 155.

43. Murray, "The Steel," in *Collected Poems*, 189.

44. Alexander, *Les Murray*, 107.

45. Missy Daniel, "Poetry Is Presence: An Interview with Les Murray," *Commonweal* 119, no. 10 (1992): 10.

itics) with "pinched unadorned belligerence and dogma,"[46] he stated, "My politics are anti-totalitarian. That's why I became a Catholic. It's for everybody. It may have a low opinion of sinners, but it's equally low of all. You're warned not to be proud, but also assured that you're of infinite worth."[47]

If it was an attraction to the Eucharist and to the inclusiveness of Catholicism that drew Murray to that faith, it was the work of the poet-priest Hopkins that principally "turned [him] on to poetry"[48] and opened to him a dimension of the craft that, many years later, he would link with the Eucharist. After reading Hopkins, "bang, I suddenly discovered this language with a live electric current through it—you know, powerful stuff. I'd been casting around for an art form for a year or so. I'd gradually been moving away from military fantasies . . . I discovered that poetry was about presence."[49]

Certainly, if poetry is about "presence" so is the Eucharist, and if the Eucharist is about the transformation of the ordinary into the divine, so too is poetry concerned with the interaction between the everyday and the absolute. As Kevin Hart has noted, Murray "sometimes follows what he calls 'an incarnational logic' in which, as Christ is both God and man, a poem is about the holy and the ordinary at once."[50] Similarly, if the Eucharist stands against "secular mythologies" that "close the possibilities of life down," so too is poetry (in what Murray calls the "celebratory mode") characterized by a "refusal of alienation and a species of humility" that "doesn't presume to understand the world, at least never reductively, and so leaves it open and expansive, with unforeclosed potentials."[51] Yet while a poem may be open to "unforeclosed potentials," it is also "a very contained thing that holds down these tremendous energies."[52] As Jennings said, poetry is, like the Eucharist, "art with its largesse and its own restraint."

The "tremendous energies" Murray refers to represent two opposed forces in his work—divine presence, on the one hand, and the need for blood sacrifice on the other:

Wait on! Human sacrifice? Surely that's an archaic horror that survives only very marginally in a few Third World groups that anthropologists write about? Sure-

46. Gig Ryan, "'And the Fetid Air and Gritty,'" *Heat* 5 (1997): 199.
47. Scammell, "Les Murray in Conversation," 36.
48. Daniel, "Poetry Is Presence," 10.
49. Ibid.
50. Kevin Hart, "'Interest' in Les A. Murray," *Australian Literary Studies* 14, no. 2 (1989): 158.
51. Les Murray, *A Working Forest: Selected Prose* (Potts Point: Duffy and Snellgrove, 1997), 360.
52. Scammell, "Les Murray in Conversation," 31.

ly the holocausts of this century in what we call "our" civilization can only be called human sacrifices in a very metaphoric sort of way? Surely there's a distinction to be made here between the literal and the metaphorical? My answer is, there may be, but I don't know of one water-tight enough to prevent the blood from seeping through it.[53]

A poem, for Murray, transforms the desire for sacrifice into a "presence" as Christ on the cross is simultaneously the victim of the sacrifice and the offerer of His presence. A poem holds down both "energies" within itself: "A poem which stays within the realm of literature completes the trinity of forebrain consciousness, dream wisdom and bodily sympathy—of reason, dream and the dance, really—without needing to embody itself in actual suffering or action, and without the need to demand blood sacrifice from us. It is thus like Christ's Crucifixion, both effectual and vicarious."[54] Elsewhere the simile is reversed: "Jesus is like a literal poem, taking these terrible energies that sacrifice people—looking for significance, to underline and stimulate it, by giving it sacrifice. He's saying, that's a superceded principle, I've taken that upon myself, it's all in here, refer to this figure, it's contained. I'm always looking for the containment of human sacrifice."[55]

Believing that a desire for human sacrifice and "significance" underpins human activity to varying degrees, Murray sets up an opposition between a resolved work of art, such as a poem, and disembodied "idols" that "demand" blood sacrifice "to embody" themselves.[56] The need for sacrifice, as such, is either resolved in ritual or art or in actual human sacrifice. Murray aims to craft a poem that is a contemplative site, the point into which human bloodlust is transformed into "a never-murderous skim / distilled," and thus to show how it shares in a Eucharistic identity, in the sense that it incarnates a presence that feeds the human desire for sacrifice and therefore, potentially, prevents such sacrifice through catharsis.[57] In this way it is both "effectual and vicarious." If poetry symbolizes for the poet the completion of his youthful journey away from "military fantasies" (and marks a rejection of them), so the Eucharist, as part of what he calls "The Iliad of peace,"[58] stands against and resolves the "human sacrifice . . . at the heart of litera-

---

53. Murray, *Working Forest*, 131–32.
54. Ibid., 321–22.
55. Scammell, "Les Murray in Conversation," 31.
56. See, for example, Murray, "The Instrument," in *Collected Poems*, 458.
57. Ibid., 458.
58. Murray, "Animal Nativity," in *Collected Poems*, 374.

ture,"[59] along with the innate need to offer blood sacrifices that military fantasies represent.

Murray's first collection of verse, *The Ilex Tree,* was published jointly with his friend Geoffrey Lehmann in 1965. Murray's contribution to the small collection contains poems that evoke the world of rural farmers and timber workers and celebrate the freshness and regenerative powers of the natural world. "Spring Hail,"[60] a poem clearly influenced by Hopkins's "Spring" and Dylan Thomas's "Fern Hill," delights in its natural setting where the numinous permeates the physical landscape—"Fresh minted hills / smoked, and the heavens swirled and blew away"—and where the experience of "spring hail" evokes an atmosphere of reverent awe before the mystery of God's creation, such that the occasion of the poem becomes (through a pun on "hail") at one with the speaker's response of praise, the perfect linguistic communion of object and subject. It strikes a note that has reverberated throughout Murray's career, one that can be heard resoundingly in his second collection, *The Weatherboard Cathedral* (1969), whose title suggests the nature of Murray's project: to craft from his humble origins something beautiful for God, "the transformation of ordinary elements into the divine," a cathedral in weatherboard. In Murray's vision, the natural world is made "vivid" by the Incarnation,[61] remanifesting Christ's presence in creation so that it can always be turned to for spiritual nourishment:

The things I write about are mainly religious or metaphysical—I'm concerned with relations between human time and eternity at the odd points where they meet and illuminate each other, eg. where matter becomes immortal, or spirit enters time "for a season." (It happens.) This heirophanic [hierophantic] thinking works both ways of course: calling on men to witness the world of spirit and, almost, calling on that world to witness us. Like Octavia Paz said in a poem I once translated: the Mass is an "incarnate pause between this and timeless time." Joints and junctions like that, arising in the oddest places, are my meat.[62]

In "Once in a Lifetime, Snow," the poet offers an example of eternity entering time "for a season," and it is interesting to note the response of the farmer to this occurrence. He eats the snow as he recognizes its numinous significance:

59. Les Murray, *The Boys Who Stole the Funeral* (Sydney: Angus and Robertson, 1980), 29.
60. Murray, *Collected Poems*, 8.
61. Murray, "Animal Nativity," in *Collected Poems*, 374.
62. Quoted in Alexander, *Les Murray*, 91.

A man of farm and fact
he stared to see
the facts of weather raised
to a mystery

white on the world he knew
and all he owned.
Snow? Here? he mused. I see.
High time I learned . . .

perceiving this much, he scuffed
his slippered feet
and scooped a handful up
to taste, and eat

in memory of the fact
that even he
might not have seen the end
of reality . . . [63]

The numinous snow, a fact of weather "raised to a mystery," assumes by analogy some of the qualities of the Eucharist in which the bread and wine are raised to the mystery of Christ's body and blood in "memory" of Christ's passion. The farmer's response is similarly Eucharistic: he tastes and eats the snow "in memory of the fact" that reality exceeds the limits of material existence (anticipating the poet's description of the Incarnation as the making "Godhead a fact").[64] Eating the snow is the means by which the farmer physically responds to the spiritual dimension of what has taken place; he incorporates it into himself both to "taste" and savor the experience as well as its significance. While the phrase "in memory of the fact" recalls Christ's words "Do this in memory of me," "Taste, and eat" also echoes part of the Eucharistic words of institution—"Take and eat"—and recalls the scriptural line, "O taste, and see that the Lord is sweet."[65] These connections are quite deliberate. By exceeding the limitations of "reality" as understood by the farmer, the event hints at all the spiritual dimensions hitherto ignored by him—the unforeclosed potentials of the natural world. Eating the snow is the means by which that which had previously been beyond the imagination

---

63. Murray, *Collected Poems*, 23.
64. Ibid., 537.
65. Psalm 33:8.

of the farmer—that which had been external to his vision—is incorporated into his imagination without being exhausted by it.

The *Weatherboard Cathedral* reveals the many-sidedness of Murray's sacramental poetic. As well as depicting a world saturated with God's presence (a dimension of Murray's work that reached its apotheosis in the 1992 collection *Translations from the Natural World*), it also shows how the sacramental enlarges to embrace the sacrificial aspects of the human and animal kingdoms. What Bernadette Ward has said of Hopkins applies equally to Murray: "To look for the intellectual core of his work is to move . . . well beyond a mere generalized feeling about something spiritually nourishing in the beauty of the world. Sacramentality is sacrificial, having to do with loss as well as joy; it perceives God's action in scenes not at all attractive to the senses."[66] In poems like "Blood" and "The Abomination," Murray uncovers the need for sacrifice at the heart of the animal kingdom. In "Blood," the speaker describes himself walking

> back up the trail of crowding flies,
> back to the knife which pours deep blood, and frees
> sun, fence and hill, each to its holy place

And notes:

> A world I thought sky-lost by leaning ships
> in the depth of our life—I'm in that world once more.
> Looking down, we praise for its firm flesh
> the creature killed according to the Law.

The pig killed according to the "Law" is an imperfect type of the true sacrifice, held aloft to the sun in a manner that recalls the elevation of the Host in the Mass. Like the snow in "Once in a Lifetime, Snow," this meat will be eaten, and the idea of "eating" in response to revelatory moments, as a means of reinforcing a sense of communion among individuals and the spiritual world, figures strongly in Murray's sacramental vision. It becomes a prominent theme in *Poems against Economics* (1972), his third collection. "Towards the Imminent Days" celebrates the sacrament of marriage, the union of lovers that "will heal the twentieth century." [67] Set in a landscape of houses and "loved fields, all wearing away into Heaven," it delights also in the

---

66. Bernadette Ward, *World as Word: Philosophical Theology in Gerard Manley Hopkins* (Washington, D.C.: The Catholic University of America Press, 2002), 131–32.

67. Murray, *Collected Poems*, 37.

earthy, hearty rituals of a country wedding: champagne and chicken sup-pers, whiskey, pumpkins, and "poddy calves," as the animal, human, and divine realms—flesh, intellect, and spirit—interconnect in a consciously in-carnational celebration of love. More darkly, *Poems against Economics* ques-tions the obverse drive in humanity, the need to make war, in "Lament for the Country Soldiers." "Vindaloo in Merthyr Tydfil," by contrast, takes a hu-morous view of a mystical experience resulting from the eating of a hot curry (reverently mocking the then-fashionable glances to the Hindu East of many Western intellectuals).[68] "Walking to the Cattle Place," meanwhile, a major sequence of fifteen poems, fuses the central ideas of the collection as it en-gages with the genuine connections—of language and cattle—between In-dian and European civilizations.[69]

In Murray's work, natural food frequently parallels supernatural food, most famously in "The Broad Bean Sermon"[70] from *Lunch and Counter Lunch* (1974), his fourth collection. In this poem, the poet explores another one of the "oddest places"—which is, at the same time, one of the most "ordinary"—where natural fecundity discloses its own inexhaustibility and invites the poet to explore the variety of its minutiae. As the title suggests, the poem is concerned with the way in which the natural world can become an un-assuming voice preaching a "sermon." The title is partly ironic, for the first image the poet uses to describe the broad beans is that of "a slack church parade / without belief, saying *trespass against us* in unison." This image illustrates the way in which, at first glance, the broad beans are a mass of seemingly indistinguishable vegetation—yet the ensuing succession of met-aphors and similes belies this impression, as the poet is drawn deeper and deeper into the world that holds his attention and deeper and deeper into his own imaginative and linguistic resources. In the second stanza, the broad beans are still discussed as a collective, while in the third the poet describes the world above "a thin bean forest." From the fourth stanza until the con-clusion, however, the poem explores the relationship between the universal "you" of the poem who goes to pick the beans and the inexhaustible diver-sity of the beans themselves. This plenitude keeps disclosing more and more variety and difference, which both the bean picker and poet seek to rein in. The rapid succession of compound images is typical of Murray at his exuber-ant best:

68. Ibid., 43, 54. 69. Ibid., 55.
70. Ibid., 112.

At every hour of daylight
appear more that you missed: ripe, knobbly ones, fleshy-sided,
thin-straight, thin-crescent, frown-shaped, bird-shouldered, boat-keeled ones,
beans knuckled and single-bulged, minute green dolphins at suck.[71]

Lunch and Counter Lunch was followed by *Ethnic Radio* (1977) and *The Boys Who Stole the Funeral* (1980), the first of Murray's two verse novels. The Eucharist, described by the poet as "food that solves the world,"[72] stands at the heart of this work, which describes an unlikely incident in which two friends, Kevin Forbutt and Cameron Reeby, sensing that Forbutt's uncle will not receive a proper funeral, steal his body. The crime propels a series of adventures during which the protagonists confront their own inadequacies and approach spiritual enlightenment, recognizing the sacred in the everyday realities of work, family, and nature. Sacrifice, again, is the dominant theme: human sacrifice—which takes the form of war, murder, abortion, and ritualized attacks on individuals—is explicitly set against God's sacrifice ("The true god / gives his flesh and blood. Idols demand yours off you").[73] In one key episode, the boys pick up a hitchhiker who elaborates what is later referred to as "his blood theology":

It was all resolved once: this is My Body, My Blood.
It's coming unsolved now.[74]

The work argues, imaginatively and forcefully, that it is not possible to ignore Christ's sacrifice without reverting to more ancient, pagan forms of sacrifice, even if these are disguised in the modern age (in the case of abortion, for example) under the veil of "progress." As Murray writes elsewhere, paraphrasing Chesterton: "who lose belief in God will not only believe / in anything. They will bring blood offerings to it."[75]

With the exception of *Translations from the Natural World,* the question of "sacrifice" is explicitly addressed in Murray's subsequent collections up to and including *Subhuman Redneck Poems* (1996), culminating in Murray's second verse novel, *Fredy Neptune* (1998). *Fredy Neptune* tells the tale of Fredy Boettcher, a German-Australian sailor who, after witnessing the geno-

71. Ibid.
72. Murray, *The Boys Who Stole the Funeral,* 35.
73. Ibid., 44. These lines reappear in "The Muddy Trench" at the end of the 2002 Australian edition of the *Collected Poems,* and in "Church," a poem dedicated to the memory of Joseph Brodsky, in Murray's collection, *The Biplane Houses* (2006). Their recent reappearance suggests their centrality to Murray's vision.
74. Murray, *The Boys Who Stole the Funeral,* 9.
75. Murray, "The Craze Field," in *Collected Poems,* 161.

cide of Armenian women at the hands of Turkish nationalists in 1917, loses feeling in his body, only to recover it when he learns to forgive his enemies. It is the poet's grand, Homeric exploration of the Enlightenment's disembodiment of humanity and the Christian alternative—the reception of a body (analogous to the reception of the Eucharist), which makes a person whole. The work forms a key part of Murray's career-long attempt to make sense of the relationship between poetry, religion, and ideology, and to find meaningful distinctions between artistic, religious, and political efforts to map experience. By an analogy evident throughout the work, the acceptance of Christ and the regaining of the body are linked with poetry, while totalitarian ideologies are linked with disembodied "poemes" (which stand to true poetry as idols stand to the true God) that seek to close people inside them.

Fredy Neptune was followed by *Conscious and Verbal* (1999), *Poems the Size of Photographs* (2002), and *The Biplane Houses* (2006), each of which confirms the recovery of Murray's earlier rhapsodic calm, his acute "everywhere focus of one devoid of boredom,"[76] that discerns grace in every corner and crevice of the human and animal kingdoms. Murray's images of sacrifice, his theory of the importance of the body for an understanding of the whole person, and his explorations of all the places where God is "caught, not imprisoned," have extended the possibilities of a sacramental poetic by showing how aesthetics embraces ethics. What Tom D'Evelyn said of *Fredy Neptune* in the *Providence Sunday Journal* applies to Murray's work as a whole: "[It] embodies the hope of a human order in an inhuman and disordered time."[77]

■ ■ ■

Drawing from a common religious tradition, in particular from Catholicism's principal ritual, the careers of Jennings and Murray reveal and extend the possibilities of a sacramental or "incarnational" tradition in modern poetry that stretches back to Hopkins. Jennings reveals the inexhaustible richness and lyrical possibilities of the "homely, the natural and the precise." Murray, who draws from the same sources, shows that sacrifice is inextricably bound up with these, as it is with human nature. The popularity and prominence of both poets ensures that the beliefs and unique preoccupations of the Catholic faith will retain a significant place in modern poetry for the foreseeable future.

76. Murray, *Collected Poems*, 203.
77. Quoted in Les Murray, *Fredy Neptune* (New York: Farrar, Straus, and Giroux, 1999), cover.

CHAPTER 13

The Estrangement of Emilio Sandoz, S.J. ▪ Othering in Mary Doria Russell's *The Sparrow*

Davin Heckman

That's right . . . the Nation of Islam is totally under Jesuit control. They are going to be used to foment anarchy and agitation, because they have an army called "the fruit of Islam," and they have millions of rounds stored in all the major cities—guns stored everywhere, so that they can start the race war. And when that happens, you see, then the brothers in Washington can implement Martial Law, suspend the Constitution, and now the Jesuits have what they want.

—Eric John Phelps, "The 'Black' Pope: The Most Powerful Man in the World"

I met Fr. Bill Mackey, S.J. after [my wife] and I served as Jesuit volunteers in Micronesia. Jane had gone to work for the Upper Canada Province of the Jesuit order, while I was a doctoral student in Toronto . . . When Fr. Bill returned for a visit in 1995, shortly after his biography called *The Jesuit and the Dragon* (written by Howard Solverson) had been published . . . He told me plainly of having his teeth pulled (and I am quite sure it was all of them) before he left for the Himalayas, because he had bad teeth and didn't want to deal with tooth aches and rot in a remote area sans medical care.

—Joseph Quinn Raab (personal correspondence with the author)

The mere mention of the Society of Jesus, the Jesuit order, evokes strong responses, both positive and negative, among those who know the name. Even the *Oxford English Dictionary*, based on popular usage, gives "a dissembling person; a prevaricator" as one definition of "Jesuit." These ambiguous feelings are not confined to members of the Roman Catholic faith, to whom the Jesuits belong. Though the order was formally suppressed by Pope Clement XIV in 1773 (and later restored by Pope Pius VII in 1814), until recently their bitterest rivals were the Protestant sects like the Calvinists and Lutherans, whose theology and doctrines the Jesuits were formed to challenge. In recent history, the Jesuits have found themselves despised by

such divergent segments of the world population as the Nazis, the Communist Party of China, and anticommunist factions in El Salvador, all of whom
have targeted them, contributing to the killing of more than three hundred
Jesuits worldwide throughout the twentieth century.[1] Milder forms of anti-
Jesuit sentiment can be found inside the Catholic Church, coming especially from critics of liberation theology who claim that the Jesuits have tainted
the mission of the Church by making Christianity amenable to Marxist ideology, and from outside the Church, coming from hard-right Protestant con-
spiracists who see Jesuit meddling in events ranging from the assassination
of Abraham Lincoln to the World Trade Towers tragedy of September 11th.
The work of conspiracy theorist Eric John Phelps, for example, positions the
Jesuits on multiple sides of virtually all large-scale modern-day conflicts—
behind Hitler, Stalin, Roosevelt, Israel, the Nation of Islam, illegal immigra-
tion—and even as manipulating the world toward the coming reign of the
antichrist. The Jesuits' fame, or infamy, is derived partially from the historical fact of the order's intrepid travels, intellectual rigor, innovative theology,
and fearless intensity. It also stems from the remnants of Reformation-era
anti-Catholic propaganda and grows out of political power struggles within
and against the Catholic Church. For better or worse, the Jesuits are viewed
by many as spiritual provocateurs.

It is not surprising, then, that Jesuits appear with notable frequency in
science fiction, a literary genre linked in the popular imagination to a scientific, technological worldview. The worlds of the science fiction text typically
exist in some future realm where the human creature is explored against the
backdrop of changes in the material world. In *Metamorphoses of Science Fiction*, Darko Suvin defines the genre: science fiction, he states, is *"a literary
genre whose necessary and sufficient conditions are the presence and interaction of estrangement and cognition, and whose main formal device is an imaginative framework alternative to the author's empirical environment"*[2] (italics
in original). But, as Suvin notes, "cognitive estrangement" must be distinguished from the "supernatural" or "metaphysical" forms of estrangement
that operate in myth, fantasy, and religious texts.[3] In other words, science
fiction may be defined primarily by its capacity to work on the cognitive, log-

1. Jaime Castellon Covarrubias, "What Martyrdom Means," trans. John O'Callaghan, *Society of Jesus* website (2000), http://sjweb.info.

2. Darko Suvin, *Metamorphoses of Science Fiction: On the Poetics and History of a Literary Genre*
(New Haven, Conn.: Yale University Press, 1979), 7–8.

3. Ibid., 7.

ical aspects of human knowledge. This does not mean that future technology does not, in the science fiction text, exert its influences on the spiritual state of the subject. It simply means that the empirical features of the fictional world must serve as a primary vehicle for estrangement and the expansion of consciousness, even when spirituality is addressed.

Still, it might strike non–science fiction readers as curious that the Jesuits, members of a Catholic religious order, are popular operators in the science fiction world. According to an article on the topic at Adherents.com, "It seems that ordained Catholics are more common in science fiction than practicing lay Catholics."[4] And among ordained Catholics, an index on the same site, "Religion in Literature," notes that the Jesuits are the most represented, with eighty-one science fiction works referencing the Society of Jesus (their nearest competitor, the Franciscans, only appear in the index fifteen times).[5] Thus it is not entirely surprising that the Jesuits figure prominently in Mary Doria Russell's science fiction novel, *The Sparrow.*

While Russell's novel deals quite sophisticatedly with profound spiritual issues, particularly the question of evil in a universe created by a good and all-powerful God, this is not the topic I choose to deal with here. For readers interested in this question of theodicy, I refer you to Martin Warren's essay on the topic, "Is God in Charge? Mary Doria Russell's *The Sparrow,* Deconstruction, and Theodicy."[6] Warren's article cuts to the core of Russell's work in its theme of the problem of evil. Here, though, I aim to address a more peripheral matter, but one that speaks to an important cultural question: why would Russell, who was born Catholic, spent twenty-five years as an atheist, and then converted to Judaism, use the Jesuits to explore her profound questions about faith in the postmodern world?

The answer to this question does not rest in the Jesuits' spiritual practices and beliefs (although these beliefs and practices breathe life into the aura associated with the Jesuit order). Nor do I believe that Russell chose the Jesuits through mere lack of originality or imagination, writing yet another science fiction story about Jesuits. In an interview Russell has, in fact, denied

4. "Jesuits in SF/F: Mainstream Science Fiction and Fantasy with Jesuit Characters and References," July 20, 2004, www.adherents.com.

5. "Religion in Literature," April, 23, 2007, www.adherents.com. Adherents.com is a collaboratively authored site supported by independent scholar and computer programmer Preston Hunter. The indices offered on the site have a very work-in-progress feel and are not necessarily a complete record of all the Jesuits that appear in science fiction works.

6. Martin Warren, "Is God in Charge? Mary Doria Russell's *The Sparrow,* Deconstruction, and Theodicy," *Journal of Religion and Popular Culture* 9 (Spring 2005), www.usask.ca/relst/jrpc.

the charge that her Jesuit character Emilio Sandoz was influenced by a Jesuit with a similar name in James Blish's novel *A Case of Conscience*.[7] Rather, Russell's use of the Jesuits rests in the cultural cache of the Society of Jesus: the legendary devotion to their mission, even at the expense of themselves; their perpetual status as outsiders, even within their home cultures; and their reputation for fearless travel, even in the face of almost certain martyrdom. The Jesuits, in other words, already occupy the uneasy place of Suvin's "cognitive estrangement"—it is their way of life.

Published in 1996, *The Sparrow* is Mary Doria Russell's first novel. It opens with a brief but ominous prologue that begins, "It was predictable, in hindsight."[8] After a cursory discussion of the Jesuits' tradition of exploration comes a synopsis of the future history of the Jesuits' discreet mission to the planet of Rakhat, a mission authorized by the pope so that the Church can embrace the children of God that might reside there. Russell concludes the prologue, "They meant no harm."[9] From the very beginning, then, the author lets readers know that, in spite of the best intentions, something went horribly wrong on the Jesuit mission to Rakhat. Then, in the first chapter, we are told that Father Emilio Sandoz, S.J., was the sole survivor of that mission, that he is extremely ill, and that he has been physically maimed. Furthermore, Sandoz's conduct on the planet of Rakhat is now surrounded by controversy. A fellow Jesuit, Johannes Voelker, refers to Sandoz as a "whore" who "killed a child" and should be expelled from the order.[10] And Sandoz himself expresses his desire to leave the Jesuit order. So, here at the novel's

---

7. James Blish, *A Case of Conscience* (London: Arrow, 1979). In the interview, Russell explained, "I am always hugely amused by the suggestion that Emilio Sandoz was named in homage to Blish's Spanish Jesuit, Ruiz-Sanchez. Actually, Emilio's last name came off a medicine bottle—my son had a cold when I started the book, and he was taking Dimetapp, made by Sandoz Pharmaceuticals. That's where I got the name! I just liked the sound of it" (Nick Gevers, "Of Prayers and Predators: An Interview with Mary Doria Russell," *Infinity Plus* (Aug. 28, 1999), www.infinityplus.co.uk. Still, fans and critics insist on Blish's influence on *The Sparrow*. According to Damien Broderick, "The most insistent voices apparently contesting behind the words of the text are those of Dr. Baines, from Blish's *Black Easter* (1967), and Father Ruiz-Sanchez from his *A Case of Conscience*, yet Russell denies being influenced by those texts—although the similarity in names of Blish's Ruiz-Sanchez, S.J., and Russell's Sandoz, S.J., smacks of honest *hommage*" (Damien Broderick, *Transrealist Fiction: Writing in the Slipstream of Science* [Westport, Conn.: Greenwood, 2000], 71). More pointedly, in a 1998 review of the text, John D. Owen claims that Russell's work comes dangerously close to the "sacrilege" of "ripping off" James Blish. But Owen ultimately concludes that Russell's work may simply be a case of "unconscious plagiarism," and a "successful" one at that (John D. Owen, "A Case of Conscience for Mary Doria Russell," *Infinity Plus* [1998], www.infinityplus.co.uk).

8. Mary Doria Russell, *The Sparrow* (New York: Ballantine, 2004), 3.

9. Ibid.

10. Ibid., 6, 11.

start, we already know its end: Emilio Sandoz, the handsome Jesuit from a Puerto Rican ghetto, goes to space, spends time on another planet, and has now returned to Earth broken, faithless, and alone.

From the moment Sandoz's astronomer friend, Jimmy Quinn, decides that his friends—Anne and George Edwards, a married couple; Sofia Mendes, an artificial intelligence programmer; and Emilio—will be the first to learn about his discovery that music is coming from a nearby planet, a chain of events is initiated that, against all odds, culminates in the mission to Rakhat. When these friends gather at the observatory where Jimmy works, Sandoz has the sudden inspiration that they should go to the planet to meet "the Singers."[11] As he points out, together this group already has the skills needed to conduct a successful mission: besides his own abilities as a linguist, Jimmy has the navigational expertise; Sofia, the contacts and programming experience; George, the technological skills; and Anne, the anthropological and medical experience.[12] Because of the eagerness and expertise of this nucleus of friends, the mission is soon approved by the Catholic hierarchy, the money lined up, the vehicle arranged, and the crew is rounded out by the addition of D. W. Yarbrough, S.J., a former marine airman from Texas and Sandoz's mentor, assigned to be the crew's leader; Alan Pace, S.J., a musicologist; and Marc Robichaux, S.J., an artist and naturalist.

From this hopeful beginning, readers follow the trajectory of the Jesuit mission as it progresses toward its tragic conclusion. As they prepare for landfall on the Eden-like landscape of Rakhat, readers learn that they all, including those crew members who previously would have described themselves as nonbelievers, came to feel great love of God.[13] They spend the first few weeks rapturously exploring a beautiful uninhabited wilderness on Rakhat. The first death on the Jesuit mission occurs when the musicologist Alan Pace, S.J., dies suddenly and mysteriously during this phase of the exploration.[14] This event foreshadows for readers the tragedy ahead but does little to dampen the enthusiasm of the mission as a whole. The first encounter with a peaceful, beautiful alien species, the Runa, among whom they end up living happily for over a year, reaffirms the sign of a benevolent hand guiding the mission. Through all these early events, Sandoz moves toward greater faith and love, surrendering himself more and more completely to God's will. Ac-

11. Ibid., 94. 12. Ibid., 98.
13. Ibid., 189. 14. Ibid., 195.

cording to his mentor, Fr. D. W. Yarbrough, he may even be on the verge of sainthood: "wedded to God at certain moments, in full communion with divine love."[15]

But things take a dramatic turn when the party makes first contact with the other intelligent species on Rakhat, the Jana'ata—the very singers whose music has lured them to Rakhat. The Jana'ata are, as Sandoz explains, "carnivores, with a dentition and forelimb adapted for killing" and a well developed society that evolved due to "cooperative hunting."[16] And, as we discover, the Jana'ata apply strict population controls on the Runa, whom they use for both labor and meat. A Jana'ata marauder kills Anne and D. W. And when the farming techniques employed by the Jesuit missionaries inadvertently lead to a population boom in the Runa village, the Jana'ata send a party to slaughter the infants, killing the recently married Jimmy and Sofia, their unborn child, and George in the process. Robichaux and Sandoz are captured by the Jana'ata but then "rescued" by the trader Supaari, who subjects the two to a cruel cosmetic procedure called "*hasta'akala*," designed to make the hands "look like trailing branches of ivy . . . to symbolize and enforce dependence."[17] In the aftermath of the grisly procedure, Robichaux dies of starvation, as he refuses to eat the butchered Runa that his captors offer him for sustenance.

Even after the rest of his party has been destroyed, Sandoz does not lose all hope. Russell describes the moment when he finds himself in the presence of Hlavin Kitheri, the great Jana'ata poet and the singer whose beautiful music has brought the party to Rakhat in the first place: "The joy of that moment took his breath away. He had been brought here . . . to meet this man: Hlavin Kitheri, a poet—perhaps even a prophet—who of all of his kind might know the God whom Emilio Sandoz served."[18] Instead, Sandoz is raped by Kitheri and left "bleeding and sobbing"—his holy hope now utterly decimated.[19] Eerily, the rape is transformed into a pornographic rhapsody: "Extemporaneous poetry was recited. Songs were written describing the experience. And the concerts were broadcast, of course, just like the songs we heard."[20] As Sandoz plunged into deep despair in his solitary cell in Kitheri's harem, he resolved to murder whoever stepped next through the door. He never expected that person would be Askama, a Runa child whom he had

15. Ibid., 251.
17. Ibid., 382.
19. Ibid., 393.

16. Ibid., 328.
18. Ibid., 390.
20. Ibid., 395.

loved like a daughter and who was, at that moment, leading to his cell representatives from a U.N.-sanctioned mission to Rakhat. She believed them to be his family come to save him. Sandoz confesses that his "nerves fired without my telling them to. I crashed into [Askama] so hard . . . I could hear the bones in her chest snap."[21] And now, Emilio Sandoz is utterly alone and ashamed, incapacitated by despair.

In Sandoz's mind, he has been led unquestionably by the hand of God to his destiny in Rakhat. In the process, he has fallen deeply in love with God. He has trusted in God and what he understands to be God's plan for him completely and without reservation. When this "plan" culminates in his spiritual, emotional, and physical ruin, Sandoz can imagine only two possible explanations. God is a monster who led him down the path of destruction. Or God was never with him in the first place.

Russell remarked in an interview that her use of the Jesuits in *The Sparrow* "was simple logic. If we were to receive incontrovertible evidence of an extraterrestrial culture that could be reached in a human lifespan, who would go? I thought of the Jesuits because they have a long history of first contact with cultures other than their own."[22] To Russell, an anthropologist by training, the important role of the Jesuits in the age of exploration made them an obvious choice for a novel about alien contact. After reading "dozens and dozens of autobiographies of priests and ex-priests," she also found in the Jesuits an ideal vehicle for examining the troubling theological issues that she was concerned with at the time, issues that finally led her to reject the Catholic Church for the Jewish faith.[23]

The key to understanding the history of the militant devotion of the Society of Jesus to their mission rests in the order's Spiritual Exercises. Stemming from St. Ignatius, who founded the Jesuit order, the Spiritual Exercises are based on the notion that true learning must begin with a process of unlearning. According to Alban Goodier, S.J., in order to proceed, "a man must be lifted out of his surroundings. He must be taught to get outside of himself, to look upon himself as a thing apart; to set his life in perspective of the greater whole, not in that of his own advantage or concern, so putting a new light on all that his life contains."[24] The radical reframing of the ego

---

21. Ibid., 397.
22. Russell, "A Conversation with Mary Doria Russell," in *The Sparrow* (New York: Ballantine, 2004), 414.
23. Ibid.
24. Alban Goodier, S.J., *The Jesuits* (London: Sheed and Ward, 1929), 40.

that takes place when one is forced to "unlearn" makes sense when choosing to dedicate oneself to a religious life bound by the countercultural vows of poverty, obedience, and chastity. But beyond their religious purpose in orienting the self towards religious life, as James J. Daly, S.J., notes, these practices are the vehicle for expanding consciousness in general. The basic premise of the Spiritual Exercises is the very question of human existence itself. In his discussion of the Spiritual Exercises, Daly provides a narrative of the stages through which one passes. He writes of these stages as weeks, though their actual duration may vary.[25] In the first week, a retreatant is bid to meditate on the following:

Here I am, then, on the back of a great flying bullet in a wilderness of space. How come I am here? And why? This is not time for spinning subtle speculations or blindfolding conscience or playing nice academic games . . . God created the universe with its planets and flaming suns. He created this flying bullet and He created me and my immortal soul and put me on it. Why?[26]

Thus the profound experience of interrogating one's very existence in relation to the cosmos becomes a technique for producing estrangement from the self.

The interrogation continues in the second week, this time in the context of sin and human failure. As the retreatant meditates on war, ignorance, pain, and suffering, he or she asks the questions, "What is to become of me, caught as I am in this tremendous catastrophe? I am a poor, weak thing pitted against the enormous forces around me and the violent passions within me. What can I do in this vast spiritual maelstrom sucking me down into the depths?"[27] The second week culminates in an understanding of one's duty to resist sin and turn to God. Subsequently, the third and fourth weeks are focused on deepening one's obedience to God. What characterizes the Ignatian approach to spiritual formation is a commitment to a rational understanding of the self in relation to the world. The logic with which one arrives at the smallness of the individual and our helplessness against even our own impulses demands that power be located elsewhere, if it exists at all. Strength is achieved through obedience to a higher law. In fact, the Jesuit motto—*Ad Majorem Dei Gloriam* (For the Greater Glory of God)—is a powerful

---

25. James J. Daly, S.J., *The Jesuit in Focus* (Milwaukee, Wisc.: Bruce, 1940), 38.
26. Ibid., 18.
27. Ibid., 25.

guiding principle that resonates strongly with human feelings of weakness and inadequacy. Nietzsche called for "supermen" to transcend the limits of the human. The Jesuits believe in a greater good, positioned outside of the self: God. And the way to excel in life is to know that we are made to advance toward this good.

It is against the backdrop of this religious formation that the estrangement of Emilio Sandoz becomes most meaningful. Though many of the characters in *The Sparrow* deal with aspects of self-estrangement, for Sandoz this estrangement is multiplied. For one thing, he is estranged from his family in Puerto Rico. Although a handsome and passionate man, he has distanced himself from his sexuality due to his acceptance of a celibate life. Then, he has the experience of the first contact with the alien culture on Rakhat and, later, of being the sole survivor in an alien world. Sandoz returns to Earth in shame, vilified by society at large and placed at odds with his own religious community. As a result of his trauma, Sandoz, although a skilled linguist, struggles clumsily with language and, instead, often chooses silence. So the matter of estrangement is felt deeply by Sandoz for a variety of reasons throughout the novel.

But Russell is careful to link Sandoz's personal experience of estrangement to his identity as a Jesuit. "Like Ignatius of Loyola," we are informed, "Emilio Sandoz had known brutality and death and stinking fear, and as the days of silence . . . passed, he had a past worthy of the name to reconsider and to turn away from."[28] Russell's awareness of Jesuit history and practice is evidenced in Father General Vincenzo Giuliani's frustrated criticism of Sandoz's silence:

There is no form of death or violence that Jesuit missionaries have not met. Jesuits have been hanged, drawn and quartered in London . . . Disemboweled in Ethiopia. Burned alive by the Iroquois. Poisoned in Germany, crucified in Thailand. Starved to death in Argentina, beheaded in Japan, drowned in Madagascar, gunned down in El Salvador . . . We have been terrorized and intimidated. We have been reviled, falsely accused, imprisoned for life. We have been beaten. Maimed. Sodomized. Tortured. And broken.[29]

After this historically accurate litany of abuses suffered by Jesuits, Giuliani turns away from the physical torments to focus on the more intimate

28. Russell, *The Sparrow*, 107.
29. Ibid., 78–79.

pains that Jesuits have suffered: their own failures and mistakes. Giuliani explains to Sandoz, "We . . . have made decisions, alone and unsupported, that have given scandal and ended in tragedy. Alone, we have made horrifying mistakes that would never have occurred in a community."[30] Still unable to draw Sandoz out, however, he now abandons his account of such abuses and failures altogether to address the question of faith. "Did you think you were the only one ever to wonder if what we do is worth the price we pay?" he demands of Sandoz. "Did you honestly believe that you alone, of all those who have gone, were the single man to lose God?"[31] But even this pointed argument fails to cut through Sandoz's despair. Ultimately, Giuliani instructs Sandoz to allow his body to heal and to strive to yield the burden of responsibility for the disaster on Rakhat to the Jesuit order that ordained the mission in the first place.[32]

In a 1999 interview, Russell stated that she considers *The Sparrow* to be the story of her departure from Catholicism and acceptance of the Jewish faith:

In a private way, *The Sparrow* was about giving Catholicism one last chance to claim my soul. While writing it, I became increasingly certain that I wasn't simply not-a-Christian, that I was in fact a Jew. Of course, having eliminated the Incarnation and all its allied dogmas about virgin birth, salvation from original sin by blood sacrifice, and resurrection theology, I was diving into the problems associated with post-Holocaust Jewish theology.[33]

While she describes the novel as an attempt to address "post-Holocaust Jewish theology," it is interesting that she relegates its only Jewish character, Sofia Mendes, to the sidelines and chooses to make a Catholic Jesuit the center of this exploration. But perhaps this is less surprising when we examine the ways that the Society of Jesus itself is rendered as a plausible and meaningful "other" through which Russell can explore questions of faith. Here, we can consider the dominant culture's very limited understanding of priestly celibacy, for example, or the many myths that circulate around the Jesuits. However, what most fascinated Russell, we can conclude, are the similarities between the Jesuits and the Jews, making the Jesuits an apt vehicle for Russell's interfaith religious exploration. Both groups have distinguished traditions of intellectual, philosophical, and theological excellence. Both

30. Ibid., 79.
31. Ibid.
32. Ibid., 80.
33. Gevers, "Prayers and Predators."

are in part defined by the experience of leaving home or of being marginalized within their homes. Both abide by ritual and spiritual practices that put them at odds with the prevailing society. And as a result of all this, both Jews and Jesuits have long been accused of intrigue and conspiracy. However, as Russell confesses of her turn from atheism and return to faith, "the Incarnation is an insuperable barrier to faith . . . [and] it occurred to me at last that Judaism was the source of the ethics and morality I valued in Catholicism, and all the theological problems associated with the Incarnation simply evaporated."[34] In *The Sparrow*, Russell dramatizes a highly personal story of moral and ethical engagement with suffering and tragedy, even going so far as to set Sandoz up as a possible Christ figure, but subverts this parallel by withholding redemption. For Russell, as for many, the Christian concept of the Incarnation seems both unimaginable and unable to contain the extremes of human experience. Naturally, she chooses a faith that makes sense to her, but not without providing a powerful occasion for Catholics to reflect.

Russell's use of the Jesuits and her account of Catholic life resonate with the experience of the faithful in the postmodern moment. To put it somewhat simplistically, contemporary attitudes toward religion tend to fall into two camps. One, the pragmatic approach, privileges reason and empiricism and accepts religion, if at all, simply because it "works" in a practical sense. The other, the subjective approach, privileges emotions and feeling and asks believers to interpret all things through the lens of faith. The differences in religious expression in these two camps often serve to distort our public perception of them, with pragmatists disparaged as "secularists" and subjectivists marginalized as "extremists." But it is striking that these two positions in today's postmodern climate agree on the same basic assumption: that reason and faith are opposing terms. To put "faith" in opposition to "reason" is an overly simplistic postmodern assumption. As with Ihab Hassan's famous list in his article, "Toward a Concept of Postmodernism," which identifies modern sensibilities and their postmodern counterparts, early contributions to the study of the postmodern often identified it as an opposing reaction to the Enlightenment modernist worldview. Along this line of thinking, for example, where modernism privileges "purpose," postmodernism privileges "play"; where modernism looks to the "root," postmodernism looks to the

34. Ibid.

"rhizome"; where modernism values "determinacy," postmodernism values "indeterminacy."[35] A more sophisticated view of this dialectical thinking, however, can be found in a work like Donna Haraway's "Cyborg Manifesto." Rather than a mere negation of the modernist impulse through the assertion of its opposite, Haraway concludes that "Cyborg imagery can suggest a way out of the maze of dualisms in which we have explained our bodies and our tools to ourselves."[36] Here, the cyborg is a metaphor for hybridity, an alternative to the either/or dichotomies like nature/culture and human/machine. The tendency to simplify things by parsing them down into discrete categories is, in this theory, counterbalanced by the ever-present tendency to hybridize as well. If contemporary religious movements simply offer dialectical refutations of modernism, then these responses are no great improvement over it. However, if postmodern subjects can resist the simplistic historical allure of mere "post-ness" to "modernism" and embrace the richness and complexity of hybridization akin to that put forward by Haraway, then we can move toward an understanding of religion that can potentially reconcile faith with reason.

Here our postmodern culture can learn from the Jesuits. Founded in 1533, the Society of Jesus overlaps significantly with the rise of humanism, and rooted in that humanism is the beginning of the modern era with its belief in the supremacy of reason, the scientific method, and human progress. The tradition of humanism spawned corresponding egalitarian impulses like literacy, democracy, and human rights for all persons. Contributing to and drawing from this emerging sense of human potential came the period of spiritual upheaval, the Protestant Reformation, sparked by grievances with the Catholic Church. The Jesuit order was founded largely in response to the Protestant Reformation as an attempt to reconcile the premodern, prehumanist Church of the medieval era with emerging humanist ideals. The result was a new Catholic worldview, one that combined traditional virtues of faith, obedience, and a code of chivalry with a corresponding emphasis on reason, freedom of conscience, and democratic principles. In other words, the Jesuits were compelled by historical exigency to occupy the uneasy state of hybrid thinking.

35. Ihab Hassan, "Toward a Concept of Postmodernism," in *Postmodernism: A Reader*, ed. Thomas Docherty (New York: Columbia University Press, 1993), 152.
36. Donna J. Haraway, *Simians, Cyborgs, and Women: The Reinvention of Nature* (New York: Routledge, 1991), 181.

In this light, the Spiritual Exercises of the Society of Jesus take on a new dimension. The Jesuits' intensive practice of progressive estrangement that begins with spiritual formation and continues with missionary work maps onto the intellectual hybridity that underscores the order's ideology. Perhaps this estrangement, the Jesuit as "other," is best seen in the Jesuits' relationship to society today. Even to Catholics, the role of religious is not always understood. Freely choosing the three vows of poverty, obedience, and chastity seems utterly at odds with contemporary mainstream life, particularly in the United States. It is not surprising, therefore, that in recent years, along with many religious orders, the Jesuits' numbers have sharply declined. Though the Jesuits remain committed to serving the most vulnerable people in society, society at large seems to have fallen out of touch with them. But perhaps our current cultural moment resonates with the role Jesuits play in *The Sparrow*. In the novel Russell, like, no doubt, the majority of her readers, observes the Jesuits with an anthropological eye, as figures that evoke curiosity. As Russell has stated, she knew no Jesuits when she began the novel, so every stroke of her pen, even when she came to care for her character Sandoz, was an exercise in "othering." As such, even though *The Sparrow* marks Russell's personal farewell to the Catholic faith, the novel serves to capture the experience of many today, Catholics and non-Catholics alike, who often do not understand the Church and who feel estranged from it. In a metaphorical sense, Emilio Sandoz, S.J., is, then, a typical postmodern subject—a person teetering on the border of faith and reason, torn between the empirical realities (post-Holocaust, post-liberal, and post-human) and subjective fantasies (consumerist, media-driven, and faith-based) of the twenty-first century.

Furthermore, if we consider the relationship between Catholics and the culture at large, *The Sparrow* captures yet another layer of estrangement. Although many Catholics may currently stand in an ambiguous relationship to the faith they abide by, the cultural split between faith and reason is much more dramatic in the larger context of American society. While there are perhaps some Catholics, for instance, who doubt the theory of evolution, Pope John Paul II formally declared in 1996 that "evolution is no longer a mere hypothesis," adding the weight of official Church teaching to the views held by Vatican scientists for decades.[37] Yet in American society at large, the debate over evolution continues at a fevered pace, with many Christians hold-

37. Mark Lombard, "Intelligent Design Belittles God, Vatican Director Says," *Catholic Online* (Jan. 30, 2006), www.catholic.org.

ing that "intelligent design" or "creationism" are articles of faith that must be believed despite the large body of scientific evidence to the contrary. In this case and in others like it, faith is seen in Abrahamic terms, as something that must be unquestioningly assented to even if it flies in the face of reason or is otherwise contrary to human nature or human experience. Just as God commanded Abraham to sacrifice his son Isaac, so the faithful must be willing to do the same. To the radical adherents of this type of faith-based Christianity, Catholics appear as a compromised, even apostate, church, in league with secular humanist forces.

But for all of its opposition to such Christian fundamentalism, the Catholic Church also has few friends among those strict adherents to the other side of the divide, radical empiricists. In its very essence as a community of faith, the Church cannot be reconciled with a dogmatically atheistic or agnostic worldview. Its ritualistic practices, especially surrounding the Eucharist, are frequently perceived as superstitious—a throwback to the Dark Ages—by those whose primary standards of judgment are reason and its close ally, efficiency. In this light, it is obvious why Church teaching appears to many to conflict sharply with secular or liberal positions on contemporary issues like abortion, gay marriage, and even aspects of global warming. Ironically, although Catholicism sees itself as at significant odds with fundamentalist Christianity, radical empiricists, threatened by any notion of faith, view all Christians—including Catholics—as part of an antirational cultural movement. Thus, in a sense, Catholics today are marginalized from both sides of the American cultural divide. They are perpetually the "other," misunderstood by those who can think only in factional terms. In addition, the Church has often failed to communicate adequately the message of the essential unity between faith and reason that indeed underscores its teaching. And thus the Jesuit Sandoz can be read as a metaphor for today's Catholic in the world who feels this conflict every day whether in large or small matters.

The Sparrow is a well-written postmodern novel, and although it does show some trace of Russell's personal inclinations, it does not pursue them pedantically. As the author crafts a tale of multiple levels of estrangement in the course of documenting her own religious estrangement, it is possible for readers to discover within this very estrangement a powerful corrective to the dialectical thinking that pits reason against faith. Among its other merits, *The Sparrow* manages to affirm, even as it challenges, the values of Catholicism as a faith irrevocably wedded to reason. Thus, its message is highly appropriate for today's Catholics. To illustrate this appropriateness, let us consider briefly a recent event that turned into, albeit far from its original intent, a significant moment in popular culture. Most will remember Pope Benedict XVI's 2006 address at the University of Regensburg for the widespread criticism in the world media and the protests and violence that it sparked.[38] Ironically, the address was actually designed as a critique of the theological program of de-Hellenization, particularly in the work of (more irony here) a Jesuit, Roger Haight, and as an affirmation of the utter necessity of *both* faith and reason.[39]

In his address, Pope Benedict explains, "This attempt . . . at a critique of modern reason from within has nothing to do with putting the clock back to the time before the Enlightenment and rejecting the insights of the modern age."[40] He continues,

The scientific ethos, moreover, is . . . the will to be obedient to the truth, and, as such, it embodies an attitude which belongs to the essential decisions of the Christian Spirit . . . While we rejoice in the new possibilities open to humanity, we also see the dangers arising from these possibilities and we must ask ourselves how we can overcome them. We will succeed in doing so only if reason and faith come together in a new way, if we overcome the self-imposed limitation of reason to the empirically falsifiable, and if we once more disclose its vast horizons. In this sense theology rightly belongs in the university and within the wide-ranging dialogue of sciences . . . as inquiry into the rationality of faith.[41]

At once, Benedict refutes the "postmodern" notion that theologians can or even should "de-Hellenize" Christianity by removing the Greek culture's philosophical and linguistic contributions to Christian thought, particularly its emphasis on the unity of faith and reason. He offers a more sophisticated (and more properly postmodern) notion: that we cannot separate language, belief, and culture. Moreover, this is for the best, since "a reason which is deaf to the divine and which relegates religion into the realm of subcultures

38. In his speech, Benedict made reference to a fourteenth-century statement by Byzantine Emperor Manuel II Palaiologos in his exchanges with a Persian diplomat: "Show me just what Muhammad brought that was new and there you will find things only bad and inhuman, such as his command to spread by the sword the faith he preached." Though this was but a passing statement in the address, the media focused solely on it, and it sparked mass protests and death threats against the pope in the Muslim world and criticism of him in the Christian world.

39. Raab, personal correspondence.

40. Pope Benedict XVI, "Three Stages in the Program of De-Hellenization," *Zenit: The World Seen from Rome* (Sept. 12, 2006), www.zenit.org.

41. Ibid.

is incapable of entering the dialogue of cultures. At the same time . . . modern scientific reason with its intrinsically Platonic element bears within itself a question which points beyond itself and beyond the possibilities of its methodology." In other words, only a commitment to both faith and reason can lead to "that genuine dialogue of cultures and religions so urgently needed today."[42]

And so we return to the estrangement of Emilio Sandoz, S.J. Though the Catholic Church and the Jesuits are hardly postmodern phenomena, the Jesuits' approach to faith, Catholics' relationship with American society, and Emilio Sandoz's struggles with belief are situated along the very questions of faith and reason to which Pope Benedict XVI refers in his address. Whether in the face of alien life or in the face of personal tragedy, these questions remain central to the human experience. And, in the case of *The Sparrow*, they peer into the heart of religious belief, dramatizing the subjective space of the Catholic faith. If one accepts the close relationship between faith and reason, the estranged role of the Catholic within the postmodern world might, for all its bristling restlessness, be to serve as missionaries for the integration of faith and reason, as facilitators of dialogue, and as mediators in a world torn by binary thinking.

42. Ibid.

CHAPTER 14

Restoring the *Imago Dei* ▪ Transcendental Realism in the Fiction of Michael D. O'Brien

Dominic Manganiello

Catholic fiction in Canada has often been marked by a strong integral humanism. Contemporary Canadian writers such as Morley Callaghan and Hugh Hood both acknowledged the seminal influence the philosophy of Jacques Maritain exerted on their work, especially his emphasis on the dignity of the human person rooted in the Incarnation. Michael D. O'Brien's recent novels in *The Children of the Last Days* series reflect the same personalism espoused by his predecessors, but with some important nuances. While Morley Callaghan expressed his fascination with the struggle between good and evil that stirs continually in the human heart, literary critics have pointed to the "flabbiness" of his moral vision.[1] The sympathetic treatment of the sinful individual who shuns divine grace prompted Callaghan, in this view, to shift his focus gradually away from a theocentric to an anthropocentric humanism. As Barbara Helen Pell puts it, "Too often [Callaghan's] Christian humanism, with its emphasis on human identification, is not balanced by a clear vision of the Christian Gospel."[2] Hugh Hood adopted a clearer ethical position than his mentor had in an attempt to be "more 'real' than the realists, yet more transcendent than the most vaporous allegorist."[3] Despite his use of traditional Christian allegory, however, Hood's religious optimism led some reviewers to accuse him of failing to engage adequately the truth of original sin. For example, Pell comments that, on account of his "religious

---

1. Desmond Pacey, *Creative Writing in Canada,* 2d ed. (Toronto: McGraw-Hill Ryerson, 1961), 211.
2. Barbara Helen Pell, "Faith and Fiction: The Novels of Callaghan and Hood," *Journal of Canadian Studies* 18, no. 2 (1983): 7.
3. Hugh Hood and John Mills, "Hugh Hood and John Mills in Epistolary Conversation," *Fiddlehead* 116 (Winter 1978): 145.

optimism," Hood "finds it difficult to depict imaginatively sin and evil."[4] Michael O'Brien, however, avoids the potential pitfalls of such Manichaeism on the one hand and Pelagianism on the other by grounding his depiction of human nature in what Maritain calls "transcendental realism," or in the "*spiritual* resemblance" that exists between the Creator and his creature.[5] In a 1997 talk, "The Vocation of the Christian Novelist," O'Brien commented on the formative influence Maritain's work has exerted on him.[6] He identifies the *Imago Dei,* lost when Adam fell and restored to the original unity of image and likeness with Christ's redemption, as providing the "hidden dynamic" that sustains the Western literary imagination.[7] In what follows, I examine the trajectory of the search for "man's complete identity"[8] in what are perhaps the two most distinctive novels of O'Brien's project, *Father Elijah: An Apocalypse* (1996) and *Strangers and Sojourners: A Novel* (1997). The first shows the adverse effects of an atheistic humanism in a supernatural thriller set in the Vatican, while the second charts Anne Delaney's journey to British Columbia and her discovery that "a hidden and sacred image [lies] within the icons of [human] faces."[9]

Father Elijah

The renewal of culture occupies a central place in Michael O'Brien's critical writing. In an incisive article published in 1997 devoted exclusively to the subject, the writer invokes a host of prominent Catholic thinkers to help him diagnose the present spiritual malaise of Western civilization and to provide a timeless antidote in timely fashion. At the end of his masterly survey of the history of the artistic imagination, O'Brien echoes Pope John Paul II's emphatic warning against the dangers of a pervasive materialism that "seeks to erase 'the whole truth about man,'" especially concerning his transcendent origin.[10] (The timbre of the late pontiff's voice resonates throughout the

---

4. Pell, "Faith and Fiction," 12.

5. Jacques Maritain, *Art and Scholasticism with Other Essays,* trans. J. F. Scanlan (London: Sheed and Ward, 1943), 96.

6. Michael D. O'Brien, "The Vocation of the Christian Novelist," talk given at St. Paul University, Ottawa, Canada, November 18, 1997.

7. Michael D. O'Brien, "Historical Imagination and the Renewal of Culture," in *Eternity in Time: Christopher Dawson and the Catholic Idea of History,* ed. Stratford Caldecott and John Morrill (Edinburgh, Scot.: T. and T. Clark, 1997), 164.

8. Ibid.

9. Michael D. O'Brien, *Strangers and Sojourners: A Novel* (San Francisco: Ignatius, 1997), 445.

10. O'Brien, "Historical Imagination," 190.

pages of *Father Elijah*.) For O'Brien the germs of a materialistic ethos began to incubate in the Renaissance and spread over the centuries into a diabolic contagion that today threatens the very survival of humanity. The more modern humanism divorces itself from "the Catholic sense of the *Imago Dei*," he maintains, the closer mankind gets to the brink of self-annihilation.[11] The remedy lies in building a "new iconography,"[12] which will restore the human soul to its proper place in what was once called the "great chain of being."[13] This call for a "return to our true identity"[14] seconds the appeal John Paul II made in *Redemptor hominis* for people to draw near again to the One who is "the 'image of the invisible God' (Col. 1:15), is himself the perfect man who has restored in the children of Adam that likeness to God which has been disfigured ever since the first sin."[15] Only through Christ the new Adam, O'Brien similarly affirms, can man come to the fullness of truth about himself. "What I hope to point out in all of my books," the author has stated, "is that there is a kind of universal onslaught underway at the very foundations of reality itself, and that the one voice that is the bulwark standing in the path of the juggernaut is orthodox Christianity, because it dares, in season or out of season, to speak the whole truth about man."[16]

When John Paul II issued "the challenge of creating a new authentic and integral humanism," he alluded to the signature idea of the modern neo-Thomist philosopher whose pioneering work has served as a main source of inspiration for O'Brien.[17] In *Humanisme Intégral* (1936), Jacques Maritain identified three defining historical moments that gave birth to modern culture and continue to sustain it. The first moment occurred during the Renaissance when man, though still cognizant of a Christian cultural pattern inherited from previous ages, inaugurated a human order by the power of human reason alone. The age of classical humanism in the sixteenth and seventeenth centuries gradually separated itself from its "transcendent vivi-

11. Ibid., 174.

12. Ibid., 191.

13. Michael D. O'Brien, "Barometer Falling: Landscapes of Unreality in Art and Society," *Canadian Catholic Review* (February 1990): 47.

14. O'Brien, "Historical Imagination," 174.

15. John Paul II, *Redemptor hominis* (Ottawa: Canadian Conference of Catholic Bishops, 1979), 24. The Pope quoted a passage from the Vatican II document, *Gaudium et spes*. For an expression of the high esteem in which O'Brien held Pope John Paul II, see, for example, Ronald McCloskey, "An Interview with Michael O'Brien," *Gilbert!* 1, no. 9 (1998): 10–16.

16. McCloskey, "Interview with Michael O'Brien," 11.

17. John Paul II, "Homily of John Paul II for Jubilee of University Professors, Sunday 10 September 2000," www.vatican.va.

fying principle," however, and spawned the second moment of "rationalist optimism" in the next two centuries.[18] This dominant philosophical outlook produced the *"revolutionary* moment" of the twentieth century with its bitter fruit.[19] The Enlightenment belief in human perfectibility triggered a "materialistic overthrow of values" with the purpose of making a "wholly new humanity rise out of a radical atheism."[20] The paradigm shift that characterizes this third cultural moment is best captured in the unsettling question posed by Nietzsche, which Maritain paraphrased as follows: "How could God still live in a world from which His image, that is to say the free and spiritual personality of man, is in the act of being effaced?"[21] The only adequate response to this threat, in Maritain's view, is for the individual to allow his Maker to retrace the divine image in his soul and thereby transform the "old man" into a "new man."[22] A wounded humanity transfigured by the power of grace according to a biblical model of the person would usher in a new age of Christian culture.

These competing visions of humanism, one atheistic, the other Christian, fuel the culture wars that are waged in *Father Elijah.* O'Brien draws the battle lines with subtle gradations that become more apparent the closer the eponymous hero of his novel gets to the heart of real evil. Elijah Schäfer, an introspective Carmelite priest with an unusual past, is unexpectedly summoned to Rome to undertake a delicate mission with universal repercussions. A Jew who barely escaped the Holocaust as a child in his native Warsaw, Schäfer later emerged as a rising star in the Israeli government of the day and went on to become a well-known prosecutor of war criminals. The loss of his beloved wife to a terrorist bomb during this period, however, radically altered the course of his life. Shortly after this tragic incident he abandoned his public career, converted to Christianity, was eventually ordained to the priesthood, and withdrew to a monastery to lead the religious life of a contemplative. The Vatican hierarchy believes these intensely lived experiences, along with his current expertise in biblical archaeology, will stand Father Elijah in good stead for the crucial test that lies ahead.

At the dawn of the third millennium the Church faces growing hostility on an unprecedented scale from vocal enemies within and outside her

---

18. Jacques Maritain, *Integral Humanism: Temporal and Spiritual Problems of a New Christendom,* trans. Joseph W. Evans (South Bend, Ind.: University of Notre Dame Press, 1973), 26, 31.

19. Ibid., 31. 20. Ibid.

21. Ibid., 34. 22. Ibid., 93.

walls. In an early conversation with Father Elijah, Monsignor Billy Strangsby identifies some of the telltale symptoms of the mounting crisis. Chief among these are the consistently violent diatribes unleashed against the orthodoxy of the Magisterium. Those critics who demonize the successor of Peter as an ironhanded leader, the Monsignor observes with wry irony, have no qualms about becoming their own pope and declaring the infallibility of personal opinion. For his part, the reigning pontiff tells Elijah that the world in the twentieth century came under the sway of atheistic materialism in its various forms, labeled interchangeably fascism, socialism, or capitalism by its proponents, an alarming phenomenon that caused man to forget the fact of his dual citizenship in the two cities. The modern revolutionary, in other words, pursues the self-defeating logic perceptively described by Camus in *The Rebel:* "To kill God and to build a Church are the constant and contradictory purpose of rebellion."[23] The arch rebel who will turn into the future antichrist, the pope believes, will not plan a frontal attack on the Mystical Body, nor will he appear on the scene with great fanfare, but will do so quietly in the guise of a "secular saint."[24] There are compelling reasons, he adds, to suspect that the current president of the Federation of European States, an affable humanist, is lurking in the wings in order to play this very role in an unfolding apocalyptic script. Father Elijah's task is, consequently, to befriend the president and to warn him that continuing his adversarial course would endanger the salvation of his soul and plunge the world into the chaos of the end times.

During their initial encounter in his private marina at Capri, however, the president extends a warm welcome to the papal emissary. After exchanging pleasantries, the two men also exchange the gift of significant books. To his great surprise, Father Elijah receives from the president the original manuscript of Aristotle's lost treatise *On Justice* for safekeeping as a token of the joint commitment Church and state have made to the advancement of civilization. The host in turn gratefully accepts from his guest a copy of the report of the Pontifical Commission for Biblical Archaeology that dates newly discovered scrolls of the Gospels to apostolic times and confirms the accuracy of standard translations but makes no comment about these recent findings that go against the grain of modernist biblical criticism. The president only remarks that the two might have become allies earlier had Schäfer pursued

23. Albert Camus, *The Rebel,* trans. Anthony Bower (New York: Vintage, 1959), 103.
24. Michael D. O'Brien, *Father Elijah: An Apocalypse* (San Francisco: Ignatius, 1996), 64.

his brief yet illustrious career in politics. The suggestion flusters the priest, who feels unable to defend the reasonableness of his faith. The urbanity of the skeptic makes the believer think that he is acting as nothing more than the official "ambassador of a myth."[25]

When Father Elijah confesses his failure upon returning to Rome, the pope gently reminds the downcast envoy of the biblical paradox that only when one realizes his weakness can he claim to be strong. The president, on the other hand, does not believe in the efficacy of grace and relies instead on the power of unaided human reason. He fails to recognize the truth of Christianity because, in his worldview, all religions are one. This relativistic outlook, moreover, allows him to say, in the same breath, that the conflicting tenets of religion and rationalism are both right. An illogical conclusion of the sort violates Aristotle's key principle of noncontradiction, the pope implies, and amounts to "madness."[26] The president's intellectual confusion destroys the authentic meaning of the person as a composite being made up of a body and soul. The false reasoning that denies man's transcendent dimension in this instance foreshadows the "universal madness" that will break out, as in Nietzsche's famous apocalyptic parable of the madman, once mankind learns about the death of God.[27] This fall into irrationality stems from what O'Brien calls the "sad and vicious circle" described by Pope John Paul II in *Evangelium vitae:* "When the sense of God is lost, there is also a tendency to lose the sense of man."[28]

This twofold loss is reflected in the new world vision that the president outlines in his keynote address at a conference held in Warsaw to celebrate the central theme of *unitas.* In his introductory remarks, the conference coordinator refers to the main speaker as a visionary and healer who aims to usher in an era of cosmic harmony between diverse cultures and nations. As he steps onto the stage, the man of the moment receives thunderous applause that grows into a form of adulation. He enthralls his audience with the idea that a unique opportunity for a "transcultural" rebirth is in the offing as the third millennium approaches, one that will allow the global community to liberate itself from ancient myths such as Judgment Day that have been the source of universal terror over the ages. In the place of these dreadful men-

---

25. Ibid., 166.

26. Ibid., 168.

27. Walter Kaufmann, *Nietzsche: Philosopher, Psychologist, Antichrist* (New York: Viking, 1968), 97.

28. O'Brien quotes this passage in his booklet, *The Family and the New Totalitarianism* (Killaloe, Canada: White Horse, 1995), 66.

tal constructs, man will have the power to reinvent himself by devising a new creation story to live by. According to this alternate Scripture, tyrants will die, while a superior "race of creators" will be born to guide the inhabitants of the planet in the appreciation of art, mysticism, spirituality, and the like. Each master will appear carrying an individual flame emanating from the "universal light" prepared to divulge "the one great truth" about human destiny hidden from the beginning of time. Human beings will thereby be inspired to put away their weapons, overcome their divisions, and recognize the glory of divinity radiating from the other person's eyes. Only then will the meaning of "worshipping in spirit and in truth," the proverbial phrase found in St. John's Gospel, be truly understood. Humans will withdraw into their spiritual selves, from where they will gradually evolve into the higher species of a world-soul. Spiritual exiles no longer, they will realize their full potential by making Earth their final home.[29]

Although some of the president's remarks retain vestiges of a vague religiosity, the tenor of his speech runs counter to the account of human destiny contained in Sacred Scripture. As Father Elijah explains, the Bible depicts man as a stranger and sojourner in search of a permanent home because he knows that no continual city can be found here. In stark contrast, the president's earthbound vision does not allow either for the pilgrim's sense of "transcendental homelessness"[30] or for the eventuality of a New Jerusalem descending as a celestial gift upon man after his sinfulness destroys the world. Instead, the presidential project promises a new Babel with the prospect of self-made men ascending to heaven by their own efforts and proclaiming their divinity as a result. The architect of the earthly paradise is an "eminently sane human being," in the words of Cardinal Vettore, "one who will build the City of God for us if we won't build it ourselves."[31] However, Father Elijah reminds the president that "no man can save the world, least of all by saving a fallen humanity from itself."[32] Only one Savior is able to redeem his creatures. These opposing views set the stage for the last battle that will pit the Word against the anti-Word.[33]

29. O'Brien, *Father Elijah*, 329–32.

30. This phrase is used by Georg Lukács in *The Theory of the Novel*, trans. Anna Bostock (Cambridge, Mass.: MIT Press, 1971), 61.

31. O'Brien, *Father Elijah*, 512.

32. Ibid., 349.

33. O'Brien borrows the term "anti-Word" from Karol Wojtyla (later Pope John Paul II). Analyzing the interaction between the serpent and Eve in the garden of Eden, Wojtyla comments: "Here, in the third chapter of Genesis . . . it becomes clear that the history of mankind, and with it the history of the

Father Elijah stakes out his position on the subject clearly at the Warsaw conference. The recent discovery of the Dead Sea Scrolls and related manuscripts, he maintains, refutes the tenuous theories of modern exegetes who claim that some early Christians revised the life of Christ rendered in the Gospels to suit their own particular theological orientation. This misguided approach takes its cue from Rudolf Bultmann, who founded the famous school of demythology that stressed the need to strip the New Testament of its supernatural dimension. In his influential essay, "New Testament and Mythology," Bultmann, a German theologian, disposed of the traditional "three-storied structure" of the universe consisting of "the earth in the centre, the heaven above, and the underworld beneath" in favor of flattening it to the level of everyday experience.[34] Bultmann undermined the credibility of the Gospels by effectively repudiating the myth that became fact. This deconstructive strategy paved the way for his successors to rewrite the *mythos* of Christianity in accordance with Gnostic principles, an act of revisionism that O'Brien characterizes as showing "colossal pride."[35] In his talk, Father Elijah also highlights the subjective bias of a new biblical criticism that serves merely to confirm the "near-infallible superiority" of its practitioners. "Perhaps," he concludes with gentle irony, "it is the demythologizers who need to be demythologized."[36]

The only person in the audience to lend a sympathetic ear to Father Elijah's presentation is an Italian judge who is poised to deliver an equally unpopular paper at the conference. Anna Benedetti views human rights from an international legal perspective that challenges the prevailing orthodoxies embraced by other speakers. Although an eclectic group has gathered together to address the topic of "unity," she points out that a tacit "uniformity" underlies the general discussion among participants.[37] Anna terms the philosophical thread that runs through the speeches "neo-monism," the belief that reality is an indivisible, universal organism. Indeed, the president pro-

---

world with which man is united through the work of divine creation, will be both subject to rule by the Word and the anti-Word, the Gospel and the anti-Gospel" (Karol Wojytla [Pope John Paul II], *Sign of Contradiction* [New York: Seabury, 1979], 29).

34. Rudolf Bultmann et al., *Kerygma and Myth: A Theological Debate*, ed. Hans Warner Bartsch (New York: Harper and Row, 1961), 1.

35. See O'Brien, "Barometer Falling," 47. In this article O'Brien highlights three main features of modern Gnosticism: "a) the devaluation of creation, b) the making of new myths, c) knowledge as salvation" (46).

36. O'Brien, *Father Elijah*, 338.

37. Ibid., 340–41.

pounds precisely this one-dimensional vision of existence that, in effect, not only blurs ethical distinctions but also suppresses genuine differences between people in the body politic that form part of their human identity.

The thrust of the president's totalizing impulse therefore concerns Judge Anna Benedetti. She intends to warn her listeners that certain notions of man might appear "humanistic" on the surface but might actually give rise to several human rights violations and even the wholesale destruction of people's lives. The danger signs of a "seemingly benign totalitarianism" at work in contemporary society are plain for those willing to read them.[38] In fact, the modern tyrant, the cardinal nicknamed "Stato" later tells Elijah, never comes across at first as a monster to his subjects because he announces in his public platform that the ostensible aim of his government is to improve humanity. Echoing the historian Christopher Dawson, the cardinal adds that this tyrant, while apparently "motivated by the highest principles," actually proceeds to perpetrate great evil that goes undetected until it is too late for anyone to stop him.[39] Thus the tyrant who poses as a humanitarian deviously exercises his ruthless will to power, robbing human beings of their dignity and freedom while appearing to do them good.

The hero of O'Brien's novel exposes the "true face" of evil in a climactic scene at Capri. Father Elijah travels to the island in a last attempt to dissuade the president from pursuing the path of destruction for, as the pope put it, "The loss of even one soul [would be] catastrophic."[40] "A person of virtue . . . a man of great intelligence, great integrity, a peacemaker . . . with a highly developed ethical system" (as O'Brien described his president in an interview), the world's most powerful man could perhaps still be convinced to accomplish the good.[41] With a heightened sense of urgency, then, Father Elijah begins his critical conversation by noting that though the power of darkness makes itself visible in many forms, "its worst face masquerades as light."[42] His recalcitrant interlocutor, however, dismisses the point as idle theological speculation based on outdated biblical myths designed to dupe the masses. Surely, the president adds, the visitor realizes that he is "one of the few capa-

---

38. O'Brien, *The Family and the New Totalitarianism*, 71.

39. O'Brien, *Father Elijah*, 439. O'Brien refers to this point in *The Family and the New Totalitarianism*, 64. The cardinal's first point is one made by the philosopher Josef Pieper, which O'Brien also cites on page 63 of the same work.

40. O'Brien, *Father Elijah*, 531, 66.

41. McCloskey, "Interview with Michael O'Brien," 11.

42. O'Brien, *Father Elijah*, 531.

ble of becoming free by [his] own efforts." This Pelagian rejoinder causes a medley of voices to resonate in Father Elijah's soul, each sowing doubt about his undertaking: *"This is a good and noble man . . . He will restore the world to sanity . . . You have misjudged him."* Temporarily confused, Father Elijah regains his presence of mind when he notices a dark shadow passing "across and through and behind" the president's eyes.[43] Suspecting a case of demonic possession about to take place, the exorcist lays a reliquary on his lap and pronounces some prayers for the victim's release. But the gesture angers the president, and he hurls the receptacle containing the splinter of wood soaked in the Redeemer's blood into the fire, denounces the "little Christ" crucified long ago, and promptly proclaims himself the messiah of the new age. Father Elijah resists the blasphemous outburst by affirming the one and only Christ of the living God. Cognizant of Cardinal John Henry Newman's prediction that the antichrist would raise himself as an "anti-icon" demanding to be worshipped, Father Elijah makes his final appeal to the president: "This is the moment of choice. [God] offers it to you because, regardless of your crimes, you are a child of Adam. You were created in His image, like all others born of woman. You are a man, no more, no less. You have been led into captivity, but this bondage is not yet absolute. Turn from Satan!"[44] Evil alters and destroys the personality for, as Chesterton observed, "the denial of identity is the very signature of Satan."[45] After completing the rite of exorcism, Father Elijah escapes the heavily guarded compound with security alarms ringing in his ears, a clear signal that the president has decided against allowing for the restoration of the divine image in his soul.

Although Father Elijah will eventually suffer martyrdom for his failed attempt to convert the president, hope remains the keynote of the novel. O'Brien weaves a beautiful novella within the main narrative in order to provide what he describes as "a counterpoint or a counter-reflection to the spiritual evil of the character of the President."[46] The dramatic contrapuntal encounter occurs in Warsaw prior to the conference. Father Elijah visits his old childhood haunts in the Polish capital with the aim of seeing, perhaps for the last time, the room where he hid from the Nazis as a young boy under the protection of Pawel Tarnowski, a kindhearted bookseller. In order to fulfill

---

43. Ibid., 532, 533, 537.
44. Ibid., 540, 447, 541–42.
45. G. K. Chesterton, *The Uses of Diversity* (London: Methuen, 1926), 78.
46. McCloskey, "Interview with Michael O'Brien," 11.

his desire, the priest contacts a dying man known as Count Smokrev, owner of the property that once housed Tarnowski's bookstore. Cagey and uncooperative at first, the nobleman reluctantly grants the request. Father Elijah's return to the premises he knew so well brings back a flood of memories of a fatherly benefactor who loved to tell his young visitor stories.

Of these tales that Father Elijah vividly recalls, the one concerning the artist who recognized "Christ hidden in the ruined face of an old sinner" seems particularly apt, as it highlights the challenge the priest faces after hearing some of the landlord's unsettling personal confessions.[47] The count reveals that his life, morally speaking, started hitting rock bottom from the time in his youth when he sexually corrupted a boy named Piotr. The first of a series of transgressions appalled Smokrev, until he discovered in later life that his fellow creatures were just as depraved as he was. Gaining this important insight gradually convinced him that no "pure, unsullied, unselfish love" exists. On account of his conviction, Smokrev forewarns Father Elijah that "no conversions are possible here."[48] His attentive listener disagrees, maintaining that human beings were not created to lead a life without love. This initial exchange launches the two into a serious discussion of the perplexing question concerning the apparent triumph of evil in a world supposedly governed by a benevolent deity. Aware that it would be practically impossible to justify God's ways to man in the brief time available, Father Elijah in his response focuses primarily on the salient point that the mystery of evil hinges on the interplay between human freedom and divine mercy. Christ's suffering redeems the pain of his fallen creatures, especially those who have plumbed the depths of despair. The palpable presence of evil in the world undermines Smokrev's belief that Satan is a figment of the human imagination, a mere symbol of a person's "dark side."[49] Father Elijah therefore encourages the dying man to avoid falling into the "deeper darkness" of impenitence by considering the beauty of opening his heart to the final grace being poured on him: "In every person's soul there is an icon of what he is meant to be. An image of Love is hidden there. Each soul is beloved beyond imagining. Each soul is beautiful in the eyes of God. Our sins and faults, and those committed against us, bury this original image. We can no longer see ourselves as we really are."[50] The count, however, forestalls his decision so

47. O'Brien, *Father Elijah*, 251. 48. Ibid., 261.
49. Ibid., 307. 50. Ibid., 305.

as to disclose a terrible secret: he killed Pawel Tarnowski by sending him to the gas chambers. This bombshell stuns the priest, who suffers in silent agony for some interminable moments before regaining his composure. Taunted all the while by Smokrev to avenge the murder, Father Elijah slowly approaches the bed-stricken man and kisses him on both cheeks instead. The poignant gesture takes Smokrev by surprise this time, softening his resistance. The unexpected expression of *caritas* prompts him to admit that he had, indeed, *not* killed Tarnowski, and then to make a full confession of his sins. Through his deathbed conversion the count recovers his spiritual nobility. The hidden icon of Love that resides within his soul points to the ultimate "victory of light," for even in the midst of abysmal failure, Father Elijah affirms, the Cross offers the brokenhearted "limitless hope."[51]

O'Brien's redemptive vision places *Father Elijah* firmly within the Catholic literary tradition. The monitory center of his apocalyptic tale evokes Robert Hugh Benson's classic treatment of the antichrist theme in his 1907 bestseller, *Lord of the World,* which depicts the near demise of a besieged Church doing battle with a secularist elite promoting the anti-Gospel message that god is man. Flannery O'Connor's presentation of the Incarnation as "the ultimate reality" in her fiction,[52] moreover, finds an equally strong resonance in *Father Elijah.* Like the American writer he admires,[53] O'Brien adopts an incarnational poetic that allows him to face the formidable challenge of addressing a contemporary audience that accepts as fact the proposition that God is dead. O'Connor alerted her readers to the dangers of subscribing to such a nihilist philosophy by injecting a sense of "mystery" in her stories and by reintroducing the biblical concept of "the devil as a real spirit who must be made to name himself, and not simply to name himself as vague evil, but to name himself with his specific personality for every occasion."[54] O'Brien employs a similar narrative strategy by offering tangible evidence the devil exists through the machinations of the president on the world stage. But the somber tone that pervades such moments in the novel does not derive from the mythic plot of Gnosticism, which posits a dualism of two coeternal and radically opposed principles, light and dark, locked together in

51. Ibid., 304–5.

52. Flannery O'Connor, *The Habit of Being,* ed. Sally Fitzgerald (New York: Vintage, 1979), 92.

53. McCloskey, "Interview with Michael O'Brien," 16.

54. Flannery O'Connor, *Mystery and Manners,* ed. Sally and Robert Fitzgerald (New York: Farrar, Straus, and Giroux, 1969), 117.

perpetual battle. Rather, O'Brien rejects the tragic view of the world as being intrinsically evil and, accordingly, dramatizes the need for the individual to be on guard against false messiahs.[55] The subplot involving Count Smokrev, for example, shows the protagonist not only recognizing sin as sin but also being brought to a new life as a naturally Christian soul. Father Elijah participates actively in this providential outcome by imitating the memorable gesture of the Christ figure who imparts a simple kiss upon his dumbfounded accuser in the famous exchange with the grand inquisitor in Dostoevsky's *The Brothers Karamazov*. The ethos of charity at work in this scene, as well as in *Father Elijah* as a whole, reflects the subject O'Connor identified as being distinctively Catholic in modern fiction: "the action of grace [operating] in territory largely held by the devil."[56]

One of the finer points of O'Brien's artistry concerns his ability to portray the depths of the human soul as it engages in an intense moral struggle between good and evil. The modernist experimental novel of a James Joyce or a Virginia Woolf typically presents the flow of a character's consciousness through the medium of an interior monologue of the mind with itself. This subjective mode of what has been termed "psychological realism," though effective in revealing secret personal thoughts, preempted the narrative presence of God, since it focused exclusively on the mental operations of an introspective individual who ignored the spiritual dimension of his or her inner life. O'Brien, on the other hand, presents his hero speaking not in isolation but as one individual to other individuals in dialogic interaction. In his many intimate moments of prayer, moreover, Father Elijah imbues his word with such a keen awareness of the divine "other" that it results in a genuine dialogue of an "I" with a "Thou." O'Brien's transcendental realism, then, not only helps him to avoid the literary pitfall of vapid characterization, but it also allows the novelist to represent the whole person in his dignity as a spiritual being communicating and living in communion with his Maker.

Strangers and Sojourners

Like Father Elijah, the protagonist of *Strangers and Sojourners* is plagued by various forms of darkness throughout her life. Anne Ashton leaves her native England as a young woman in order to take up a job teaching in Can-

---

55. Cf. Mark 13:21–23.
56. O'Connor, *Mystery and Manners*, 118.

ada, but before long she finds herself married to Stephen Delaney, bearing him children and eventually becoming a grandmother. The rest of her days are spent in the isolated outpost of Swiftcreek, British Columbia. The geographical displacement is overshadowed, however, by the arduous interior journey she takes across a wasteland of despair before advancing toward an "unknown land with hope."[57] The novel opens with her traumatic childhood memory of being transported against her will by her father and sister to participate in an occult ritual. During the séance, a voice purporting to be that of her dead mother is heard through the power of a medium. Anne breaks the magic circle of participants, reaches into her pocket, and clutches there her grandmother's little cross for protection. The eerie episode leaves a "horrid smell in the mind" of "something corrupt" at work that continues to haunt her years later.[58]

This early experience serves as the main point of reference for Anne's subsequent encounters with a malevolent presence. Her first day in Canada, in fact, is marked by a terrifying vision of shadows swirling against a September sky, transforming themselves into myriad beastly forms at once of a giant panther, a bear, and a dragon. As she peers through the train window to get a better look at the protean animal, it stares back at her with cold, malicious eyes and comes to a standstill with "one forepaw lifted in mid-stride." The eidetic image stirs in Anne's mind especially during her recurring bouts of depression, symbolizing the hideous type of darkness she defines simply as "the enemy of light." The threat seems so real that it makes Anne feel "as if an evil archon were officiating at a liturgy of hell and she were the sacrificial victim."[59] The growing fear of becoming the burnt offering in a Black Mass culminates one winter morning when Stephen is away, and Anne's acute sense of loneliness leaves her particularly vulnerable to a spiritual attack. At that very moment, the shadow beast Anne first spotted on the train ride reappears at her doorstep, threatening to devour the Delaney children as well as the rest of the family. Trembling yet defiant, the housewife manages to stare down the monstrous shape until it departs from the vicinity.

For the greater part of her life, however, Anne is unable to chase away the shadows and wonders whether she will ever find inner peace. Unsure at first precisely what good and evil mean, she nevertheless recognizes a few of the "nastier" devils when they cross her path. Calling their bluff might

57. O'Brien, *Strangers and Sojourners*, 445.   58. Ibid., 74.
59. Ibid., 48, 204.

stall the advance of bad spirits, but an act of sheer willpower, she discovers, does not prevent them from returning to her psychological hinterland. Her son Ashley, on the other hand, disapproves of his mother's shadowboxing. He maintains that because evil will never go away, one should embrace the dark as well as the light side of the human personality. Drawing on her painful experience, Anne finds this Jungian conception of evil entirely unconvincing. "If your house is full of shadows, it won't be fit to live in," she tells her grandson Nathaniel. The development of the whole person requires "a house of love [to] be flooded with light." The attempt to reconcile the bestial or demonic self with its better half is bound to fail because the principle of integration used in depth psychology blurs the distinction between good and evil or love and hatred. These opposing forces wage a perpetual war inside the human soul. The facile optimism of Ashley's "religion of shadows" reflects, in his mother's view, "a lack of hope in anything outside his own mind." Although the reason why each person must engage in an ongoing internal battle, or *psychomachia*, remains a "very deep mystery," Anne believes the answer lies "somewhere beyond the mind without excluding it."[60]

The process of finding a credible explanation for the problem of evil takes Anne on a lifelong search for the meaning of what is truly human. Her early anthropocentric view of the world leads her, like Shakespeare's Hamlet, to exclaim, "What a piece of work is man!" The wonder of her being later gives rise to a query: "Do we create ourselves, or are we created?"[61] Left unanswered, this central question simmers in the back of her mind until her young protégé Nigel unwittingly brings it to the foreground again. During a lesson the gifted student quotes a striking passage from *The Divine Comedy:* "O human race, born to take flight and soar / Why fall ye, for one breath of wind, to earth?"[62] As a teenager, Anne marveled at the flight of birds and considered it "unfair" that man, who aspires to climb to the dizziest heights, is born without wings. The medieval masterpiece provides a rationale for this apparent injustice. The gravity of original sin hindered the soul's ascent toward its heavenly destination, just as the earthbound worm, naturally des-

---

60. Ibid., 444, 445, 446.

61. Ibid., 39, 45.

62. Ibid., 274. This translation of Dante's *Purgatorio* XII.95–96 is by Dorothy L. Sayers, *The Divine Comedy I–III: Inferno, Purgatorio, Paradiso* (Harmondsworth: Penguin, 1949–1962). O'Brien quotes this passage in his article "Historical Imagination" and comments, "Unless there is a return to the search for the *Imago Dei* man will continue to fall down two main false trails: on one hand an increasing sterility, rage, absurdity and nihilism; and on the other hand a return to cultic paganism" (183).

tined to become an "angelic butterfly," cannot pretend to fly without wings.[63] Grace supplies what fallen human nature lacks, elevating the lowly pilgrim above the dark wood of error and into the realm of "pure intellectual light, fulfilled with love / Love of the true Good."[64] The exaltation of the humble soul Dante depicts in his famous epic compels Anne to reconsider her cherished ideal of human perfectibility.

The real danger of making man the measure of all things dawns on Anne for the first time during a stimulating conversation with her sister: "Suppose there really is a God, Emily, and let's say that he knows full well that this *hubris* of ours, this damnable pride, is a thing that eventually destroys us. Would it not be an act of kindness on his part to bring down the temple in which we worship an image of ourselves?"[65] Anne imagines the possibility of a good God saving his presumptuous creatures from suffering irreparable harm by destroying the inner sanctuary where they practice the cult of self-worship. The providential scenario she envisages opens up a new vista that exists beyond the ken of "proud . . . intellects."[66] From the perspective of eternal wisdom, the pristine image of man, though marred by sin, retains hidden traces of its divine likeness, the way, one might say, the fingerprints of the potter cling to the clay vessel he molds. Anne later advances a related hypothesis: "Suppose there is a great Love behind creation, but the original unity of this vast work of art has been damaged, and all of existence as we know it is merely a brief moment during which the artist repairs his masterpiece."[67] The first author of beauty touches up the erratic dabs of paint human hands apply to the canvas of creation and, through his mercy, delivers a masterstroke that restores the blemished images to their original splendor.

The prospect of this supreme Artist coming to heal her wounded nature fills Anne's final days with hope. The road to recovery begins when she sees reflected in the injured eye of a townswoman, Wanda Tobac, a broken image of herself that requires mending. The shock of recognition allows Anne to identify for the first time the root cause of her recurring malaise: "Depression . . . is the reaction of my inner self to a lie, to a false concept of the self." To overcome the deep discouragement such self-delusion breeds, she decides to follow the advice the local parish priest, Father Andrei, gives her: "The false

---

63. This passage is from the Sayers's translation of *Purgatorio* X.124–25.
64. This passage is from the Sayers's translation of *Paradiso* XXX.40–41.
65. O'Brien, *Strangers and Sojourners*, 338.   66. Ibid., 339.
67. Ibid., 542.

self must die in order for the true self to be born."[68] This radical change of heart, she suspects, does not occur overnight for newcomers to the idea. Believers, like Stephen Delaney, alleviate their spiritual hunger by consuming their Lord in the Eucharist, whereas those "starved for the unknown God," like Anne, seek nourishment in the aridity of the desert where no manna seems miraculously supplied to them as it was to the ancient Israelites.[69] In spite of its apparent futility, Anne's personal pilgrimage proves to be a fruitful one in the end. The presence that eludes her for so long becomes real, paradoxically, just at the moment when she is about to resign herself to living in the incertitude of the void. While attending a Catholic Mass with her family in the early days of her marriage, Anne paused for a moment upon hearing the congregation utter the last petition of the Lord's Prayer in Latin, *sed libera nos a malo,* and asked the "benign Presence" silently, *"Deliver me from the shadow in my mind."*[70] This silent plea is later answered on her deathbed. After Father Andrei performs the last rites, Anne accepts the grace of conversion and tells her husband that the shadows, as well as her fears, have finally disappeared. The gift of self with which she closes the book of her life vivifies Anne's hope of attending the "victory feast,"[71] or Great Banquet, which Josef Pieper stated "takes place beyond time and above the heavens."[72]

The trust Anne places ultimately in the One whose beauty she saw reflected in human faces becomes her most enduring legacy. As a mother, she worried constantly about the deep psychological scars her son suffered from long after he was physically attacked by a grizzly bear: "Would Ashley one day see through the broken image to find the mutilated face of a poor man hung on a tree?"[73] Although the question of whether Ashley eventually averts the danger of going beyond good and evil is left open in the novel, Nathaniel clearly vindicates his grandmother's philosophy of life. Confronted in a cave by the same "phantom bear" that terrorized his extended family

---

68. Ibid., 342, 300. 69. Ibid., 190.
70. Ibid., 201. 71. Ibid., 541.

72. See Josef Pieper, *Josef Pieper: An Anthology* (San Francisco: Ignatius, 1989), 233. Pieper comments that the "great banquet" Plato speaks of in the *Phaedrus* serves as one of the memorable "images of hope" in philosophy. "But," he adds, "the communal meal in which Christians, while still in the world of history, apprehend and, in a real sense, celebrate the beginning and their foretaste of their life of beatitude at the table of God—this kind of fellowship, this kind of banquet is something which Plato never dreamed of" (233). O'Brien has mentioned that he makes a point of reading the piece from which this extract is taken, titled "The Art of Not Yielding to Despair," several times each year. See McCloskey, "Interview with Michael O'Brien," 11.

73. O'Brien, *Strangers and Sojourners,* 445.

in previous generations, the young man finds himself at the crossroads. The cunning beast exhorts his potential victim to abandon his *"childish image"* of evil and to accept an offer of the "goodness" that is synonymous with *"unlimited power to change mankind"* (italics in the original).[74] Nathaniel hears the same siren song that enchanted some of his ancestors—that salvation can be attained through knowledge or gnosis—but he rejects the modest proposal. Holding up a stone cross, he breaks the spell and banishes the shadow. By choosing to dedicate himself to a life of making beauty, Nathaniel, like Anne before him, stands ready to play his part in a divine comedy rather than in a human tragedy.

In both *Father Elijah* and *Strangers and Sojourners*, fragmented human figures stagger in an interior landscape, a *paysage intérieur*, in search of their lost faces. Modern thinkers such as Nietzsche argue that man is a stranger to himself because he does not create the moral order of things, while Jung maintained that alienation results from the failure to balance the chiaroscuro shading of the human psyche. The diverse experiences of a Father Elijah or an Anne Delaney point instead to man's old dream of deifying the ego through his own efforts, along with the loss of the sense of sin, as being the real source of the problem. The rupture of the original unity of body and soul highlighted in the book of Genesis left a fallen humanity struggling to comprehend its true nature. Manichaeism maintained that the postlapsarian soul remained imprisoned in matter and could only be liberated by accessing an arcane wisdom. In addition to falsifying Scripture, according to O'Brien, this claim denies the freedom of the human agent and transfers responsibility for his actions to a primeval darkness or an amorphous principle of evil residing in a person. In response O'Brien affirms the benevolence of the primal creation: "Matter is good, very good." "But," he cautions, "[matter] is not an end in itself."[75] The crucial distinction between means and end led an atheistic humanism, in O'Brien's view, to present man as a being made of matter alone without a spiritual core. This opposite extreme to Manichaeism generated another major misconception: that man possesses the power to perfect himself on his own. The notion of human perfectibility stemmed from the centuries-old belief that original sin failed to damage human nature. Pelagianism conveniently disregarded man's propensity

---

74. Ibid., 564.
75. O'Brien, "Historical Imagination," 169.

for evil and over-optimistically exalted human nature's capacity for good. In his fiction, O'Brien has shown his ability to steer a middle course between the Scylla of Manichaeism and the Charybdis of Pelagianism, because both philosophies paint a misleading and distorted picture of what it means to be human. As Maritain has pointed out, a humanism of the Manichaen type rejects the religious dimension of the creature and discards in the process "a whole part of the human heritage."[76] The same can be said of a Pelagian-inspired humanism. To counter these reductionist theories, O'Brien grounds the meaning of personhood in his fiction on the biblical drama of the fall and redemption. His guiding principle, therefore, is that, on the one hand, humanity cannot escape from the fundamental problem of sin and, on the other, no real change, individually or collectively, is possible without the aid of divine grace.

The solution to the problem of evil for O'Brien's characters lies in striving to orient their lives, consciously or unconsciously, in accordance with what Maritain called an integral humanism. The authentic integration of the human and divine, they discover, is only made possible by Christ's Incarnation. O'Brien's portrayal of Anne Delaney, for instance, is in keeping with the biblical view of man as wayfarer—a stranger and sojourner in this world. One of O'Brien's favorite writers, Walker Percy, defined the narrative of the quest as being "nothing else than a recipe for the best novel-writing from Dante to Dostoevsky." The Judeo-Christian emphasis on the value of the person, coupled with the sacramental realism of Catholicism, provides, Percy adds, an antidote to despair. Emerging from this traditional anthropology, "you have a man in a predicament and on the move in a real world of real things, a world which is a sacrament and a mystery; a pilgrim whose life is a searching and a finding."[77] Following this paradigm, Anne is searching, in other words, for the face that reveals the person and, above all, for the visage of God.[78] Like Dante the pilgrim at the end of the *Paradiso,* she has a vision of the humanness of the incarnate God. In the words of O'Brien, "God revealed an image of himself, but so much more than an image—a *person* with a heart, a mind, a soul, and a face. To our shock and disbelief it is a human face. It is our own face restored to the original image and likeness of

76. Maritain, *Integral Humanism,* 91.

77. Walker Percy, *Signposts in a Strange Land,* ed. Patrick Samway (New York: Farrar, Straus, and Giroux, 1991), 369.

78. Cf. Psalm 26:8.

God."[79] By presenting compelling epiphanies of man's true face refigured according to the *Imago Dei* in his novels, Michael O'Brien joins the front ranks of modern artists of hope. As he has put it, "The artist of hope creates images of man restored to the *imago Dei*, the image and likeness of God within us."[80]

---

79. O'Brien, "Historical Imagination," 160.

80. O'Brien, "The Decline and Renewal of Christian Art," *Second Spring* (August/September 1994): 34.

CHAPTER 15

Maiden Mothers and Little Sisters ▪ The Convent Novel Grows Up

Meoghan B. Cronin

It appears at first glance that the convent girl is a figure lost to contemporary Catholic fiction. The convent itself, as a literary setting, suggests the quaintness of a castle, the mysterious and silent remains of old oppressions. Without its inhabitants, the cloister is but a curiosity, a relic with none but emblematic meaning in fiction. In late-twentieth- and early-twenty-first-century fiction, girls are no longer sent to convent school to await directives from God or man, in either the form of a vocation or an approved suitor. Mention convent fiction (as I do often) and you are usually asked about *In This House of Brede* (1969) by Rumer Godden or *The Prime of Miss Jean Brodie* (1961) by Muriel Spark, novels written more than forty years ago.

But the last two decades have seen a light flurry of literary fiction about nuns in convents, most notably the American novels *Mariette in Ecstasy* (1991) by Ron Hansen and *Lying Awake* (2000) by Mark Salzman and the British novel *Daughters of the House* (1992) by Michèle Roberts. In recent popular fiction, too, nuns have appeared in period novels such as Sarah Dunant's *The Birth of Venus* (2003), set in the Renaissance; Kate Horsley's *Confessions of a Pagan Nun* (2002), set in the first century A.D.; and Catherine Monroe's *The King's Nun* (2007), set in the time of Charlemagne. Liberated and liberal sisters create an unorthodox but spiritually fulfilling convent in Susan Leonardi's *And Then They Were Nuns* (2003). Nuns have also emerged as detectives, such as Monica Quill's Sister Mary Theresa and Carol Anne O'Marie's Sister Mary Helen, and as political activists, as in Julia Alvarez's *In the Time of the Butterflies* (1995).

In addition to their literary excellence, what distinguishes the novels by Hansen, Roberts, and Salzman, however, is their focus on the central cruxes of convent fiction: the role of the nun in community and the conflicting though confluent development of girlhood and sisterhood. The convent's unique, all-female community-for-life draws attention to gender issues and gender roles in ways that no other setting can, examining a woman's search for meaning in a distinctive setting that "freezes" female sexual and social development while overdetermining a woman's physical purity and spiritual self. Like major convent novels of an earlier period, such as Godden's *In This House of Brede* and Antonia White's *Frost in May* (1933), Roberts, Hansen, and Salzman focus narrowly on women's physical and metaphysical relationships with each other, with their families, and with God. While invoking some older conventions of religious fiction, these contemporary novelists raise persistent modern questions concerning female identity, social roles, and spirituality while they explore, in particular, the relationship between sexual and spiritual desire.

Moreover, the figure of the nun allows Hansen, Roberts, and Salzman to reexamine the roles of woman, sister, and mother. With a fastidious eye and subjective—often multiple—narrative voice, each of their novels observes womanhood developing on parallel planes, so to speak, as female experience is examined in both the closed convent system and outside of it in the larger world. Within the convent, girls and adult women are depicted in generational relationships that mimic and replace family roles. At the same time, girlhood development in the convent is compared to womanliness outside the convent, where sexuality and fertility are represented in nature and in girls who become wives of men, not spouses of Christ. In each of the novels I examine here, religious experience is inseparable from family dynamics, and spiritual crisis is cast in terms of both personal loss and the conflict between body and soul. As such, each novel underlines the most ambiguous and terrifying elements of a woman's experience of the supernatural: the human suspicion and rejection occasioned by her mystical or miraculous communion with the divine.

One can argue that contemporary convent fiction offers the same dynamic between the self and family as other domestic fiction, and that it does so in the same central setting, the family home. Indeed, the convent house ascribes strict roles to sister, Mother, and Father: a woman's place in the sisterhood is defined through a hierarchy of rank that begins with postulant, novice, and sister, and then, for some, Mother Superior or abbess. All sisters vow obedience to the order, and they adhere to the overarching authority of their assigned priest, or Father, who is mostly absent from the physical setting of the house. At age seventeen, Ron Hansen's Mariette Baptiste in *Mariette in Ecstasy* leaves her father's lavish world to enter the Convent of Our Lady of Sorrows, where her thirty-seven-year-old biological sister is the prioress. Carmelite Sister John of the Cross, the elderly main character of Mark Salzman's *Lying Awake*, remembers her own girlhood entrance into the cloister, which she associates with the abandonment of childhood and her relationship with her long-absent mother. In Michèle Roberts's *Daughters of the House,* the adult Leonie and her cousin Thérèse uncover family identities as they piece together their secret memories of their adolescent summers in Normandy, just before Thérèse entered the enclosed cloister. In each novel, the little family of individuals is subsumed and rewritten by the larger Church structure. The bringing together of young girls and older women shows the maturation of sexuality and spirit as influenced by the patriarchy of the Church and a matriarchy of maidens in a community that mortifies the senses and denies the body while also redirecting desire onto Christ and the natural world. The female collective settings reveal developing sexuality as natural but also transgressive as it is contrasted with feminine self-sacrifice and renunciation of sensual pleasure.

In addition, these works explore the possibility of finding satisfying answers to the questions of self-transformation that arise when girl meets not boy but God. In her work on autobiographical Catholic girlhood narratives, Jeana DelRosso discusses the difference between the way that religious women see their vocation and the way that they are seen by others. She notes that "many feminist theologians . . . read the convent as a site of feminist awareness and achievement," but that nuns are also seen as "dangerous, alternative women" who reject the roles of wife, mother, and even daughter and define themselves apart from marriage and men.[1] Thus, even in her obedience and self-abnegation, the nun can be as perceived as self-indulgent. Indeed, her mortifications of the body and resistance of temptation must necessarily become "paths toward the self"[2] or she has no self; her ripening sensual desire must become an intense longing to know Christ intimately or her desire is barren. Today, this type of female spirituality, the nun's life, is so odd and

1. Jeana Delrosso, *Writing Catholic Women: Contemporary International Catholic Girlhood Narratives* (New York: Palgrave Macmillan, 2005), 187.
2. Elizabeth N. Evasdaughter, *Catholic Girlhood Narratives: The Church and Self-Denial* (Boston: Northeastern University Press, 1996), 4.

paradoxical that it can seem disturbing. But in these recent novels, the convent's institutional oppressions of the self are balanced by the detailed portraits of a type of female mystical experience that is spiritually, emotionally, and even physically fulfilling.

Readers have noted both contrasts and connections among these three novels. In their religious attitudes, Hansen, Salzman, and Roberts are quite different, at least on the surface. Ron Hansen grew up in a devout Catholic family, attended Catholic schools, and holds the Gerard Manley Hopkins professorship at Santa Clara University. A daily communicant, he has written often about his faith and about the relationship between religion and literature, especially in his book of essays, *A Stay against Confusion* (2001). Michèle Roberts brings the experience of convent education to her fiction but speaks frequently of her struggle with the Church, which she, at times, has felt is repressive and misogynist in its teachings. Her dual French-Catholic, English-Protestant background, she says, has attuned her to the dialectical positions expressed in Catholic culture and practices, especially as they affect women. Mark Salzman, a self-labeled agnostic, found the creative difficulties of writing *Lying Awake* much like the spiritual dryness often experienced by saints and mystics, and his intensive research on the Carmelite order repeatedly revealed to him previously unseen connections between the spiritual pilgrim's dark night of the soul and the creative aridity and emotional darkness suffered by the writer.

What primarily links these novelists is their interest in exploring the state of the afflicted female soul. Each of the three works relies upon historical and spiritual writings by women, in particular the life of Thérèse of Lisieux, Saint Thérèse of the Child Jesus. Roberts's *Daughters of the House* and Hansen's *Mariette in Ecstasy* are directly informed by Saint Thérèse's autobiography, *Story of a Soul*, and it is also referred to in *Lying Awake*. The three novels also allude to other famous religious figures such as Dame Julian of Norwich and Teresa of Avila. At her profession, Helen Nye in *Lying Awake* takes the name of the mystic St. John of the Cross and later experiences his dark night of the soul and dryness of spirit. As he has stated, Salzman's first idea for *Lying Awake* occurred after reading an Oliver Sacks essay about temporal lobe epilepsy, particularly symptoms "where the person would experience an intensification of interest in religion and spirituality."[3] He discov-

3. Quoted in Carol Lloyd, "A Conversation with Mark Salzman," *Salon* (Jan. 10, 2001), www.archive.salon.com.

ered that Teresa of Avila, "the founder of the Carmelite order[,] had all sorts of terrible illnesses and headaches along with her visions" and may have suffered from epilepsy.[4] While it is clear that his character Sister John's me-nangioma is causing her seizures, her religious raptures may not be purely pathological in their origin. Like Hansen and Roberts, Salzman does not shut down entirely the possibility that his character communes with the divine directly, and none of the novels provides unequivocal explanations for the central religious mystery in their stories. The truth of their supernatural experiences is known only by the novels' characters, even as they are scrutinized by their communities. One critic's point, that in *Mariette in Ecstasy* the reader "observes and evaluates miracles simultaneously," is true for each of these novels.[5]

The language and structure of the three novels are also illuminated by comparison. All three authors shape the narratives through multiple forms of telling. The third-person narrator in each case expresses the thoughts and feelings of one or all of the characters, and this overarching narrative is cut through with first-person writings and utterances in the form of journals, poetry, recorded visions, letters, and, in *Mariette in Ecstasy*, the priest's official "Extracts of an Inquiry into Certain Wonderful Events at the Priory of Our Lady of Sorrows Having to Do with Mariette Baptiste." These different viewpoints on and articulations of the female experience of the divine demonstrate the essential ambiguity of such occurrences, the fluidity of the characters' consciousnesses, and the subjectivity through which the meaning of experience evolves and is understood. At the same time, however, Hansen's and Salzman's novels use more objective secular and liturgical calendars as well as the strictures of monastic time to emphasize the mundane routine of convent life. The language of each of the three works is lucidly imagistic and impressionistic. The novels' subjective interiority and shifting points of view, contrasted with their sections of detailed earthy realism, manipulate and alter the figure of the stereotypical nun that readers thought they knew and raise questions about the interpenetration of the divine and human realms.

The heavy and layered subjectivity of these works emphasizes the mind and body of the character who experiences the mystical moment: each wom-

---

4. Ibid.

5. Mark Cronin, "Ron Hansen: *Mariette in Ecstasy*," in *Encyclopedia of Catholic Literature*, vol. 1, ed. Mary R. Reichardt (Westport, Conn.: Greenwood, 2004), 313.

an's own emotional and physical feelings affect her perceptions and cloud objective ways to evaluate her experience. The themes of disease and writing further locate religious mystery within the subjective self. Like Salzman's Sister John, Hansen's Mariette and Roberts's Thérèse are confronted by people who necessarily equate religious experience with pathology. Mariette's own physician-father is called to the convent to diagnose his daughter's wounds; Sister John's tumor is removed; and Thérèse Martin heads to the convent knowing that she has discredited her cousin's confused vision of the golden-red Lady. In this latter novel, the village *curé* has accused the girls of having "heated imaginations. Hysteria," and of spouting "dangerous pagan nonsense"[6]—all typical reactions to female claims of divine favor.

The Convent in Popular Culture: Nuns and Lovers

While they depict the contemplative life with detailed accuracy and psychological realism, Hansen, Salzman, and Roberts subvert readers' familiarity with popular depictions of nuns and convents. Despite her obsolescence, the nun as a cultural figure feels like a familiar relic, especially in her comic identity made popular by Catholic school memoirs, stage comedies, and films such as *The Sound of Music* (1965), Mary O'Malley's *Once a Catholic* (1978), *Nunsense* (1985), and others. The artistic use of widely held stereotypes of convents and nuns was common in the eighteenth and nineteenth century as well, but rather than comic nostalgia, the attitudes behind the portrayals often reflected Protestant anxieties about the Roman Church. The earliest popular works to feature convents prominently were British gothic novels with their delight in the decorative and evocative possibilities of dark-habited clerics, papist rituals, and imprisoning cells. The nearly unvarying sameness of convents in gothic fiction gave nineteenth-century writers like Mary Shelley and Charlotte Brontë a set of predictable sensations to choose from for their novels *Valperga* (1823) and *Villette* (1853), respectively. Despite the fact that England had almost no active Roman Catholic convents from about 1535 to the 1790s (and Katharine M. Rogers makes the point that convents in English literature had to be "drawn from imagination" rather than from life),[7] by the nineteenth century the convent abbey, vaults, and garden

6. Michèle Roberts, *Daughters of the House* (New York: Picador, 1992), 113–14.
7. Katharine M. Rogers, "Fantasy and Reality in the Fictional Convents of the Eighteenth Century," *Comparative Literature Studies* 22, no. 3 (1985): 313.

had currency as stock images in literature and art, largely due to the popularity of earlier novels like Ann Radcliffe's *The Italian* and Matthew Lewis's *The Monk,* both published in 1796. Most commonly, the convent was depicted as a stronghold where young women were kept away from unsuitable lovers or a sanctuary to which they fled in despair when forbidden to marry the man of their choice. *The Italian,* like many eighteenth-century gothic novels, uses the convent literally as a prison setting where a young woman is deprived of her will and punished for her desires. Critic Manuela Mourão says that the convent in gothic fiction serves to heighten the "lurid and claustrophobic effect,"[8] but, in addition, the consistent suggestion of sexuality in the gothic version reflects Protestant perceptions of convents as Catholic brothels as well as English and American fears that the Church would steal girls away from their natural, proper place with fathers and husbands, the "true" owners of female virginity.

The gothic variant itself relied on other established depictions of nuns and convents. In the eighteenth century, one way for writers to emphasize the importance of rationalism and enlightened social values was to condemn or caricature the opposing values, superstition, error, and religious oppression, all of which were aligned with the Catholic Church. Post-Reformation anti-Catholicism and stereotypes derived from European literature also influenced these portrayals. Mourão points out that in the seventeenth and eighteenth centuries, women frequently entered convents to withdraw from male authority and control but that literature often inverts this important element of vocation.[9] Rather, fictional nuns typically long for their lovers; they are brokenhearted, fallen, or mad because of men. Claude Barbin's *Les Lettres portugaises* (1669), Aphra Behn's *The History of the Nun, or the Fair Vow-Breaker* (1689), Diderot's *La Religieuse* (1780–83), Chateaubriand's *Rene* (1802), and Alessandro Manzoni's wildly popular *I Promessi Sposi* (1827) featured "risqué adventures of nuns" and reflected stereotypical images of vow-violating novices and convents ruled by sadistic priests and lesbian abbesses.[10] In America, tales of "escaped nuns" became a phenomenon of literary culture, and two of these supposedly true stories, Rebecca Reed's *Six Months in a Convent* (1835) and Maria Monk's *Awful Disclosures of the Hotel Dieu* (1836), were sensa-

---

8. Manuela Mourão, *Altered Habits: Reconsidering the Nun in Fiction* (Gainesville: University of Florida Press, 2002), 35.
9. Ibid., 1.
10. Ibid., 15.

tional bestsellers despite their disputed authenticity.[11] While later nineteenth-century religious novels left behind some of this gothic sensationalism, both Protestant and Catholic writers expressed the conflicting values arising from the girl's act of leaving the world. In particular, what Margaret Maison terms "cloister-hearth conflicts" disturb the Catholic or convert girl.[12]

In the twentieth century, Antonia White's *Frost in May* stands, arguably, as the finest literary portrayal of convent school life. Not as well known as Godden's *Brede,* it precedes that novel by thirty years and provides a young woman's story that contrasts with the older widow's convent tale in Godden's work. *Frost in May* depicts Nanda Grey's coming of age in terms of familiar, grand-scale narrative values: displacement, suffering, friendship, love, and education. As a setting, The Convent of the Five Wounds is a home that is strictly ruled and surveilled; in this enclosure, the Church represents an omnipotent authority against which rebellion is both forbidden and fruitless, and any expression of a woman's imagination or affection is perceived as transgressive. *Frost in May*'s power lies in the novel's dual depiction of the suffocating grip of convent routine and oppression of Nanda's individual will and of "the presence of very genuine beauty, devotion and love" she discovers in her relationship with God.[13]

Rumer Godden's *In This House of Brede* provides an intimate portrayal of businesswoman Philippa Talbot's call to Brede Abbey and her life as first a novice and then a professed nun in the cloistered Benedictine order. One commentator expresses a widely held opinion of the novel in calling it "the most accessible, accurate and sympathetic presentation of monastic life in all of English literature."[14] Godden's is considered the first popular novel to depict both the spiritual beauty and the human pettiness present in a religious community. *Brede* focuses entirely on the interior spaces of the convent and inner chambers of the nuns' personalities, revealing a routine that is both comforting and numbing and the experience of sisterhood as alternately intimate and alienating, rewarding and disappointing, communal and excruciatingly lonely. Dame Philippa's greatest challenge is not her faith

11. Susan Griffin, *Anti-Catholicism and Nineteenth-Century Fiction* (Cambridge: Cambridge University Press, 2004), 39.

12. Margaret M. Maison, *The Victorian Vision: Studies in the Religious Novel* (New York: Sheed and Ward, 1962), 159.

13. Thomas Woodman, *Faithful Fictions: The Catholic Novel in British Literature* (Philadelphia: Open University Press, 1991), 27.

14. Phyllis Tickle, intro. to Rumer Godden, *In This House of Brede* (Chicago: Loyola Press, 2005), ix.

or commitment to her vocation, but her vow of obedience within the rigid hierarchy of the cloister, an organization that strictly limits personal friendships and redirects even the emotions of love and grief toward the service of God. Both *Frost in May* and *In This House of Brede* served to establish a modern, realistic view of convent life, especially in their detailed descriptions of the appearance and layout of the house, the daily routine of the sisters, and the strict practices of convent rule. Nonetheless, the fictionalized convents in these novels retain the mysterious, even exotic atmosphere of earlier convent fiction. Within the Catholic universe—a subculture with its own language, its own calendar, and its own class system—the convent remains a world of its own. The achievement of White's and Godden's convent novels is their creation of "the paradoxical combination of strangeness and yet utterly taken for granted routine in the day-to-day life" of this world.[15]

"Tell My Beloved That I Am Sick with Love"

In August 1906, Mariette Baptiste enters the Couvent de Notre-Dame des Afflictions in upstate New York, leaving behind her father's world of wealth, status, and eligible suitors. Earlier on this day Mariette "is upstairs in a great country house and sitting at a Duchess desk in a pink satin nightgown as she pens instructions . . . saying to whom her jewelry and porcelains and laces and gowns ought to go."[16] She is "pretty and naked and seventeen. She skeins her chocolate-brown hair. She pouts her mouth. She esteems her full breasts as she has seen men esteem them. She haunts her milk-white skin with her hands. *Even this I give you.*"[17] In the convent, the beautiful postulant both charms and offends the other sisters young and old. Although she is full of entertaining wit and youthful high spirits, Mariette's greatest desire is to be consumed by Christ and to suffer greatly for Him. When she appears to experience this suffering as physical pain of an excessive nature—she receives the stigmata of Christ's wounds—her sister-nuns respond in a human manner: they are at once awed, envious, and suspicious of this supposed lavish display of love for the Beloved. When Mariette is dismissed from the convent six months later, this love has not diminished. But the novel remains purposely ambiguous as to whether the girl's wounds are divine, psychosomatic, or self-inflicted. Perhaps they are all three.

15. Woodman, *Faithful Fictions*, 27.
16. Ron Hansen, *Mariette in Ecstasy* (New York: Harper Perennial, 1991), 8.
17. Ibid.

Mariette in Ecstasy earned Ron Hansen broad critical praise. While his other novels generally reflect themes of sin and redemption, *Mariette in Ecstasy* is his most explicitly Catholic novel to date. Its focus on a young girl ecstatic to share the pain of the dying Christ seems, to a modern audience, both shocking and extreme. Indeed (and, ironically, despite their order's name) some of the Sisters of the Crucifixion consider Mariette's stigmata to be merely further evidence of her theatrical nature and unseemly fanaticism, and Mariette's own words to her confessor Father Marriott are disturbing: she longs, she states, to "feel the horrors and terrors of death just as Christ did."[18] While the novel's central mystery concerns the source of Mariette's bleeding wounds, its commanding idea exposes the paradox in the Christian view of the human person: Mariette is both a sensuous creature and a spiritual soul, a body weak and carnal and a daughter of God Incarnate.

Hansen depicts the world of the convent as representing this paradox. The novel's fragmented, impressionistic language captures both the silent contemplation and the monastic Rule of Saint Benedict by which the nuns live: "Church windows and thirty nuns singing the Night Office in Gregorian chant. Matins. Lauds." But the convent is also a place of abundant earthiness. The sisters' work reveals this harmony of flesh and spirit. One sister prays as she kneads bread dough, which "rolls as slowly as a white pig"; another sews the "corporal for the holy chalice."[19] The sensory language of color and light creates a unique earth-heaven that is free of all superfluity but full of soulful life: "Troughs of sunlight angle into the oratory like green and blue and pink bolts of cloth grandly flung down from the high, painted windows. Still present are the wood oil smells and habit starch and an incense of styrax and cascarilla bark."[20] Hansen uses both structure and imagistic prose to create an effect of almost oriental spareness that is employed to elide flowingly from one observation to the next or to point to jarring contrasts. As the narrative perspective sweeps from outside to inside the convent and then back outside again, the seasons of the natural world and the progress of the liturgical year are brought into synchrony. But at other times the descriptive contrast is violent, as when the Latin missal lies next to a five-dollar bill, when Mariette removes her mother's ornate bridal gown for the black habit and wooden work shoes, and when the brisk dialogue of Father Marriott's formal inquiry into Mariette's affliction interrupts the narrator's lyrical observations of natural images.

18. Ibid., 40.
20. Ibid., 32.

19. Ibid., 3, 4.

In Mariette, this natural-supernaturalism finds expression as an apparent conflict of body and soul. The other nuns are drawn to and repelled by the same qualities in Mariette that discomfort and attract us as readers: excess, whether of sensuality or piety, is unnerving, and Mariette's love for the Lord is excessive in both ways. When asked to testify, her sister-nuns are quick to list her faults: "She has been a snare and a worldliness to me and a terrible impediment to the . . . interests of the Holy Spirit," reports one.[21] Mariette's mortifications of body are also extreme. Secretly, she twines rabbit wire beneath her breasts and around her upper thigh, "just under her sex." Her pain brings her rapture and her raptures bring disapproving attention. But the playlet from the Song of Songs performed by the novices provides the biblical precedent for such lush, excessive desire for the divine Bridegroom. Mariette the bride is sick with love, mad for consummation with Christ. When her physician-father is called to evaluate her wounds, she asks him, "Are you trying to turn it into a disease?"[22]

About the authenticity of Mariette's vocation, the novel provides only her explicit motive: her wish "to be a great saint."[23] But in his descriptions of the Baptiste family, Hansen presents additional possibilities for Mariette's call, and the progress of Mariette's suffering is clearly driven forward by her personal grief. Her mother dead from cancer, the home life Mariette leaves is dominated by her father, an imposing male figure who is terribly angry when he loses his second daughter to the convent. As a postulant, Mariette reunites with her blood sister Annie, now Mother Céline, who nevertheless coldly distances herself from Mariette. Cancer takes Mother Céline on Christmas Eve, and Mariette's hands begin to bleed on Christmas Day. Her first words in the novel—"even this I give you"—shift and reshape their meaning as her body expresses both Christ's passion and her own desire for earthly love. As her father examines her rent flesh, Mariette "turns to [him] in her nakedness. 'Je vous en prie,' she says. At your service."[24]

Throughout her stay in the convent, Mariette has recorded her ecstasies for Father Marriott, and it is in these letters—essentially love letters to Christ—that we hear her spiritual and self-doubts. Fittingly, then, the novel ends with a letter from the now forty-year-old Mariette to the convent's new Mother Philomene. Mariette writes to her old friend, "I have been a troubled bride pining each night for a husband who is lost without a trace."[25]

21. Ibid., 88.
23. Ibid., 19.
25. Ibid., 179.

22. 103, 171.
24. Ibid., 172.

"Comforter, Where, Where Is Your Comforting?"

Mark Salzman's middle-aged Sister John of the Cross is not lovely, nor was she pretty when she entered the convent as the overweight postulant Helen Nye, but her desire for God is no less passionate than Mariette's. She lives her enclosed life in the state that Saint Augustine describes as "an exercise of holy desire. You do not see what you long for, but the very act of desiring prepares you, so that when He comes you may . . . be utterly satisfied."[26] And God does come to Sister John of the Discalced Carmelites: like Mariette, she stands out in her religious house because she is visited by ecstasies of love for God. These raptures provide visions and, afterward, reflections, which Sister John describes in popular books that have become a needed source of income for the convent. Medical inquiry into her headaches reveals the likely pathological, rather than mystical, nature of her experiences.

Like *Mariette in Ecstasy, Lying Awake* is organized around the calendar of Catholic feast days, and the novel notes the double label of each day, the secular date and the saints' name day. The present day narrative begins on July 25, 1997, or Saint James, Apostle, and it ends on November 1, All Saints Day; within this frame the story ranges back to young Helen Nye's "call" in 1969 and to her spiritual crises of 1982 and 1994. Sister John's spiritual journey falls into several parts, each of which becomes central to her identity and her faith. She recalls a childhood spent under a slanted attic bedroom ceiling; awaiting the rare letters from her runaway mother; her spiritual guide Sister Priscilla who tells Helen, "[God's] after you"; her "desert" time of torturous spiritual dryness; and the "rain from heaven" or headaches that bring unconsciousness and "crimson flowers," visual experiences of God's presence. As these visions become frequent, she welcomes the intense pain, "knowing that those who love more want to suffer more."[27]

Life in the Carmelite cloister is based on renunciation of the world, though the monastery itself is surrounded by worldliness, "with the Golden State Freeway to the east, Chinatown to the south, the Police Academy to the north, and Dodger Stadium a mile to the west." Though "the Sisters . . . prayed from the very heart of Los Angeles," the natural world is fruitful and intimately close at hand: "Desert poppies opened like the sun . . . a dewdrop caught in a spider's web flashed like a prism."[28] These moments

26. Mark Salzman, *Lying Awake* (New York: Knopf, 2000), 25.
27. Ibid., 91, 109, 15.
28. Ibid., 8, 50.

are sacramental for Sister John, who has learned to see God in every thing and in every person, from the young novice Sister Miriam to the oldest nun Mother Mary Joseph, the Living Rule. The cloister world of constant prayer is reflected in Salzman's narrative structure, which interrupts the flow of the story's plot with the community rituals of daily prayer, Sister John's personal prayers, and her recorded visions and poems. This prayerful way of seeing allows Sister John to connect the convent with the alien world around it. For example, she begins to see God when she enters the hospital, a place she initially regards only as one of feverish hurry and wastefulness. For her impending surgery, she changes into "a gown as white as the bridal dress she had worn at her Clothing Ceremony."[29]

Several of the feast days marking time in the novel celebrate holy men and women who are called "virgin and doctor," such as Teresa of Avila and Thérèse of the Child Jesus. The link of cloister and hospital, of course, is Salzman's analogy for the interweaving of Sister John's epileptic and spiritual episodes, and Sister John begins to realize that she cannot unwind the strands to determine if, indeed, the God she so ardently desires, especially during her dark night of the soul, has really visited her at all. The notebooks she fills with her visions have come to constitute her identity, and she guiltily acknowledges that "writing had become as important as prayer to her—It was prayer."[30] With the strands of self and soul inextricably bound, Sister John is terrified of losing both. Her prayer asks, "Have I been worshipping reflections of my own neediness?"[31]

Mother Emmanuel is aware that such extraordinary gifts of grace "[make] the soul especially vulnerable to the sin of pride. Was Sister John putting her own interests before those of the community?"[32] When Sister John's headaches cause her to faint, or she lingers in her cell to experience or record a vision, she is late to prayer. Like Mariette's stigmata, Sister John's visions disrupt the rule of the cloister and the regulated lives of the other sisters. The desires of the self conflict with the family life of the cloister; as Sister John herself realizes, "too many blessings received by one person could be a problem. In the spiritual life, individual success often came at the expense of community harmony."[33] Struggling with the understanding that her personal communion with God might be an organically produced illusion of the

29. Ibid., 149.
31. Ibid., 128.
33. Ibid., 27.

30. Ibid., 35.
32. Ibid., 34.

brain, Sister John decides to have her tumor removed, knowing that, in doing so, she might never see her Beloved again. Thus, in this decision, she
apprehends Saint Augustine's command: "The vessel must be emptied of its
contents and then be cleansed . . . even if you have to scour it." Re-clothed
after the ordeal in her habit, Sister John feels no longer herself: "The gar-
ment she had cherished for so long looked strange, like a costume." But the
novel ends with Sister John witnessing a novice's profession and praying to
be more like the sparrows, who "answered yes to everything."[34]

"A Serious House on Serious Earth"

In *Daughters of the House,* the religious girl is "split," so to speak, into
two characters of the same age, Thérèse and Leonie, one of whom enters the
convent while the other remains outside of it, giving up her virginity and
stripped of her religious vision. The novel is set decades after the Second
World War, but most of the plot occurs around the summer that cousins Leonie and Thérèse are thirteen and living in the old family home in the village of Blemont-la-Fontaine, Normandy. Leonie and Thérèse claim to have
seen the Virgin Mary in the woods behind the house, where an old peasants' shrine to the Blessed Mother once was located. In reconstructing their
visions and reinterpreting the stories of the house, the girls discover the
town's secret—a mass grave of murdered Jews at the shrine and the Frenchman who tried to protect them—as well as the family secret that they are not
actually cousins but rather twin sisters. The girls piece together the town's
past and their own identities in two ways, by knitting together stories re-
called by Victorine, the house maid, and Rose Taille, a farm woman, and by
reading the secret letters of Thérèse's mother Antoinette to her sister Soeur
Dosithée, a nun in the Visitation convent. These shreds of the past serve to
impel Thérèse into the cloister in part, perhaps, as her chosen penance for
her illegitimate origins and her fear of her physical nature. Reuniting in the
Martin house in their late thirties, both women—the cloistered nun Thérèse
and the worldly sensualist Leonie—feel that they have been robbed of their
authentic identity by their family, by the Church, and by each other.

Several of Roberts's other novels, such as *The Wild Girl* (1984), *Impossible
Saints* (1997), and *The Secret Gospel of Mary Magdalene* (2007), involve reli-

34. Ibid., 24–25, 165, 181

gious women. The thread that unifies these works is the focus on religion as one of the "forces shaping gender identity."[35] *Daughters of the House* is one of Roberts's novels that critic Rosie White calls "reconstructive narratives,"[36] works that revise, concentrate, and fictionalize history, memory, space, and time. Roberts has described her interest in rewriting women's stories as a "feminist wish to resurrect lost, dead, gone, [female] voices,"[37] and this intent seems to underscore, albeit unconsciously for them, the task that Leonie and Thérèse undertake. In their quest, memory, truth, and story cease to matter as "real" or "false" experiences or events and instead become authenticated only by the girls' feelings about how the sources they discover fit into their own histories. Roberts has stated that, to her, stories about girl saints usually express the "rebellion of the daughter in various ways,"[38] and both Leonie and Thérèse rebel against authority in their own way. After the visions, Thérèse manipulates the adults and priests into accepting her authenticity as a holy seer, and Leonie, whose version of the events has been rejected, abandons them to embrace the rural woods, the pleasures of food and flesh, and the things of the house.

The convent that Thérèse enters is not the house of the novel's title. In *Daughters of the House,* the convent remains offstage, and only its effect on Thérèse is described. Rather, the family house and cousin/sister Leonie that Thérèse leaves behind when she enters religious life take center stage as the elements of the past that she wants to deny and that have both formed and deformed her relationship with her family and with God. For Thérèse, the house is one of secrets linked to the core questions of identity, represented by bones in the wine cellar, letters in the biscuit tin, and Jewish bodies under the holy shrine. For Leonie, however, the house's physical objects become equated with her body and her memory, and she cherishes their physicality. Each of the novel's chapters is named for an object or item of the house which the adult Leonie dreams is bounded by skin, ordered by rules, and full of "forbidden places."[39] The novel begins from Leonie's point of view: "It was a changeable house. Sometimes it felt safe as a church, and some-

---

35. Susan Rowland, "Michèle Roberts's Virgins: Contesting Gender in Fictions. Re-writing Jungian Theory and Christian Myth," *Journal of Gender Studies* 8, no. 1 (1999): 35–42. Academic Search Premier.
36. Rosie White, "Permeable Borders, Possible Worlds: History and Identity in the Novel of Michèle Roberts," *Studies in the Literary Imagination* 36, no. 2 (2003): 71.
37. Patricia Bastida Rodriguez, "On Women, Christianity, and History: An Interview with Michèle Roberts," *Atlantis* 25, no. 1 (2003): 98.
38. Ibid., 99.
39. Roberts, *Daughters of the House,* 1.

times it shivered and then cracked apart." On the other hand, unlike Leonie, Thérèse's convent life has made her, so to speak, frozen in time. On her trip home, she notices primarily that the world has changed but the house has not. Dark Algerian men now ride the train; ads promote alien items ("What was cellulite?" she wonders); but "the clock had not changed" and "the buffet stood in its old place."[40]

Though both Leonie and Thérèse feel like "daughters of the house," Leonie remains the outsider. Throughout the novel, whether in the present or in her memories, she defines herself as Thérèse's opposite—as sexual, worldly, English, married. Thérèse thinks of them as opposites, too: "One married and one not, one plump and one thin, one truthful and one a liar, one who belongs and one who doesn't."[41] The unfolding story of Leonie's and Thérèse's identity is organized around the significance of the writing table, the bed, the looking-glass, the photographs, the biscuit tin, the recipe book, the cellar key, the statue of the Virgin—material objects given meaning by Leonie's associations of them with herself, her cousin/sister, and their mothers. When Leonie glances into Thérèse's spiritual notebook, she notices that "Thérèse had listed words like soul, God, sin, miracle, prayer. Leonie's inventory sang a litany of beds and tables and chairs."[42] When Thérèse, on returning home from the convent, finds herself touching remembered treasured objects, "Too much attachment to objects," she scold[s] herself,[43] recalling her long discipline in mortifying the senses. Leonie describes Thérèse's thin frame by sarcastically reiterating the logic of spirituality: "Deny the body's needs and advance in holiness." This is the crux of the women's estrangement: each twin has rejected the other's perception of the relationship of body and soul but, in doing so, has also renounced a part of herself. Finally, Thérèse announces that she plans to leave the convent for the sake of "something unfinished here." She will write an autobiography, and she wants Leonie to help her remember the past. But "Leave my childhood alone," Leonie commands, though she also "long[s] for" her twin "like a lover." Their irreconcilable stories of body and soul determine only that, for all their differences, they are indeed "sisters under the skin."[44]

■ ■ ■

In each of these novels, a type of spiritual pride provokes a woman to feel especially chosen as witness to the immanent presence of the divine. For

40. Ibid., 1, 7, 11.   41. Ibid., 21.
42. Ibid., 19.   43. Ibid., 13.
44. Ibid., 12, 22, 23, 3, 21.

each, too, the experience is sensual, known and measured in terms of physical feeling as well as inexplicable emotional transformation. The events become so valued that the women guard them possessively, though they also feel urged to express them or evangelize to others. Each mystical experience, then, becomes a cherished personal possession and an exhilarating possibility for the faith community. The essential theological paradox in each case involves the central role of the woman's body and self—her pain, her sexuality, her bleeding hands—in her experience of divine presence. Her intense feeling of desire takes over the physical self, even to the point of pathology, but the communion with God also raises her out of and beyond the self. In one of her raptures, Sister John "splintered like broken glass, she became all edges and points and she was sure this had to be death, it had to be the end of everything, then her suffering blinked off."[45] She then writes:

> an invisible sun
>> a shock wave of pure Being
>> swept my pain away, swept everything away
>> until all that was left was God . . . His presence is the only reality.[46]

In *Daughters of the House,* when Leonie runs to the old shrine, "She saw it. Saw the fine rainy air become solid and golden and red, form itself into the shape of a living and breathing woman . . . Something outside of her, mysterious and huge, put out a kindly exploring hand and touched her. Something was restored to her which she had lost . . . The deepest pleasure she had ever known."[47]

This restoration of love and emphasis on self is opposed in each novel by the mystic realization that, as Sister John reflects, "Selfhood had been an illusion, a dream."[48] The novelists' reliance on Thérèse of Lisieux draws attention to the value she placed on the "little way," the humble life of self-forgetfulness. Before the surgery to remove her tumor, Sister John recalls in prayer that Saint Thérèse's "only ambition had been to love."[49] But to be mad with desire for God is, in these novels, physical, sensual, and crucial to identity. Thomas Wendorf writes that in both *Mariette in Ecstasy* and *Lying Awake,* "God and world, spirit and body involve separate and competing imperatives, and the way to God is through a denial of the one for the sake

45. Salzman, *Lying Awake,* 37.
46. Ibid.
47. Roberts, *Daughters of the House,* 86.
48. Salzman, *Lying Awake,* 18.
49. Ibid., 154.

of the other."[50] This is the painful reality that Hansen's, Salzman's, and Roberts's characters face, and the truth represented by the insistent rule of the convent. "A serious house on serious earth," it does indeed evoke the image of a chapel in Philip Larkin's poem, "Church-Going."

One particular sacrifice required of the nun that Hansen, Roberts, and Salzman emphasize is the loss of family. To leave the outside world involves denying the affection of mother and of father as well. In all three novels, *Mariette in Ecstasy, Lying Awake,* and *Daughters of the House,* the girls' mothers are explicitly and palpably absent. The mothers of Mariette and Sister John have been gone since they were small girls, and both novels connect the loss of the mother to the call to enter the convent. Mariette's father underlines the absence of her mother both in his cold physical presence and in his obvious grief for the loss of his wife, older daughter, and now Mariette. Salzman's narrative directly juxtaposes the end of young Helen's long futile wait for her mother with her decision to enter the cloister. And the entire recollected story that makes up *Daughters of the House* reconstructs the girls' memories of the mother Antoinette and the effects of her death. The deformed/reformed family of Roberts's novel, even more than the other two books, equates the search for the spiritual "other" with the search for the mother.

This theme of the loss of family is common to convent fiction of all eras. And though contemporary convent fiction has largely left Protestant fears and gothic sensationalism behind, the convent as a setting has not lost its mystery. It is still a place of buried secrets, a place of desire. Eighteenth- and nineteenth-century novels often suggested that the Catholic Church tempted women to abandon their proper roles as obedient daughter, wife, and mother, and more recent convent fiction retains this theme of the competition between devotion to family and love for God. Following White's *Frost in May* and Godden's *In This House of Brede,* modern convent novels portray women as developing within an alternate family structure and by an altered progression from girlhood to womanhood—one in which sisters are fixed in time, physically and emotionally. In this convent community, old family rules apply but are also subverted, and the modern convent novel has become the story of the female self developing within complex family dynamics and against institutional obstacles. White's *Frost in May* was ground-

<hr>

50. Thomas Wendorf, "Body, Soul, and Beyond: Mystical Experience in Ron Hansen's *Mariette in Ecstasy* and Mark Salzman's *Lying Awake," Logos: A Journal of Catholic Thought* 7, no. 4 (2004): 43.

breaking in its portrayal of the multiple and contradictory developments of a girl's nature: her intense intimacy with God, affectionate heart and creative mind, and hard fist of rebellious will. In the novel, Nanda Grey recognizes the change that the convent school has effected in her: "She felt so much unpicked and resewn and made over to a different pattern."[51] Regardless of the techniques and approaches through which they view this transformation, the same questions arise in all convent fiction since White: How does the Catholic girl fulfill the Christian paradox? Must she lose her self to give herself to God?

51. Antonia White, *Frost in May* (New York: Dial, 1980), 36.

Bibliography

This list includes major primary and secondary sources cited in the essays and some additional works in Catholic literary criticism.

Abbott, Claude Colleer, ed. *Further Letters of Gerard Manley Hopkins*. Oxford: Oxford University Press, 1956.

Alexander, Peter F. *Les Murray: A Life in Progress*. Melbourne: Oxford University Press, 2000.

Alexie, Sherman. *The Summer of Black Widows*. Brooklyn, N.Y.: Hanging Loose, 1996.

———. *Ten Little Indians*. New York: Grove, 2003.

Arkins, Brian. *Desmond Egan: A Critical Study*. Little Rock, Ark.: Milestone, 1992.

Arnold, Matthew. *Essays in Criticism* (Second Series). London: Macmillan, 1903.

Barton, Shelle, Sheyene Foster Heller, and Jennifer Henderson. "'We Were Such a Generation'—Memoir, Truthfulness, and History: An Interview with Patricia Hampl." *River Teeth* 5, no. 2 (2004): 129–42.

Beevor, Antony. *The Spanish Civil War*. New York: Penguin, 2001.

Bergonzi, Bernard. "A Conspicuous Absentee: The Decline and Fall of the Catholic Novel." *Encounter* 55, no. 2–3 (1980): 44–57.

———. *David Lodge*. Plymouth, Engl.: Northcote House, 1995.

———. "A Religious Romance: David Lodge in Conversation." *The Critic* 47 (Fall 1992): 69–73.

Berkouwer, G. C. *The Second Vatican Council and the New Catholicism*. Translated by Lewis B. Smedes. Grand Rapids, Mich.: Eerdmans, 1965.

Blish, James. *A Case of Conscience*. London: Arrow, 1979.

Bosco, Mark, SJ. *Graham Greene's Catholic Imagination*. Oxford: Oxford University Press, 2005.

Boyer, Nicholaus. *Sacred and Secular Scriptures: A Catholic Approach to Literature*. Notre Dame, Ind.: University of Notre Dame Press, 2005.

Brennan, Michael G. "Graham Greene's Catholic Conversion: The Early Writings (1923–29) and *The Man Within*." *Logos* 9, no. 3 (2006): 134–57.

Broderick, Damien. *Transrealist Fiction: Writing in the Slipstream of Science*. Westport, Conn.: Greenwood, 2000.

Brodrick, William. *The Gardens of the Dead*. New York: Viking Penguin, 2006.

———. *The Sixth Lamentation*. New York: Viking Penguin, 2003.

———. *A Whispered Name*. London: Little, Brown 2008.

Brophy, Don. *One Hundred Great Catholic Books: From the Early Centuries to the Present.* New York: Blue Bridge, 2007.

Brown, David, and Ann Loades, eds. *Christ: The Sacramental Word—Incarnation, Sacrament and Poetry.* London: Society for Promoting Christian Knowledge, 1996.

Campbell, Debra. *Graceful Exits: Catholic Women and the Art of Departure.* Bloomington: Indiana University Press, 2003.

Camus, Albert. *The Rebel.* Translated by Anthony Bower. New York: Vintage, 1959.

Carlson, Julia. *Banned in Ireland: Censorship and the Irish Writer.* Athens: University of Georgia Press, 1990.

Cascone, Gina. *Pagan Babies and Other Catholic Memories.* New York: Washington Square, 1982.

Chesterton, G. K. *The Uses of Diversity.* London: Methuen, 1926.

Childs, J. D., Robert Feduccia Jr., Michael C. Jordan, and Jerry Windley-Daoust, eds. *Great Catholic Writings: Thought, Literature, Spirituality, Social Action.* Winona, Minn.: Saint Mary's, 2006.

Clark, Edward William. *Five Great Catholic Ideas.* New York: Crossroad, 1998.

Cohn, Dorrit. *Transparent Minds: Narrative Modes for Presenting Consciousness in Fiction.* Princeton, N.J.: Princeton University Press, 1978.

Cotter, James Finn. "The Inshape of Inscape." *Victorian Poetry* 42, no. 2 (2004): 195–200.

Crowe, Marion E. "A Modern Psychomachia: The Catholic Fiction of Piers Paul Read." *Christianity and Literature* 47, no. 3 (1998): 309–29.

Daly, James J., SJ. *The Jesuit in Focus.* Milwaukee, Wisc.: Bruce, 1940.

Daniel, Missy. "Poetry is Presence: An Interview with Les Murray." *Commonweal* 119, no. 10 (1992): 9–12.

Delibes, Miguel. *Five Hours with Mario.* Translated by Frances M. López-Morillas. New York: Columbia University Press, 1988.

———. *The Heretic.* Translated by Alfred MacAdam. New York: Overlook, 2006.

———. *Las ratas.* In *Obra completa. Tomo III,* by Miguel Delibes, 445–570. Barcelona: Destino, 1968.

Delrosso, Jeana. *Writing Catholic Women: Contemporary International Catholic Girlhood Narratives.* New York: Palgrave Macmillan, 2005.

Detwiler, Robert, and David Jaspar. *Religion and Literature.* Louisville, Ky.: Westminster John Knox, 2007.

DiPasquale, Theresa. *Literature and Sacrament: The Sacred and the Secular in John Donne.* Cambridge: James Clarke, 2001.

Donofrio, Beverly. *Looking for Mary: Or, the Blessed Mother and Me.* New York: Penguin Compass, 2000.

Durán, Leopoldo. *Graham Greene: Friend and Brother.* Translated by Euan Cameron. London: HarperCollins, 1995.

Eagleton, Terry. "The Silences of David Lodge." *New Left Review* 172 (1988): 93–102.

Eco, Umberto. *The Name of the Rose*. San Diego: Harcourt Brace, 1994.

Egan, Desmond. *The Death of Metaphor*. Newbridge, Ire.: Kavanagh, 1990.

———. *Selected Poems*. Newbridge, Ire.: Kavanagh, 1992.

Eire, Carlos M. N. *From Madrid to Purgatory: The Art and Craft of Dying in Sixteenth-Century Spain*. Cambridge: Cambridge University Press, 2002.

Ellis, Alice Thomas. *The Inn at the Edge of the World*. Pleasantville, N.Y.: Akadine, 2000.

———. *Serpent on the Rock: A Personal View of Christianity*. N. Pomfret, Vt.: Trafalgar Square, 1995.

———. *The Sin Eater*. Kingston, R.I.: Moyer Bell, 1998.

Ellsberg, Margaret R. *Created to Praise: The Language of Gerard Manley Hopkins*. Oxford: Oxford University Press, 1987.

Endō, Shūsaku. *The Samurai*. Translated by Van C. Gessel. New York: New Directions, 1982.

English, Richard. *Irish Freedom: The History of Nationalism in Ireland*. London: Macmillan, 2006.

Evasdaughter, Elizabeth N. *Catholic Girlhood Narratives: The Church and Self-Denial*. Boston: Northeastern University Press, 1996.

Ewing, Dorothy. "The Religious Significance of Miguel Delibes's *Las ratas*." *Romance Notes* 11, no. 3 (1970): 492–97.

Fallon, Brian. *An Age of Innocence: Irish Culture 1930–1960*. Dublin: Gill and Macmillan, 1998.

Ferreter, Luke. *Towards a Christian Literary Theory*. Houndsmills, Basingstoke, Engl.: Palgrave Macmillan, 2003.

Flannery, Austin, OP, ed. *Vatican Council II: The Conciliar and Post-Conciliar Documents*. Wilmington, Del.: Scholarly Resources, 1975.

Frye, Northrop. "The Argument of Comedy." In *Shakespeare's Comedies*, edited by Laurence Lerner, 317–25. Harmondsworth, Engl.: Penguin, 1967.

Fuller, Louise. *Irish Catholicism since 1950: The Undoing of a Culture*. Dublin: Gill and Macmillan, 2004.

Gable, Mariella. *The Literature of Spiritual Values and Catholic Fiction*. Edited by Nancy Hynes, OSB. Lanham, Md.: University Press of America, 1996.

Gallick, Sarah. *The Big Book of Women Saints*. San Francisco: HarperCollins, 2007.

Gandolfo, Anita. *Faith and Fiction: Christian Literature in America Today*. Westport, Conn.: Praeger, 2007.

———. *Testing the Faith: The New Catholic Fiction in America*. Westport, Conn.: Greenwood, 1992.

Gelpi, Albert. "The Catholic Presence in American Culture." *American Literary History* 11, no. 1 (1999): 196–212.

Gevers, Nick. "Of Prayers and Predators: An Interview with Mary Doria Russell." *Infinity Plus* (Aug. 28, 1999). www.infinityplus.co.uk.

Giles, Paul. *American Catholic Arts and Fictions: Culture, Ideology, Aesthetics.* Cambridge: Cambridge University Press, 1992.

Gioia, Dana. *Interrogations at Noon.* St. Paul, Minn.: Graywolf, 2001.

Goodier, Alban, SJ. *The Jesuits.* London: Sheed and Ward, 1929.

Gordon, Mary. "Appetite for the Absolute." In *The Best American Spiritual Writing 2005,* edited by Philip Zaleski, 89–97. Boston: Houghton Mifflin, 2005.

———. Interview by Barbara A. Bannon. *Publishers Weekly* (Feb. 6, 1981): 274.

———. *Men and Angels.* New York: Random House, 1985.

Greeley, Andrew. *The Catholic Imagination.* Berkeley: University of California Press, 2001.

Greene, Graham. *The Man Within.* London: William Heinemann, 1929.

———. *Monsignor Quixote.* Harmondsworth, Engl.: Penguin, 1983.

———. *Ways of Escape.* London: Bodley Head, 1980.

Griffin, Susan. *Anti-Catholicism and Nineteenth-Century Fiction.* Cambridge: Cambridge University Press, 2004.

Halton, Thomas. "The Catholic Writer." *Christus Rex* 29, no. 2 (1957): 707–18.

Hampl, Patricia. *Blue Arabesque: A Search for the Sublime.* Orlando, Fla.: Harcourt, 2006.

———. *The Florist's Daughter.* New York: Harcourt, 2007.

———. *I Could Tell You Stories: Sojourns in the Land of Memory.* New York: Norton, 1999.

———. *A Romantic Education.* New York: Norton, 1999.

———. *Virgin Time: In Search of the Contemplative Life.* New York: North Point, 1992.

Hansen, Ron. *Mariette in Ecstasy.* New York: Harper Perennial, 1991.

———. *A Stay against Confusion.* New York: HarperCollins, 2002.

Haraway, Donna J. *Simians, Cyborgs, and Women: The Reinvention of Nature.* New York: Routledge, 1991.

Harmon, Maurice. *Maurice Harmon: Selected Essays.* Edited by Barbara Brown. Dublin: Irish Academic Press, 2006.

Hart, Kevin. "'Interest' in Les A. Murray." *Australian Literary Studies* 14, no. 2 (1989): 147–59.

Hassan, Ihab. "Toward a Concept of Postmodernism." In *Postmodernism: A Reader,* edited by Thomas Docherty, 147–56. New York: Columbia University Press, 1993.

Hassler, Jon. "A Conversation with Jon Hassler." *Image: A Journal of the Arts and Religion* 19 (Summer 1998): 41–58.

———. *The Life and Death of Nancy Clancy's Nephew.* In *The Staggerford Murders,* by Jon Hassler, 105–98. New York: Penguin/Plume, 2004.

———. *North of Hope.* New York: Ballantine, 1990.

———. *Staggerford.* New York: Ballantine, 1993.

Homza, Lu Ann. "Erasmus as Hero, or Heretic? Spanish Humanism and the Valladolid Assembly of 1527." *Renaissance Quarterly* 50, no. 1 (1997): 78–118.

Hood, Hugh, and John Mills. "Hugh Hood and John Mills in Epistolary Conversation." *Fiddlehead* 116 (Winter 1978): 133–46.

Hopko, Thomas. *All the Fullness of God: Essays on Orthodoxy, Ecumenism and Modern Society.* Crestwood, N.Y.: St. Vladimir's Seminary Press, 1982.

Hutcheon, Linda. *The Canadian Postmodern: A Study of Contemporary English Canadian Fiction.* Oxford: Oxford University Press, 1989.

———. *A Poetics of Postmodernism: History, Theory, and Fiction.* New York: Routledge, 1988.

Iser, Wolfgang. *The Implied Reader.* Baltimore: Johns Hopkins University Press, 1974.

Jaspar, David. *The Sacred Desert: Religion, Literature, Art, Culture.* Malden, Mass.: Blackwell, 2004.

Jennings, Elizabeth. *Every Changing Shape.* London: Andre Deutsch, 1961.

———. *New Collected Poems.* Manchester: Carcanet, 2002.

———. "Saved by Poetry." *The Tablet* (May 15, 1993): 613–14.

John Paul II (Pope). *Letter to Artists.* 1999. www.vatican.va.

Jones, David. *The Anathemata.* London: Faber and Faber, 1952.

———. *The Dying Gaul and Other Writings.* London: Faber and Faber, 1978.

Kamen, Henry. *The Spanish Inquisition: A Historical Revision.* New Haven, Conn.: Yale University Press, 1997.

Karr, Mary. *Abacus.* Pittsburgh, Pa.: Carnegie Mellon University Press, 2007.

———. *Cherry.* New York: Penguin, 2001.

———. *The Devil's Tour.* New York: New Directions, 1993.

———. *The Liars' Club.* New York: Penguin, 1996.

———. *Sinners Welcome.* New York: HarperCollins, 2006.

Kaufmann, Walter. *Nietzsche: Philosopher, Psychologist, Antichrist.* New York: Viking, 1968.

Keble, John. *Lectures on Poetry: 1832–1841.* Bristol, Engl.: Thoemmes, 2003.

Kenny, Colum. *Moments That Changed Us.* Dublin: Gill and Macmillan, 2005.

Ker, Ian. *The Catholic Revival in English Literature, 1845–1961.* Notre Dame, Ind.: University of Notre Dame Press, 2003.

Labrie, Ross. *The Catholic Imagination in American Literature.* Columbia: University of Missouri Press, 1997.

Lamott, Anne. *Traveling Mercies: Some Thoughts of Faith.* New York: Pantheon, 1999.

Lawson, Mark. "Catholicism's Indelible Mark on the Page." *The Tablet* (April 29, 2006): 16–17.

Leigh, David J. *Circuitous Journeys: Modern Spiritual Autobiography.* New York: Fordham University Press, 2000.

Lenoski, Daniel S. "The Catholic Carnival: The Novels of David Lodge." *Ultimate Reality and Meaning* 28, no. 4 (2005): 315–29.

Lichtmann, Maria "The Incarnational Aesthetic of Gerard Manley Hopkins." *Religion and Literature* 23, no. 1 (1991): 37–50.

Lodge, David. *The British Museum Is Falling Down*. London: Penguin, 1983.

———. *How Far Can You Go?* London: Penguin, 1981.

———. *The Modes of Modern Writing*. Ithaca, N.Y.: Cornell University Press, 1977.

———. *Therapy*. London: Penguin, 1995.

———. *Write On: Occasional Essays 1964–85*. London: Penguin, 1986.

Lukács, Georg. *The Theory of the Novel*. Translated by Anna Bostock. Cambridge, Mass.: MIT Press, 1971.

MacCulloch, Diarmaid. *The Reformation: A History*. New York: Viking, 2004.

Maison, Margaret M. *The Victorian Vision: Studies in the Religious Novel*. New York: Sheed and Ward, 1962.

Maritain, Jacques. *Art and Scholasticism* and *The Frontiers of Poetry*. Translated by Joseph W. Evans. Notre Dame, Ind.: University of Notre Dame Press, 1974.

———. *Integral Humanism: Temporal and Spiritual Problems of a New Christendom*. Translated by Joseph W. Evans. South Bend, Ind.: University of Notre Dame Press, 1973.

Martin, Augustine. "Inherited Dissent." In *Bearing Witness: Essays on Anglo-Irish Literature*, edited by Anthony Roche, 81–99. Dublin: University College Dublin Press, 1996.

Mason, Emma, and Mark Knight. *Nineteenth Century Religion and Literature*. Oxford: Oxford University Press, 2007.

McCloskey, Ronald. "An Interview with Michael O'Brien." *Gilbert!* 1, no. 9 (1998): 10–16.

McDermott, Alice. *After This*. New York: Farrar, Straus, and Giroux, 2006.

———. *At Weddings and Wakes*. New York: Random House, 1992.

———. *Charming Billy*. New York: Random House, 1998.

———. "Confessions of a Reluctant Catholic." *Commonweal* 127, no. 3 (2000): 12–16.

———. "The Lunatic in the Pew." *Boston College Magazine* 64, no. 3 (2003): 35–37.

———. *That Night*. New York: Random House, 1987.

McGahern, John. "The Church and Its Spire." In *Soho Square* 6: *New Writing from Ireland*, edited by Colm Toibin, 17–27. London: Bloomsbury, 1993.

———. *The Dark*. London: Faber and Faber, 1963.

———. *Memoir*. London: Faber and Faber, 2006.

———. *That They May Face the Rising Sun*. London: Faber and Faber, 2002.

McHale, Brian. *Postmodernist Fiction*. New York: Methuen, 1967.

McNees, Eleanor. *Eucharistic Poetry: The Search for Presence in the Writings of John Donne, Gerard Manley Hopkins, Dylan Thomas and Geoffrey Hill*. Lewisburg, Pa.: Bucknell University Press, 1992.

McVeigh, Daniel, and Patricia Schnapp, eds. *The Best American Catholic Short Stories*. New York: Rowman and Littlefield / Sheed and Ward, 2007.

Miller, Patricia Cox, ed. *Women in Early Christianity: Translations from Greek Texts*. Washington, D.C.: The Catholic University of America Press, 2005.

Moore, Brian. *Catholics*. 2nd ed. London: Triad/Panther, 1983.

———. *Cold Heaven*. London: Triad/Panther, 1985.

Motion, Andrew. *Philip Larkin: A Writer's Life*. London: Faber and Faber, 1993.

Mourão, Manuela. *Altered Habits: Reconsidering the Nun in Fiction*. Gainesville: University of Florida Press, 2002.

Murdoch, Iris. *The Fire and the Sun*. Oxford: Clarendon, 1977.

Murphy, Francesca Aran. *Christ the Form of Beauty: A Study of Theology and Literature*. Edinburgh: T. and T. Clark, 1995.

Murray, Les. *The Boys Who Stole the Funeral*. Sydney: Angus and Robertson, 1980.

———. *Collected Poems: 1961–2002*. Potts Point: Duffy and Snellgrove, 2002.

———. *Fredy Neptune*. New York: Farrar, Straus, and Giroux, 1999.

———. *The People's Otherworld*. Sydney: Angus and Robertson, 1983.

———. *A Working Forest: Selected Prose*. Potts Point: Duffy and Snellgrove, 1997.

Newman, John Henry. *The Idea of a University*. New York: Holt, Rinehart and Winston, 1960.

Norris, Kathleen. *Amazing Grace: A Vocabulary of Faith*. New York: Riverhead, 1998.

———. *The Cloister Walk*. New York: Riverhead, 1996.

———. "A Word Made Flesh: Incarnational Language and the Writer." In *The Incarnation: An Interdisciplinary Symposium on the Incarnation of the Son of God*, edited by Stephen T. Davis, Daniel Kendall, and Gerald O'Collins, 303–12. Oxford: Oxford University Press, 2002.

O'Brien, Michael D. "Barometer Falling: Landscapes of Unreality in Art and Society." *Canadian Catholic Review* (February 1990): 44–54.

———. "The Decline and Renewal of Christian Art." *Second Spring* (August/September 1994): 30–36.

———. *The Family and the New Totalitarianism*. Killaloe, Can.: White Horse, 1995.

———. *Father Elijah: An Apocalypse*. San Francisco: Ignatius, 1996.

———. "Historical Imagination and the Renewal of Culture." In *Eternity in Time: Christopher Dawson and the Catholic Idea of History*, edited by Stratford Caldecott and John Morrill, 151–91. Edinburgh: T. and T. Clark, 1997.

———. *Strangers and Sojourners: A Novel*. San Francisco: Ignatius, 1997.

O'Connor, Flannery. *The Habit of Being*. Edited by Sally Fitzgerald. New York: Vintage, 1979.

———. *Mystery and Manners*. Edited by Sally and Robert Fitzgerald. New York: Farrar, Straus, and Giroux, 1969.

Ó Faoláin, Seán. "The Modern Novel: A Catholic Point of View." *Virginia Quarterly Review* 2 (1935): 339–51.

Okada, Sumie. *Japanese Writers and the West*. New York: Palgrave Macmillan, 2003.

O'Rourke, Brian. *The Conscience of the Race: Sex and Religion in Irish and French Novels 1941–1973*. Dublin: Four Courts, 1980.

Ortiz, Gaye, and Clara A. B. Joseph, eds. *Theology and Literature: Rethinking Reader Responsibility*. New York: Palgrave Macmillan, 2006.

O'Toole, Fintan. *The Ex-Isle of Erin*. Dublin: New Island, 1997.

———. *The Lie of the Land*. Dublin: New Island, 1998.

Owen, John D. "A Case of Conscience for Mary Doria Russell." *Infinity Plus* (1998). www.infinityplus.co.uk.

Pacey, Desmond. *Creative Writing in Canada*. 2nd ed. Toronto: McGraw-Hill Ryerson, 1961.

Pavel, Thomas. "Tragedy and the Sacred: Notes towards a Semantic Characterization of a Fictional Genre." *Poetics* 10, no. 2–3 (1981): 231–42.

Payne, Stanley G. *Spanish Catholicism: An Historical Overview*. Madison: University of Wisconsin Press, 1984.

Pearce, Joseph. *Literary Converts: Spiritual Inspiration in an Age of Unbelief*. San Francisco: Ignatius, 2000.

———. *Literary Giants, Literary Catholics*. San Francisco: Ignatius, 2005.

Pell, Barbara Helen. "Faith and Fiction: The Novels of Callaghan and Hood." *Journal of Canadian Studies* 18, no. 2 (1983): 5–17.

Percy, Walker. *Signposts in a Strange Land*. Edited by Patrick Samway. New York: Farrar, Straus, and Giroux, 1991.

Pieper, Josef. *Josef Pieper: An Anthology*. San Francisco: Ignatius, 1989.

Rafroidi, Patrick. "Pilgrim's Progress." In *Desmond Egan: The Poet and His Work*, edited by Hugh Kenner, 36–46. Orono, Maine: Northern Lights, 1990.

Read, Piers Paul. *Hell and Other Destinations*. London: Longman, Darton, Todd, 2006.

———. *A Season in the West*. London: Secker and Warburg, 1988.

Reichardt, Mary R., ed. *Catholic Women Writers: A Bio-Bibliographical Sourcebook*. Westport, Conn.: Greenwood, 2001.

———. *Encyclopedia of Catholic Literature*. 2 vols. Westport, Conn.: Greenwood, 2004.

———. *Exploring Catholic Literature*. Lanham, Md.: Rowman and Littlefield / Sheed and Ward, 2003.

———. "Literature and the Catholic Perspective." In *Ethics, Literature, Theory: An Introductory Reader*, edited by Stephen K. George, 173–79. Lanham, Md.: Rowman and Littlefield / Sheed and Ward, 2005.

Roberts, Michèle. *Daughters of the House*. New York: Picador, 1992.

Rodriguez, Patricia Bastida. "On Women, Christianity, and History: An Interview with Michèle Roberts." *Atlantis* 25, no. 1 (2003): 93–107.

Rogers, Katharine M. "Fantasy and Reality in the Fictional Convents of the Eighteenth Century." *Comparative Literature Studies* 22, no. 3 (1985): 297–316.

Rowland, Susan. "Michèle Roberts's Virgins: Contesting Gender in Fictions. Rewriting Jungian Theory and Christian Myth." *Journal of Gender Studies* 8, no. 1 (1999): 35–42.

Russell, Mary Doria. "A Conversation with Mary Doria Russell." In *The Sparrow*, 411–16. New York: Ballantine, 2004.

———. *The Sparrow*. New York: Ballantine, 2004.

Ryan, Gig. "'And the Fetid Air and Gritty.'" *Heat* 5 (1997): 196–203.

Salzman, Mark. *Lying Awake.* New York: Knopf, 2000.

Sampson, Denis. *Outstaring Nature's Eye: The Fiction of John McGahern.* Washington, D.C.: The Catholic University of America Press, 1993.

Scammell, William. "Les Murray in Conversation." *PN Review* 25, no. 2 (1998): 29–36.

Scott, Malcolm. *The Struggle for the Soul of the French Novel: French Catholic and Realist Novelists 1850–1970.* London: Macmillan, 1989.

Sharrock, Roger. *Saints, Sinners and Comedians: The Novels of Graham Greene.* Tunbridge Wells: Burns and Oates, 1984.

Sherry, Norman. *The Life of Graham Greene.* Vol. 1: *1904–1939.* London and Toronto: Jonathan Cape and Lester and Orpen Denys, 1989.

———. *The Life of Graham Greene.* Vol. 3: *1955–1991.* London: Jonathan Cape, 2004.

Smith, Sidonie, and Julia Watson. *Reading Autobiography: A Guide for Interpreting Life Narratives.* Minneapolis: University of Minnesota Press, 2001.

Suvin, Darko. *Metamorphoses of Science Fiction: On the Poetics and History of a Literary Genre.* New Haven, Conn.: Yale University Press, 1979.

Tracy, David. *The Analogical Imagination: Christian Theology and the Culture of Pluralism.* New York: Crossroad, 1981.

Tulloch, Jonathan. *Give Us This Day.* London: Jonathan Cape, 2005.

———. *The Lottery.* London: Vintage, 2003.

Unamuno, Miguel. *The Tragic Sense of Life in Men and Nation.* Translated by Anthony Kerrigan. Princeton, N.J.: Princeton University Press, 1972.

von Balthasar, Hans Urs. *The Grain of Wheat.* San Francisco: Ignatius, 1995.

Walcott, Derek. *What the Twilight Says: Essays.* London: Faber and Faber, 1998.

Ward, Bernadette. *World as Word: Philosophical Theology in Gerard Manley Hopkins.* Washington, D.C.: The Catholic University of America Press, 2002.

Warren, Martin. "Is God in Charge? Mary Doria Russell's *The Sparrow,* Deconstruction, and Theodicy." *Journal of Religion and Popular Culture* 9 (Spring 2005). www.usask.ca/relst/jrpc.

Watts, Cedric. *A Preface to Greene.* Harlow, Engl.: Longman, Pearson Education, 1997.

Wendorf, Thomas. "Body, Soul, and Beyond: Mystical Experience in Ron Hansen's *Mariette in Ecstasy* and Mark Salzman's *Lying Awake.*" *Logos: A Journal of Catholic Thought and Culture* 7, no. 4 (2004): 37–64.

White, Antonia. *Frost in May.* New York: Dial, 1980.

White, Rosie. "Permeable Borders, Possible Worlds: History and Identity in the Novel of Michèle Roberts." *Studies in the Literary Imagination* 36, no. 2 (2003): 71–90.

Whitehouse, J. C. *Catholics on Literature.* Dublin: Four Courts, 1997.

Whyte, James. *History, Myth and Ritual in the Fiction of John McGahern: Strategies of Transcendence.* Lewiston, N.Y.: Edwin Mellen, 2002.

Woodman, Thomas. *Faithful Fictions: The Catholic Novel in British Literature.* Philadelphia, Pa.: Open University Press, 1991.

About the Editor and Contributors

Editor

Mary R. Reichardt is a professor of Catholic Studies and literature at the University of St. Thomas in St. Paul, Minnesota. She received a PhD in English from the University of Wisconsin–Madison in 1987. Her teaching and research interests include Catholic literature, American literature, and literature by women. The author of eight scholarly books, her previous works on Catholic literature include *Encyclopedia of Catholic Literature* (2 volumes, Greenwood 2004); *Exploring Catholic Literature: A Companion and Resource Guide* (Rowman and Littlefield 2003); and *Catholic Women Writers: A Bio-Bibliographical Sourcebook* (Greenwood 2001). She is also an editor for Ignatius Press's critical editions series.

Contributors

Ed Block received his PhD in English and Comparative Literature from Stanford University. He is a professor of English at Marquette University in Milwaukee, Wisconsin, and edits the journal *Renascence: Essays on Values in Literature*. He has published widely on Victorian literature, the relationship of science, literature, and values in the Victorian era, the dramatic theory of the late Swiss humanist and theologian, Hans Urs von Balthasar, and the poetry of Denise Levertov. His books include *Critical Essays on John Henry Newman* (University of Victoria 1992); *Rituals of Dis-Integration: Romance and Madness in the Victorian Psychomythic Tale* (Garland 1993); and *Glory, Grace, and Culture: The Work of Hans Urs von Balthasar* (Paulist 2005). His critical essays have appeared in such journals as *Victorian Studies, Journal of the History of Ideas, Journal of Dramatic Criticism and Theory,* and *Logos.* He is currently at work on a critical study of Jon Hassler.

Gary M. Bouchard has been a professor of English at Saint Anselm College in Manchester, New Hampshire, for the past twenty-one years, serving as the college's executive vice president from 1998 to 2003. He earned his undergraduate degree from Benedictine College in Atchison, Kansas, and his PhD from Loyola University of Chicago. A specialist in early modern poetry, he has published numerous articles on the works of sixteenth- and seventeenth-century poets, with particular emphasis on pastoral and metaphysical poetry. More recently, he has focused his scholarship on the poetry of the Catholic recusant and martyr Robert Southwell. His book *Colin's Campus: Cambridge Life and the English Eclogue* was published in 2000 by Susquehanna University Press.

Michael G. Brennan (MA, Oxford and Cambridge; DPhil, Oxford) is professor of Renaissance Studies at the University of Leeds, where he has taught since 1984. He has conducted an MA course on Graham Greene's writings for the past fifteen years and has published articles on various aspects of Greene's Catholicism. He is currently writing a book on Graham Greene, *Fictions, Faith and Authorship*, forthcoming from Continuum Publishing. His recent books in the area of renaissance studies and travel writing include *The Sidneys of Penhurst and the Monarchy, 1500–1700* (Ashgate 2006) and *The Origins of the Grand Tour* (Hakluyt Society 2004).

Meoghan B. Cronin is an associate professor of English at Saint Anselm College in New Hampshire, where she teaches courses in nineteenth-century British literature, specializing in the Victorian novel. Her scholarship has focused on superstition and folklore in Victorian fiction, particularly the novels of Thomas Hardy. Her recent work concerns the subject of religion and girlhood in nineteenth- and twentieth-century British novels. She contributed an essay on these themes in Antonia White's novels to Mary R. Reichardt's *Encyclopedia of Catholic Literature* (Greenwood 2004). In 2006, she received the New Hampshire Excellence in Education Award for postsecondary education.

Davin Heckman is an assistant professor at Siena Heights University in Adrian, Michigan, where he teaches English and communications. He is the author of *A Small World: Smart Houses and the Dream of the Perfect Day* (Duke University Press 2008), which analyzes the intersection of technology, popular culture, and daily life. He is cofounder of the journal *Reconstruction: Studies in Contemporary Culture* and has published scholarly articles on diverse topics from games to graffiti, from Marcel Duchamp to the war on terror. Current research includes a book-length study of labor and identity and the gothic mood in American literature as well as an ongoing study of electronic literature. Davin's wife, Carrie Heckman, assisted in writing and editing the essay on Mary Doria Russell's *The Sparrow* in this collection.

Daniel S. Lenoski received his MA degree from the University of Manitoba and his PhD from Queens University in Kingston, Ontario. He teaches modern Canadian, British, and Catholic Studies at St. Paul's College, an affiliated college of the University of Manitoba in Winnipeg. He has published and edited extensively in these areas (over ninety publications) in five countries, and he was for many years both a founding owner and editor of Turnstone Press, a Canadian literary press based in Winnipeg. He has also been both dean of studies and acting rector of St. Paul's College and has just finished his third appointment to the latter position.

Robert P. Lewis is professor emeritus of English at Marist College in Poughkeepsie, New York, where he has taught courses in Victorian literature, the English novel, Shakespeare, and religious themes in literature. He holds degrees from Manhattan College (BA), Columbia University (MA), and New York University (PhD). He has published articles and reviews on Victorian literature and on modern Catholic writers. He maintains a scholarly interest in the work of Bernard Lonergan for the light it casts on questions of theological anthropology, literary interpretation, and interdisciplinary methodology.

Eamon Maher is director of the National Centre for Franco-Irish Studies at the Institute of Technology, Tallaght (Dublin), where he also lectures in humanities. He is the author of numerous articles and books, the majority of which focus on the links between literature and Christianity. He wrote his PhD dissertation on the theme of marginality in the work and life of the French priest-writer Jean Sulivan (1913–80), and a monograph on this topic for the French publisher L'Harmattan is now available. He is general editor of the Studies in Franco-Irish Relations and the Reimagining Ireland series, both with Peter Lang. His books include *Crosscurrents and Confluences: Echoes of Religion in Twentieth Century Fiction* (Veritas 2000) and *John McGahern: From the Local to the Universal* (Liffey 2003). His coedited books include *Irish and Catholic? Towards an Understanding of Identity*, with Louise Fuller and John Littleton (Columba 2006); and *Contemporary Catholicism in Ireland: A Critical Appraisal*, with John Littleton (Columba 2008).

Dominic Manganiello received his BA from McGill University and his DPhil from the University of Oxford. He is currently professor of English literature at the University of Ottawa, where he has taught since 1979. He has also taught at Laval University and Augustine College. The author of *Joyce's Politics* (Routledge and Kegan Paul 1980) and *T. S. Eliot and Dante* (Macmillan 1989), he has also coauthored with David L. Jeffrey *Rethinking the Future of the University* (University of Ottawa Press 1998). He has written extensively on the culture of modernism and on twentieth-century Catholic authors, including articles on Oscar Wilde, G. K. Chesterton, Evelyn Waugh, Walter Miller Jr., J. R. R. Tolkien, and Seamus Heaney.

Stephen McInerney lectures in literature at Campion College, Sydney, Australia. He received his PhD from the University of Sydney in 2006, and was awarded the University Medal with his bachelor of arts by the Australian National University in 2000. He is the author of *In Your Absence: Poems 1994–2002* (Indigo/Ginninderra), a 2002 *Times Literary Supplement* "Books of the Year" recommendation. His poem "After Wendy Cope" appears in the new anthology *100 Australian Poems You Need to Know*, edited by Jamie Grant (Hardie Grant 2008).

Nan Metzger is currently completing a PhD in English and is teaching at Mount Mary College in Milwaukee, Wisconsin. Her article "Towards Constructing a 'Poetics of Space' for the Sentimental Novel: A Topo-Analysis of Charlotte Smith's *The Old House Manor*" appears in the book *Romanticism: Comparative Discourses*, edited by Larry H. Peer and Diane Long Hoeveler (Ashgate 2006). Her main areas of interest include nature writing, narrative theory, and autobiography.

Salvador A. Oropesa is professor of Spanish and American Ethnic Studies at Kansas State University, where he has taught since 1992. He received a PhD in 1990 from Arizona State University. He is currently on the editorial board of five journals, including *Chasqui* and *Studies in Twentieth and Twenty-First Century Literature*. His books include *The Contemporáneos Group: Rewriting Mexico in the Thirties and Forties* (University of Texas Press 2003), *La novelística de Antonio Muñoz Molina: Sociedad civil y literatura lúdica* (Universidad de Jaén 1999), and *La obra de Ariel Dorfman: Ficción y critica* (Pliegos 1992). He has also published numerous journal articles and book reviews.

Patricia L. Schnapp is a Sister of Mercy. She earned an MA in English from Marquette University in Milwaukee, Wisconsin, and a PhD in English from Bowling Green State University in Ohio. Her dissertation was entitled "The Liberation Theology of James Baldwin." For the past twenty years she has taught literature and writing at Siena Heights University in Adrian, Michigan, where she is currently an associate professor. In 2007 she coedited *The Best American Catholic Short Stories* with Daniel McVeigh (Rowman and Littlefield). Her article on Catholic poet Francis Thompson, "The Poet of the Return to God," appeared in *America* the same year. She has lectured and authored articles on the issue of restorative justice, and her poems frequently appear in *Review for Religious* and the *National Catholic Reporter*. In 2000 she won the first place award for poetry by the Catholic Press Association.

Nancy Ann Watanabe is a professor of comparative literature at the University of Oklahoma and is currently on sabbatical to pursue Pacific Rim research at the University of Washington libraries. She has also taught literature and technical writing at the University of Alaska–Fairbanks and literature at Boise State University. She holds an MA from the University of Washington and a PhD from Indiana University–Bloomington. Her award-nominated books include *Beloved Image: The Drama of W. B. Yeats, 1865–1939* (University Press of America 1995) and *Love Eclipsed: Joyce Carol Oates's Faustian Moral Vision* (University Press of America 1998). She has contributed essays and chapters to ten scholarly books. Among her academic honors are Fulbright research grants and National Endowment for the Humanities faculty fellowship awards.

Wendy A. Weaver is an assistant professor at Mount Mary College in Milwaukee, Wisconsin. She recently earned her PhD in English from Marquette University. She previously worked as an editorial assistant for *Renascence: Essays on Values in Literature*. She has published an article in *Logos: A Journal of Catholic Thought and Culture* and has contributed entries to both the *Encyclopedia of Catholic Literature* and *Encyclopedia of Women's Autobiography*. Her main areas of interest are autobiography, poetry, and spirituality in literature.

J. C. Whitehouse works as an independent scholar, writer, and translator. He is now retired from the position of senior lecturer in French and reader in comparative literature in the School of Modern Languages, University of Bradford, England. His publications include *Catholics on Literature* (Four Courts 1997); *Vertical Man: The Human Being in the Novels of Graham Greene, Sigrid Undset, and Georges Bernanos* (Saint Austin 1999); an essay on Piers Paul Read in Mary R. Reichardt's *Encyclopedia of Catholic Literature* (Greenwood 2004); and articles in many refereed journals in Britain, France, the U.S., Germany, and Brazil. He has also published translations of three of Georges Bernanos's novels, *Mouchette* (London: Bodley Head; New York: Holt, Rinehart and Winston 1966), *The Impostor* (Bison 1999), and *Under Satan's Sun* (Bison 2001).

Index

Index

Mills, John, 242n3
Milosz, Czeslaw, 68
Modernism, Antimodernism and Postmodernism, 41. *See also* Lodge, David
Modes of Modern Writing, The, 41, 44, 49n52. *See also* Lodge, David
Monk, Maria, 268
Monk Dawson, 178, 180. *See also* Read, Piers Paul
Monroe, Catherine, 262
Monsignor Quixote, 11, 154–70. *See also* Greene, Graham
Moore, Brian, 8, 9, 69, 70, 71, 73, 75
Morrill, John, 243n7
Morton, Andrew, 211n21, n23
Mourão, Manuela, 268
Moynihan, Patrick, 137
Murdoch, Iris, 207, 211
Murray, Les, 12, 13, 207–9, 216–25

Name of the Rose, The, 42. *See also* Eco, Umberto
New Catholic Encyclopedia, 19
New Collected Poems, 12, 209–16. *See also* Jennings, Elizabeth
Newman, John Henry, 5, 171, 172, 251
New Woman, The, 129. *See also* Hassler, Jon
Nice Work, 33. *See also* Lodge, David
Nietzsche, Friedrich, 65, 234, 245, 259
Nims, John Fredrick, 136
Norris, Kathleen, 107, 110, 111, 208n6
North of Hope, 10, 119, 120, 126–29. *See also* Hassler, Jon

O'Brien, Michael D., 13, 242–61
O'Collins, Gerald, 208n6
O'Connor, Flannery, 1, 3, 6, 119, 136, 204, 253, 254
Ó Faoláin, Sean, 74, 75
O'Hagan, Andrew, 172
Okada, Sumie, 196
O'Malley, Mary, 267
O'Marie, Carol Anne, 262
Once a Catholic, 267. *See also* O'Malley, Mary
O'Neill, Joseph, 15
O'Rourke, Brian, 85
Other Side of the Fire, The, 176. *See also* Ellis, Alice Thomas
O'Toole, Fintan, 69, 84
Our Man in Havana, 155. *See also* Greene, Graham

Owens, John D., 229n7
Owenson, Sydney (Lady Morgan), 72

Pacem in terris (Pope John XXIII), 88
Pacey, Desmond, 242n1
Pagan Babies and Other Catholic Memories, 108–9. *See also* Cascone, Gina
Paradise News, 33. *See also* Lodge, David
Passion of Sts. Perpetua and Felicity, The, 5
Patriot in Berlin, A, 178. *See also* Read, Piers Paul
Paul VI, Pope, 73, 163, 173, 188
Pavel, Thomas, 41
Payne, Stanley G., 89n4, 90n9
Paz, Octavia, 220
Pearce, Joseph, 171
Peelman, Achiel, 49
Pell, Barbara Helen, 242–43
People's Otherworld, The, 216. *See also* Murray, Les
Percy, Walker, 136, 260
Phelps, Eric John, 226, 227
Picture-Goers, The, 32. *See also* Lodge, David
Pieper, Josef, 258
Pilgrim's Progress, The, 124, 206. *See also* Bunyan, John
Pillars of Gold, 177. *See also* Ellis, Alice Thomas
Pius VII, Pope, 226
Pius XI, Pope, 90
Pius XII, Pope, 90
Plath, Sylvia, 210
Poems, 212. *See also* Jennings, Elizabeth
Poems against Economics, 222, 223. *See also* Murray, Les
Poems the Size of Photographs, 225. *See also* Murray, Les
Porter, Katharine Anne, 136
Power and the Glory, The, 5, 11, 135, 155, 163, 169. *See also* Greene, Graham
Praise, 215. *See also* Jennings, Elizabeth
Prime of Miss Jean Brodie, The, 262. *See also* Spark, Muriel
Promessi Sposi, I, 268. *See also* Manzoni, Alessandro

Quill, Monica, 262
Quinn, Peter, 16
Quo Vadis: The Subversion of the Catholic Church, 178, 179. *See also* Read, Piers Paul